T0318438

Community Filmmaking

Community Filmmaking takes up central issues in contemporary media studies, from representational politics and public policy to screen culture and civic engagement, in a unique and productive fashion. Theoretically sophisticated and empirically rich, this volume is a welcome addition to a growing body of scholarship on community, participatory and collaborative media practices.

—*Kevin Howley, DePauw University, USA*

This book examines the role of community filmmaking in society and its connection with issues of cultural diversity, innovation, policy and practice in various places. Deploying a range of examples from Europe, North America, Australia and Hong Kong, the chapters show that film emerging from outside the mainstream film industries and within community contexts can lead to innovation in terms of both content and processes and a better representation of the cultural diversity of a range of communities and places. The book aims to situate the community filmmaker as the central node in the complex network of relationships between diverse communities, funding bodies, policy and the film industries.

Sarita Malik is Professor of Media, Culture and Communications at Brunel University London. Her research explores questions of social change, inequality, communities and cultural representation. Over the past twenty years, Sarita has published several articles on race, representation, diversity and the media and led several research projects related to these areas.

Caroline Chapain is a Lecturer in Economic Development at the Business School, University of Birmingham, UK. Her research focuses on topics related to the creative industries, creative clusters, innovation, creative citizenship, creative cities and local and regional economic development and policies. In the last 10 years she has undertaken research on these topics within the UK and in collaboration with colleagues across Europe.

Roberta Comunian is Lecturer in Cultural and Creative Industries at the Department for Culture, Media and Creative Industries at King's College London, UK. Her research interests include: relationship between public and private investments in the arts, art and cultural regeneration projects, cultural and creative industries, creativity and competitiveness. Her most recent works have been published in *Geoforum, Journal of Education and Work, International Journal of Cultural and Creative Industries* and *Cultural Trends.*

Routledge Studies in Media and Cultural Industries

1 **Community Filmmaking**
   Diversity, Practices and Places
   Edited by Sarita Malik, Caroline Chapain
   and Roberta Comunian

Community Filmmaking
Diversity, Practices and Places

Edited by Sarita Malik,
Caroline Chapain
and Roberta Comunian

Routledge
Taylor & Francis Group

LONDON AND NEW YORK

First published 2017 by Routledge

2 Park Square, Milton Park, Abingdon, Oxfordshire OX14 4RN
52 Vanderbilt Avenue, New York, NY 10017

Routledge is an imprint of the Taylor & Francis Group, an informa business

First issued in paperback 2019

Library of Congress Cataloging-in-Publication Data
CIP data has been applied for.

ISBN: 978-1-138-18806-8 (hbk)
ISBN: 978-0-367-87649-4 (pbk)

Typeset in Sabon
by codeMantra

Contents

List of Figures and Table

Figures

Table

Preface

Yudhishthir Raj Isar

It is a real privilege to contribute a Preface to such a ground-breaking collection of chapters on community filmmaking across the world. It was even more of a privilege to have served on the Advisory Committee of the Community Filmmaking and Cultural Diversity project that generated these writings, an experience that considerably broadened my acquaintance with this key arena of cultural practice, commentary and representation.

I was also honoured to have been invited to deliver the opening address at the project's rich January 2014 conference. At that moment, I had recently completed work on the *United Nations Creative Economy Report 2013*, sub-titled "Widening Local Development Pathways".[1] Although the community filmmaking research project was UK-based, centring on questions raised within and on behalf of the country's diverse cultural strands, its community focus necessarily foregrounded issues that are common to many settings. Many of these issues were taken up in the UN report, for example, the key point that particular lenses are required in order to analyse the conditions on which, across all the domains of the cultural economy, success at the local scale depends and also the need to envision differently the policy frameworks that are conducive to such success, as many of the contributions to this volume make clear. The critical success factors include both organic development and deliberate policy initiatives, which in turn consist of a wide range of characteristics, conditions or variables. These include financing; key agents, intermediaries and institutions; an ethic of service to people and their aspirations; effective intellectual property rights; ethical decision making by local actors and communities; transnational connections and flows, or the global-local relationship, including access to global markets and digital connectivity; specific mechanisms scaled for local, enterprise development and the value chain; capacity building for technical, entrepreneurial, leadership and networking skills; community development and welfare; and, last but not least, education. Taken together, these factors make up a specifically calibrated road map; many of these factors have been examined by the contributors to this volume, as they explore different facets of community filmmaking in a variety of settings.

Since the broad cultural economy canvas covers more creative forms than community filmmaking, however, I shall take the liberty here of sharing a few rather more general considerations with the reader: first, the need to see any dimension of the cultural economy not as an abstraction, but as grounded, built by actors, intermediaries and consumers in specific circumstances. This requires more than broad-brush accounting for the production, distribution and consumption of cultural products. Instead, we need to understand how the economic emanates from and is entwined within culture. Culture is not a 'bedrock' or separate 'layer' to the economy, as the UN report pointed out, but the filter through which 'economic' activities in daily life are mediated: the rich meshwork of human and social relationships *are* the economic practices that converge and accumulate over time and in different places to form specific cultural and creative industries. They summon us to carry out careful local analysis so that we can think through a palette of options in the context of people's aspirations.

Second, grounded understandings of causality and agency are also always essential. If the economy is not an abstraction 'out there', but rather a human construct that is built and rebuilt by key actors, then it invites reflection on exactly how things get done, by whom, and whether these actions suit the aspirations and capacities of the people concerned. In this view, all manner of economic transactions, exchanges and functions are mediated by ethical considerations, quandaries and decisions. Yet we still do not know exactly how ethical decision making emerges in this context and how people in challenging circumstances negotiate constraints to produce truly community-relevant work. These constraints necessarily include the claims of personal gain. Building cultural and creative industries as community enterprises upholding ethical and social goals often requires lengthy gestation periods, good communication and intricate negotiations, of both principles and the distribution of benefits.

Third, the expressive and emotive dimensions of any kind of cultural creativity often involve dissonant or contestatory expression – a key dimension of much community filmmaking in both North and South. The risk of making policy making 'safe' – for either investors or governments – is of watering down goals to the point where it loses cultural meaning and merely becomes old wine in new bottles, a business-as-usual co-opting of cultural expression for entrenched interests, all the while missing opportunities to enhance dialogue, debate and ultimately new forms of development for marginalized people (that might initially stem from sub-cultural or oppositional roots).

That said, there are issues specific to community filmmaking that intersect with such broader cultural economy concerns in ways that are explored admirably in this volume. For example, how their work is impacted by the policies of any country's major cultural institutions, the dynamic relationship that exists between the individual filmmaker and her community or the combination of representation (of the community) and engagement (by the community) that such work often embodies, hence placing it squarely within social and political alternatives as a locus of counterhegemonic assertion. As the editors point out in their Introduction to this volume, the issues and practices at stake around community filmmaking emerged in the 1960s and 1970s, not just in the UK but also in many other Western European countries. In this context, it is appropriate to return to two pairs of politically oriented notions (the pairs are interlinked) articulated at that time, which are 'old wine' that has matured, regardless of whether the kinds of bottles containing it are old or new. They remain central challenges of cultural policy and practice. The two binomials were/are cultural 'democratisation' and cultural 'democracy' on the one hand; cultural 'exclusion' and 'inclusion' on the other. Both pairs require not an 'either/or' but a 'both/and'. In particular, 'inclusion' cannot be achieved without both 'cultural democratisation' and 'cultural democracy'.

From the 1960s onwards, governments across Europe sought to 'democratise' access to and participation in the arts and heritage. This approach appears distinctly elitist in retrospect, since it tended to imply that a single cultural canon determined on high could be propagated to 'the masses'. Nor has it ever been entirely successful, quite simply because the unequal distribution of 'cultural capital' in Bourdieu's sense has made access to the arts and arts institutions either difficult or unsolicited by the intended beneficiaries. Moreover, in recent years, the growing presence of market-driven cultural industries has reduced the reach of subsidised cultural provision. And yet, access and participation have been broadened and their promotion remains a fundamental policy principle for all European governments. *Cultural democracy* on the other hand emerged as an alternative to democratisation strategies. It seeks to augment and diversify access to the means of cultural production and distribution instead of merely attempting to increase cultural consumption. This agenda has been singularly advanced – and transformed – by the digital media and other new technologies, *inter alia* through the forms of 'produsage' to which the Introduction refers, affording community filmmakers among others direct access to and indeed often control of the means of production.

The itineraries of the terms are also inextricably bound up with the broader master narrative of 'cultural diversity', holding out challenges on a Europe-wide, indeed global scale, since both European integration and globalisation make it imperative to look beyond the purely national level so as to identify the forces and flows that are changing the 'grammar' of national cultures (often in disconcerting terms, as recent attitudinal trends in the UK that contributed to and followed Brexit have starkly revealed).

What patterns and forces in the cultural economy pre-determine certain kinds of exclusion as regards cultural expression, goods and services? Our societies have broadened the notion of 'inclusiveness', seen mainly in class terms when the debate began, to include many different dimensions of difference – as well as to the excluding ideas and behaviours that must be overcome. The focus of attention is clearly on claims, as Tony Bennett has put it, of "ethnically marked cultural differences associated with the international movement of peoples, and within national territories, the claims to difference associated with the protracted struggles of indigenous minorities to maintain their identity".[2] The contributions to this volume remind us of how the discourses of democracy and inclusion, heretofore largely confined to countering income inequality and the unequal distribution of social and cultural capital within societies that had become relatively homogeneous culturally, now emphasise new categories of the 'excluded' created by the migratory flows that have diversified the composition of all societies. Within each nation, therefore, the task of enabling all the groups that henceforth constitute the national community to assume ownership of an evolving, composite cultural identity has become the question of the hour. This is not simply a matter of combating intolerance and exclusion, but also of giving dignity, voice and recognition in the public sphere to different cultural groups while constructing – negotiating – a sense of national community. Four principles enumerated by Bennett reflect the more general perspectives of cultural democracy and the needs of citizenship; each of them also relates to what community filmmakers, like any creative producers actually seek and do. Since they are highly apposite to the purposes of this volume, an adapted version of the four principles is worth citing below:

1   An entitlement to equal opportunity to participate in the full range of activities that constitute the field defined as 'culture' in the society in question;
2   The entitlement of all members of society to be provided with the means of functioning effectively as cultural actors without being required to change their cultural allegiances, affiliations or identities;
3   The obligation of governments and other authorities to nurture the sources of diversity through imaginative mechanisms, arrived at through consultation, for sustaining and developing the different cultures that are active within the populations for which they are responsible;
4   The obligation to foster ongoing interactions between differentiated cultures, rather than their flourishing as separate enclaves, so as to transform the ground on which cultural identities are formed in ways that will favour a continuing dynamic for diversity.

As regards the last point – "ongoing interactions between differentiated cultures" – many 'multiculturalist' policies have tended to freeze 'identities' into fixed categories. This is where the creative and ethical choices of the filmmaker, co-creative practice and community participation can have a significant impact, as several chapters show.

Finally, actually existing cultural diversity policies across Europe also tend to disregard social and/or economic stratification. Some have 'culturalised' inequality. Yet cultural and economic exclusion often go hand in hand, as has been the case particularly with the Roma population in Central and Eastern Europe and with most immigrant groups in Western and Northern Europe over the last few decades. In this perspective, the concern is not merely with the inclusion of 'minorities' but rather with the nature of society as a whole. As the Indian-born British political scientist Bhikhu Parekh famously wrote, "'we' cannot integrate 'them' as long as 'we' remain 'we'; 'we' must be loosened up to create a new common space in which 'they' can be accommodated and become part of a newly constituted 'we'".[3] The overarching challenge is to reconstitute the national – and European – 'we' within a public space that cherishes both plurality and the shared identity of common citizenship. Community filmmaking is one of the principal creative forms that is rising to this challenge, as the contributions to this volume eloquently demonstrate.

Notes

1. UNESCO/UNDP. 2013. *United Nations Creative Economy Report 2013. Special Edition. Widening Local Development Pathways.* New York: UNDP.
2. Bennett, T. 2001. *Differing Diversities: cultural policy and cultural diversity.* Strasbourg: Council of Europe Publishing.
3. Parekh, B. 2000. *Rethinking Multiculturalism – Cultural Diversity and Political Rights.* London: Macmillan.

Acknowledgments

A collection of this scale is only made possible through the input of a range of supportive people. The book has emerged from an Arts and Humanities Research Council (AHRC) funded project as part of the Connected Communities programme. This commitment from the AHRC for the Community Filmmaking and Cultural Diversity project has made a number of collaborations possible. Most importantly, it has provided the time and space to reflect, with others, on community filmmaking and to approach this aspect of our contemporary culture from an interdisciplinary perspective. We thank all the community filmmakers who gave up their time to speak to us about their practice as we conducted this research.

The two-day conference hosted at the British Film Institute in 2014 was a major part of the project, and it is here that a number of academics, filmmakers and other practitioners came together to talk about the interactions made possible by community filmmaking and also of the complexities that are involved in terms of community engagement and participation, creative practice, policy and funding. We would like to take this opportunity to thank our research partners, the British Film Institute, City-Eye, Lighthouse and WORLDwrite; members of the Advisory Committee; and the Associate Researchers, Dr Clive James Nwonka and Dr Patricia Romeiro. All the authors whose work is published here have shown a consistent level of support, professionalism and expertise, and we are truly appreciative of each of their excellent contributions to the debate. Special thanks also goes to Professor Yudhishthir Raj Isar for acting as Chair of the Advisory Committee, for his inspiring keynote address at the British Film Institute and for agreeing to write the Preface to this collection – his continuous support for the wider project has been hugely beneficial as well as his expertise on issues of creativity and cultural diversity. Finally, we are grateful to Routledge for their interest in this field of research and for their patience and guidance through the process of assembling this new collection.

1 Community Filmmaking Diversity, Practices and Places

An Introduction

Sarita Malik, Caroline Chapain and Roberta Comunian

1 Background to the Collection: Investigating Community Filmmaking and Cultural Diversity

This collection has emerged following a UK government Arts and Humanities Research Council-funded project (2013–2014) led by the three editors of this collection. The one-year interdisciplinary study, *Community Filmmaking and Cultural Diversity,* researched the relationship between community filmmaking and cultural diversity in the UK. The main objective was to examine how cultural diversity and community filmmaking are understood and enacted by community filmmakers themselves and to what extent the practices and processes involved support cultural diversity in the film sector today. Within the project, we were keen to make a distinction between community filmmaking and other forms of participatory communication, such as community, ethnic and alternative or oppositional media. Therefore, the origins of this book are multifaceted, and the book itself builds on a number of interactions, including an international conference that took place at the British Film Institute in 2014, in addition to interviews with community filmmakers and a workshop with academics and practitioners from the UK and Europe.

One of the important consequences of such exchanges was that an opportunity was created to capture various understandings of key concepts, such as 'community filmmaking' and 'cultural diversity,' terms that are opened up further in this collection. For example, participants at our workshop, which included academics, facilitators and practitioners, recognised that community filmmaking is a broad concept that can be understood and produced in different ways. On one level, there is participatory community filmmaking, where the filmmaking process is wholly managed and undertaken by the community involved. At the other end of the spectrum, there are community filmmakers who might film community issues but do not involve communities in participatory ways. In this book, a range of scholars and practitioners put forward their own interpretations of community filmmaking.

The levels at which community filmmaking operates are themselves incredibly diverse, ranging from filmmaking as everyday cultural practice *for* multiple communities and cultural groups so that they may engage in forms of self-representation, to films that are *about* local communities and have been produced for and screened to wide audiences, including on national television. There is a larger emphasis in this book on the former mode, particularly in relation to the diverse civic agendas that are so often to be found in participatory modes of community filmmaking. If 'community filmmaking' is a contested concept within this area of study, then so too is the notion of 'cultural diversity'. Participants at our workshop highlighted that cultural diversity can be experienced in different ways depending on the filmmaker, community and context in question. As a consequence, a broad definition of cultural diversity is used in this book in order to better accommodate analysis of how various filmmakers and communities experience it. Within the collection, cultural diversity includes notion of gender, ethnicity, geography, social class and sexual orientation, and many of the chapters engage with the discursive processes at work in how these different dimensions of diversity are framed. The flexible nature of these key concepts permeates the selection of the chapters to be found here and represents the complexity of community filmmaking practices and politics that each of them interrogates.

1.1 Project Framework and Complexity Approach to Community Filmmaking within this Book

Within mainstream film studies, there is limited research on community filmmaking (Coyer 2007). There is more evidence of research on participatory video and amateur filmmaking (Zimmerman 1986, Odin 1999, Fox 2004), especially with the new affordance that digital technologies have supported in lowering the need for access to filmmaking tools (Fox 2004, Conway 2004, Kattelle 2004). Therefore, the community mode of filmmaking as a field of enquiry has been characterised by a lack of academic writings integrating theory and empirical fieldwork (Shand 2008). We suggest that many of the interdisciplinary areas of concern, including issues around skills, training and networks, the role that place and policies may have on community filmmaking practices and the role of cultural intermediaries, all require further academic research across disciplines, including media studies, business studies and creative industries research.

In recent years, a number of authors have highlighted the usefulness of applying complexity theory to better understand the creative industries. These industries sit at the junction of various rationales and dimensions – cultural, social, economic and civic. These are expressed in various ways in different places and are supported by policy in different ways. Comunian and Chapain have both, for example, used this complexity approach in their work (Comunian 2011, Comunian, Alexiou and Chapain 2012, Andres and Chapain 2015, Comunian and Alexiou 2015, Chapain and Hargreaves 2016). There is a growing amount of literature that applies this approach to the creative industries, given their transversal role in contemporary society (see Hartley et al. 2013 for a discussion). Using a complexity framework can also be helpful in reconciling creative acts taking place at the boundaries between amateur and professional such as community filmmaking (Chapain and Hargreaves 2016). As such, the use of complexity theory to support understandings of community filmmaking is relevant because it too sits at the junction of various dimensions, is expressed by different community filmmakers in particular communities and places and typically brings together both professional and amateur filmmaking activities. Recognising the complex set of cultural, economic and social relationships, goals and engagements in community filmmaking, our research adopts a complexity and multidisciplinary framework to use a wider perspective to consider the cascade of connections behind community filmmakers' engagement with communities, industries, supporting institutions and audiences and may impact on the cultural product and experience delivered as well as on urban/local development (Comunian 2011). In the research at the origin of this book, we framed this by decomposing the relationship between cultural diversity and community filmmaking along five key sub-dimensions: 1) identity and representation; 2) film as a media; 3) film between arts and commercial practices; 4) innovation, skills and networks and 5) policy and place (see Figure 1.1). Many of these dimensions appear in the various contributions, but the chapters have been grouped in four different parts to reflect the main dimension that the author focuses on in his or her discussion.

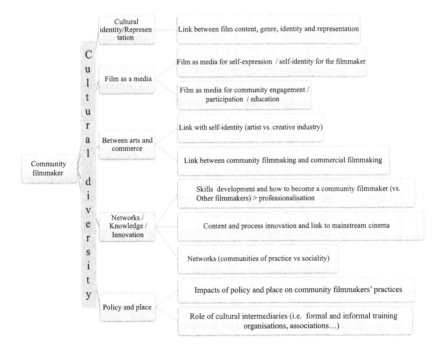

Figure 1.1 Understanding community filmmaking and cultural diversity through a complexity framework.

More specifically, our complexity framework can be understood from two perspectives: first as a theoretical framework that allows us to bring together a range of theories and understandings of community filmmaking from a multi-level analysis and second as a practical tool that allows us to bring together multidisciplinary contributions and to consider the value they add to our understanding, without prioritising any single perspective. The first theoretical advantage comes from the opportunity to consider the range of interactions and their scales taking place within the community filmmaking ecology. The micro level – the individual filmmaker and its decision-making process – sets the foundation for our understanding. However, we are aware that this micro level also needs to be reconciled with the role of networks, communities and practices ie. the meso level.

Our complexity approach to community filmmaking considers filmmakers as the key intermediary in community filmmaking processes. As such, we consider community filmmaking as a process in which the community filmmaker works in participatory ways with communities. We examine the role that lived (rather than discursively framed) cultural diversity plays in these filmmakers' work and practice and how they experience this diversity. Similarly, communities, networks and individuals do not act in a vacuum but, at the macro level, have to deal with (both influencing and being influenced by) policy, place and macro structure that regulates the film sector and other relevant sectors (such as community policy) in society. With this insight, these various levels and their influences on each other become the scope of the research and the range of contributions assembled here to address this understanding (with a variety of foci), helping build a coherent and in-depth picture of the community filmmaking ecology. Second, from a practical perspective, the complexity framework adopted in the book expresses itself also in the way the collection is structured around various elements of community filmmaking as well as in the different theoretical understandings underpinning each individual chapter.

The existing literature on community filmmaking emerges primarily from Cultural and Media Studies, and there is much to be gained from bringing in further perspectives that deal with economic, social and spatial dynamics. One of the main objectives of the book, then, is to offer a more holistic and nuanced approach to the study of community filmmaking by looking at it from multidimensional and multidisciplinary perspectives. This is reflected in the four parts around which the book is organised and that sit at the heart of our research: cultural diversity, practices, place and the different ways community filmmaking engages communities through participatory processes. As such, the way we approach community filmmaking here is based on a complexity framework reflected in the structure of the book, its title, the range of themes addressed in its distinctive parts and the multidisciplinary background of the contributors.

1.2 Community Filmmaking and Diversity: A Research Agenda

The original research project and the chapters in this book engage with three key areas of importance in the understanding of community filmmaking and its practice in relation to issues of diversity. We believe these areas offer the potential to draw a new research agenda for the sector and its future development.

1.2.1 *Diversity, Representation and Engagement in the Context of Community Filmmaking*

The obvious relationship between different kinds of cinema (to the mainstream) and different kinds of (otherwise marginalised) cultural perspectives provided by community filmmaking positions it as a critical site of cultural and community significance. The community arts movement of the 1960s and 1970s was predicated on the ideological basis that community-led activity was representative of the people and merited public investment (Braden 1978). A range of community art forms, from theatre to dance to film have, since then, commonly been based around active participation and dialogue and geared towards notions of cultural democracy, community development and social transformation (Mayo 2000). Within the significant body of scholarly research around community media in general, important work has pointed to the range of tensions and power relations within different forms of participatory arts practice (Price 2015). This includes the work of those who have argued that the model of community arts and media of the 1960s and 1970s has shifted away from a collective, political basis to a depoliticised reflux in which the interest of the individual dominates (Mattaraso 2013). Community filmmaking also introduces us to some of the tensions and politics that have been identified as being at work in a range of other contexts of community arts and media.

The public and academic debates around the significance of cultural diversity to film culture are part of a broader set of debates around minorities and the media. These discussions have foregrounded questions of representation; for example how diverse communities of identity use cultural spaces for political and aesthetic projects that seek to rework or re-imagine dominant cultural representations; an alternative (or oppositional cinema) to the mainstream (cinema) (Pines and Willemen 1989, Mercer 1988, Hill 2004). Filmmaking that has emerged from the margins and is created and controlled by a community has typically involved a struggle over identity and cultural representation that has been activated on two fronts: the first in relation to material issues (both opportunities and constraints) such as funding, distribution and exhibition and the second in relation to aesthetics such as how new paradigms, languages and agendas might be formed through and within innovative modes of filmmaking that operate outside of a mainstream, institutionalised context (Malik 1996).

Running parallel are how other agendas – policy, economic, socio-political – have shaped the language and nature of engagement and participation that underpins traditional community-led filmmaking. Take, for example, the black and Asian-led collectively managed film workshops that emerged in the UK in the 1980s and that were to be deeply impacted on by these kinds of wider agendas and contexts. At the time, this screen workshop movement signalled a community commitment to the film-form, as well as an engagement with communities 'from within' and a distinctive creative practice (political, aesthetic and economic) outside of the mainstream film sector. Importantly, the wider independent collective film movement demonstrated "a commitment to the local community, and to pressure groups such as trade unions, feminist organizations and anti-racist bodies" (Petley 1989, 6). It is beyond the scope of this introduction to outline the changing conditions that led to the eventual demise of the workshop sector in the 1990s (see Malik 1996); however, it is a useful example of how community filmmaking, like any other cultural form, is necessarily caught up in the fluctuating cultural politics of arts subsidy and policy frames in addition to fast-moving technological changes that continue to redefine what film is and how it is produced, distributed and exhibited.

With regards to film policy, this tends to be based around the mainstream film sector rather than community filmmaking contexts and has today a strong emphasis on how film supports trading and sustainability, as well as cultural expression. Whilst the 2016 UNESCO report, "Diversity in the Film Industry", specifically addresses the relationship between film and diversity, the focus is on the mainstream film industry on a global level. For Richard Curtis, the UK filmmaker and Advocate for UN Global Goals, as he marked the tenth anniversary of UNESCO's 2005 Convention on the Protection and the Promotion of the Diversity of Cultural Expressions, "film has the power to give societies a sense of what needs to be done and can bring about positive changes (Curtis 2016). The connection that is frequently built between film and ideas of social change is notable, but discussions about the potential contribution of community filmmaking here remain limited. So there is a further motivation within this collection: to put the spotlight on the cultural and civic dimension of community filmmaking and the diverse forms of cultural expression that it facilitates through its processes of production and its dynamic contributions to the media environment, whilst at the same time engaging critically with issues of diversity, practices and places.

1.2.2 *The Role of Networks and Diverse Practices in Community Filmmaking*

The chapters highlight the importance of networks and networking for community filmmakers. This is also apparent in the general literature on creative industries and creative work (Comunian 2012, Jones 2010) as well as the commercial filmmaking sector (Cattani and Ferriani 2008). However, in the specific case of community filmmaking, the variety and range of networks involves spans beyond the sector, gatekeepers and funders to reach specific communities and social activist networks as well as charities and other social groups working on specific causes. Malik, Chapain and Comunian (2015) highlight that there are five main constituencies in the work of community filmmakers and summarise the range of platforms and organisations they need to engage and network with (see figure 1.2). These are essential to understand the practices that are explored in the book and their sustainability. These five constituencies are the main actors and agents identified in the community filmmaking eco-system:

1   **Communities and community leaders.** Most of the community filmmaking projects that are examined in this collection derive from a range of collaborations and negotiations between filmmakers (with a range of professionalism and expertise) and community groups and their representatives. Independently from the nature of the projects, there is a need to translate issues and content between community filmmakers and communities; these negotiation skills are essential to enable diversity and a range of voices to emerge in the project. These networks are also likely to be the ones that create a reputation for the filmmakers themselves, as they move to new projects and engage with new communities and constituencies.

   Charities and third-sector organisations. In addition to establishing direct networks with communities, community filmmakers have a range of connections with the third sector, including with charities and 'not-for-profit' organisations that are also key to engaging with communities and to giving filmmakers new projects. These organisations are often the funders or brokers that can support community projects and engage with diverse communities and stakeholders.

2   These organisations are often the funders or brokers that can support community projects and engage with diverse communities and stakeholders.

3   **Funding bodies and organisations.** In different national and international settings, as also highlighted in the book, community filmmakers experience different kinds of formal and informal support from funding bodies and policy organisations. In general, there is

recognition that because of its non-commercial nature as well as it community-driven content, the funding streams, which often privilege more commercially orientated productions or auteur-driven films, often marginalise community filmmaking. However, the role of new forms of funding such as crowdfunding also needs further exploration (Sørensen 2012).

4   **Platforms for training, showcasing and archiving.** Alongside networks with communities, charities and support organisations, there seems to be a burgeoning of festivals and organic filmmakers associations to help access information and other networks and reach critical mass. Another important element of networks connects with the need for training of community filmmakers (Glow and Johanson 2010). As many filmmakers do not have economic resources for continuous professional development, relying on networks with peers and institutions that provide training is extremely valuable.

5   **Community of filmmakers.** The final element highlighted throughout the collection is the strong community of practice (Wenger 1998) that is present amongst community filmmakers. There is an acknowledgement of the great wealth of knowledge and support that is shared amongst peers in community filmmaking projects and how these same projects are often developed through asking for informal help and support within groups and collectives that are able to shape practice and engagement.

Figure 1.2 Representation of the network of organisations and communities with whom community filmmakers work.

Overall, community filmmaking relies on a range of networks and stakeholders that make it a valuable example of creative and cultural production, spanning across private, public and not for profit economies. However, it is important to reflect on how diversity further impacts on the range of networks and opportunities and helps to develop new content. The aspiration to engage with a range of diverse communities and stakeholders or to reach new audiences in fact creates a 'multiplier effect' for many community filmmaking projects, which result in vital connections with place and participation.

1.2.3 Place and Participation in Community Filmmaking

As discussed previously, our complexity approach to community filmmaking and diversity means that, in contrast to much of the existing research on community media, we consider the role of place in the practice of community filmmaking. Indeed, beyond the role that place can have in terms of how it inspires the content of the films produced, some contributions in this book explore how place can both constrain and enable community filmmaking practices, on the one hand, and how community filmmaking can influence the development of place, on the other. Place here is understood in a wider sense and can encompass various geographical scales, be they neighbourhoods, cities or countries. Our research shows that community filmmaking tends to be one element of filmmakers' portfolio of activities (Malik, Chapain and Comunian 2015). Much has been written on the economic geography of the creative industries – filmmaking within them – in the last 20 years (see, for example, some of the contributions from the editors of this book (i.e. Chapain and De Propris 2009; Comunian, Chapain and Clifton 2010, Chapain, Clifton and Comunian 2013, Comunian, Chapain and Clifton 2014, Clifton, Chapain and Comunian 2016). Overall, this literature discusses how creative workers and industries are embedded within place in terms of inspiration, cultural framework, economic dynamics, skills and professional practices and supporting infrastructure – local and national idiosyncrasies, economic and social contexts and policies play a role – in addition to connecting with global networks and economic dynamics. Recently, there has also been a call to examine and better understand the role of cultural and creative intermediaries, i.e. 'arts and cultural councils, policy networks, economic development agencies, foundations and unions to artist collectives, cultural centres, creative industries incubators, festivals and tradeshows' (Jakob and Van Heur 2015, 357) in mediating the usage and practices of the creative industries. Our research on community filmmaking in the UK has highlighted the importance of cultural intermediaries in supporting community filmmaking and its various objectives (Malik, Chapain and Comunian 2015). Some chapters in the book further contribute to this debate.

Another important dimension touched upon is the role that community filmmaking can play in the cultural and social development of place. There has been a longstanding debate about the contribution of creative activities to urban development and the regeneration of place in fostering social cohesion, generating new cultural amenities for both residents and visitors, and supporting new cultural representations of place, etc. (see for example, Bianchini and Parkinson 1993, Evans and Shaw 2004; Markusen and Gadwa 2010 for a more in-depth discussion). Community filmmaking is a particular form of creative activity, by supporting the participation of communities in the filmmaking and creative processes and by collaborating with communities to broaden cultural expressions. It connects the everyday acts of creativity and self-expression with the cultural, civic and social goals of amateur practices of groups and communities to the professional skills of filmmakers or in other terms the creative citizenship to the creative economy (Chapain and Hargreaves 2016). Many of the chapters discuss the way community filmmakers mediate this participation, which can cover a wide range of activities depending on projects as defined by Jackson and Herranz (2003):

> Participation is not just attendance, observation, consumption, or even audience participation. It includes many other categories of action – making, doing, teaching, learning, presenting, promoting, judging, supporting – and spans many artistic disciplines. It can be amateur or professional, active or passive, individual or collective, continuous or episodic, public or private. (13)

Chapters reflect on the impacts this participation has on individuals and communities and the challenges that such participatory practices can generate both for filmmakers and communities at times. Finally, some contributors also emphasise the potential that community filmmaking can offer for local and regional development. In doing so, the book offers a more rounded perspective on this area of practice and its impacts on both people and place.

2 Overview of the Chapters

We recognise that our collection has a greater emphasis on community filmmaking and community filmmaking contexts in the Global North than on the contexts of Global South. However, the collection has the potential to provide impetus for subsequent work on the rich community filmmaking traditions of Latin America, Africa and elsewhere. As our Conclusion to the collection notes, we call for subsequent work to address a wider geographical coverage, something that would be relevant, probably for a larger collection. We suggest that our focus on the Global North allows us to present a more unified collection. Whilst this primarily addresses the Anglophone tradition of filmmaking, the diversity of chapters and case studies also means that we are able to present contrasts, with examples from across the UK, Ireland, Germany, Spain, Canada, Australia and Hong Kong. The chapters that are presented here have indeed resulted from a 'global' call for papers that was certainly not designed to be exclusionary. The objective of the book is indeed more focused on addressing particular issues around community filmmaking as highlighted by the four main parts' distinctive foci, and therefore perhaps less directed at representing global geography. As asserted by Yudhishthir Raj Isar in his Preface to the book, such a focus offers an opportunity to reflect on "exactly how things get done, by whom, and whether these actions suit the aspirations and capacities of the people concerned."

The chapters are organised in four main sections: Part 1: *Diversity, representation and community filmmaking;* Part 2: *Networks and intermediaries in community filmmaking*; Part 3: *community filmmaking: practices in place and for place;* and Part 4: *Engagement and participation in community filmmaking.* Each of these parts has a short introduction to its key themes, outlining how the chapters included in those sections relate to those themes. There are, quite rightly, overlapping themes across individual chapters and, indeed, across the sections themselves. We now provide an overview of the chapters that form each of the four parts of the book.

3.1 Part 1: Diversity, Representation and Community Filmmaking

Issues of diversity and representation are salient themes for an analysis of the practices of community filmmaking. The short introduction, written by Malik, outlines the relevance of bringing together community filmmaking and cultural diversity in academic research. It notes cultural representation's significant role in how community filmmakers themselves describe their work and in relation to the communities with whom they work and set themselves up to serve. Community filmmaking is utilised as a cultural space in which communities, for example communities of identity, can be re-imagined and directly involved in reworking cultural representations.

Daniel Ashton, in his chapter about participatory documentary projects in the UK, explores the possibilities and tensions in creating culturally diverse representations of everyday life through film. Engaging with critical perspectives on participatory cultures, Ashton asks whether the open invitation to a wide number of potential participants in participatory film projects equals diverse forms of self-representation. In Chapter 2, he interrogates the discourses of inclusion and empowerment presented in participatory film projects and engages with recent scholarship on diversity in cultural representation. Tackling head on the questions of diversity and representation that are addressed in the book, Ashton asks the critical question of whether diversifying levels of participation – in this case through encouraging the mass participation of 'the crowd' – inevitably translates into diversity in content.

Casey Burkholder addresses the politics of participation in community filmmaking in relation to themes of diversity and representation, and in a quite different global context. Her chapter outlines an empirical study on ethnic minority young people and civic engagement in contemporary Hong Kong. Chapter 3 combines ethnographic and participatory visual research in order to discuss ethnic minority young people's participation in and reaction to Hong Kong's Umbrella Revolution and how concepts of self and citizenship are negotiated and represented by the participants. Burkholder engages with the literature and practices of participatory visual methodologies, specifically drawing on the use of cellphilms (participatory video using cell phones), which have been employed as a tool to encourage ethnic minority youth to document notions of resistance, senses of belonging and civic engagement.

Using a historical approach, Alistair Scott's chapter focuses on community filmmaking in Scotland and traces how the representation of local communities on screen has evolved, by examining its associations with the projection of ideas of Scottish cultural identity. He shows how community filmmaking in Scotland today draws upon creative practices developed in a number of different periods since the early twentieth century and explores how the representation of cultural identity has altered over this period as a result of shifting attitudes to class and gender and, most significantly, with the establishment of communities of Scots from a range of ethnic backgrounds. Chapter 4 takes on particular resonance in the light of the UK's vote in 2016 to leave the European Union (EU). Against the call for Britain to exit the EU, Scott reminds us that the Scottish Government, local authorities and the Scottish public largely welcome new refugees and immigrants, leading to an even wider range of projects that can be categorised as community filmmaking than at any other time.

3.2 Part 2: Networks and Intermediaries in Community Filmmaking

In the second part of the book, introduced by Comunian, we look at the role played by different groups of intermediaries and a diverse range of networks in facilitating the production and distribution of community films. From the production perspective, it is important to consider how community filmmaking is seen as a collective endeavour and therefore to reflect on the value of collective creativity and the often unwritten rules of these collaborations. Furthermore, we consider the value of social innovation and the role of intermediaries in shaping local contexts and also the work of communities and participants.

Murray and Dooley's contribution in Chapter 5 presents an interesting case study from Australia. The low-budget feature film *52 Tuesdays* and its online companion project *My52Tuesdays* are used to reflect on how cultural diversity comes to the forefront in the representation of modern families and gender identities through filming the journey of Jane, a transgender parent, and Billie, her teenage daughter. As the authors highlight, the film benefits from the input of communities and networks in its development, with the weekly writing, pre-production and production occurring simultaneously and involving the real lives of the cast and crew in the process. An emotional connection is also evident when examining *My52Tuesdays,* an interactive, online extension of the film, which builds on notions of authenticity to further engage interested audience members globally. In the ever-changing world of filmmaking, *52 Tuesdays* is an example of an alternate way forward for community filmmaking. It offers variations on forms of community filmmaking through innovative responses to government film policy initiatives. With a foot in both camps, the film was able to benefit from mainstream infrastructure, which increased local, and international audience access. At the same time its filmmaking process anchored *52 Tuesdays* within its community, while providing constantly dynamic subject matter and authenticity, which ultimately enabled it to resonate globally.

The second case study presented in this part comes from *Spain.* Asier Aranzubia, Miguel Fernández Labayen and Aitor Iturriza reflect in Chapter 6 on the way collaborative practices and artist networks come together in the case of 'Colectivo Cine sin Autor' (lit. Authorless Cinema Collective). The case study of this established and longstanding Collective, founded in Madrid in 2007, allows the authors to reflect on the opportunity that filmmaking as a process and practice can offer when it is not driven by individual recognition and authority. They consider the importance of this format in allowing a redistribution of the creative power and decision-making processes, adopting a non-hierarchical structure in the writing and producing of films. The collective, they suggest, acts almost as an intermediary between the community of producers and their audiences, and taking this intermediary role, they propose, could be considered an example of 'good cultural practice' that allows cultural diversity to emerge without constraints. They reflect on this case study as an emerging form of filmmaking, not simply in terms of its content and production, but also on the practice as a methodology to enable new content and communities to emerge.

Jonathan Dovey, Shawn Sobers and Emma Agusita present a case study from the UK (Bristol) and consider further the role of network and intermediaries and their agency and contribution to local innovative practices. Reflecting on the case study of community video production and exchange in the case of *South Blessed* (Bristol) they consider how young people involved in community media activities engage with issues of representation and self-expression as well as participation and personal realisation by engaging in community media. They reflect on how this engagement and their commitment to local networks in itself can produce new assets for the local communities and creative milieu. In their findings it is clear that resources, especially technology that enables the production, are key factors. However, they argue that the motivation and values of the individuals involved, and their shared agenda, constitute a much more powerful driver. Chapter 7 concludes with their suggestion that this attitude towards creating a community of interest and interaction, and offering training and peer support, represents for the individuals involved the most important aspect of community video practice.

3.3 Part 3: Community Filmmaking: Practices in Place and for Place

In this third part of the book, introduced by Chapain, we look at the practices of community filmmaking in various places as well as how community filmmaking can participate in the development of these places. When looking at community filmmaking practices, it is important to understand how the national cultural, social and policy frameworks, as well as the local contexts within which community filmmaking is undertaken, delineate, support and impact these practices. Like other creative practices, the film content produced within community filmmaking projects and the way it is produced will be dependent on the knowledge and skills developed by filmmakers within these particular contexts. In addition, given its participatory nature, it will be dependent on the mediation of community cultural representations, creative aspirations and skills as well as the particular objectives of the film project in question. Finally, community filmmaking, like any other creative participatory practices, can contribute to the cultural and social development of communities and places.

Chapter 8, by Daniel Mutibwa, examines the opportunities and challenges that British and German filmmakers face in their community filmmaking practices. This chapter is based on secondary and primary research looking at the production and practice of four companies engaged in community filmmaking; two in Britain and two in Germany. The chapter discusses how filmmakers navigate and reconcile their artistic, professional and commercial imperatives with the civic and at times oppositional functions usually associated with community filmmaking. In particular, it highlights the influence that socio-economic and socio-political circumstances can have in this process. Filmmakers apply their professionalism in the undertaking of community filmmaking in

terms of research and documentation that support each project. However, their creative vision and directorship need, at times, to be compromised to ensure the community participatory process inherent to letting
communities lead the filming process, on the one hand. On the other
hand, at times, the original intent of a particular project, seen as too
radical, has to be tweaked to allow filmmakers to obtain funds for their
films and sustain their practices. The notions of autonomy, creative freedom and experimentation are nevertheless seen as crucial to the practice
of community filmmaking. Mutibwa calls for a better recognition of
this practice within the wider film landscape and its social relevance for
communities.

Eileen Leahy, who studies various participatory processes used in
community filmmaking and their impacts on communities experiencing urban regeneration and social exclusion phenomena, explores these
issues further in Chapter 9. Initially challenging the assumed positive
benefits of cultural participation such as participation in community
filmmaking projects, her case studies' analysis highlights that these
projects can indeed help communities reclaim part of the spaces from
which they may be excluded. Indeed, being involved in filmmaking
projects with professional filmmakers allows communities to (re)invest
some spaces from which they feel excluded or associate new meanings
and identities to these spaces. In doing so, communities can "redefine
themselves in the face of change and thus preserve, build or maintain
community". Her analysis also highlights the diversity of creative and
community engagement processes at play and the range of interplay between amateur and professional practices within community filmmaking projects. Professional practices can help in terms of legitimation of
the activities but also in terms of community development through the
acquisition of new skills. She concludes by suggesting that community
filmmaking can serve in the process of local cultural development within
'globalising creative cities'.

Chapter 10 by Sharon Karsten offers a similar proposition in discussing the potential of community video in supporting the cultural
mapping of "the multiplicity of histories, identities and desires
(i.e. intangible assets) housed within place" within Canadian cities. As
such, after reviewing the debate around the concept of cultural mapping and the history of the Canadian community movement, Sharon
discusses the case of the *Where is here* project, a community video
project exploring the connections of local residents with place and
the potential of such a project to serve in both cultural mapping and
urban planning processes. Indeed, community video may offer easier
avenues to marginalised communities to express themselves on the one
hand and then on the other hand could be a way for urban planners
to "tap into new, and 'hard to grasp' (within a planning and development context), understandings of place", she suggests. Nevertheless,

she concludes that such an approach to cultural mapping and its use within urban policies would require the development of new epistemological approaches.

3.4 Part 4: Engagement and Participation in Community Filmmaking

The last section of the book, introduced by Malik, Chapain and Comunian, considers the role of community filmmaking as a driver for engagement and participation. Community filmmaking has been used in policy interventions as an example of creative and cultural practice that can facilitate dialogue and community engagement. However, there is limited research that highlights the challenges and rewards of engaging communities with film and what this implies for artists as well as audiences involved.

Chapter 11 by Roberta Mock, Kayla Parker and Ruth Way reflects on their experience of making the community film, *Heaven is a place*. As per their description, it is "a short dance film, made in 2014 in collaboration with members of the lesbian, gay, bisexual and transsexual community in Plymouth in South West England". The film explores the politics and poetics of LGBT location in a community dance film and brings together the work of Jean Genet as an artist and activist and the experiences of Plymouth's LBGT communities past and the mythogeography of Plymouth itself. The authors argued that by using dance as a tool to engage LGBT participants to dialogue with each other and express their own voices, the poetic of Jean Genet and the use of particular places in Plymouth, the film constitutes a "queer counter-public cartography" of the city. Like other community filmmakers, they comment on the difficulties of reconciling conflicting expectations about filmmaking within the project as well as the imperatives of creative and social engaged practices. Nevertheless, overall, the film resulted in the strengthening of bonds and relationships within the LGBT community in Plymouth and was seen as contributing positively to the representation of the community in the city.

Steve Presence addresses the issue of exhibition by focusing on a national (UK) network infrastructure that supports radical film culture in the UK. Presence situates the network in the context of the contemporary radical film culture from which it has emerged and argues that this culture has expanded significantly in recent years, as access to digital technologies has meshed with socio-economic, political and environmental contexts marked by crisis and discontent. As a result, he argues in Chapter 12, those organisations that remain from the radical film cultures of the 1960s to 1990s have been joined by a plethora of more recent groups, and there now exists a wealth of organisations dedicated to the production, distribution and exhibition of films broadly aligned with the politics of the radical left but also discusses the state of precarity for those working in radical activist cinema. Located as it is in the section on engagement and participation, Presence discusses the specific issues involved in negotiating engagement with local audiences of radical activist cinema. He examines how organisations involved in radical film exhibition negotiate such precarious conditions and how these conditions shape their approach to exhibition.

In Chapter 13 Alicia Blum-Ross explores another important dimension of community filmmaking engagement and participation: work with youth in the UK. She considers how youth media projects are reflective not only of the young filmmakers, but also of the adult intermediaries (facilitators and funders) who provide and access the resources to run them. Adopting a complexity approach, she articulates how youth filmmaking projects operate at a 'micro' grassroots level, but also incorporate the 'meso' level of youth media funding and the 'macro' level of youth policy and young people in popular media discourse. Drawing on extensive ethnographic research with youth media organisations in London, she shows how youth filmmaking is justified as a form of empowerment of youth to "express themselves" and give them a sense of belonging. However, she also highlights how this is often built on negative assumptions about young people as apathetic or disengaged, while at the same time "digital natives". Her work helps us consider how engagement and participation objectives sometimes build on stereotypes and simplified understanding of communities, which do not completely value their diversity.

The last chapter in the collection, co-written by Kate Pahl and Steve Pool, revisits their work as an ethnographer and visual artist respectively, as they encounter video within co-produced community-research projects. They explore the uses of film in community-oriented research and how this relates to power inequalities both within and beyond projects with a particular focus on engagement and participation. Pahl and Pool draw on the respective fields of ethnographic research and engaged critical art practice and discuss the intersections with the field of participatory film. For the authors, it is increasingly clear that the digital capture of the moving image has become an everyday cultural practice and that this has changed the possibilities and implications of its use within research. Through a close analysis of three film projects with children and young people in which they were involved, they demonstrate in Chapter 14 how film became a space of practice where young people could develop articulations of their lived experience and their ideas. At the same time, they assert that it is in community co-production contexts that filmmaking can provide the most accessible and meaningful form of community engagement but that this is an outcome that is marginalised in the context of knowledge production and transfer in academic discourse.

References

Andres, Lauren and Caroline Chapain. 2015. "Creative Systems: a new integrated approach to understanding the complexity of cultural and creative industries in Eastern and Western countries." In *The Handbook of Service Business*, edited by John Bryson and Peter Daniels. Cheltenham: Edward Elgar.

Bianchini, Franco and Michael Parkinson. Eds. 1993. *Cultural Policy and Urban Regeneration: The West European Experience*. Manchester: Manchester University Press.

Braden, Su. 1978. *Artists and People*. London: Routledge and Kegan Paul.

Cattani, Gino and Simone Ferriani. 2008. "A Core/Periphery Perspective on Individual Creative Performance: social networks and cinematic achievements in the Hollywood film industry." *Organization Science* 19(6): 824–844.

Chapain Caroline, Nick Clifton and Roberta Comunian. 2013. "Understanding Creative Regions: bridging the gap between global discourses and regional and national contexts." Special issue, *Regional Studies* 47(2).

Chapain, Caroline and Lisa De Propris. 2009. "Drivers and Processes of Creative Industries in Cities and Regions." Special Issue, *Creative Industries Journal* 2(1).

Chapain Caroline and Ian Hargreaves. 2016. "Citizenship in the Creative Economy." in *The Creative Citizen Unbound: how social media and DIY culture contribute to democracy, communities and the creative economy*, edited by Ian Hargreaves and John Hartley. Bristol: Policy Press.

Clifton Nick, Caroline Chapain and Roberta Comunian. eds. 2016. *Creative regions in Europe*. Oxon: Routledge.

Comunian, Roberta. 2011. "Rethinking the Creative City: the role of complexity, networks and interactions in the urban creative economy." *Urban Studies* 48: 1157–1179.

Comunian, Roberta. 2012. "Exploring the Role of Networks in the Creative Economy of North East England: economic and cultural dynamics." In *Encounters and Engagement between Economic Cultural Geography*, 143–157, Edited by Barney Warf. Netherlands: Springer.

Comunian, Roberta and Katerina Alexiou. 2015. "Mapping the Complexity of Creative Practice: using cognitive maps to follow creative ideas and collaborations." In *Cultural Mapping as Cultural Inquiry*, edited by Duxbury Nancy, William Francis Garrett-Petts and David Maclennan. London: Routledge.

Comunian, Roberta, Katerina Alexiou and Caroline Chapain. 2012. *The Role of Complexity in the Creative Economy: connecting people, ideas and practices*. Report presented to the AHRC Connected Communities Programme.

Comunian Roberta, Caroline Chapain and Nick Clifton. 2014. "Creative Industries and Creative Policies: a European perspective?" Special issue, *City, Culture and Society* 5(2).

Comunian Roberta, Caroline Chapain and Nick Clifton. 2010, "Location, Location, Location: exploring the complex relationship between creative industries and place." Special issue, *Creative Industries Journal* 3(1).

Conway, Kyle. 2004. "Digital Video, Microcinema, and the Rhetoric of Media Democratization." *Spectator* 24(1): 42–52.

Coyer, Kate. Tony Dowmunt and Alan Fountain. 2007. *The Alternative Media Handbook*. London: Routledge.

Curtis, Richard. 2016. "Support Creativity & the Diversity of Cultural Expressions around the World." http://en.unesco.org/creativity/news/support-creativity-diversity-cultural-expressions-around-world-richard-curtis-advocate-un.

Evans, Graeme and Phyllida Shaw. 2004. *The Contribution of Culture Regeneration in the UK: a review of evidence.* A report to the Department for Culture Media and Sport. London: London Metropolitan University.

Fox, Broderick 2004. "Rethinking the Amateur: acts of media production in the digital age." *Spectator* 24(1): 5–16.

Glow, Hilary and Katya Johanson. 2010. "Building Capacity or Burning out? Supporting Indigenous Performing Artists and Filmmakers." *Media International Australia* 136(1): 71–84.

Hill, J. 2004 "UK Film Policy, Cultural Capital and Social Exclusion." *Cultural Trends* 13 (2): 29–39.

Jackson, Maria-Rosario and Joaquim Herranz. 2003. *Culture Counts in Community: a framework for measurement.* Washington: The Urban Institute.

Jakob Doreen and Bas Van Heur. 2015. "Editorial: taking matters into third hands: intermediaries and the organisation of the creative economy." *Regional Studies* 49(3): 357–361.

Jones, Candace. 2010. "Finding a Place in History: symbolic and social networks in creative careers and collective memory." *Journal of Organizational Behavior* 31: 726–748.

Kattelle, Alan 2004. "Once, There Was Film... looking back at amateur motion picture technologies." *Spectator* 24 (1): 53–64.

Hartley John, Jason Potts, Stuart Cunningham, Terry Flew, Michael Keane and John Banks. 2013. *Key Concepts in the Creative Industries.* London: Sage.

Malik, Sarita. 1996. "'Beyond "The Cinema of Duty'? The Pleasures of Hybridity: black British film of the 1980s and 1990s." In *Dissolving Views: key writings on British cinema.* Edited by Andrew Higson. London: Cassell: 202–215.

Malik, Sarita, Caroline Chapain and Roberta Comunian. 2014. *Spotlight on Community Filmmaking: a report on community filmmaking and cultural diversity research.* Birmingham and London, UK: Brunel University, the University of Birmingham and King's College.

Markusen, Ann and Anne Gadwa. 2010. *Creative Placemaking.* Washington: Markusen Economic Research Services and Metris Arts Consulting.

Mattaraso, Francois. 2013. "All in the Together': the depoliticastion of community art in Britain, 1970–2011. *Community, Art, Power,* Rotterdam: ICAF.

Mayo, Marjorie. 2000. *Cultures, Communities, Identities: cultural strategies for participation and empowerment.* Basingstoke: Palgrave Macmillan.

Mercer, K. 1988. Ed. *Black Film, British Cinema.* London: Institute of Contemporary Arts.

Odin, Roger. 1999. Ed. *Le cinema en amateur.* Communications. Ecole des Hautes Etudes en Sciences Sociales – Centre d'Etudes Transdisciplinaires (Sociologie, Anthropoligie, Histoire), Paris: Seuil.

Petley, Julian. 1989. "Background and Development of Film and Video Workshops." *Landmarks.* London: British Council.

Pines, J. and P. Willemen. 1989. *Questions of Third Cinema.* London: British Film Institute.

Price, Jonathan. 2015. "Contested agendas of participation in the arts." *Journal of Arts and Communities* 7. 2(3): 17–31.

Shand, Ryan. 2008. "Theorizing Amateur Cinema: limitations and possibilities." *The Moving Image* 8(2): 36–60.

Sørensen, Inge. 2012. "Crowdsourcing and Outsourcing: the impact of online funding and distribution on the documentary film industry in the UK." *Media, Culture & Society* 34(6): 726–743.

Wenger, Étienne. 1998. *Communities of Practice: Learning, Meaning and Identity, Cambridge*, MA: Cambridge University Press.

Zimmerman, Patricia. 1986. "The Amateur, the Avant-Garde and Ideologies of Art." *Journal of Film and Video* 38(3/4): 63–85.

Part I

Diversity, Representation and Community Filmmaking – a Short Introduction

Sarita Malik

Questions of diversity frame this collection. The book highlights the important relationship between the community mode of filmmaking and diversity through practice; between different kinds of cinema (to the mainstream) and different kinds of (otherwise marginalised) cultural perspectives. Community filmmaking is therefore identified as a critical site of both cultural and community significance and a useful example that can help inform wider debates about diversity and the media.

This short introduction sets the context for the three chapters in Part 1 of the book and also introduces a range of concerns that are apparent across the entire collection. Each of these three chapters, in various ways and focusing on different contexts, highlights how the social and political are at the centre of the community filmmaking process and how it can function as a critical counterhegemonic space in contemporary culture. Issues of culture and identity have indeed become a central concern within the humanities and social sciences, particularly since the 1990s, as we have seen a rise of solidarity and collective identities alongside processes of civic communication in relation to, for example, new media forms. However, more traditional forms of media such as film have been relatively overlooked in terms of their contribution to communicative participation. Cultural Studies, which has established itself across a range of disciplines, has been particularly notable for its scholarly contribution to debates about diversity and the media in general and around representation and community media specifically. This is hardly surprising, given the focus within cultural theory on the political dynamics of contemporary culture, communities and identities and on critical questions of the relationship between power, culture and ideology.

'Community', Margins and Mainstream

The idea that communities can have a 'common identity' is problematic and whilst various 'communities' are discussed in the book, the flexibility of the idea of 'communities of identity' – whether racial, sexual, class or otherwise – is taken on board throughout the collection. At the same time, when groups of individuals or networks define themselves as communities, for example, the Hong Kong population that self-identifies as ethnic minority youth in Burkholder's chapter or the diverse Scots in Scott's chapter, this is also explored as an interesting facet of diversity and (self)representation. Community becomes for us in this collection an act of being, rather than a fixed state. How these multifaceted ideas of community and connectivity are constructed or acted upon also underlines the importance of seeing communities as action, process and activity (Walkerdine and Studdert 2011) and of further exploring issues of positionality for the community filmmaker in relation to 'community'. This idea of cultures and communities in motion also mirrors the complex processes at work in how community filmmaking is produced and enacted.

One element of analysis within the academic literature has focused on how communities of identity, themselves often marginalised in mainstream contexts, use cultural spaces for political and aesthetic projects that seek to rework or reimagine dominant cultural representations or provide an alternative (or oppositional cinema) to the mainstream (cinema) (Mercer 1988; Pines and Willemen 1989). A tension or 'ambivalence of community' (Bauman 2001) is manifest therefore between how 'community' is chosen as part of a 'social imaginary' (Taylor 2004) within community filmmaking contexts because it enables certain modes of cultural identification and solidarity, and in other instances 'community' is resisted because of the essentialist identity paradigms and deindividualising processes it helps produce and sustain. There is a notable growth in media and cultural studies that address the relationship between civic agency and social change. As some of this work points out, the role of the media in such processes is central here both because of its powerful role in "the shaping of popular understandings of citizenship (its insides and outsides)" (Jackson et al. 2015, 2) through, for example, regimes of cultural stereotyping and because of its "potential to allow the intervention of marginalised voices into the mainstream" (ibid. 3).

The politics of representation through these participatory modes of production does mean (as has been noted elsewhere in the book) that community filmmakers are able to actively engage to reshape and reposition their practice within alternative business models and without rendering any aspirations for civic, social or political change as instruments of a neoliberal agenda or industry-led diversity policy paradigms such as 'creative diversity' (Malik 2013). Community filmmaking can be enacted therefore as a group practice and mode of expression that sets in motion bell hooks' idea of 'communities of resistance', which she describes as "places where we know we are not alone" (1989).

The idea that communities, often with strong civic agendas, are constantly being created and reformulated and reproducing themselves – through the medium of film and through new forms of social affiliation – is deeply apparent in each of the three chapters presented here. Ashton, Burkholder and Scott all demonstrate how new communities are created through community-engaged film. Ashton also points to some of the tensions in trying to reflect these processes of engagement when approached by the mainstream (in this case the British Broadcasting Corporation (BBC)). The particular value of these discussions is in how they bring together elements of a media and cultural studies approach to questions of diversity and the politics of representation, whilst also addressing questions of praxis within community filmmaking contexts.

Community, Identity and Representation

In our research, we have found that one of the important facets of community filmmaking is how it builds conditions for creative sharing and how, within this, there is a strong motivation to elicit social change. Much of the work that is presented here focuses on how different groups come together and mobilise through the process of making film together and thus pays particular attention to the matter of praxis. It considers how particular groups that are routinely marginalised in society and also in cultural representation use film to deliberately challenge the notion that meanings, ideologies and 'community' are fixed, by facilitating or producing work that reworks or renegotiates existing representations.

A point of concern is what this then produces in terms of textual representations – that is whether more diverse representation in the production process necessarily leads to more diverse representations within the media text itself. This is a question that has been taken up recently (Saha 2016) and is further explored here in Ashton's chapter when he asks, "does the open invitation to a wide number of potential participants equal diverse forms of self-representation?" For the purpose of this collection, our focus on representation is primarily in terms of the creative process itself (rather than what actually ends up on screen), and many of the chapters indicate that film work that takes place within community contexts facilitates a significant range of diversity to be articulated, particularly through processes of production.

There are two cautionary points here. The first is in relation to access and networks and how this overlaps with questions of representation. Traditional problems around gaining access and barriers to entry that have been widely discussed in critical cultural production studies

(Saha 2016) in relation to mainstream cultural industries are tackled, we suggest, through an ethos of participation and co-creation that can be found in community filmmaking contexts. However, as Comunian points out in her introduction to Part 2 on networks and intermediaries, the networks that can be found in community filmmaking contexts can also often give rise to forms of exclusion or create cliques that might discourage new entrants or 'outsiders' to engage with the cultural exchange process. Community filmmaking is therefore not exempt from wider social processes of inequality and exclusion that are enacted within the creative sector, inequalities that have been repeatedly identified within academic research (O'Brien and Oakley 2015; Eikhof 2013).

The second is in relation to representational politics. Whilst diversity manifests itself and is 'made visible' within the process itself and in the labour of making film within these more or less participative, community-engaged contexts, the question of whether this directly translates to diverse content on screen remains open. It is the case then that there is a potential tension between diversity in terms of production process and diversity in terms of textual representation.

This is reminiscent of a point made by Scott in Chapter 4: that community filmmaking (and he uses the example of the workshop movement in which he was involved in Scotland during the 1980s) produces a constant tension between *process* and *production*. This is a tension that is linked to this relationship between diversity and representation, communities and film, and we start to address it here. As Scott says, for some involved in the film workshop movement, being represented through the collaborative process of making films was important, but for others it was "the product, the completed film, [that] was seen as a useful outcome but less important than the collaborative work and participation during production".

Diversity and Community Filmmaking

The lack of diversity within the creative industries is one of the major contexts in which this collection of chapters is assembled. As outlined in Chapter 1, the media is, for example, being questioned for how it grapples with social diversity in a broad sense, and cultural diversity in particular. A lack of cultural diversity within screen representation (on-screen) and also in the workforce (off-screen) has been acknowledged within academic research (O'Loughlin 2006) and industry reports (Creative Skillset 2012). For example, mirroring the 2016 American Oscars' controversy, the 2015 and 2016 British Academy of Film and Television (BAFTA) shortlists suggest ongoing exclusion of women and black people within the mainstream film sector (O'Brien and Oakley 2015). Given the opportunities that appear to be produced within community filmmaking contexts, the question for us is whether media and cultural production that emerges from outside of formal, mainstream structures, facilitates an alternative politics or creative practice that supports social diversity and expression. And if this is the case, we are interested in knowing what processes or frameworks allow this to happen. Furthermore, with regards to film and representation, what specifically does the film form offer community filmmakers in terms of the possibilities of diverse representation, and why does community film remain pervasive even in the midst of complex modes of migration, globalisation and media consumption?

References

Bauman, Zygmunt. 2001. *Community: seeking safety in an insecure world.* Cambridge: Polity Press.

Creative Skillset. 2012. Employment Census of the Creative Media Industries, http://creativeskillset.org/assets/0000/5070/2012_Employment_Census_of_the_Creative_Media_Industries.pdf.

Eikhof, Ruth. 2013. "The Promised Land? Why Social Inequalities Are Systemic in the Creative Industries." *Employee Relations* 5: 495–508.

hooks, bell. 1989. Talking Back: thinking feminist, thinking black. Toronto: Between the Lines.

Jackson, Daniel, Alexander, Jenny, Thorsen, Einar and Savigny, Heather. 2015. "Introduction." In *Media, Margins and Civic Agency,* edited by Einar Thorsen, Daniel Jackson, Heather Savigny and Jenny Alexander. Basingstoke: Palgrave Macmillan.

Malik Sarita. 2013. "Creative Diversity": UK public service broadcasting after multiculturalism. *Popular Communication* 11(3): 227–241.

Mercer Kobena. 1988. Ed. *Black Film, British Cinema.* London: Institute of Contemporary Arts.

O'Brien Dave and Oakley Kate. 2015. *Cultural Value and Inequality: a critical literature review,* AHRC. http://www.ahrc.ac.uk/documents/project-reports-and-reviews/cultural-value-and-inequality-a-critical-literature-review (accessed 20th November 2015).

O'Loughlin, Ben. 2006. "The Operationalization of the Concept 'Cultural Diversity' in British Television Policy and Governance." Centre for Research on Socio-Cultural Change, *Working Paper* no. 27. http://www.cresc.ac.uk/medialibrary/workingpapers/wp27.pdf.

Pines Jim and Willemen Paul. 1989. *Questions of Third Cinema.* London: British Film Institute.

Saha, Anamik. 2016. "From the Politics of Representation to the Politics of Production." In *Media and Minorities: Questions of Representation from an International Perspective,* edited by G. Ruhrmann, Y. Shooman and P. Widmann, 39–49. Vandenhoeck & Ruprecht.

Taylor Charles. 2004. *Modern Social Imaginaries.* Durham, NC: Duke University Press.

Walkerdine, Valerie and David Studdert. 2011. *Concepts and Meanings of Community in the Social Sciences.* Connected Communities Discussion Paper. http://www.ahrc.ac.uk/documents/project-reports-and-reviews/connected-communities/concepts-and-meanings-of-community-in-the-social-sciences/.

2 Digital Stories, Participatory Practices and *Life/Britain in a Day*

Framing Creativity and Debating Diversity

Daniel Ashton

Introduction

This chapter examines the *Life in a Day* and *Britain in a Day* participatory documentary projects to explore the possibilities and tensions in creating culturally diverse representations of everyday life through film. Operating across different national and global scales, these projects share common ground in facilitating participation in cultural production and developing a 'crowd' (Surowiecki 2004) approach to representing everyday life.

Life in a Day was compiled from video footage recorded by members of the public on 24th July 2010 and then submitted to YouTube. The final 95-minute documentary was edited together from 80,000 submissions to create a "paean to what it means to be human in the world today" (IMDB 2011). Likewise, the 2012 documentary that followed in its footsteps, *Britain in a Day*, invited footage captured in Britain on 12th November 2012. The final 95-minute documentary was edited together from 11,526 submissions to offer "remarkable insight into the lives, loves, fears and hopes of people living in Britain today" (BBC 2012).

This chapter presents findings from a research project mapping the 'life' of the ... *in a Day* projects. The three aims of this larger project are to (1) identify the ways in which the contributions of participants to the crowdsourced documentaries *Britain in a Day* and *Life in a Day* were framed through instructional and guidance materials; (2) analyse the narrative themes and content of the films; and (3) evaluate the public response to the guidance materials and finished films. Research findings analysed in this chapter focus on the agendas of the ... *in a Day* projects to encourage and facilitate wide participation in representing everyday life (aim one) and the associated tensions expressed by potential participants concerning the constraint and framing of their creative agency within the production (aim three).

First, this chapter outlines the wider research project and presents the rationale and methodological approach for researching the ... *in a Day* projects. Second, this chapter connects the ... *in a Day* projects with the critical approaches of Malik (2013) and Saha (2013a) to address issues of participation and diversity. Their arguments concerning diversity in representation provide a useful point of reference for critically evaluating the 'diversity through numbers' dimensions common to both recent media and cultural policy discourses and the ... *in a Day* projects. To examine the meeting points between production frameworks and public experiences, this chapter engages with critical perspectives on participatory cultures (Carpentier 2003, Muller 2009) and documentary filmmaking (Dovey and Rose 2013, Dovey 2014). Specifically, this chapter examines three dimensions of the ... *in a Day* projects: the invitation stage; the participatory processes; and the public responses. In doing so this chapter asks, does the open invitation to a wide number of potential participants equal diverse forms of self-representation?

Researching ... *in a Day*

Life in a Day was developed in collaboration with YouTube and drew inspiration from the Mass Observation Movement approach of giving a voice in documenting everyday life to those outside of the elite (see Watercutter 2011). *Britain in a Day* was developed in collaboration with the British Broadcasting Corporation (BBC) and emerged out of a UK context in which the BBC under its public service broadcaster remit had been involved with the similar *Video Nation* and *Capture Wales* digital storytelling projects (see Carpentier 2003, Kidd 2009). The ... *in a Day* projects can be located within a longer history of digital storytelling and efforts to capture expressions of everyday life on film. The distinctive aspect of the ... *in a Day* documentary projects is their approach to mass participation. Crowdsourcing contributions for the goal of documenting life on earth/in a country on one day continues to gain momentum with recent projects under the ... *in a Day* banner taking place in Italy (26th October 2013) and India (10th October 2015). The continued use of the crowdsourced approach for generating and distributing stories suggests that everyday stories will continue to be of wide media and public accessibility and interest. That this growth is through the ... *in a Day* brand and led by a particular production company, Scott Free Productions, raises questions around the contexts and conditions under which "digital stories are exchanged, referred to, treated as a resource and given recognition and authority" (Couldry 2008, 388).

The primary research sites of the project explored in this chapter are the *Life in a Day* YouTube channel and the *Britain in a Day* YouTube channel and BBC webpages. The continued availability of the YouTube channels, the videos and the comments threads provide a 'living' (Burgess and Green 2009) and 'informal' (Pietrobruno 2013) archive for this research project. Specifically, these 'paratextual' (Caldwell 2014) guidance materials were examined in terms of their capacity to 'scaffold' or 'prefigure' (Barker 2004) participation. The videos posted by the production team and the comments thread made in response, come together on the YouTube page – a "complex configuration of semiotic components" (Androutsopoulos and Tereick 2015, 356). Indeed, the role of YouTube in the origination, design and execution of the projects and the engagement of the 'YouTube community' (see Macdonald in Dodes 2011) signal the importance of analysing comments threads.

The *Life in a Day* channel in total has 59 videos and 25,116 comments in response. Videos included: trailers for the project to generate interest; 'about the film' and 'guidance' videos with members of the production team; messages from the production team on the process; interviews with the projects' participating 'filmmakers'; the film made available on 11th January 2011; and videos one year later created by participants or recorded with the production team. The *Britain in a Day* channel has 18 videos and 215 comments in response. Videos include: trailers for the project to generate interest; teasers; and 'about the film' videos. The film itself is not available on the YouTube channel, so for this research project the version broadcast on Monday 11th June 2012 at 9pm on BBC2 was accessed using *Box of Broadcasts*. In addition, the guidance provided face to face during workshops delivered by Rosa Productions for *Britain in a Day* was discussed through a face-to-face semi-structured interview with one of the organisers of the workshops.

Through an iterative process, the following six themes were identified and used to code the documentary films, the YouTube videos and the comments: participation; technology; authorship and ownership; narrative and style; expertise and society. The approach with this chapter is not to include comments as 'evidence'. Indeed, some of the challenges of researching YouTube concern who is speaking and the practical challenges of following how comments connect to each other. Given the volume of responses, there is an issue that certain viewpoints might be over-represented whilst others are marginalised. Comments are included within this chapter with the 'LD' identifier for *Life in a Day* and the 'BD' identifier for *Britain in a Day*, as well as a comment number. Whilst there are challenges with the "one commentator said" approach to including quotes and comments (see Taylor 2012), each comment provides an important way to explore how invited participants responded to the guidance on how to participate. There are several other important further considerations, limitations and challenges to note for this research.

There are certainly relevant connections and comparisons to be made across the two projects, but there are also important distinctions including the public service broadcasting underpinnings and the use of workshops for *Britain in a Day*. Similarly the larger project from which this chapter draws seeks to make links with other projects with alternative ways of working (for example, *One Day on Earth* – a project name-checked by several commenters addressing the originality of the Scott Free Productions). Further to the interview with the workshop organiser, there also remain significant openings for empirical research with those involved in the productions. Notwithstanding these points, the comments presented in this analysis are an important part of understanding how 'the crowd' can evaluate the participatory promises and practices of the ... *in a Day* projects. This is relevant for issues of community filmmaking, because it allows us to also understand the perceptions and experiences of communities themselves. One of long-standing debates in studies of community media concerns the relationships between facilitators and participants and the differing emphasis on 'process' and 'product' (see for example Sobers 2009). Connecting with these wider debates addressing the role of power dynamics in facilitating participation in community filmmaking, this chapter investigates how the management and usage of user generated content (the film footage) can be examined through analysing user generated content (the comments threads).

Participation and Diversity: "A wonderful patchwork of our nations"

In one of the guidance videos (BD1) for *Britain in a Day*, Director Morgan Matthews addresses potential participants and enthuses that when video footage has been sent in, "we can create this wonderful patchwork of our nations that reflects anything and everything about us and what it means to be British and what we're going through in our lives today". The aim of these projects to document human life clearly aligns with the efforts to source the documentary materials from a wide range of participants. There were no restrictions or limitations on who could send in footage. Similarly, there was no specific participant profile. As will be addressed in relation to 'the invitation' in the next section, there were explicit efforts to support certain groups in creating and submitting footage. This was less about having a certain type of documentary participant and more about having a range and diversity of participants.

Related to questions of participation in media making, Malik (2013) examines a shift in media and cultural policy from multiculturalism and cultural diversity to creative diversity. This is an agenda that "formulates ideas of quality and creativity over (structural) questions of (in)equality" (Malik 2013, 233). Malik (2013, 233) identifies the 'all-encompassing' nature of this re-framing – an approach to participation that is also obvious with the ... *in a Day* projects and the stated concern to get lots of footage from lots of people. With reference to other commentators, Malik (2013, 233) goes on to suggest that this move towards being all-encompassing includes and contains "all possible forms of diversity in society" (van Ejiwk, 2011) and claims to broaden access "to the widest possible range of cultural experiences" (Garnham 2005, 27). The approach to wide access is common to public service broadcasting in the UK, and seeing this agenda with the *Britain in a Day* project is unsurprising given the involvement of the BBC alongside Scott Free Productions. Indeed, the *Britain in a Day* project has obvious connections with at least two of the six 'public purposes' set out by the BBC (2016): "stimulating creativity and cultural excellence" and "representing the UK, its nations, regions, and communities". The aim of opening participation operates at two levels: the possible cultural experiences included as content in the films and diversity in production.

The examination of (diverse) representations within the actual content of these participatory documentaries is part of the wider research project but beyond the scope of this chapter's focus on production frameworks and dynamics. That said, the politics of production and politics of representation are intricately connected. Indeed, these projects present a distinctive way of responding to Hall's (2000) 'multicultural question' concerning different groups of people occupying the same social space and living together in difference. Specifically, these documentary projects attempt a filmic 'patchwork' representing diversity by seeking to create an on-screen shared presence. A further dimension to this on-screen 'patchwork' of diversity comes with material being contributed by the public rather than purposefully created. Indeed, many of the claims made concerning the diverse representations of Britain/Life that these projects create are based on the participation of the 'crowd'. Clearly, the 'patchwork' of representations presented in the final films would not be possible if these people, experiences and events did not exist and if the footage was not submitted for inclusion. That said, each stage of these projects involves a carefully crafted process of selection and organisation. Alongside the representations of Britain/Life presented within the final films, attention must focus on how efforts to generate high participation numbers were located within specific cultures of production.

Efforts to increase participation and extend the diversity profile of those working in the cultural and creative industries have been critically reviewed by both Malik (2013) and Saha (2013a). With the ... *in a Day* projects a corresponding effort to promote industry workforce/production team is not explicitly on the agenda. Rather, the distinctive approach here is of inviting public contributions and having credits that include 'filmed by you'. On this, there is an understanding both in the discourses that Malik and Saha address and in the ... *in a Day* projects of how diversity in production voices translates into diversity in content.

With regard to workforce diversity in the creative and cultural industries, Saha (2013a, 214) identifies "numerous initiatives launched across both corporate and subsidized cultural sectors that have made efforts to increase and encourage participation from 'Black Minority Ethnic (BME) groups'". Both Malik (2013) and Saha (2013a) address the limitations of a quantitative approach of increasing diversity through increasing numbers. They caution against assuming a connection between steps to increase workforce diversity and corresponding changes in representation and content. Specifically, Saha (2013a, 219) argues that the discourse of representation in the labour market has a sole focus on the quantitative that:

> [...] not only ignores the *quality* of output and the politics of representation, but more crucially, fails to understand the relation between cultures of production and the agency of the cultural worker through which symbols of 'race' and ethnicity are created.

Here we see a cautionary note to take care of simple claims that diverse content and representation necessarily flow from the involvement of a diverse range of participants. What is crucial from Saha's (2013a) account is the issue of creative agency. As the following addresses, the tension between *who* is involved and *how* runs throughout this analysis.

Invitation: "It was very important to involve as many people as possible"

In introducing *Life in a Day*, director Kevin Macdonald describes it as a "portrait of the world" and as "a time capsule" (LD1). Similarly, in the trailer for *Britain in a Day* (BD2), the invitation is extended to "pick up your cameras and join us" to become, as TV presenter Mel Giedroyc puts it, "part of British film history". These projects have a clear view towards contributing to social history and establishing their cultural commentary 'legacy' (Gratton and Preuss 2008). To secure involvement, these projects had to make consistent efforts to generate interest. Indeed, Beresford and Schwarz (2014, 67) address how "online digital PR underpinned the whole process" of *Life in a Day*. For one YouTube commenter to a video on the *Life in Day* channel, the sustained high profile coverage was a point of frustration:

> I don't really mind these kinds of special projects but I wish Youtube wouldn't keep spamming my homepage with this stuff over and over. I've seen the lifeinaday channel about a hundred times over the last 2 days. I get it, it's all very trendy and hip, but it's getting on my nerves now (LD1 comment 1)

The promotion on YouTube and by the BBC to generate attention, the use of celebrities (with *Britain in Day*) to encourage and the (arguably) novel aims and approaches were all factors driving the call to participate.

Referencing digital literacy projects, Poletti (2011, 75) suggests that, "an invitation to 'tell your story' is but one of many experienced by people in everyday life" (see also Kidd 2009). The plentiful opportunities for self-representation were consistently pointed out in the comments thread responses to the *Life in a Day* YouTube channel videos. The following offer some insights:

> This is stupid because people make documentaries everyday. They can just watch old news clips or read articles online. (LD1 comment 2)

> ok this idea is FUCKIN STUPID! it doe not make any sense at all. we already VlOg and film our everday life anyways[...]! (LD1 comment 3)

The first comment points to the range of mass media 'time capsule' materials already in operation, and the second comment, along with others, highlight that this is happening on an ordinary basis through YouTube anyway. To summarise, commenters raised questions of "why this project" and "why with/for you?" These are questions that resonate with Dovey's (2012, 22) analysis of participatory documentary when he discusses "framing the call to action" and positioning a project within a "wider social, political or cultural framework".

Previous analysis of *Life in a Day* by Wilson (2012, 113) argued that, "the discourse established by the production is one of inclusion and empowerment, and this agenda, whether or not it is authentic, is the key element of the project". The specific materials through which Wilson makes this argument are not clear, but the analysis undertaken within this project of the YouTube invitation and guidance materials thoroughly supports it. For example, an 'empowerment' celebratory account is presented by a woman in a swimming pool in "Britain in a Day is about YOU" (BD3) who suggests, it is a "great way of showcasing to the rest of the world what a great country we have here in Britain". In the same video, a sense of social coherence comes across in the comments from a man in a garden who states the importance of the project in bringing "people together in these very difficult times. We need to share each others' lives and help each other". In reflecting on the BBC *Capture Wales* project, Kidd (2009, 175) notes how the personal can often be "dismissed in favour of dialogue about community and inclusion". The creation/choice of messages for the 'call to action' in trailers resonates with the emphasis on dialogues around community and inclusion. In turn, the emphasis on the personal was a strong dimension. The most explicit invitation to contribute stories that are personal in nature comes in the "Advice from Morgan Matthews and producer Ridley Scott" video in which Scott states, "film anything, but most of all make it personal" (BD1). Likewise with *Life in a Day*, Ridley Scott (LD2) emphasises, "It should be personal. It must be personal. That's what we are looking for". These projects seek to address issues of the social and political through individual narratives and personal stories.

Addressing the 'mosaic aesthetics' of "life on earth" projects, including *Life in a Day*, Gaudenzi (2014, 137) points out how the "the number of participants is essential to the artefact itself [...]. Without that the project is meaningless and risks dying". The link can be re-established here to Saha's (2013a) analysis that cultural diversity comes through agency in symbol creation rather than diversity targets. Whilst there are not 'diversity targets' in the same sense, there is a similarity with the ... *in a Day* projects concerning numbers and scale. Although there were few expectations stated by the directors on how many submissions there would be, the goal it would seem was always to represent as widely as possible. The invitations attempt to speak to as many people as possible though promotional videos and trailers. As the following comments from the directors of each film make clear, a project priority was diversity and representation:

> It was very important to involve as many people as possible, because if the film doesn't represent the length and breadth of the country, if it doesn't represent the diversity of the country, then it doesn't represent us.
>
> (Matthews BD4)

> It was important to represent the whole world.
>
> (Macdonald cited in Dodes 2011)

Both directors recognise what is at stake with these projects in needing to receive footage from a wide diversity of potential participants. These comments should also be taken alongside other comments from the directors showing that they view the projects still in terms of their directorial vision and that their interest could be in drawing out narratives and themes (for example, see Macdonald in Dodes 2011 and Matthews in BD5). Overall though, the shared approach of the ... *in a Day* projects is entirely consistent with 'crowdsourcing' approach – encouraging a lot of contributions and bringing these together to show life across the world/in Britain. The calling card of the ... *in a Day* projects comes with the multiplicity of voices that come together. By examining the participatory production processes, a firmer sense of how these aims for (self)representation are actualised can be determined.

Participation: "We want you to pick up your cameras and join us"

In his discussion of British national identity, Colls (2012, 103) makes the point that, "images of national identity are not always to be trusted as true representations, even when they are multi-sourced, as in the case of the BBC's 2012 "Britain in a Day" documentary". Colls (2012, 103) continues to suggest that, "national identity is not the same as its passing image". With the ... *in a Day* projects, the claims only ever extend to creating a snapshot. There is recognition that the world of 24th July 2010 and the Britain of 21st November 2011 would of course be different from the days before and that follow. Indeed, it is recognising the changing nature of life in the world/Britain that drives efforts to create a narrative of timeless themes in the documentaries (and as prompted in the questions by Macdonald and Mathews). That said, Colls' comments highlight that a larger number of contributors does not necessarily lead to 'truer' representations. In one respect, this is about the authenticity of the material captured. Indeed, YouTube commenters flagged up that exciting versions of the day or purposeful activities would be submitted. In another respect, this is an issue of participatory production processes and the kind of involvement available in constructing the representations.

Alongside the issue of authenticity concerning discourses of inclusion and empowerment, there has been sustained academic analysis concerning the ways in which participants were actually able to participate. For Vickers (2012, 106), with *Life in a Day*, "conventional hierarchical power structures remain". Similarly, Dovey (2014, 21), argues that "the invitation to contribute your footage for free to be cut by someone else with no editorial rights is a very minimal collaboration". Elsewhere (Ashton 2015), I engaged with Muller's (2009) concept of the quality discourse to argue that the guidance materials speak to potential contributors as amateurs whose contributions would extend only to providing raw material for expert and professional editing. For this chapter, the distinctive concern is with the 'open invitation' to participate and how this was followed up in the terms of participation that were in place.

With *Life in a Day*, there were steps to bring in global perspectives through sending out "400 cameras to parts of the developing world" (Macdonald, cited in Wattercutter 2011). These 'outreach cameras' resulted in 5,000 clips (Walker LD3) and show the practical steps to realise claims to inclusion and wide representation. In planning and developing the *Britain in a Day* project, Rosemary Richards from Rosa Productions, the company commissioned by the BBC to lead workshops, describes an awareness concerning the diversity in the range of participants to *Life in a Day*, with specific mention of the number of film and media students. Building on the methods established with the BBC's *Video Nation* project, an approach to facilitating participation through workshops was implemented (Richards 2015). These workshops were part of a wider call for participation that included relationships with further and higher education institutions and public promotion through trailers broadcast on BBC channels and on YouTube. Thirty workshops were organised across the UK, often using local community media and arts organisations as both the host venue and a way to access existing community networks established by those organisations.

The Facebook page for Rosa Productions documents the workshops. Clear examples of engagement with existing community film and media organisations, include the workshops with Glasgow Media Access Centre (09.11.11) and Oxford Film (28.10.11). The explicit efforts to engage a wide range of contributions can be seen with the workshop at BUILD in Norwich (09.11.11) involving "a mixture of adults and young people with varying degrees of learning difficulties", and the Nerve Centre in Derry (25.11.11) with three groups: Action Hearing Loss; Rathmore 5+ and Northwest Lifelong Learning Ltd. In terms of nationality and ethnic diversity, there were workshops at the Meridian Society in London (06.11.11), an organisation that "promotes Chinese culture with the aim of fostering better understanding between people of Chinese origin and those from other ethnic backgrounds, both in the UK and worldwide", and with 'the Polish Community' at media 19 in Gateshead (29.10.11). Other workshops included: Silent Cities in Sheffield (19.10.11); Council for Voluntary Service, Blackpool Wyre and Fylde (11.11.11); and Lumiere Arts in Leicester (26.10.11). Workshops with education institutions included Belfast Metropolitan College (08.11.11), Newport Film School and Ravensbourne (11.11.11).

Previous analysis (Ashton 2015) of the ... *in a Day* projects addressed the distinction between the digital storytelling approach and that of inviting and then using materials contributed through crowdsourcing. The workshops for *Britain in a Day* show a concerted effort to raise awareness within specific contexts to encourage a wide range of contributions. Engagement with participants in workshops included support with exploring ideas through the 'story circle' (see Lundby 2008) and with the technical dimensions (these two elements were the basis for morning and afternoon activities). That said, tensions remain in how contributions to *Britain in a Day* were framed more broadly, and a small number of YouTube commenters were critical of the aims of the project and its geographical coverage. The following section presents a more detailed analysis of the potential disconnection between the aims and public guidance materials presented by the production teams and the views of potential participants and the 'pre-existing community of people' on YouTube (Macdonald, cited in Watercutter 2011).

Contestation: "You just want our footage..."

Returning to Malik (2013) and Saha's (2013a) account of the 'numbers' approach to diversity, there were clear steps with both projects to have concrete actions to go alongside the aims of open and far-reaching participation. Having considered how invitations to participate positioned potential contributors as individuals with stories to tell towards a "portrait of the world" (Macdonald)/"a wonderful patchwork of Britain" (Matthews) and how there were processes in place to try and support a range of contributing voices, this final section will consider how these discourses and processes were evaluated, critiqued and contested within public comments threads.

There are, as noted above in the methods overview, several points of caution concerning research with YouTube comments. Nevertheless, the comments provide a valuable source for understanding how the public/YouTube community being spoken to by the production team responded. In many respects the critical points articulated by academic commentators (Ashton 2015, Caldwell 2014, Dovey 2014, Vickers 2012) have already found voice in these comments threads. Given that these comments were made in direct response to videos posted by the production teams, they are arguably more potent interventions.

Beresford and Schwarz (2014, 67) assert that the YouTube materials posted on the *Life in a Day* channel represent "a continuous dialogue online with participants and audiences for over a year". In contrast to Beresford and Schwarz's comments, the analysis undertaken for this research across both the … in a Day projects reveals that comments from the production team only extend to practicalities around what was required and how to submit footage. Rather than a 'continuous dialogue', the few responses by the production team were only made in relation to issues of collecting footage. The range of other concerns voiced regarding free labour, intellectual property rights, limitations on access by age and country and the shaping of creative agency were not responded to. Of course, the language and mode of address of certain posts addressing these issues might not invite dialogue and response by the production teams:

> Here we go again, more meaningless blather to get "you" involved, even though "you" will never be involved…. these people just want to cash in, make it look like "art" or whatever it is…. more bs for mindless slaves to chew on…. eat it up assholes….' (LD2 comment 1)

Nevertheless, articulated here are concerns around power relationships, the nature and extent of participation, ownership and finances.

The workshops organised by the BBC for *Britain in a Day* represent steps to engage participants in learning, exchange and dialogue. Accounts of the workshops (Richards 2015) point to the value of the workshops for participants. With regard to the crowdsourcing dimension of the … in a Day projects, "potential contributors were cynical of their involvement as 'sources' providing content for media professionals to use"' (Ashton 2015, 109). The following addresses the extent to which the promises of the production team for the documentary projects were realised, or not, as they engaged with potential participants. Certainly, for some the projects were held to form a meaningful part of their lives. This was much more difficult to gauge with *Britain in a Day* due to the limited number of comments. With *Life in a Day* there were video accounts by participants (for example, "One Year Later: Christopher Brian" LD4), and in the comments thread to the film other (assumed) participants would add their positive and enthusiastic accounts. There were however also express concerns by YouTube commenters/potential participants on the possibilities for access and involvement and on creative agency and the terms of (self)presentation.

For *Life in a* Day, commenters addressed the limitations of who could participate – particularly relevant given the discourses of inclusion. These limitations were expressed in relation to religion:

> It's a shame that it is on Saturday when Jews cannot use a camera. I would love to participate next time if it isn't on Saturday (LD1 comment 4)

For the following commenter it was restrictions on countries ("a resident of Cuba, Iran, North Korea, Sudan, Myanmar/Burma, Syria, or any other U.S. sanctioned country") from which participants could contribute:

> [...] it was so disappointing to know that you had banned nations from the countries who have the deepest passions to picture. I am deeply sorry for you SIR SCOTT. You banned people not governments (LD1 comment 5)

For another commenter it was age:

> Oh sorry, I guess my sister's not alive nor does she matter since she's younger than 18. A portrait of the world in a day includes EVERYONE of all ages (LD1 comment 6)

One commenter responding to a *Britain in a Day* trailer raised a point of accessibility in relation to technical preferences and choices:

> What about people wanting to shoot on film? a week is not enough time to process and have the film telecined. All formats should be encouraged for a diverse view of the nation. Great concept mind… (BD6 comment 1)

With regard to issues of wide representation, the following comments go further in challenging whether wide numbers from a range of positions would be achievable. For a number of commenters, there was scepticism around who would actually be able to participate:

> Life on earth as experienced by people rich enough to own a movie camera. Not exactly representational (LD1 comment 7)

> i believe that most of the world today is in poverty and this film will not capture the world today as we know it (LD1 comment 8)

> SOUNDS INTERESTING but . through selection its gonna be your portrait of the world in a day . this project will never show a true day in peoples lives (LD1 comment 9)

> Life in the day across the whole world of people affluent enough to own ways to record and post on youtube. Interesting idea but to say it represents the whole planet on this day would be ridiculous (LD1 comment 10)

For one commenter to *Britain in a Day* (BD7), similar concerns were raised in relation to class:

> "you'll make your audience feel queasy" No Julie, that happened when we watched our hard earned money spent on this BS [...] The working man & woman are being mugged off by the ruling classes and are brazen enough not to give a shit, Fuck off and take the bankers, politicians, FTSE directors, Footballers, "Celebs" et al with you (BD7 comment 1)
> You are being shafted, do you really believe your point of view means shit to this global cartel? [...] This is about the haves vs the have nots. The coming times are going to be hard unless you were born into privilege. Forget race, colour or creed, If you aren't in their circle, you're fucked! (BD2 comment 1)

The questions raised by easty971 connect with Malik's comments on the 'structural'. Whilst this commenter is writing before *Britain in a Day* had been filmed, edited and broadcast, there was anger in anticipation of what those 'in charge' and behind the production would address. A similar point was made in a comment made for *Life in a Day*:

> This would REALLY be interesting if someone in GAZA did this but I'm sure that JewTube would NEVER show Israeli terrorists dropping white phosphorus on the Palestinian children or israeli tanks shooting young boys for throwing deadly rocks at their tanks! (LD1 comment 11)

The claims to extensive open participation are challenged in a number of respects in these comments. Moreover, significant concerns were expressed in comments threads on the editing and organisation of materials *within* the documentary.

As discussed elsewhere (Ashton 2015), editing was an express point of challenge and contestation in comments to the video "The Film Editor's how-to guide for Life in a Day" (LD5). The clearest articulation of the issues of power dynamics identified by Vickers (2012) and Dovey (2014) made in response to the YouTube channel materials comes with the comments by Simme808 in response to this video: 'you just want our footage so you can edit it' (for more on tensions around editing, see Dovey and Rose 2013, Ashton 2015). The question of editing and who was able to do what also emerged in the less-populated comments threads to *Britain in a Day*: "Funny how his 'example clip' has music and is edited, two of the things you're NOT MEANT TO DO" (BD8 comment 1). Addressing editing, but extending to the whole process, the following comments directly address the issue of creative agency: "they edit together clips. they don't want us involve in the creative process of the movie" (LD3 comment 1). At stake here is the difference between being able to participate and the terms of that participation.

Discussion

This chapter has examined the discourses of inclusion and empowerment presented in the *… in a Day* projects invitation and guidance materials. Engaging with recent scholarship on diversity in cultural representation, this chapter has raised questions on whether an open invitation and the encouragement of diversity through the mass participation of 'the crowd' translates into diversity in content. Whilst recognising that diverse forms of representation can be addressed with regard to the documentaries' content, this chapter has analysed the paratextual materials to examine the participatory processes through which the representations were created. In other words, how diversity in production operated in these participatory documentary projects.

Saha (2013b) has argued that the conditions of the cultural industries steer the work of minority cultural producers. Specifically, he addresses an "arts funding governmentality" that places "an expectation on the work that culturally diverse companies are supposed to produce – work that stresses the cultural diversity or differences of their narratives" (Saha 2013b, 832). With *Britain in a Day* and its connections to the BBC, the stress on cultural diversity is clearly evident. With the *… in a Day* projects it would be a difficult task to assess the processes of selection by which clips were selected for inclusion based on whether they stressed cultural diversity (although there has been some critical discussion of the rating process undertaken by a selected and trained group of filmmakers and film students – see Ashton 2015).

With the … *in a Day* projects, there is not a corresponding governmentality that places expectations on what contributions cover or that suggests contributors have a 'weight of representation' in covering cultural experiences. Rather, there is a focus on the individual and personal, and diversity is then held to flow from the multiplicity of voices. However, from Saha's (2013b) analysis there is a further point to draw out concerning how the limitations on participation and the curating/curtailing of creative agency shape culturally diverse forms of self-representation. This is a point best considered through some of Saha's observations made in his case study of the play *Curry Tales* by Rasa Productions, a Manchester-based theatre company.

Through a sociologically driven study of cultural production, Saha (2013b) pays attention to the processes and structures through which representations and symbols of difference are produced. The cultural industries context and political economy of theatre is central to Saha's analysis, and the idea of cultural production being coaxed and steered is a key dimension to this analysis. For instance, Saha (2013b, 834) questions the nature of the commercial and critical success of *Curry Tales* and examines how "enlightened and politically engaged cultural practitioners were steered" in a particular direction and how Rasa ended up making itself up in a way to fit a gap in the market reserved for Asian artists. In this respect, Saha is drawing attention to how diverse and unexpected forms of representation were re-orientated through the production contexts into well-established norms. Through this case study, Saha (2013b, 832) addresses "the politics of representation as mediated through commercial forces, frequently to the detriments of the producer's particular aesthetic and cultural politics". The focus Saha puts on production contexts and the ways in cultural production is framed resonates with this analysis of the invitation and guidance materials that frame the boundaries and practices of the … *in a Day* participatory documentaries.

For Saha, the contexts of production are intricately intertwined with the possibilities for cultural transruption – the unsettling of social norms. Specifically, the potential for cultural transruption is "based upon the degree to which the symbol creator can evade the forms of rationalized industrial production techniques that have been imposed throughout the cultural industries" (Saha 2013b, 229). Such rationalization comes through "standardized processes that restrict the autonomy of creative managers and prevents them from taking risks" (Saha 2013b, 834). In relation to participatory culture and the … *in a Day* projects examined in this chapter, the possibilities for sharing stories and creating representations were unconstrained by market pressures (see Macdonald, LD5). However, the persistence of established production techniques, hierarchies and expertise suggests that the cultural transruptions possible with these documentaries are limited. The crowdsourcing dimension saw an unprecedented number of clips from different people come together into one film. The agency of these symbol creators did though only extend to being invited and being able to participate. In this respect there was little to unsettle who is telling stories and the ways in which these stories can be told. It is pertinent to see how the formation of these digital stories is a socially and culturally situated process. The aim here is not to undermine the significance of digital stories and the importance that these life stories have within public discourses. However, this analysis is driven by the existing critical voices of those who have come to the project through the platform of the project.

Conclusions

This chapter has taken wider debates around cultural diversity in media and cultural production and examined these in relation to the ... *in a Day* participatory documentaries. This provides a distinctive meeting point for evaluating how the 'numbers' approach to diversity in content is manifest within a 'crowd' context where the numbers are in the tens of thousands.

Saha (2013a, 220) has suggested that "an effective cultural strategy needs to have less emphasis on the number of non-white bodies in the cultural industries, and a greater focus on the cultures of production through which diversity is governed". Saha's emphasis on ethnicity and diversity in cultural production (within the context of the cultural and creative industries) is equally relevant for addressing how participatory documentary filmmaking is approached. This is even more so in the case of *Britain in a Day* because of its alignment with BBC strategy. Echoing Saha's analysis of creative and cultural industries, this chapter has argued that initiatives to create diverse representations of everyday life must move beyond the 'numbers' approach to wide and diverse participation and go on to address cultures of production.

With the ... *in a Day* projects, there were identifiable efforts through a wide invitation and outreach and workshop activities to encourage a diversity of 'different bodies'. Beyond this distinctive crowdsourcing approach to encouraging involvement, there remain significant questions around creative agency. Whilst the films themselves present diverse experiences of everyday life, the processes of (self)representation suggest there is little to unsettle or transrupt culturally established forms of storytelling. As argued, the organisation and editing of content did little to unsettle who is telling stories and the ways in which these stories can be told. Given the continuation by Scott Free Productions of the ... *in a Day* projects (one every two years) there are important conversations to undertake on how participatory practices might be negotiated and redefined in future projects.

References

Androutsopoulos, Jannis and Jana Tereick. 2015. "YouTube: language and discourse practices in participatory culture." In *The Routledge Handbook of Language and Digital Communication*, edited by Alexandra Georgakopoulou and Tereza Spilioti, 354–370. London: Routledge.

Ashton, Daniel. 2015. "Producing Participatory Media: (crowd)sourcing content in *Britain/Life in a Day*." *Media International Australia* 154: 101–110.

Barker, Martin. 2004. "News, Reviews, Clues, Interviews and Other Ancillary Materials – A Critique and Research Proposal." *Scope* (February).

BBC. 2012. "Britain in a Day." Accessed April 12, 2016. http://www.bbc.co.uk/programmes/p00kqz5p.

BBC. 2016. "Public Purposes." Accessed April 12, 2016. http://www.bbc.co.uk/corporate2/insidethebbc/whoweare/publicpurposes.

Beresford, Shirley and Andreas Schwarz. 2014. "Managing Public Relations." In *Entertainment Management: towards best practice*, edited by Stuart Moss and Ben Walmsley, 60–76, Wallingford: CABI.

Burgess, Jean and Joshua Green. 2009. *YouTube: online video and participatory culture*. Cambridge: Polity.

Caldwell, John Thornton. 2014. "Para-Industry, Shadow Academy." *Cultural Studies* 28 (4): 720–740.

Carpentier, Nico. 2003. "The BBC's Video Nation as a Participatory Media Practice: signifying everyday life, cultural diversity and participation in an online community." *International Journal of Cultural Studies*, 6 (4): 425–447.

Colls, Robert. 2012. "What Is British National Identity and How Do We Get It?" *Soundings*, 52: 100–112.

Couldry, Nick. 2008. "Mediatization or Mediation? Alternative Understandings of the Emergent Space of Digital Storytelling." *New Media & Society* 10 (3): 373–391.

Dovey, Jon. 2014. "Documentary Ecosystems: collaboration and exploitation." In *Emerging Platforms, Practices and Discourses*, edited by Kate Nash, Craig Hight and Catherine Summerhayes, 11–32, Basingstoke: Palgrave Macmillan.

Dovey, Jon and Mandy Rose. 2013. "'This Great Mapping of Ourselves': new documentary forms online." In *The Documentary Film Book*, edited by Brian Winston, 366–375, Basingstoke: BFI/Palgrave Macmillan.

Gaudenzi, Sandra. 2014. "Strategies of Participation: the who, what, and when of collaborative documentaries." In *Emerging Platforms, Practices and Discourses*, edited by Kate Nash, Craig Hight and Catherine Summerhayes, 129–148, Basingstoke: Palgrave Macmillan.

Gratton, Chris and Holger Preuss. 2008. "Maximising Olympic Impacts by Building up Legacies." *The International Journal of the History of Sport* 25(14): 1922–1928.

Hall, Stuart. 2000. "Conclusion: the multicultural question." In *Un/settled Multiculturalisms: Diasporas, Entanglements, Transruptions*, edited by Barnor Hesse, 209–241, London: Zed Books.

IMDB. 2012. "Life in a Day: Plot Summary." Accessed April 12, 2016. http://www.imdb.com/title/tt1687247/plotsummary.

Kidd, Jenny. 2009. "Digital Storytelling and the Performance of Memory." In *Save As … Digital Memories*, edited by Joanne Garde-Hansen, Andrew Hoskins and Anna Reading, 167–183, Basingstoke: Palgrave Macmillan.

Lundby, Knut. 2008. "Introduction: digital storytelling, mediatized stories." In *Digital Storytelling, Mediatized Stories*, edited by Knut Lundy, 1–17, Oxford: Peter Lang.

Malik, Sarita. 2013. "'Creative Diversity': UK public service broadcasting after multiculturalism.' *Popular Communication* 11(3): 227–241.

Muller, Eggo. 2009. "Where Quality Matters: discourses on the art of making a YouTube video." In *The YouTube Reader*, edited by Pelle Snickers and Patrick Vonderau, 126–139, Stockholm: National Library of Sweden.

Pietrobruno, Sheenagh. 2013. "YouTube and the Social Archiving of Intangible Heritage." *New Media and Society* 15 (8): 1259–1276.

Poletti, Anna. 2011. "Coaxing an Intimate Public: life narrative in digital storytelling." *Continuum* 25 (1): 73–83.

Richards, Rosemary. Interview by Author. Tape recording. Oxford. November 17, 2015.

Rosa Productions, Facebook Page. Accessed November 10, 2015. https://www.facebook.com/ROSA-Productions-171821742900370/.

Saha, Anamik. 2013a. "The Cultural Industries in a Critical Multicultural Pedagogy." In *Cultural Work and Higher Education*, edited by Daniel Ashton and Caitriona Noonan, 214–231, Basingstoke: Palgrave Macmillan.

Saha, Anamik. 2013b. "'*Curry Tales*': the production of 'race' and ethnicity in the cultural industries." *Ethnicities* 13 (6): 818–837.

Sobers, Shawn. 2009. "Debating Process, Product, and Progression in Community Media." *Beyond Project Blog*. Accessed July 2, 2014. http://beyondproject.wordpress.com/2009/06/18/debating-process-product-and-progression-in-community-media/.

Surowiecki, James. 2004. *The Wisdom of Crowds*. New York: Doubleday/Anchor.

Taylor, Stephanie. 2012. "'One Participant Said …': the implications of quotations from biographical talk." *Qualitative Research* 12 (4): 388–401.

Vickers, Richard. 2012. "Convergence Media, Participation Culture and the Digital Vernacular: towards the democratisation of documentary." Paper presented at *International Conference on Communication, Media, Technology and Design*, Istanbul, May 9–11.

Watercutter, Angela. 2011. "*Life in a Day* distils 4,500 Hours of Intimate Video into Urgent Documentary." *Wired*, July 2011. Accessed November 27, 2014. http://www.wired.com/2011/07/life-in-a-day-interviews/all/1.

Wilson, James Andrew. 2012. "When Is a Performance? Temporality in the Spatial Turn." *Performance Research* 17 (5): 110–118.

… in a Day YouTube Videos
LD1: "Kevin Macdonald on Life in a Day"
<https://www.youtube.com/watch?v=C_4uii96xqM>
LD2: "Ridley Scott on Life in a Day"
<https://www.youtube.com/watch?v=kGYACultjCY>
LD3: "Life in a Day: a new type of filmmaking"
<https://www.youtube.com/watch?v=jf1AI3_qX7c>
LD4: "One Year Later: Christopher Brian"
<https://www.youtube.com/watch?v=YFiAz3diEyE>
LD5: "The Film Editor's How-to Guide for Life in a Day"
<https://www.youtube.com/watch?v=1nIIVH0R0kY>

BD1: "Advice from Morgan Matthews and Producer Ridley Scott"
<https://www.youtube.com/watch?v=V9vYjuAnB6A>
BD2: "Britain in a Day Trailer - upload by 21st November"
<https://www.youtube.com/watch?v=g3PSMbpHjo8>
BD3: "Britain in a Day Is about YOU"
<https://www.youtube.com/watch?v=b0tRYV5fycY>
BD4: "How the Documentary Was Made by the Team"
<https://www.youtube.com/watch?v=SVItmy59ReY>
BD5: "What Is the Britain in a Day Archive?"
<https://www.youtube.com/watch?v=m5rkZujIw7Q>
BD6: "Britain in a Day Teaser #1: the day begins"
<https://www.youtube.com/watch?v=hPN48PdnEGs>
BD7: "Julia Bradbury on How to Shoot Your Day for Britain in a Day"
<https://www.youtube.com/watch?v=HqZDvnHK13Q>
BD8: "Dan Snow on How to Upload Your Video to YouTube"
<https://www.youtube.com/watch?v=xTbGipW6CQ0>

Who's Hong Kong?
Cellphilming and Civic
Engagement with Ethnic
Minority Young Women

Casey Burkholder

Introduction

As Jennifer Ngo noted in a *South China Morning Post* article on
3 February 2016, ethnic minorities "fall through the cracks" of Hong
Kong society. Problematically, Hong Kong's South Asian ethnic minorities are often described in deficit terms in popular media and society.
Within these discourses, the experiences of girls and women are often
marginalized further. To address these problematic discourses, this
chapter describes a cellphilming (cellphone + filmmaking) project with
two Filipina and two Nepalese young women in post-Occupy Hong
Kong to speak back (Mitchell & De Lange 2013) to essentialized notions of difference and exclusion. Inspired by participatory video methodology, cellphilms are short videos made with cellphone technologies
to address community challenges, and to promote critical dialogue and
social action (Dockeny & Tomaselli 2009, Dockney, Tomaselli & Hart
2010, MacEntee, Burkholder & Schwab-Cartas forthcoming, Mitchell,
De Lange & Moletsane 2014). This chapter explores cellphilm production as an act of civic engagement for young women in post-Occupy
Hong Kong. It examines how four young women's experiences of community filmmaking with cellphones have influenced the ways in which
they engage politically in their young adult lives. The research presented
here asks how ethnic minority young women take up issues of identity,
belonging and civic engagement in their cellphilm productions. How is
Occupy Central positioned in relation to these women's sense of civic
engagement in the cellphilms? How might the process of cellphilming
(from brainstorming in a workshop to disseminating the cellphilms on
YouTube) be understood as distinct acts of civic engagement?

Situating the Study

Shannon Walsh (2012) argues that without situating community
filmmaking projects – and the potentially empowering stories they
produce – in historical and social realities there is "a real danger of de-
contextualizing the stories that emerge, even though it is also important

to remember that storytelling is a fundamental way through which we understand the world. Participatory video can be a tool for enlivening the art of storytelling and for collective discussion, of both where we are now and where we hope to go" (242–243). With this critique in mind, I situate this study at the time it began – January 2015 – just one month after police removed youth protesters from Occupy Central. Occupy Central was a youth-led popular movement that intensified from September to December 2014 when young people took to the streets and to digital spaces to interrogate Hong Kong's existing political system, relationship to China and distinct identity. The movement brought up key questions for Hong Kong people, including its citizens and permanent residents who self-identify as ethnic minorities. For example, who is a Hong Kong person? What distinct political and cultural values define the city and its residents? How should leaders be chosen to represent the people in Hong Kong? These youth occupied strategic commercial and consumer areas to assert dissatisfaction, demand increased representation and articulate a distinct Hong Kong political identity. After the Occupy spaces were taken over by authorities (Grundy 2015), protests continued across digital spaces, and two years later, in August 2016, the hashtags #OccupyCentral and #UmbrellaRevolution continue to be used on Twitter.

In the context of this post-Occupy Hong Kong, this study seeks to understand ethnic minority young women's articulations of self, belonging and citizenship through cellphilming (an extension of participatory video) and situate these stories within the larger political and systemic frameworks that operate on and around ethnic minority women-citizens in Hong Kong.

Hong Kong's Census and Statistics Department (2013) relate a non-Chinese identity to ethnic and racial origins, based on the self-representation of census respondents. Emerging from Hong Kong's 2011 census data, *The Thematic Report on Ethnic Minorities* (Census and Statistics Department 2013) reports that of the 6.4% of Hong Kong's population that self-identifies as ethnic minorities, 30% or 133,377 identify as Indonesian, 29% or 133,018 identify as Filipino, 12% or 55,236 identify as White, 6% or 28,616 identify as Indian, 4% or 18,042 identify as Pakistani, 4% or 16,518 identify as Nepalese, 3% or 12,580 identify as Japanese, 2% 11,213 identify as Thai, 3% 12,247 report to be 'Other Asian' and 7% 30,336 identify as 'Others' (7). The discourses of non-Chinese and ethnic minority effects actors differently based on their country of origin, socio-economic status, religion and race. This study is also framed in relation to my own identity, which raises issues about ethnographic, qualitative and participatory visual research within Hong Kong's specific socio-political context. As a female white Canadian teacher and visual researcher, I am also an ethnic minority in the context of Hong Kong. I first came to Hong Kong as a Form II (grade 8) teacher at a public secondary school in Hong Kong, where I worked from 2008–2010. At that school, students who were not ethnically Chinese – as well as those who did not speak Cantonese as a home language – were colloquially referred to as NC or non-Chinese. One significant factor that needs to be addressed within this study is 'race', and specifically my own whiteness. The unearned privileges accorded to whiteness in Hong Kong have been clearly influenced by the British colonial legacy. As Cooks (2003) argues,

> The power of whiteness extends to much more than simply racial characteristics; indeed, White culture has the power to define what is appropriate, normal, and permissible. If identities are multiple and fragmented, and take on particular meanings in specific contexts, then it stands to reason that whiteness is more about dynamics of power—the power to define what is normal and comfortable, to give spaces particular meanings and uses, to define what and who counts in a culture. (249)

As a white woman living, working and later researching in Hong Kong, I was able to access unearned privilege, including admittance to a number of structures and spaces that I might not otherwise have entered.

However, my non-white Filipina and Nepalese participants spoke of different and much more negatively marginalised and racialised realities as they migrated through language practices and social spaces. As Hue and Kennedy (2015) acknowledge, "between 2007 and 2012, the number of non-Chinese-speaking students in secondary schools increased by 94.77%, from 3272 to 6373...The majority of these students are among the lowest achievers academically; they come from low socio-economic backgrounds and experience learning difficulties" (289). When I was teaching in Hong Kong, I saw my learners systematically excluded from spaces within the school as well as access to high-quality instruction, all of which impacted their experience of otherness in the school. After two years, I realised how little systemic change I had affected, and this experience of anger and frustration led me to embark on a study with my former students for my Master's work. In that qualitative and ethnographic study, I found that the policies set out by the Hong Kong Education Bureau to promote inclusion for ethnic minorities did not align with the lived experiences of 20 of my former students (Burkholder 2013). However, I was limited in communicating the results of this study with my participants and their communities. I realised that despite my intentions, I was still managing to do research 'on' instead of research 'with' participants, and my findings were not communicated in accessible spaces. With these critiques in mind, for my doctoral work, I set out to do something different. I wanted to research notions of belonging, identity and civic engagement *with* these same folks, but to do so using cellphone video production, where we could create and disseminate our findings together across diverse publics. In this, I hoped we would create meaningful cellphilms that would speak to ethnic minority community members and speak back to dominant notions about ethnic minorities too often present in the local media (See for example Ngo 2015, Zhou 2014).

Who's Hong Kong? Situating the Participants

Ann

Ann is a Hong Kong-born Filipina who is presently studying at college, is engaged in activism and dreams of becoming a professional journalist. She writes constantly in English and Tagalog on her blog and for cultural newspapers, and her activism is focused on ethnic minority youth. Her experiences at a multi-ethnic school in Hong Kong have served as the basis for some of her writing and activist practices, including her engagement in Occupy Central. She loves travel and anime above all else.

Katrina

Katrina is a Hong Kong-born Filipina. She is a young mother who is studying at college while working part time in the service industry. Katrina speaks English and Tagalog and does not speak much Cantonese. She is incredibly driven, passionate and thoughtful. She is constantly reading and planning for the future. She was involved in the Occupy Central protests and stated that it was the first time that she really began to think about her place in Hong Kong. She has dreams of being a graphic designer, and she is very engaged in fashion, most recently starting her own Instagram-based clothing business.

Sabi

Sabi was born in Nepal and came to Hong Kong in her late teens. She is a permanent resident of Hong Kong and attends college while working full time as a hostess in a fine dining establishment. Sabi speaks Nepali and English fluently and some Cantonese. She became very involved with the Occupy Central protests, with her family's support. She described the Occupy Central protests as one of the first times she had engaged in prolonged and positive encounters with 'local' Hong Kong Chinese people.

Yuna

Yuna was born in Nepal and was raised by her grandparents while her parents worked in Hong Kong. In her early teens, Yuna joined her parents in the city, and she is now a permanent resident. She works full time as a head server (in management) in a fine dining establishment. Although she had originally planned to attend college, her father had a workplace accident, and so Yuna went to work full time to support her family. Yuna participated in the Occupy Central protests, but not to the same extent as Sabi, her best friend, because she spends a majority of her time at work.

Cellphilming and Community Filmmaking

Building from the tradition of participatory video (Milne, Mitchell & De Lange 2012) and autobiographical filmmaking (Russell 1999), I suggest that cellphilming is a participatory tool people can use to express their community concerns and ways of seeing the world. What is the nature of this participation in community filmmaking projects? Elder (1995) has argued for lateral participation where filmmaking participants shape the direction of the project, including the questions taken up, the images used and the directions of the films. The documentary filmmaker and film scholar Coffman (2009) acknowledges that videos provide avenues for new audiences to engage with critical community and organizational issues, and "rather than waiting for an individual filmmaker to identify them as storytelling 'material,' though, groups are beginning to seek filmmaking assistance on their own. Getting one's story told—well-told—is more affordable now too" (62). With cellphilming, participants tell their own stories through cellphone video-generated images, and in this specific project, they have done so with their own filmmaking technologies. Here, cellphilming is a departure from participatory video, for example, where often a researcher or filmmaker brings the filmmaking into the community, and when the project ends, the filmmaking equipment also leaves the community setting (Schwab-Cartas & Mitchell 2014). What is more, cellphilms can be produced, edited and viewed within the cellphone technology itself (Dockney & Tomaselli 2009). However, it must be noted that the ethical complexities that emerge in participatory video with regard to access, data storage, privacy and ownership of data are not diminished when a cellphone is used as the main filmmaking tool. Any time a cellphilm is created through social media or uploaded to a site, issues of consent, ownership and data storage remain.

From a media and communications studies perspective, Buckingham (2009) suggests that new media technologies are democratising as they encourage DIY (Do It Yourself) media making, which can be employed both to support and to challenge traditional media structures. Chau (2011) claims that participatory cultures are fostered by digital sharing spaces, such as YouTube, as young people reflect their own ways of knowing and benefit from these growing spaces and exchanges with other youth across global contexts. In the context of HIV/AIDS-affected South Africa, Mitchell and de Lange (2013) found that the cellphilms enabled a conversation to take place and that viewings of the cellphilms provided teachers an opportunity to create cellphilms in response to those that they had viewed, encouraging teachers to "speak back" (1) to representations they challenged or disagreed with and to be critical and reflective about the content of the initial cellphilms. In this project, cellphilms provide the opportunity to create and sustain an ongoing conversation with participants and publics.

Community Cellphilming: Beginning with the Workshop

Mitchell, De Lange and Moletsane (2014, 3), in their work on cellphilming with teachers in rural South Africa in the context of HIV/AIDS, describe their no-editing-required approach to cellphilm workshops as being inclusive of seven steps: 1) discussing the themes that guide the workshop, 2) brainstorming with prompts on a specific topic, 3) voting between participants to choose the topics to film, 4) storyboarding these ideas, 5) practicing with the filming technologies, 6) filming, 7) screening the products and immediately discussing the cellphilms in a large group. In these workshops, Mitchell et al. employed "one-shot-shoots" (OSS) where participants would shoot an entire cellphilm in a single take, as well as an "extended film with six to eight shots" where the 'pause' button would be used on the video capture device to enable multiple scenes (3). Mitchell et al. used the OSS cellphilm productions as a prompt for the longer cellphilms, where participants then went through the seven steps listed above. Mitchell et al. also note that although their workshop participants (two groups of in-service teachers in two areas in rural South Africa) had much previous experience using their cellphones as filmmaking devices, all were familiar with the workings of their own phones and were quickly able to adapt to this new usage.

In an earlier article, Mitchell and De Lange (2013) articulate:

> A strength of visual participatory work is that the productions (in this case the cellphilms) are immediately available to both participants and researchers for analysis. While the participants offered comments on the productions and their messages…we as a research team were able to carry out an additional layer of analysis on the primary texts (the productions) via what the producers said about the cellphilms (see Fiske 1989). (6)

In this project, I followed an adapted version of the Mitchell, Moletsane & De Lange (2014) workshop process, but I omit the one-shot-shoot cellphilming technique. Instead, I have encouraged participants to download free editing applications on their phones, and they began to create multi-shot cellphilms within the confines of a workshop.

Katrina, Ann, Yuna and Sabi, met with me one on one over coffee, and we talked about their notions of self, citizenship and belonging. During these conversations, I explained my interest in cellphilms and asked if they would be interested in creating short cellphilms for the project. We then scheduled a mutual agreed-upon time to hold the cellphilm workshop. Before the workshop, I created a short zine that explained the project, the cellphilm prompts and, briefly, the steps to make a cellphilm. I included a written link to a playlist of cellphilms from the *International Cellphilm Festival* – a festival I co-organize in at McGill University in Montreal, Canada – where participants could view previously produced cellphilms. I did so in order to show the breadth of topics and techniques that participants might employ in their cellphilms. The zine and playlist were also references for additional cellphilming ideas outside of the workshop environment.

Ann, Katrina, Yuna, Sabi and I began our workshop with a focus group interview where they spoke about their experiences as ethnic minority women growing up in Hong Kong, and this in-depth conversation gave them the chance to get to know one another better. After the focus group, which took place at a café, we moved to a room at an English medium university in Hong Kong. I had prepared the room in advance with snacks, drinks, drawing supplies, post-its, hand-drawn storyboard templates, coloured paper and tables with four chairs each. I had also prepared a visual presentation, which I displayed on the LCD projector. The participants arranged themselves so that Ann and Katrina sat at one table and Sabi and Yuna at another. We began by watching a few examples of cellphilms, so that the women could have a sense of the range of methods of cellphilm making. I showed two stop-motion cellphilms (one that employed Claymation, one that used Scrabble tiles) and two more that used multiple shots and focused on actors and interviews. The women then talked about their reactions to the cellphilms' content and the techniques used. We discussed whether they had used cellphones as video-production tools in the past, and all acknowledged that they had for a variety of purposes. Sabi was an especially savvy Snapchat user, and often used cellphilming to document her everyday life at work and with family and friends. I then introduced the participants to the three cellphilm prompts, 1) "Who am I in Hong Kong? What is my sense of identity?"; 2) "Where do I belong in Hong Kong?"; 3) "How do we participate as citizens of Hong Kong?" The participants brainstormed these prompts in two small groups and then created short scripts based on these conversations.

Next, the women storyboarded their scripts and began the filming process. During this process, I created a short cellphilm, documenting the cellphilm workshop and the processes of cellphilm-production (See: https://vimeo.com/138322009). At this point, the participants decided that they wanted to go home to be able to film outside of the university campus and the confines of the workshop. We screened what we had filmed thus far and discussed our ideas about where the cellphilms would continue to develop. Then the women went home and continued filming collaboratively. Sabi and Yuna created a cellphilm (2 minutes and 32 seconds) that included responses to all three prompts, named, *Ethnic Minorities in HK*. Ann and Katrina created a (60-second) cellphilm called, *Who am I in Hong Kong* that spoke to their identities as Filipina-Hong Kongers and featured Katrina as the actor and narrator. The two cellphilms that emerged from the workshop were analysed collaboratively in a screening event (detailed below), in follow-up semi-structured interviews and in my close reading.

The Cellphilm Productions

I begin my examination of civic engagement and cellphilming through a close reading of each cellphilm. The four ethnic minority women all took up issues of belonging and civic engagement in their cellphilm productions, and Occupy Central was centrally positioned in relation to each. I begin with a close reading of Ann and Katrina's *Who am I in Hong Kong?* and then move onto my reading of Yuna and Sabi's *Ethnic Minorities in HK*. Each was filmed and edited on the women's personal cellphones and then uploaded to our shared YouTube account, *We are Hong Kong Too,* named by Katrina and Ann.

Who Am I in Hong Kong?

Anne and Katrina's cellphilm opens with the title, *Who am I in Hong Kong?* in pink letters on a black background. The audience hears static, and then a female voice reads the title aloud. The next shot follows a woman in black as she walks down a long corridor. As she walks, we hear a female narrator speaking about her experiences as a Hong Kong-born Filipino woman. Then next shot is a blurry video of a secondary school classroom. The camera pans in a 360 motion around the class, and when the camera reaches the blackboard, the shot fades to black. Fading in from black, the audience sees a close-up shot of a text box, and we hear someone typing the words "Ethnic Minority students" as a tweet. The narrator simultaneously intones, "I have studied and worked here, however I am being labeled as an ethnic minority even though I am a Hong Kong resident, and have been living here all my life". The next shot is from the perspective of someone riding a bicycle down a tree-lined bicycle path. The shot fades out and fades into a shot of a woman – filmed from the left side of her body – at a table – her face obscured – writing, "Who am I? Where do I belong? How do I participate as a citizen of Hong Kong?"

The camera's perspective shifts, and the next shot examines the woman writing head-on from a medium distance. In this, the woman's face is obscured. She is sitting in a large room, writing at a yellow table, with two unoccupied office chairs in the background. The shot fades into the woman standing at the front of an LCD projector, seemingly presenting information to an unseen audience. While she is presenting, the narrator speaks: "Because of this I feel like I am in isolation. So I involve myself in workshops and community work…" The next shot shows the same woman, sitting at a computer searching Google for the term 'Umbrella Revolution'. The shot fades out, and fades into the woman opening and closing a door. As she does this, the narrator continues, "…to feel and be like a local". The cellphilm ends with the sound of the door closing loudly. To see this cellphilm in our cellphilm archive: *We are HK too*, visit: https://www.youtube.com/watch?v=d-VrXht7U4A.

Ethnic Minorities in HK

Sabi and Yuna's cellphilm opens with bouncy upbeat music, and the words "Who Am I" over a still image of Hong Kong Island's skyline seen at night. The shot fades into a tracking shot where the camera-woman is on an escalator in a metro station and continues onto a train platform. The female narrator begins speaking about her experiences as a Nepali-born woman who has grown up in Hong Kong. Both her narration and the bubbly music continue throughout the cellphilm. In the next shot, we see a large number of people rushing in and around the station platforms as the shot follows up to the train as the doors close. The next shot shows a train arriving at the station, and people rush out of the train cars. The shot fades out and fades into a shot of office buildings illuminated at night. The words, "Where do I belong?" fade into and out of a still image of the building. The cellphilm then fades into a shot of a public park in the early evening. It is still light out, but the natural light is fading, and the park becomes illuminated by city lights. The park is full of people, and the filmmaker walks around a path. Different groups of people occupy the shot, sitting, playing on the playground and, later, a group of people playing basketball. The shot fades to white and then to some pavement, where a person is walking towards the camera. The camera moves to the right, and it becomes clear that the scene has re-turned to a metro station. The shot cuts to a close up of a yellow rib-bon on a black background – a symbol that emerged from the Umbrella Revolution. The words, "How do I participate as a citizen?" fade into and out of the still image of the yellow ribbon (a popular symbol of the Occupy movement).

Next, there are two successive shots of photographs of the Occupy Central protests. The first is a crowded scene where we can see a yellow sign with a black umbrella on it. The sign reads: SUPPORT STUDENT & DEMOCRACY. The next shot is of shadows on the ground during an evening protest. The camera cuts to another still photograph, this one is a collage of three photographs that have been placed together. This collage show ethnic minorities participating in the Occupy Central protests and includes signs written in Nepali. The next shot shows a close up of a sign that is white with black text. The sign reads: Thanks for coming to sit with us and fight with us! The camera cuts to a time-lapse of evening traffic from the perspective of a city overpass. The film fades out from the time-lapse of the traffic as the narrator states, "After the protest it actually proved that even though people are from other countries, when in time of need, all the people can be one as Hong Kongers". The film fades to black. To see this cellphilm in our cellphilm archive: *We are HK too*, visit: https://www.youtube.com/watch?v=tDIZku37Afc.

After creating the cellphilms, the participants met with me in small groups to discuss the content of their cellphilms and to look at the composition of each shot (close-up, medium, long-shot), focusing on dialogue, sound, music, lighting, camera angles, use of foregrounding and backgrounding. During this collaborative analysis, participants commented on the tone and ephemeral qualities of the cellphilms. In the collaborative analysis, we discussed how we predicted that others might view these cellphilms, or what messages others might take away from them in a screening. In both of these productions, the participants noted that Occupy Central is portrayed as a moment where the women participated as citizens of Hong Kong. This was a time where they felt that they belonged in the city. Another clear finding is that cross-cultural exchanges and conversations about what it means to be a Hong Kong citizen – regardless of racial, cultural, or linguistic practices – are playing out in digital spaces and are assisted by the cellphilms – even over a year following the Umbrella Revolution. Another prominent finding that emerged from these conversations is that the Umbrella Revolution encouraged youth participants to interrogate their sense of citizenship as Hong Kong people for the first time. Katrina, Ann, Sabi and Yuna explained that they had not considered what it meant to be a Hong Kong person before the Umbrella Revolution. The protest acted as a prompt for these young women to think about their identities as ethnic minorities and as people who have grown up in Hong Kong. After we held this collaborative analysis, we decided on the different spaces where we might show the cellphilms to audiences. As a result, we planned a screening of the cellphilms at an English-medium university in the city.

Screening the Cellphilms: In Public and on YouTube

I see the process of cellphilming (from brainstorming in a workshop to disseminating the philms on YouTube) as distinct acts of civic engagement, as each element of the process is inherently political. Here I align with Buckingham (2000) who sees civic engagement in the everyday political actions of citizens, particularly youth who are so often excluded

from formal political structures (although these very structures operate on and around them). Haw (2008) noted that "issues about who
is listened to and what is listened to" (192) are ameliorated through
screenings of participant-produced videos. Here, there is huge potential
for new media, social media and digital spaces to create spaces for youth
to "screen[] truth to power" (Cinema Politica 2015), which responds to
traditional media that tends to exclude, other or commercialise youth
perspectives.

Speaking specifically to cellphilm screening events, Mitchell & De
Lange (2013) articulate that screenings are an important part of cellphilm method, as it provides opportunities for community members and
public audiences to engage with the videos and act as a way to encourage
discussion beyond the initial research participants. Screenings are used
to disseminate the cellphilms and to open up dialogue in an effort to promote social action and community change. Schwab-Cartas & Mitchell
(2014) describe two sites where they explored cellphilm method: South
Africa and Mexico. In his retelling of a screening event of a cellphilm,
No Modesta, Schwab-Cartas argues that the screening of the cellphilm
prompted community members to thoroughly discuss issues of language,
loss and revitalization.

Our public cellphilm-screening event can be understood as a form
of civic engagement: both in viewing the cellphilms and in the ensuing
discussions. After consulting with the participant schedules, we decided
to hold a screening event on a Sunday evening in May 2015. We chose
a Sunday evening because most participants worked six days a week,
and this way they would be able to attend the screening on their day of
rest. This also opened up the screenings (in theory) to other marginalised community members, including foreign domestic workers in Hong
Kong, who only get one day of rest per week by law (usually Sundays).
The screening event was free and was advertised through online spaces
(Facebook, Google +, Twitter, e-mail, Instagram) and in a poster that
I created and sent via e-mail to academics and community organisations that specialise in ethnic minority educational issues in Hong Kong.
I created a Facebook event and tried to publicise the event by word of
mouth and encouraged participants to tell other community members
about the event.

In the end, only eight people – other than my partner and me – came
to the screening. Three participants from the larger research project (out
of 11), including Ann and Katrina, attended the screening. At the last
moment, the other participants all notified me that they could not attend
because of work or family commitments. The audience was also made
up of participants' family members, a teacher of ethnic minority young
people (and a former colleague of mine) and one of my friends with
whom I used to teach English in Mainland China. We began the screening a little late (20 minutes) because Katrina's bus was stuck in traffic.

After another 20 minutes passed, she texted Ann and suggested that we begin the screening without her.

The small and intimate nature of the audience made for an interesting dynamic following the screening. My former colleague began the discussion by relaying his thoughts on ethnic minority education in Hong Kong, and how experiences in school would have necessarily affected participants' sense of identity. He also stated that most participants took up the topic of learning Cantonese in their cellphilm productions and that language acts as a barrier or a gatekeeper for participants to engage more fully in the larger community:

> The films are very diverse. In their presentations and their own styles. And they have some common themes like language, a sense of belonging, and Occupy Central. And how Occupy actually brought them together to feel that they are a part of Hong Kong. I think actually they need more opportunities to be a part of Hong Kong.

Another audience member asked how the cellphilms might have changed, or how the research project would have been affected, if the Umbrella Revolution had not happened, as these issues were raised in almost all of the participants' cellphilms. He noted that, "the Umbrella Revolution seems to have made them feel like they are a part of the city, and as they said, for the first time". Shasad (a participant in the larger project) commented on the aesthetic quality of the cellphilms and the idea that the cellphilms made him reconsider his own sense of identity, "I had never thought about it like this before, about belonging in Hong Kong from the ideas about Occupy Central". Ann spoke about the process of filming and her activist practices more generally, "I mean, I can relate to the others' experiences. I think that people will see these cellphilms and feel something. They are emotional in a really beautiful way".

As the conversation was unfolding, Katrina arrived. We paused our discussion and screened the cellphilms again. Following the second screening, we revisited the central themes of the cellphilms, and Katrina spoke about her experiences with cellphilming, "the cellphilms were interesting to make, like to show my perspective, and then to see the things that other people were talking about. They were similar. Our ideas were similar. Especially about Occupy [Central]". Katrina then talked about her reaction to the prompts and how she revisited them as she worked her way through the creation, filming and editing of the cellphilms. She also spoke about her choice to employ a voiceover and music.

After the discussion, I closed the screening room, and the entire audience walked to the train station together. As we walked, we continued to speak about what we had learned from the cellphilms. In reflecting on the audience numbers and on the reality of people's schedules and lives, we talked about showing the cellphilms in the digital realm to reach larger publics. I brought this up as we walked to the train, and Ann and Katrina suggested that we share the screening event's playlist of the cellphilms on our shared YouTube channel: *We Are Hong Kong Too* (See: https://www.youtube.com/watch?v=d-VrXht7U4A&list=PLM_ zBVIVwWeBCie8--UFeS9mtMweHtmkl). The idea to bring the participatory process that grounds the study to the dissemination phase of the participant-produced cellphilms was inspired by Park, Mitchell & De Lange's (2008) article, which explored the idea that participants should have ownership over the dissemination of the knowledge created in participatory projects (Burkholder forthcoming). As of April 2016, the cellphilms have been viewed over 1100 times, with viewers coming from Hong Kong, Canada, Australia, Japan, Thailand, Saudi Arabia and the U.S. This archive of cellphilms becomes a rich site of data, and its shared maintenance is another example of participation in the cellphilm process. As time passes, and diverse publics engage with the cellphilms, the cellphilms continue to communicate complex messages about identity, belonging, and what it means to belong and act in Hong Kong as an ethnic minority young person.

Some Concluding Thoughts

Given 2014's Occupy Central protests in Hong Kong and the growing 2016 Localist movement, this study contributes to an understanding of civic engagement and belonging in this evolving political space. Combining ethnographic and participatory visual research with four ethnic minority young women's participation in and reaction to Hong Kong's Umbrella Revolution are illuminated, as concepts of self and citizenship are negotiated and represented in the cellphone video productions. Cellphilming has been employed as a tool to encourage these young women to document notions of community, resistance, a sense of belonging and civic engagement. In their cellphilms, Sabi, Yuna, Ann and Katrina discuss notions of identity, belonging, civic engagement and what it feels like to grow up as an ethnic minority in the context of Hong Kong. These cellphilms contribute to an understanding of civic engagement from their diverse perspectives and speak back to essentialist and deficit discourses. Positioning Occupy Central at the fore of their political action and experiences of otherness, these women have articulated their ways of belonging in the territory as permanent residents and ethnic minorities. The four young women "speak back" to power through their cellphilm productions, through the screening of these cellphilms and in the disseminations of the videos in a participant-managed digital archive on YouTube. In their discussion of politics and civic engagement, and in their community cellphilming practices, the women work together to articulate their own ways of knowing and acting in Hong Kong. In so doing, they answer, Who's Hong Kong? We are HK too!

References

Buckingham, David. 2000. *The Making of Citizens: young people, news, and politics.* New York: Taylor & Francis.

Buckingham, David. 2009. "'Creative' Visual Methods in Media Research: possibilities, problems and proposals." *Media, Culture, and Society* 31 (4): 633–652. doi:10.1177/0163443709335280.

Burkholder, Casey. 2013. "Just the School Make[s] us Non-Chinese": contrasting the discourses of Hong Kong's education bureau with the lived experiences of its non-Chinese speaking secondary school population." *Educational Research for Social Change* 2 (2): 43–58.

Burkholder, Casey. Forthcoming. "We Are HK too!: disseminating cellphilms in a participatory archive." In *What's a Cellphilm?: integrating mobile phone technology into participatory arts based research and activism,* edited by Katie MacEntee, Casey Burkholder and Josh Schwab-Cartas. Rotterdam: Sense Publishers.

Census and Statistics Department (Hong Kong). 2013. "Hong Kong 2011 Population Census Thematic Report: ethnic minorities." Report. Accessed November 20, 2015. http://www.censtatd.gov.hk/hkstat/sub/sp170.jsp?productCode=B1120062.

Chau, Clement. 2010. "YouTube as a Participatory Culture." *New Directions for Youth Development* 128: 65–74.

Cinema Politica. 2015. "Cinema Politica: screening truth to power." Accessed November 20, 2015. http://www.cinemapolitica.org/.

Coffman, Elizabeth. 2009. "Documentary and Collaboration: placing the camera in the community." *Journal of Film and Video* 61 (1): 62–78.

Cooks, Leda. 2003. "Pedagogy, Performance, and Positionality: teaching about whiteness in interracial communication." *Communication Education* 52 (3–4): 245–257.

Dockney, J. and K. G. Tomaselli. 2009. "Fit for the Small(er) Screen: films, mobile TV and the new individual television experience." *Journal of African Cinema* 1 (1): 126–132.

Dockney, Jonathan, Keyan Tomaselli and T. B. Hart. 2010. "Cellphilms, Mobile Platforms and Prodsumers: hyper-individuality and film." In *The Citizen in Communication: revisiting traditional, new and community media practices in South Africa,* edited by Nathalie Hyde-Clarke, 75–96. Cape Town: Juta Press.

Elder, Sarah. 1995. "Collaborative Filmmaking: an open space for making meaning, a moral ground for ethnographic film." *Visual Anthropology Review* 11 (2): 94–101.

Grundy, Tom. 2015. "Hong Kong Free Press Lens: 'we'll be back' –the clearance of the Occupy Admiralty camp." *Hong Kong Free Press,* December 11. Accessed August 24, 2016. https://www.hongkongfp.com/2015/12/11/hkfp-lens-well-be-back-the-clearance-of-the-occupy-admiralty-camp-part-1-of-2/.

Haw, Kaye. 2008. "Voice" and Video: seen heard and listened to." In *Doing Visual Research with Children and Young People,* edited by P. Thompson, 192–207. London and New York: Routledge.

HKSAR (Hong Kong Special Administrative Region). 2011. "Hong Kong 2011 Population Census Thematic Report: ethnic minorities." Report.

Accessed November 20, 2015. http://www.censtatd.gov.hk/hkstat/sub/sp170. jsp?productCode=B1120062.

Hue, Ming-tak and Kerry John Kennedy. 2015. "Promoting Cultural Responsiveness: teachers' constructs of an assessment classroom environment for ethnic minority students in Hong Kong secondary schools." *Teachers and Teaching* 21(3): 289–304.

MacEntee, Katie, Casey Burkholder and Josh Schwab-Cartas Forthcoming. Eds. *What's a Cellphlm? Integrating Mobile Phone Technology into Participatory Arts Based Research and Activism.* Rotterdam: Sense Publishers.

Milne, E. J., Claudia Mitchell and Naydene de Lange. 2012. Eds. *The Handbook of Participatory Video.* Rotterdam: Sense Publishers.

Mitchell, Claudia and Naydene De Lange. 2011. "Community-Based Participatory Video and Social Action in Rural South Africa." In *The Sage Handbook of Visual Research Methods,* edited by Eric Margolis and Luc Pauwels, 171–185. Thousand Oaks, CA: Sage.

Mitchell, Claudia and Naydene De Lange. 2013. "What Can a Teacher Do with a Cellphone? Using Participatory Visual Research to Speak Back in Addressing HIV&AIDS." *South African Journal of Education* 33 (4): 1–13.

Mitchell, Claudia, Naydene De Lange and Relebohile Moletsane. 2014. "Me and My Cellphone: constructing change from the inside through cellphilms and participatory video in a rural community." *Area.* Accessed November 20, 2015. doi:10.1111/area.12142.

Ngo, Jennifer. 2015. "Hong Kong's Ethnic Minorities Strive to Break Down Barriers." *South China Morning Post,* July 30. Accessed November 17, 2015.

Park, Eun G., Claudia Mitchell and Naydene de Lange. 2008. "Social Uses of Digitisation within the Context of HIV/AIDS: metadata as engagement." *Online Information Review* 32 (6): 716–725.

Russell, Catherine. 1999. *Experimental Ethnography: the work of film in the age of video.* Durham, NC: Duke University Press.

Schwab-Cartas, Josh and Claudia Mitchell. 2014. "A Tale of Two Sites: cellphones, participatory video and indigeneity in community-based research." *McGill Journal of Education* 49 (3): 603–620.

Walsh, Shannon. 2012. "Challenging Knowledge Production with Participatory Video." In *The Handbook of Participatory Video,* edited by E.J. Milne, Claudia Mitchell and Naydene de Lange, 242–256. Rotterdam: Sense Publishers.

Zhou, Shirley. 2014. "Ethnic Minority Children Stereotyped and Belittled in Hong Kong Schools, Say Parents: teaching Chinese to ethnic-minority children is not enough, some parents and educators say." *South China Morning Post,* May 26. Accessed November 17, 2015.

4 Representing Scottish Communities on Screen

Alistair Scott

Introduction

This chapter will focus on community filmmaking in Scotland and trace how the representation of local communities on screen has evolved, examining ways in which this has been associated with the projection of ideas of Scottish cultural identity. This historical approach explores interconnections between community filmmaking and mainstream media, both documentary film and television, to identify changing approaches in this field. The aims are to show how community filmmaking in Scotland today draws upon creative practices developed in a number of different periods since the early twentieth century and to explore how the representation of cultural identity has altered over this period as a result of shifting attitudes to class, gender and, most significantly, with the establishment of communities of Scots from a range of ethnic backgrounds. This analysis outlines the importance of cultural diversity for contemporary community filmmaking and explores the ways in which it is now possible to reflect multiple, overlapping Scottish identities that are informed by the tradition of community filmmaking in Scotland.

The research methodology is based upon identifying relevant examples through an audit of films held in the Scottish Screen Archive and through other records, including previous published surveys of filmmaking in Scotland (McBain 1982, Blain 1990, Hardy 1990, Petrie 2000, MacPherson 2013). The history of community filmmaking in Scotland has produced a limited number of films, and the selection of case studies is also based upon my experience in this field as a filmmaker working with communities in Scotland since the late 1970s. In this way the analysis of the development of community filmmaking is informed by the critical reflection and perspective of a practitioner engaged with the changing landscape for this field of work.

Defining exactly what constitutes community filmmaking is elusive, with some writers pointing to 'multiple versions', and eliding the two concepts of community and alternative media (Atton 2015). Previous research identified a number of features such as: the participation and empowerment of non-professional 'ordinary' people; access to filmmaking skills and equipment by local groups and engagement with activist-inspired campaigns for political change. These are all aspects of filmmaking with a civic purpose or filmmaking with a radical committed agenda (Coyer et al. 2007). I want to make the case that it is also appropriate to consider films from and about local communities that have been produced and screened to a wider audience on television. The chapter will chart three phases: first, the 1970s and 1980s, when video filmmaking was introduced for community development work, when local groups were given access slots on the BBC and Channel 4 and when the first cable community television experiments were introduced. Second, the 1990s and 2000s, when the on-screen representations of local communities were shaped by new configurations of factual television programming. Finally, the current situation in which community filmmaking provides a platform for a diverse range of 'voices' competing to find their place in the crowded digital media environment. The analysis draws on knowledge gained through my personal involvement, as a community worker using video in the 1970s, as a filmmaker within the workshop sector in the 1980s and as an independent television producer collaborating with local organisations for broadcast productions in the 1990s and 2000s. Each of these phases of development has influenced the shape of community filmmaking in Scotland today.

Context

It is relevant to establish the historical context and background of this genre of film. The idea of the 'local film', representing a specific community, dates back to the earliest period of silent filmmaking in the 1900s, described as the *pre-documentary era* (Winston 2008), when filmmakers captured street scenes of ordinary life and these films were screened with short descriptive titles rather than with a developed narrative structure. Arriving in a new town, fairground exhibitors used their cameras to film as many townspeople as possible, and this footage was processed for immediate use. This local material was advertised and became a major attraction, as audiences came to see themselves on screen, with the novelty of viewing familiar everyday life in their own community (Toulmin and Loiperdinger 2005). Local content was an integral part of early film exhibition in Scotland (McBain 2007); this archive is now a rich resource for today's local history projects, and these short portraits of everyday life are the original antecedents of community filmmaking.

Following audience enthusiasm for the 'local film', early documentary filmmakers sought out subject material set within specific communities in order to reflect aspects of national cultural identity. This was particularly the case in Scotland where, from the time of *Drifters* (Grierson 1929), which told the story of the herring fishing fleet community, filmmakers recorded portrayals of Scottish working-class life. Grierson set the didactic tone of these documentaries with seven films produced by Films of Scotland for the Glasgow Empire Exhibition of 1938. This established a tradition in which the function of documentary filmmaking was a tool for educational and civic purposes (Aitken 1998). This approach was never a model for participation or engagement with community film-making, and from a later perspective the dominant mode of these films was seen as overtly paternalistic (Blain 1990). Grierson believed that government and industry should sponsor professional filmmaking and that these films with a utilitarian social purpose would lead to a more progressive society (Ellis 2000). This ethos continued from the 1940s to the 1970s with films about Scottish communities such as *Dunfermline, a plan for change* (1947), *Heart of Scotland* (1961) and *Keep your eye on Paisley* (1975) (Hardy 1990). In his analysis of the legacy of these films McArthur (1982) proposed the concept of the 'Scotland on the move' discourse as Scottish communities were always presented as modern, urban and industrial, optimistic and forward-looking. He argued that this presented unrealistic, clichéd stereotypes with no recognition of the range of social attitudes.

Despite the dominance of Grierson's influence, there were examples of different approaches, on a small scale, but relevant to the development of community filmmaking. Throughout the 1930s Jenny Gilbertson documented her local community in films including *A Crofter's Life in Shetland* (1932) and *The Rugged Island – a Shetland Lyric* (1933). Her work impressed Grierson and she was able to distribute her films through the GPO Film Library (Petrie 2000). During the same period left-wing amateur film enthusiasts established workers' film societies, such as the Glasgow Kino Club and also experimented with the production of short films about local political issues (Allen 1982). A post-war example of such an organisation was the Dawn Cine Group 1953–1957 set up as an adjunct to the Clydeside Film Society. Their productions were shot on 16mm film and recorded events such as a local rents' protest march. Their most successful film, *Let Glasgow Flourish* (1956), was a power-ful piece of propaganda calling for action to tackle the housing crisis in the city (Shand 2008). But, apart from this marginal activity, the repre-sentation of Scottish communities was dominated by the output of Films of Scotland with little opportunity for any diversity of viewpoint.

1970s – Campaign Films, the Introduction of Video and Access Broadcasting

The 1970s was a key period for the development of community film-making beginning with the emergence of independent film groups across the UK. MacPherson (2015) argues that new developments in alternative/ community media in Scotland developed later than in England because of Scotland's subordinate position as a stateless nation; however, despite the fact that there was at that time no Scottish independent film group, the movement did make an impact by documenting the landmark occupation and work-in by shipbuilding unions at UCS (the Upper Clyde Shipyard) in 1971. This was filmed by the radical independent film collective Cinema Action for *UCS1* (1971) and *Class Struggle: Film from the Clyde* (1977). These films continued the tradition of the committed, Marxist propaganda film, established by the workers' film clubs of the 1930s documenting Scottish grassroots political action,

Further new developments for community filmmaking during the 1970s came as a result of two catalysts: the use of video production as a tool within community development work and policy initiatives to give ordinary people greater 'access' to television. The introduction of the Sony Portapak video camera/recorder, which used black and white ½-inch reel-to-reel tape, brought the tools for filmmaking into the hands of local activists; and the launch of cable television experiments in a number of towns across the UK, together with a new department in the BBC, gave some communities access to the airwaves. Throughout the decade the question of how local communities could engage with possible new approaches to programme-making was integral to the debates associated with the on-going deliberations of the Annan Committee about the proposed new fourth television channel (Coyer et al. 2007). A number of cable companies were granted licences for community television channels in Bristol, Swindon, Greenwich, Sheffield, Wellingborough and Milton Keynes (Lewis 2015). In contrast to the regular community programme output from these stations, the experiments in community television in Scotland were short-lived with limited resources and were embedded in community development initiatives. Vale TV was part of a 'Quality of Life Experiment', which was managed by a consortium including Dumbarton District Development Agency, the Scottish Film Council and the Vale of Leven Neighbourhood Development Group. A small production team was established, and funding was secured for two cameras and basic video editing equipment. A licence was granted to broadcast for a six-week period from May 1976, and newspaper adverts encouraged the general public to submit programme ideas. The short experiment resulted in films about cultural and arts organisations such as the local amateur operatic society, the Loch Lomond and District Pipe Band and the Cardross Scouts. There were also issue-based programmes such as *Women in Focus* and *Vale Summerplay*. The final report noted difficult challenges but commented on the enthusiasm and appetite for local programming (Lewis 1978).

A second short community cable television project also developed from a community arts project based at the Leith Adult Education Centre in Edinburgh. The project ran throughout July 1977 serving 500 households and broadcasting via the communal aerial system for the Grampian and Cairngorm House flats in Leith. The main output from this experiment was an agit-prop, community film, presented by local teenagers, about the lack of amenities for children at these high-rise flats, *Playspace* (1977). The film was screened to the Council by the local tenants' group and, with vivid evidence expressed by local voices; the group was able to secure funding for an adventure playground and new facilities. This link between community video and neighbourhood issues was repeated across the UK, and many tenants' organisations became adept at using video to campaign and lobby local councils.

Cinema Sgire, Gaelic for 'Community Cinema', was another project defined by community development aspirations but with the additional aim to reflect linguistic diversity as an important facet of Scottish cultural identity. This project ran for two years (1977–1979), bringing film to communities across the Western Isles. As well as organising screenings in village halls, the project used portapak equipment to make a film in Gaelic about the impact of a military rocket range on local fishing and crofting. There were also video recordings of the music and oral history of the Hebrides. The project worker was Mike Russell who went on to set up the Celtic Film and TV Festival in 1980 and later to become an influential SNP politician. At the same time as the *Cinema Sgire* project, Jack Shea and Allen Moore, two American anthropologist filmmakers from Harvard University, were making *The Shepherds of Berneray* (1981) about the crofting community on a small island south of Harris (Petrie 2000). As in other countries, the representation of a vulnerable, indigenous, minority language, in this case Gaelic, and the traditional culture and way of life of the remote island communities has remained a constant strand within Scottish community filmmaking.

Access to the broadcast media was promoted throughout this decade with the explicit aim of reflecting communities who had hitherto been unrepresented. The main UK-wide initiative to give local groups access to broadcasting during this period was through the BBC's Community Programme Unit established in 1972. Organisations were invited to submit programme ideas to the *Open Door* series and, if selected, the group would retain nominal editorial control and be supported by a team of professional programme makers (Coyer et al. 2007). The aim was to increase the diversity of voices and minority interest groups represented on BBC television, but, although there were around 25 programmes made each year, the number of Scottish-based groups successful in getting ideas selected was tiny. One BBC Scotland network series, *Lilybank* (1977), did adopt elements of the Community Programme Unit approach to engage with, and present a portrait of, a Scottish community and its embryonic tenants' group; however, because there was no attempt by the producers to allow editorial input for local people, the film led to controversy.

In *Lilybank – the fourth world* the producer, David Martin, and director, Mike Tosh, set out to show that social conditions in this east-end Glasgow neighbourhood were worse than in a developing third-world country (Day 2009). The presenter, Magnus Magnusson, was filmed on location identifying the causes of deprivation and outlining the objectives of the Glasgow East End Area Renewal project (GEAR) to upgrade the neighbourhood's poor quality tenement housing. The main programme contributor was Kay Carmichael, a social worker and academic, who had previously spent three months living anonymously in a rented flat in the area, with a weekly income based on supplementary benefit, to experience first-hand the problems of unemployment and poverty. With the video diary not yet invented, she provided evidence about life in the community in the interviews with Magnusson. These were filmed walking the streets of Lilybank, in a local café and from the comfort of an armchair in a flat in Glasgow's west end with Carmichael reflecting on her experience through a prism of middle-class attitudes. The interviews are intercut with location sequences with local residents similar to content used in many *Open Door* programmes (Harvey 2000). There are film sequences following the meetings to establish a new tenants group and attempts by the group to meet with, and influence, local politicians and planners. In vox-pop clips, local residents give first-hand accounts of problems such as damp housing, overcrowding, the lack of amenities for children and teenagers, glue-sniffing and anti-social behaviour. The third and final programme is a debate, filmed as a multi-camera outside broadcast, from a local school hall with a panel of professionals chaired by Magnusson including Carmichael, other academics and representatives from the Council, the Police, the planning authorities and developers. There is an audience of local people, although throughout the programme there is no opportunity for them to participate. Towards the end a member of the tenants' committee interrupts and makes an eloquent plea for greater engagement with the community. He expresses the frustration residents feel at being excluded from decision-making. *Lilybank* is important because it was the most significant representation of a Scottish community on network television during this period and because it reveals the problem of filmmakers speaking on behalf of a local community. Yet, despite their lack of editorial control, over 30 years later the most powerful, enduring voices in these programmes are the local people themselves (*The Herald*, 17 July 2009).

1980s – The Workshop Movement and Impact of Channel 4

Initiatives to set up community filmmaking groups across Scotland were consolidated in the 1980s, and the launch of Channel 4 in 1982, with a clearly defined public service broadcasting remit to introduce new voices, encourage diversity and sponsor regional initiatives, led to funding and new opportunities for community filmmakers to make programmes for broadcast. Edinburgh Film Workshop Trust (1977) established a model for community filmmaking, with a not-for-profit organisation supported by the local authority, providing training, access to equipment, facilities and expertise for local groups and projects. This was followed by a number of other groups, Red Star Cinema (1980), Video in Pilton (1982), Glasgow Film and Video Workshop (1983) and later, Fradharc Ur on the Isle of Lewis, Alva in central Scotland and video access centres in Aberdeen and Dundee. A Scottish Association of Workshops (1983–1989) was established to share experience and liaise with Channel 4. Community film work also took place in arts projects based in the housing schemes around Glasgow such as Castlemilk and Drumchapel, and a group in Cranhill produced *Clyde Film* (1985), in the polemical tradition of the earlier work of the Dawn Cine Group (MacPherson 2013).

The workshop movement developed an approach to filmmaking where there was a constant tension between *process* and *production*. The *process,* with this kind of filmmaking, was to establish tools for community development, to introduce new communication skills for grassroots organisations, and to empower local groups who would otherwise have no voice through the media. For some groups the *product,* the completed film, was seen as a useful outcome but less important than the collaborative work and participation during production. For others in the sector securing commissions for broadcast programmes was vital in order to represent life in these communities to a wider audience. At this time production was upgraded from the Sony portapak cameras, first to ¾-inch u-matic, and later to Beta Sp colour video formats. A number of the workshops were enfranchised under the Association of Cinema and Television Technicians (ACTT) Workshop Declaration (1981) giving the professional union recognition required so that programmes made by them could be broadcast on Channel 4 (Stoneman 1992).

With strands such as *People to People,* and *11th Hour,* Channel 4's Independent Film and Video department demonstrated a commitment to funding documentaries that gave voice to sections of society and content, such as feminist history, which had previously been under-represented. *Red Skirts on the Clyde* (1984) was the first of these based on a Scottish subject. This was a film telling the story of the 1915 Glasgow Women's Rent Strike, made by women from the Sheffield Film Co-op with BFI production funding. As in the previous decade, the first move had come from an independent film group from outside Scotland; however, several later films were made for the *People to People* series presenting portrayals of different types of Scottish communities. *Wester Hailes – the Huts* (1985) presented a portrait of life on a sprawling council estate on the outskirts of Edinburgh made in collaboration with local people. The film's producer was Trevor Davies from Skyline Films. Davies had long-established links with this community as a Labour councillor, and it is evident that local groups participated closely in shaping the programme content.

The policy of Channel 4's commissioners encouraged experimentation in form (Stoneman 2005), and *The Huts* attempts a radical structure, using several different modes of documentary. Aspects of life on this estate such as the isolation of single parents, housing problems and the powerlessness felt by the long-term unemployed, are introduced through imaginative sequences, poignant and funny, delivered by local amateur actors, as direct to camera monologues, short dramatised scenes and the use of shadow puppets. Local circus workshop performers give a tour of the area led by a juggling teenage unicyclist. These sequences are intercut with interviews and documentary footage following meetings of the tenants' group and the community newspaper. These different elements combine to produce an impressionistic portrait, focusing on the participation of residents in initiatives to improve the quality of their lives. This is a film that engages with local people to present a multi-layered, creative portrayal of a community far from the conventional reportage of *Lilybank*.

Two other Scottish communities featured in the Channel 4 *People to People* strand. *The Work They Say Is Mine* (1986), filmed in Shetland by Avonbridge Films, was a drama-documentary tracing the traditional role of women in the crofting and fishing industries that built on the work of Jenny Gilbertson in the 1930s. As with the earlier film from Sheffield Film Co-op, this was made by a group of women filmmakers, tackling gender issues and exploring cultural history that had been largely forgotten. *Leithers* (1987) was an oral history programme produced by Edinburgh Film Workshop, which celebrated the community identity of Edinburgh's port, an inner-city area that had suffered industrial decline and was undergoing urban regeneration. Intercutting archive footage and interviews with local residents, the film also recorded on-going campaigns to improve housing, provide local facilities and improve community cohesion. The film documented the establishment of a Sikh community in Leith, reflecting the ways in which, as in many Scottish cities, there was now representation from different ethnic backgrounds shaping the identity of the area. This was one of the earliest examples of programme to portray this diversity as a feature of modern Scotland. As well as this production for *People to People* Edinburgh Film Workshop Trust contributed sequences about the experience of Scottish mining communities during the 1984/85 strike for the award-winning film *The Miners Tapes* (1985). The variety of approaches adopted through these productions demonstrated a new vitality for Scottish community filmmaking.

From 1989, Channel 4's commissioning policy changed and moved away from supporting these types of programmes, and by the early

1990s there was no further on-going commitment for the Workshop sector. The organisations adopted a variety of strategies to secure alternative support. Edinburgh Film Workshop Trust produced a number of non-broadcast documentaries through its Women's Production Unit, *Your health's your wealth* (1990) looking at women's health issues, and *Behind closed doors* (1991) about combatting domestic abuse. Other organisations such as Glasgow Film and Video Workshop focused on access to equipment and training. Two drama productions came as a result of work with local arts organisations, *The Priest and the Pirate* (1994) from Video in Pilton and *Butterfly Man* (1996) from Edinburgh Film Workshop Trust leading to on-going involvement in the production of independent short films.

1990s – New 'hybrid' Formats for Factual Television

The changes in commissioning policy by the broadcasters resulted in more competitive scheduling and the blurring of programme genres. It has been argued that innovative strategies first seen on community television influenced the new styles of factual programming during the 1990s (Biressi and Nunn 2005). The introduction of hybrid docusoap formats led to extensive reframing of broadcast television programmes addressing ideas of community identity. On the mainstream channels there were increasing demands for programmes to entertain as well as to inform. This led to a 'hybridising impulse' with a shift from presenting an overview of a community to concentrating on individual human stories (Hill 2007). This also led to the adoption of storytelling devices from genres such as television soap operas, with 'characters' that could represent specific social issues. With new light-weight video cameras it was easier to adopt an observational documentary approach for filming and to present real life by creating a narrative structure that would interweave these scenes and characters, presenting life in working-class communities in an entertaining style (Bruzzi 2007).

Examples of this type of approach to filming communities in Scotland included *Heartland FM* (Peat, BBC, 1999), about the Moray Firth Community Radio station and the community it served; *Postcards from Sighthill* (Scott, STV, 1999) about asylum-seekers and refugees rehoused by Glasgow Council and *Raploch Stories* (Scott, BBC, 2002), a longitudinal documentary series following a year on a housing estate in Stirling. These films placed character development at the heart of the narrative, and this became the predominant way for local communities to be presented by broadcasters. Later series have been accused of reinforcing negative stereotypes of community life in order to create a compelling narrative. *The Scheme* (Friel Kean Films, BBC 2010, and 2011) portrayed the lives of people living on the Onthank Estate in Kilmarnock and, by following the interlinking lives of six families over several months, dealt with issues such as unemployment, inter-generational conflict and drug addiction. *The Scheme* demonstrates how in an increasingly competitive environment for broadcasting there is pressure to depict extreme situations as, rather than representing a typical cross-section from the Onthank community, the contributors in *The Scheme* all come from dysfunctional households. The process of 'casting' these characters has identified households where everyone is unemployed and at least one person is living a chaotic lifestyle. The focus on this section of the community led to public debate about the series leading some commentators to brand the series 'poverty porn' (*The Scotsman* 28 May 2010).

This approach to storytelling continues to be the way in which local communities in Scotland are portrayed on mainstream television. *Commonwealth City* (Bennett, BBC, 2014) was a series of three documentaries filmed over a four-year period, tracking upheaval and change in Dalmarnock, a community in the east end of Glasgow, redeveloped to be home to major sporting venues for the 2014 Commonwealth Games. The films followed local residents and community activists and recorded the impact that the transformation of the neighbourhood had on their lives. The series interweaves the stories of Darren, a local shop-keeper, Stephen, a teenager construction trainee, Margaret, a long-time resident who resists compulsory eviction when her tenement is scheduled for demolition to make way for the Athletes' Village, and Yvonne, who campaigns for a legacy of improved community facilities alongside the new sports complexes and whose personal journey leads to her election as a local councillor. It is fast-moving, entertaining, factual television that establishes these real people as characters whose lives are emblematic of social issues such as the benefits and disadvantages for communities transformed by urban regeneration.

The current Situation for Community Filmmaking in Scotland

Community filmmaking across Scotland today has been shaped by the legacy of the approaches from the earlier phases outlined in this chapter. New developments in technology, on-going innovation with new high-definition digital video cameras, computer-based editing and Internet distribution have transformed the ways in which films can be produced and distributed. Social media has introduced new channels of communication for local groups to collaborate and participate in creative productions. Also, since 1999 the devolution of powers to the Scottish Parliament has contributed to changing attitudes about national and community representation across Scotland. The ways in which attitudes increasingly differ from other parts of the UK was demonstrated by voting patterns in the 2016 UK EU Referendum. In Scotland 62% of voters wanted to remain in the EU (compared with 46.6% in England

and 48.1% overall) with only 38% of Scots voting to leave (compared with 53.4% in England and 62% overall). With Scottish Government, local authorities and public opinion polls welcoming new refugees and immigrants (*The Guardian* 3ʳᵈ September 2016) there is now a wider range of projects that can be categorised as community filmmaking than ever before.

There are local groups that have clearly defined specialist interest projects, such as using participatory filmmaking to create social networks to document aspects of community life and history. In Govan in Glasgow, Plantation Productions has worked with a local senior citizens' group and a group of local mental health service users on films such as *The Govan Banners* (2010) and *You Play Your Part* (2011). Macleod (2015) analyses her role as a facilitator and director and reflects on these projects "as social processes that nurture knowledge through participation in production". In the initial stages the research by the group drew upon work from an earlier phase by screening *Red Skirts on Clydeside* (1984). The story of the 1915 Glasgow Women's Rent Strike, led by Mary Barbour, acted as a catalyst for these women to share their own memories of their involvement in and contributions to political campaigns. This led to collaboration in making films that explored how their personal experiences gave new insights into the history of the fight for equal pay and equality for women. With filmed interviews, for example about their involvement with the UCS work-in, the films developed new perspectives on the role of women in the community. The 'after-life' of the film was also significant, with the presence of the women filmmakers at post-screening discussions, such as at Scottish Women's Library and the Glasgow Film Theatre on International Women's Day, leading to impact and recognition from other communities.

Alongside groups operating in local neighbourhoods, community filmmaking in Scotland today includes media activism with global links, using the Internet and social media, to share content with groups across the world and also reflecting the increasing diversity of Scottish communities. Media Co-op, established in 2004, produces content for, and with, the voluntary sector and social action groups in Scotland and abroad, with a track record of encouraging the participation of community organisations. Camcorder Guerrillas, a Scottish-based collective formed at an Indymedia meeting in 2002, has been active in a number of political interventions such as *Welcome* (2005), a film documenting how asylum-seekers and refugees were treated by the authorities. Camcorder Guerrillas also worked with international partners to provide alternative journalistic coverage of the G8 Conference held at Gleneagles in 2005 (Hadzi 2007).

Another innovative project that integrated community filmmaking with new ways of networking through social media and the Internet was the *Northern Lights* project. This was a crowd-sourced documentary film, funded through a Scottish Government initiative with National Lottery support, about the communities and people of Scotland. The project advertised for submissions and set up a team to run workshops giving an introduction to filmmaking and basic training in over 50 communities across Scotland. Between March and June 2012 there were a total of 1500 submissions and, using over 300 hours of this original material, the creative director, Nick Higgins, with film editor, Colin Monie, shaped a multi-perspective, feature-length film that presented a "kaleidoscopic documentary portrait of Scotland and its communities" that they described as "identity as assemblage". *We are Northern Lights* (2013) was premiered at the Glasgow Film Festival and then screened at cinemas across Scotland and abroad.

Alongside these new approaches to community filmmaking the legacy of the workshop movement has evolved and continues to be important. The two main centres for community filmmaking in Edinburgh and Glasgow both trace their history back to the 1980s. Video in Pilton, first established in 1981, now operates as Screen Education Edinburgh having changed its name in 2012, and Glasgow Film and Video Workshop was renamed GMAC (Glasgow Media Access Centre) in 2000. Both of these organisations have redefined their profiles with an emphasis on education, training and community development. From the mid-1990s they have benefited from local authority revenue funding, especially for their work with young people from disadvantaged areas, and have also attracted support from the National Lottery. Video in Pilton was originally set up to work in a single community in north Edinburgh, but from 1995 the organisation was given a city-wide remit to support long-term development including diversity work funded through the City Council's Children and Families department. An example of a community filmmaking that grew from this was *Then and Now* (2003), a film following a family of asylum-seekers from Iraq and the integration of the family's two teenage girls in the local community. Video in Pilton also continued to develop local short filmmakers with projects such as *Colours* (2013), developed with local young men serving sentences in Polmont Young Offenders Institution. There are on-going links with the Edinburgh International Film Festival for film education and for screening completed work. They also act as the host organisation for the annual BFI Film Academy in south-east Scotland.

GMAC in Glasgow is also a social enterprise with charitable status with a mission to act as a bridge between the screen industries and the community. As with Screen Education Edinburgh, GMAC is focused on talent development, access to equipment and training, to raise the aspirations and confidence of young people from areas of high deprivation and from the Black and Minority Ethnic (BAME) communities in the city. There are regular networking events, screenings and a partnership agreement to deliver the BFI Film Academy workshops. Initiatives such

as Second Light, advertised locally through Radio Ramadan, have offered apprenticeships for trainees from the ethnic communities. This is
now starting to result in new production work, such as the short film
Meet Me by the Water (2016), written and directed by Raisha Ahmed.
Along with Screen Education Scotland and Station House Media Unit
(SHMU) in Aberdeen they are involved in Film Access Network
Scotland (FANS). These partnerships are implementing a strategy to
reflect the multicultural communities across Scotland today. Another
example is the work of on-line community video activists such as the
artist/filmmaker Basharat Khan with projects such as *Albert Drive TV*
based in the Pollokshaws and Govanhill areas of Glasgow where there is
a large Scots/Pakistani community.

New community television projects have also built on the early cable
TV experiments of the 1970s. Dave Rushton, who was part of local
Edinburgh group Red Star Cinema, established the Institute of Local TV
and led a sustained campaign for innovative, democratic access to broadcast television (Rushton 1993). This group now delivers community programming, via the web, with Summerhall TV, based at an Edinburgh
arts centre. There are other organisations, such as Fife TV, serving communities with Internet television services in other regions of the country.
There have also been a new 'city' TV services on mainstream broadcast
television with the launch of the local digital TV network (LDTVN).
To date two Scottish stations have started transmission, STV Glasgow
in June 2014 and STV Edinburgh in January 2015. Ofcom has granted
licences to further stations in Aberdeen, Dundee and Ayr. In every case
in Scotland the successful bid for a new LDTVN franchise has been
awarded to STV in partnership with a local university, and their proposals have emphasised the importance of providing slots for community
programming.

From the small cable experiments of the 1970s and the modest output
of Clyde Cablevision and Aberdeen Cable in the 1990s once again local
TV is key part of the media landscape. At the outset the LTVDN network was hailed as a major initiative to extend choice for UK audiences
and to introduce a new tier within the national framework of broadcasting with channels in around 50 locations across the UK granted initial
licences for 12 years. STV is the only ITV franchise licence holder that
sought to be included in the local network. This means that, unlike other
local stations, they can use cross-channel promotion, with trails for the
local stations on the main ITV channel and with local stations available
'on-demand' on the STV player. The content on both stations is based
around flagship 'live' magazine programmes, *The Riverside Show* in
Glasgow and *The Fountainbridge Show* in Edinburgh, but community
interest programmes are being introduced and making an impact. The
channels have developed local history programmes such as *Glasgow's
Murder Mysteries,* and both the Glasgow and Edinburgh stations have

given exposure to local bands with the programme *Grassroots Music,* with other community-focused programmes such as *Christmas Choirs* from local schools. It is too early to assess the extent that these new local channels will contribute to the idea of public service broadcasting by providing an outlet for community filmmakers, as set out in their franchise bids. However, they certainly represent a potential opportunity to develop new types of local content on broadcast television.

There are now many different approaches for community filmmaking across Scotland, drawing on the all the previous stages of development. The legacy of early work by pioneers such as Jenny Gilbertson still continues to be relevant, with recent screenings of her 1930s documentaries for the community in Shetland. Filmmaker, Shona Main, has drawn inspiration from Gilbertson's work for her film, *Clavel* (2015) about crofting today. This was screened alongside Gilbertson's work at the Inverness Film Festival linking past and present. The work of the Dawn Cine Group has also been rediscovered, and a group of musicians and filmmakers have completed their unfinished project, *Lost Treasure* (1956), which was the story of the Scottish Highlands from a socialist perspective. The new version of the film, with a contemporary score, opened the Glasgow Short Film Festival 2016. In Glasgow there are local independent filmmakers working closely with community organisations, with Alison Irvine at the Red Road flats and Chris Leslie, with his film *(Re)Imagining Glasgow,* reversioning earlier documentary work directed by Oscar Marzaroli such as the film *Glasgow 1980* (1970).

The diversity and variety of subject material illustrates the multiple cultural identities that are part of contemporary Scotland. Festivals such as *Africa in Motion* (established in 2005), the SQIFF (the Scottish Queer International Film Festival) and the Scottish Mental Health Arts and Film Festival all incorporate new work from local community filmmakers for local audiences. In the Scottish Borders, Alchemy Film and Arts based in Hawick has recently introduced a new initiative for aspiring young filmmakers funded by Creative Scotland. Since 2007 FilmG has co-ordinated an annual community filmmaking competition, operated in partnership with BBC Alba, to encourage grassroots filmmaking in the Gaelic language. Filmmaker Andy Mackinnon has also set up Uist Media in The Hebrides. From the small-scale achievements of *Cinema Sgire* in the 1970s Gaelic filmmaking has continued to grow and is now part of the range of community filmmaking reflecting regional cultural identities across different parts of Scotland.

Conclusion

This historical overview traces how community filmmaking has always been an integral part of Scottish screen culture. It also shows how filmmakers today draw directly from the legacy of earlier creative practice.

One of the foundations on which this has been built is the survival and evolution of organisations formed during the 1980s. They have adapted to develop up-to-date training and production initiatives and to promote grassroots filmmaking with an emphasis on diversity. There is now an increasingly complex representation of modern Scottish cultural life reflecting the multiple, overlapping identities of twenty-first-century Scots. Each individual community film project leads to greater empowerment for those participating; however, this is limited in scale, and institutional policy is focused on skills development rather than on opening up democratic access to the media. The broadcast media has always produced programmes portraying local communities and has been influential in recording changing Scottish cultural identity and attitudes for a mainstream audience. The authenticity of this representation has been shaped by the changing approaches of the programme commissioners. New forms of distribution, through the web and, perhaps on the local TV digital network, offer opportunities to create exciting ways for community filmmaking to reach a wider audience in the future.

References

Aitken, Ian. 1998. *The Documentary Film Movement, an Anthology,* Edinburgh: Edinburgh University Press.

Allen, D. 1982. "Workers' Films: Scotland's hidden film culture." In *Scotch Reels, Scotland in Cinema and Television*, edited by Colin MacArthur. London: British Film Institute.

Atton, C. 2015. Ed. *The Routledge Companion to Alternative and Community Media*. London: Routledge.

Biressi, A. and Nunn, H. 2005. *Reality TV: realism and revelation,* London: Wallflower Press.

Blain, Neil. 1990. "A Scotland as Good as Any Other - Documentary Film 1937–82." In *From Limelight to Satellite: a Scottish film book*, edited by Eddie Dick. London: British Film Institute.

Bruzzi, Stella. 2007. *New Documentary, a Critical Introduction.* London: Routledge.

Coyer, Kate, Tony Dowmunt and Alan Fountain. 2007. *The Alternative Media Handbook*. London: Routledge.

Day, Daniel. 2009. "Nation Shall Speak Peace unto Nation': the BBC and the projection of a new Britain 1967–82." In *Narrating Media History*, edited by M. Bailey. Abingdon: Routledge.

Ellis, Jack C. 2000. *John Grierson: life, contributions, influence.* Carbondale: Southern Illinois University Press.

Hadzi, A. 2007. "New(er) Technologies." In *The Alternative Media Handbook,* edited by Kate Coyer, Tony Dowmunt and Alan Fountain. London: Routledge.

Hardy, Forsyth. 1990. *Scotland in Film.* Edinburgh: Edinburgh University Press.

Harvey, Sylvia. 2000. "Access, Authorship and Voice: the emergence of community programming at the BBC." In *From Grierson to Socusoaps*, edited by John Izod, Richard Kilborn and Matthew Hibberd. Luton: University of Luton Press.

Hill, Annette. 2007. *Restyling Factual TV: audiences and news, documentary and reality genres.* London: Routledge.

Lewis, Peter M. 1978. *Community Television and Cable in Britain.* London: British Film Institute.

Lewis, Peter M. 2015. "Community Media Policy." In *The Routledge Companion to Alternative and Community Media,* edited by Chris Atton. London: Routledge.

Macleod, Kirsten. 2015. "I Film Therefore I Am: process and participation, networks and knowledge – examples from Scottish community media projects." In *The Routledge Companion to Alternative and Community Media,* edited by Chris Atton. London: Routledge.

MacPherson, Robin. 2013. "Radical and Engaged Cinema in Scotland." In *The Directory of World Cinema, Vol 27 Scotland,* Bristol: Intellect.

MacPherson, Robin. 2015. "Peripheral Visions? Alternative Film in a Stateless Nation." In *The Routledge Companion to Alternative and Community Media,* edited by Chris Atton. London: Routledge.

McArthur, Colin 1982. Ed. *Scotch Reels, Scotland in Cinema and television.* London: British Film Institute.

McBain. Janet. 2007. "Green's Picturedromes." *Film Studies* 10 (Spring).

Petrie, Duncan. 2000. *Screening Scotland.* London: British Film Institute.

Rushton, Dave 1993. Ed. *Citizen Television: a local dimension to public service broadcasting.* London: John Libbey.

Shand, Ryan. 2008. "Theorizing Amateur Cinema: limitations and possibilities." *The Moving Image* 8 (2): 36–60.

Stoneman, Rod. 1992. "The Sins of Commission." *Screen* 33 (2).

Stoneman, Rod. 2005. "The Sins of Commission 2." *Screen* 46 (2).

Toulmin, Vanessa and Loiperdinger, Martin. 2005. "Is It you? Recognition, Representation and Response in Relation to the Local Film." *Film History* 17 (1) Local Film: 7–15, University of Indiana.

Winston, Brian. 2008. *Claiming the Real, Documentary: Grierson and beyond.* London: Palgrave.

Part II

Networks and Intermediaries in Community Filmmaking – a Short Introduction

Roberta Comunian

Introduction

As we explore how community filmmaking is organised and delivered across a range of countries and communities of interests (Wenger 1998), two key elements emerge as central to its functioning, in reference to production and consumption: networks and intermediaries. In this respect, community filmmaking can be strongly reconnected with filmmaking in general (Blair 2003, Cattani and Ferriani 2008) and even more broadly with the creative economy, as networks and intermediaries are considered key features of the working of these sectors (Comunian 2012, Jakob and van Heur 2015). Networks and intermediaries are also strongly connected with the literature on cultural and creative work as they represent structures and modes of work that facilitate and enable cultural production and the coming together of different knowledge and skills in paid and unpaid labour structures (McKinlay and Smith 2009, Conor et al. 2015). The sector and its workers have to face issues of uncertainty and risk (the 'nobody knows' principle proposed by Caves 2002), as well as the precarity that derives from the project-based nature of these industries. In the specific case of the film industry, the importance of temporary contracts (Blair 2001), biased forms of networking to access opportunities, and reputation-based careers (Zafirau 2008) is even stronger. While we can recognise that community filmmaking shares many connections with the broader filmmaking sector and creative economy, it is important to consider also how it challenges assumptions about traditional value chains and the role of networks but also the interconnection of the creative industries with the wider economy and social innovation (Bakhshi et al. 2008). While there is increased emphasis on the business argument within policy initiatives and funding (Creative England 2015), these schemes are often in great contrast with the account of independent producers that, far from wanting to lead profit-driven businesses, are focusing their energy on delivering innovative ideas and engaging with specific cultural or social issues for a specific audience (Comunian 2009). There are signs of a 'contested' creative identity – often portrayed as business-minded but, on the contrary, also led by socio-cultural aspirations, a voice of dissent and critical engagement through which socio-cultural interventions are produced.

Community filmmakers have usually actively engaged to reshape and reposition their practice within alternative business models, to deliver their aspirations without making them instruments of a neoliberal agenda or industry-led paradigms such as 'creative diversity' (Malik 2013). Beyond the business models that might be adopted in this sector, creative industries practitioners are specifically recognised for their ability to establish networks and through intermediaries and engagement with a range of stakeholders to drive the agenda (Comunian 2012). This is very much the case with community filmmaking where every independent project needs to source funding, engage communities and potential markets as well as gatekeepers in order to be completed. For community filmmaking, communities are a defining part of the job and contribute significantly to the content developed within projects – communities are often also stakeholders and (financial) supporters of projects and a key element in how success within the community filmmaking sectors is measured. Although the policy perspective is not strongly present in the chapters in this section, it is important to keep in mind how community filmmaking and diversity are also part of institutional and policy concerns, which are themselves often developed or implemented, supporting local networks and community organisations. In this brief introduction, we explore in more detail the role of these networks and intermediaries for community filmmakers.

The Role of Networks and Intermediaries in Community Filmmaking

Building on the existing literature on filmmaking as well as creative and cultural entrepreneurship, it is easy to identify some key roles played by networks (and networking) to enable both production and consumption of films (Negus 2002). It is also easy to consider how specific intermediaries might facilitate or inhibit opportunities for development and can play a crucial role. Focusing specifically on community filmmaking, we have identified four main roles played by networks and intermediaries that mirror some of the reflections proposed here.

Networks and Intermediaries as Access to Projects and Creative Labour

The chapters within this section of the book highlight how networks and intermediaries, such as community organisations and individual brokers

(Blum-Ross 2015) are key to the ecology of the work of community film-makers. Whether such community filmmakers strongly identify them-selves with this definition or profile, or whether they prefer to define themselves as artists, animators or filmmakers, they all recognise the importance that networking across projects, institutions and communi-ties play in enabling them to secure projects and potentially work and in-come. As Somers (1994) highlights, it is interesting to consider how their identity is defined in a relational way, depending on their networks and practices. This also seems to support previous research that highlights the complex portfolio of work experienced by creative practitioners (Gornostaeva and Campbell, 2012), with community filmmaking being one of many identities adopted by filmmakers. This is one of the key ele-ments in the case study of *South Blessed* that is presented in Chapter 7.

Networks and Intermediaries as Social/Support and Professional Development Structure

Networks are project based and valuable for the development of differ-ent projects, but they are also personally valuable for filmmakers as they allow a degree of personal support and professional development. In sec-tors like community filmmaking where there is a high degree of informal training and learning 'on the job', networks become a very valuable form of knowledge exchange (Comunian 2016), developing communities of practice around the making process but also accompanying individuals throughout their careers. This is highlighted in all the case studies and chapters to be found in this section.

Networks and Intermediaries as Access to Funding and Opportunities

Connected to the previous point, but expanding on the opportunity for community filmmakers to tap into funding streams and other re-sources to dedicate to their practice, networks seems particularly valu-able towards making stronger connections with specific funding bodies (at local, national and international levels) as well as accessing a range of opportunities. Networks become also an opportunity to share valu-able resources and the means of cultural production. For example, in the case of *Colectivo Cine sin Autor* (Authorless Cinema Collective) in Chapter 6, the cultural network is aimed at providing access to audio-visual means to communities and collectives that would otherwise not have the opportunity to work with these resources. If we look at the importance of funding, this can be viewed from both directions. On the one hand, community filmmakers are networked with institutions and funders to access support; on the other, public and third sectors are also closely interlinked with cultural practitioners and rely on these networks to make sure projects are delivered and reach the desired audiences

(Comunian 2012). This is the reason networks are often grassroots organisations developed by producers, but sometimes funding bodies or other organisations can initiate networks to support a range of people and initiatives, through funding and training (Comunian 2012).

Networks and Intermediaries to Access Audiences and Markets

Another important role of networks and intermediaries is in relation to connecting audiences and markets. This is very well documented in the filmmaking literature (Negus 2002; Fu 2015). However, as the community filmmaking sector cannot benefit from the same levels of funding towards marketing and promotion as the commercial film sector, the importance of networking is even greater. This is very well documented in the filmmaking literature (Negus 2002; Fu 2015); however, it is just as important in community filmmaking, especially as often there is no funding directed towards marketing and promotion, as in the for-profit filmmaking sector. It is important to notice how the same networks and community infrastructure that come together in community filmmaking projects to produce new work is strongly connected with community audiences and that often these are made up of the same people who co-produce the work. This is the case for many case studies and projects in this book. However, networks and often online social media can also play a role in enhancing the audiences and markets for community filmmaking projects. This is true for the case study of *52 Tuesdays* in Chapter 5 by Murray and Dooley. Here we see the importance of connecting with audiences in the production as well as consumption process.

This short introduction has allowed us to reflect on some of the themes emerging in the following three chapters, highlighting how a network perspective ties together a lot of the processes of co-production and development as well as distribution/consumption for community filmmakers. It is important to remember also that networks and intermediaries are not a panacea and can sometimes inhibit cultural processes and development as much as help them (Vorley et al. 2012). In particular, as diversity is a specific concern of the chapters in this book, it is worth considering how networks can often give rise to forms of exclusion or create cliques that might discourage new entrants or 'outsiders' from engaging with the cultural exchange process. Nonetheless they provide a valuable lens for researchers to investigate and explore how practitioners make community filmmaking happen and the level of formal and informal networks they rely on to achieve their own goals or the objectives of the communities with whom they are working. A challenge that remains open for researchers in the field of community filmmaking is how to capture the evolving nature of networks. This collection of chapters helps to introduce some of the key issue and processes, but further research is needed to better identify the value of these networks in ever-evolving part-time and temporary community projects in order to create a better awareness for practitioners and their communities of the value of managing and interacting within and across networks.

References

Bakhshi, Hasan, Eric McVittie and James Simmie. 2008. *Creating Innovation: Do the Creative Industries Support Innovation in the Wider Economy?* London: NESTA.

Blair, Helen. 2001. "'You're Only as Good as Your Last Job': the labour process and labour market in the British film industry." *Work, Employment and Society* 15: 149–169.

Blair, Helen. 2003. "Winning and Losing in Flexible Labour Markets: the formation and operation of networks of interdependence in the UK film industry." *Sociology* 37: 677–694.

Blum-Ross, Alicia. 2015. "Filmmakers/Educators/Facilitators? Understanding the Role of Adult Intermediaries in Youth Media Production in the UK and the USA." *Journal of Children and Media* 9(3): 308–324.

Cattani, Gino and Simone Ferriani. 2008. "A Core/Periphery Perspective on Individual Creative Performance: social networks and cinematic achievements in the Hollywood film industry." *Organization Science* 19: 824–844.

Caves, Richard. 2002. *Creative Industries, Contracts between Art and Commerce.* Cambridge, MA: Harvard University Press.

Comunian, Roberta. 2009. "Questioning Creative Work as Driver of Economic Development: the case of Newcastle-Gateshead." *Creative Industries Journal* 2: 57–71.

Comunian, Roberta. 2012. "Exploring the Role of Networks in the Creative Economy of North East England: economic and cultural dynamics." In *Encounters and Engagements between Economic and Cultural Geography*, edited by B. Warf, 143–157. Netherlands: Springer.

Comunian, Roberta. 2016. "Temporary Clusters and Communities of Practice in the Creative Economy: festivals as temporary knowledge networks." *Space and Culture*, online before print July 25, 2016, doi: 10.1177/1206331216660318.

Conor, Bridget, Rosalind Gill and Stephanie Taylor. 2015. "Gender and Creative Labour". *The Sociological Review* 63: 1–22.

Creative England. 2015. *Creative England's Film Enterprise Guide*, http://applications.creativeengland.co.uk/assets/public/resource/145.pdf (accessed 27th November 2015).

Foster, Pacey, Stephan Manning and David Terkla. 2015. "The Rise of Hollywood East: regional film offices as intermediaries in film and television production clusters." *Regional Studies* 49(3): 433–450.

Fu, Yongchun. 2015. "Movie Matchmakers: the intermediaries between Hollywood and China in the early twentieth century." *Journal of Chinese Cinemas* 9(1): 8–22.

Gornostaeva, Galina and Campbell Noel. 2012. "The Creative Underclass in the Production of Place: example of Camden Town in London." *Journal of Urban Affairs* 34(2): 169–188.

Jakob, Doreen and Bas van Heur. 2015. Editorial: Taking Matters into Third Hands: intermediaries and the organization of the creative economy. *Regional Studies* 49(3): 357–361.

Malik, Sarita. 2013. ""Creative Diversity": UK public service broadcasting after multiculturalism." *Popular Communication* 11(3): 227–241.

McKinlay, Alan and Chris Smith. 2009. *Creative Labour: working in the creative industries,* Basingstoke: Palgrave MacMillan.

Negus, Keith. 2002. "The Work of Cultural Intermediaries and the Enduring Distance between Production and Consumption." *Cultural Studies* 16 (4): 501–515.

Somers, Margaret. 1994. "The Narrative Construction of Identity: A relational and networks approach." *Theory and Society* 23: 605–649.

Vorley, Tim, Oli Mould and Richard Courtney. 2012. "My Networking Is Not Working! Conceptualizing the Latent and Dysfunctional Dimensions of the Network Paradigm." *Economic Geography* 88: 77–96.

Wenger, Étienne. 1998. *Communities of Practice: Learning, Meaning and Identity, Cambridge,* MA: Cambridge University Press.

Zafirau, Stephen. 2008. "Reputation Work in Selling Film and Television: life in the Hollywood talent industry." *Qualitative Sociology* 31(2): 99–127.

5 *52 Tuesdays*

Community Filmmaking in a Global Context

Virginia Murray and Kath Dooley

Introduction

The Australian feature film *52 Tuesdays*, developed and part-funded by the South Australian Film Corporation (SAFC) opened theatrically in 2013. The narrative appears straightforward: Jane and her teenage daughter Billie meet every Tuesday, and so the story develops. Jane has, though, just declared her intention to transition from female to male. Exploring family dynamics from a transgender perspective is unusual, but what makes the film distinctive is its production methodology: filming occurred over 52 consecutive Tuesdays, with a script that developed as filming progressed. *52 Tuesdays* opened at the Adelaide Film Festival with its online companion project *My 52 Tuesdays*. Like the film, the online project explores issues of identity and gender but does this by encouraging online participants to record their own journey in a series of photographs posted weekly over a year.

This chapter examines *52 Tuesdays* as a case study of cinema that both draws upon and creates local and global networks. The film and the online companion project engage with both local and global individuals and community groups who are participants in the production process and/or its world-wide audience. In community cinema the act of reaching out beyond oneself is central and in the contemporary world the act of reaching out may be global as easily as local. Engagement with others beyond the self operates on two levels in *52 Tuesdays*. Global connections are made in two ways: within the film's narrative and by the film itself. Story writing credits are shared by screenwriter Matthew Cormack and director Sophie Hyde, but local and global collaborators sourced through a range of networks shaped the project's realisation during the year-long production process. Quotes by the filmmakers are from discussions with the authors in 2014 and 2015.

As noted by Thomas, utilising the filmmaking process to engage communities and tell new stories is a well-recognised practice (2011, 27). Specifically, he observes that filmmaking can be used as "a tool to amplify community voices and strengthen local identities by constructing stories about issues that are of concern" (2011, 27). Similarly, Orbach, Rain and Contreras describe an experience of "working with video as a medium for community based research and knowledge-sharing" (2015, 479). Further, Internet culture now enables media expressions that facilitate "the questioning of an increasingly homogenised mass media, which often simplifies cultural expressions in its representations" (Thomas 2011, 28). While the makers of *52 Tuesdays* did not enter into the project with the aim of amplifying community concerns, particularly in relation to transgender communities, the film's year-long production process maximised the participation potential of the community. In this sense both the film and the *My 52 Tuesdays* project can be considered 'participatory video', which "engages producers and viewers in a process of self-definition and identification" (Bery 2003, 108).

Furthermore, the filmmakers' interaction and dialogue with participants and community groups through social media intermediaries, film festivals and the *My 52 Tuesdays* website was a mutually beneficial exchange that provided support and knowledge on both a social and creative level. Considering the project's low budget and the small production team, it is apt to consider Comunian's point that "networks have proven to be valuable forms of support for small to medium sized companies as a means to access support, information and knowledge" (2012, 153). In *52 Tuesdays,* the themes of identity and gender are explored through a dialogue that occurs throughout the film's production process: interactions with cast and crew; advice sought from local and international transgender groups and exchanges with supporters accessed via social media networks. *My 52 Tuesdays* continues this exploratory process by asking participants (members of the public) to become producers of media content, creating a world-wide imaginary online community.

As the title *52 Tuesdays* explains, the starting point of the film was the form. Two people met every week on Tuesday for a year. The filming took place only on Tuesdays and evolved with the seasons and what was going on in the protagonists' lives. This simple concept determined not only the content, but also the process and finally the marketing of the film. The process was cumulative so that perhaps the best way of understanding the global impact of the form and its effects in terms of local and global engagement is to examine first how the form functioned during production.

The Filmmaking Process

The concept of two people meeting once a week for a year formed a single-page story idea submitted in 2011 to the South Australian Film Corporation's now defunct 'Film Lab' program by director Sophie Hyde, writer Matt Cormack and cinematographer/editor Bryan Mason. A handful of ideas, rather than scripts, were chosen by Film Lab to be developed and produced as low-budget feature films.

Lengthy discussions followed on who the protagonists might be. The form initially suggested a love affair between two people. Once the filmmakers thought about spending a year with the characters, the idea of a family surfaced quickly. Hyde explains: "We were interested in a family, people [who] were familiar to us, that we didn't get to see much on screen ... a queer family for want of a better term ... we were questioning the rules of how we live". Gradually two characters on the cusp of change emerged: 16-year-old Billie lives with her mother Jane in suburban Adelaide. Jane announces that she wants to become James. The transition process will take a year and during that time Billie will live with her father, Tom. In order to maintain contact with Billie, Jane suggests they spend every Tuesday evening together.

52 Tuesdays went into production based on a story outline, character profiles and the first 25 pages of script. Cormack wrote the remainder of the script in weekly increments over the year-long period, with the strength of performances and the logistic constraints of performer and location access constant variables. To maintain the integrity of the concept the filmmakers devised a set of rules (Figure 5.1).

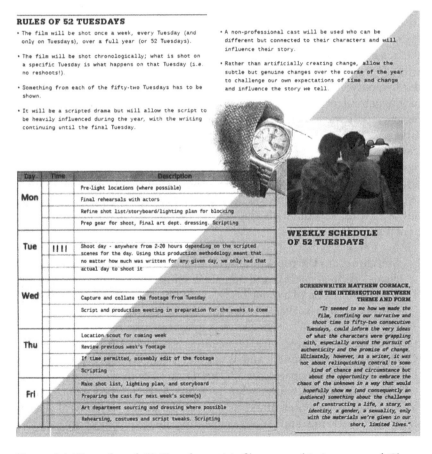

RULES OF 52 TUESDAYS

• The film will be shot once a week, every Tuesday (and only on Tuesdays), over a full year (or 52 Tuesdays).

• The film will be shot chronologically; what is shot on a specific Tuesday is what happens on that Tuesday (i.e. no reshoots!).

• Something from each of the fifty-two Tuesdays has to be shown.

• It will be a scripted drama but will allow the script to be heavily influenced during the year, with the writing continuing until the final Tuesday.

• A non-professional cast will be used who can be different but connected to their characters and will influence their story.

• Rather than artificially creating change, allow the subtle but genuine changes over the course of the year to challenge our own expectations of time and change and influence the story we tell.

Day	Time	Description
Mon		Pre-light locations (where possible)
		Final rehearsals with actors
		Refine shot list/storyboard/lighting plan for blocking
		Prep gear for shoot, Final art dept. dressing. Scripting
Tue	!!!!	Shoot day - anywhere from 2-20 hours depending on the scripted scenes for the day. Using this production methodology meant that no matter how much was written for any given day, we only had that actual day to shoot it
Wed		Capture and collate the footage from Tuesday
		Script and production meeting in preparation for the weeks to come
Thu		Location scout for coming week
		Review previous week's footage
		If time permitted, assembly edit of the footage
		Scripting
Fri		Make shot list, lighting plan, and storyboard
		Preparing the cast for next week's scene(s)
		Art department sourcing and dressing where possible
		Rehearsing, costumes and script tweaks. Scripting

WEEKLY SCHEDULE OF 52 TUESDAYS

SCREENWRITER MATTHEW CORMACK, ON THE INTERSECTION BETWEEN THEME AND FORM

"It seemed to me how we made the film, confining our narrative and shoot time to fifty-two consecutive Tuesdays, could inform the very ideas of what the characters were grappling with, especially around the pursuit of authenticity and the promise of change. Ultimately, however, as a writer, it was not about relinquishing control to some kind of chance and circumstance but about the opportunity to embrace the chaos of the unknown in a way that would hopefully show me (and consequently an audience) something about the challenge of constructing a life, a story, an identity, a gender, a sexuality, only with the materials we're given in our short, limited lives."

Figure 5.1 The rules of *52 Tuesdays*: visit films press kit (courtesy of Closer Productions).

This approach challenged traditional feature-filmmaking practices of filming a finished script. It meant that "the film's conception and development was closely linked with its execution, with the process of screenwriting not only *driving* production, but also being *driven by* production" (Dooley 2014, 2). Most importantly, the unusually long period of pre-production and production meant that the cast's lived experience was implicated in the production.

Production: Connecting Locally – the Cast

The cast of *52 Tuesdays* was mostly inexperienced, non-professional actors auditioned from the local community. The original story outline focused equally on Billie's and James' journeys; however, it was Billie's point of view that became prominent as shooting progressed. Cormack recalls that the filmmakers set out to make a film "that was more equal in terms of narrative time and access to James and Billie, and as the process went along, that changed". For Cormack this change was a result of the surprisingly strong initial performance of Tilda Cobham-Hervey, while Hyde notes that "emotionally (the filmmakers) had more access to Tilda the actor than we did to Del (Herbert Jane) the actor". Herbert Jane, who identifies as gender nonconforming, also occupied the role of 'gender diversity consultant' on the production. Hyde observes that "none of [the actors] are like themselves exactly but all of them ... brought experience that was talked about, elements that are investigated" (Dooley 2014, 9). These experiences formed a major component of the film with lead actor Tilda Cobham-Hervey's contribution to the film being the most obvious.

Cobham-Hervey was 16 when shooting began, and character Billie's search for identity was mirrored by Cobham-Hervey's. Hyde recalls an initial casting session with the actress, where Cobham-Hervey questioned her self-identity:

> She came into the room and [said] "I feel like I've always been really clearly defined as this kind of girl – I drink tea, I don't party like my friends, I'm a bit of a home body, ... and maybe that's not completely who I am, maybe there's room for something else".

As Hyde observes, "the idea of identity was right up in the front of [Cobham-Hervey's] mind" and was something that she was working through whilst participating in *52 Tuesdays*.

Unlike James who knows who he wants to be, Billie's gender identity is a particular point of exploration in *52 Tuesdays*. Several scenes show her observing and finally, engaging, in sexual experimentation with two school friends, Josh (Sam Althuizen) and Jasmine (Imogen Archer). These moments of contact take place late at night in an empty warehouse and are filmed by Billie as part of an ambiguous 'art project'. For example, one scene sees Billie film Jasmine as she removes her top and then engages in sex play with Josh. The specifics of their contact are determined by Jasmine, who sets up a series of rules related to touching. A later scene sees Jasmine kiss Billie after similar rules for their contact have been established.

52 Tuesdays' teenage cast directly influenced the writing of these scenes. Filmed material was developed in workshops that involved the three actors, Hyde and Cormack (as observer). Part of this workshop process involved "a series of 'set exercises' involving questions and answers" (Dooley 2014, 9). Cormack notes that "in early story documents we knew that there was an art project that was presented to the world in a broader sense. We didn't know how much of the kids and what they filmed would be in that" (2014, 8). Similarly, Hyde comments that "the part of the film that is about the videoing and what happens with the teenagers – that wasn't something that was originally part of our plan" (2014, 8). This material was developed as production progressed and could be considered a form of 'writing with bodies', that was fostered by *52 Tuesdays'* particular production methodology. Hyde notes that, while no particular cast member's story is written into the script, "all of their emotional experience … factored into the film and we pulled on that and we pulled on our own the experience of making the film". Hyde also acknowledges a connection between the filmmakers and the friends of three teenage actors during filming: "We had a lot of them in [as] extras, [and so] they became a group of people that were around the film that we kept bringing back in". This young community of actors and their friends could therefore be considered key to the filmmaking process, as well as to the final film text.

Production: Connecting Locally – Community Networks

The cast had a significant influence on the production content, but the impact of crew, volunteers and community groups, though less obvious, is no less important. The filmmakers encouraged outside input. According to Cormack, this approach was linked to "an idea of authenticity" that was important. "I don't think we … went into a community and activated it in any way in terms of … want[ing] to tell a specific story of that community. We did feel that we were accessing different communities". These communities included transgender groups and a network of supporters who were approached personally or through social media.

The low budget (A\$700,000) available for production meant that the filmmakers needed support from the local community. Over the year, a small rotating crew was all paid the same fixed daily rate and was allowed to drop in and out of the production process. Additionally, a Facebook page was set up and functioned as an intermediary: a means of engaging the public with *52 Tuesdays'* progress and a method of community sourcing. While a film made 20 years earlier may have relied on the limited audience of local notice boards in supermarkets, by utilising social media intermediaries such as Facebook, the makers of *52 Tuesdays* were able to reach out to a large online audience for logistical and material support. In addition to locations and equipment, the filmmakers called out for weekly caterers. By paying for food ingredients only, a potentially large production expense was transformed into an opportunity for community engagement. Meals were regularly photographed, and the weekly caterers were thanked on Facebook.

At the time of writing the *52 Tuesdays* Facebook page has 3,688 likes and material about the film's release around the world continues to be posted. Hyde describes the development of the film's Facebook following as "a very organic thing" that occurred as film production progressed and a way to publicly acknowledge the project's many supporters. Through Facebook the filmmakers were able to include the film's followers in its production. They continually updated information about the production's activities; supplied access to its content through links to transgender magazines such as *Original Plumbing* and *Dude Magazine* and issued invitations to followers to participate as extras. In so doing the makers of *52 Tuesdays* developed an online community of supporters who would also become a core audience for the film. This social media intermediary could therefore be considered a form of support infrastructure for the filmmakers, as well as a market building strategy.

Production: Connecting Globally – Content

Initially the subject matter of *52 Tuesdays* appears localised, even parochial. The filmmakers wanted to depict a family that they knew well but one that wasn't often shown. This was the 'queer family' Hyde describes earlier. Through such a family the filmmakers could interrogate the rules of how to live, or more specifically, how one might live a life true to oneself. Sociologist Ken Plummer writes that increasingly, these issues have become major questions of contemporary late modern human existence in the Western world. Plummer argues that now and progressively more in the future, the day-to-day problems that will concern us will be intimate ones that involve making ethical choices around "bodies, relationships, representations, identities and gender experiences" ([1995] 1997, 151 in Murray 2015). These are the questions that occupy the characters in *52 Tuesdays* and provide the means by which the film connects with the wider community.

One of these questions is the dynamic nature of identity formation both within and outside of the family. From one perspective *52 Tuesdays* is a teenage coming-of-age film, but Hyde notes that Jane/James's story extends the concept of coming of age to one that we experience "over and over at different times of our life". Further, events that take place in *52 Tuesdays* verify the central argument of queer theory that identity is fluid and as Hyde says, "shifts and changes across your life". Plummer writes that increasingly the intimate stories he has encountered concern the deconstruction of gender and question its innateness. *52 Tuesdays* broadly supports Judith Butler's argument that gender is "the repeated stylisation of the body, a set of repeated acts within a highly regulated frame that congeal over time to produce the appearance of substance, of a natural sort of being" (1990, 33). Seen this way it is easy to understand that gender is involuntary although socially constructed. In *52 Tuesdays*, the involuntary nature of gender and mental and physical suffering of transition forms a central part of James's narrative. Initially James plans to use testosterone to transition but has to abandon it when he develops a potentially fatal liver reaction. Billie discovers him drunk and depressed after missing one of their Tuesday appointments. The film is sympathetic towards James' frailty, and these intimate insights invite the audience to share and learn from James' experience.

Increasingly lesbian and gay families are being positioned as the "pioneer outpost of the postmodern family condition confronting most directly its features of improvisation, ambiguity, diversity, contradiction, self-reflection and flux" (Stacey 1996, 142). Sally Hines (2006) writing on transgender family experiences in the United Kingdom argues for the inclusion of transgender families as many of them include children and children are central to narratives of intimacy. She argues that if experiences are integrated into the contemporary studies of intimacy, an even richer understanding of changing patterns of parenting, partnering and friendship can be achieved (2006, 353). One example used by Hines is that of telling children about decisions to undergo gender transition. The decision to transition is a central issue for transgender parents because it must be articulated, and the decision of when to transition is often influenced by parenting commitments. Many of the transgender parents in Hines' studies saw transitioning as a means to having a more open and honest relationship with their child and a way of affirming their new gender. In *52 Tuesdays* James and Billie's negotiation of these issues in their roles of parent and child is relevant not only to the transgender community but to the wider community in terms of providing a richer understanding of gender diversity.

Production: Networking Globally – Transgender Groups

Ken Plummer's work on intimate citizenship discussed above argues that the intimate questions about gender, relationships and ethics being asked globally are ultimately political. Never before has the personal been so political. The act of defining identities and establishing political rights originates from the links between the public and intimate spheres of relationships, bodies and feelings. This process of self-identification and understanding others begins with listening to and telling each other stories.

When James begins taking testosterone he films himself to keep a record of his progress for himself and Billie. Early in the film as part of his identification process he shows Billie pictures of trans men who identify as men after using testosterone. After James is forced to stop testosterone he searches online for communities who identify as trans men who don't take hormones. He travels to San Francisco to learn from them how to become the man he wants to be. The men he interviews identify themselves in different ways: as gender queers, trans guys and as men who don't need hormones to identify as men. Writing on intimate citizenship Plummer writes that one's interior identity (Who am I?) is determined by the choices available in the wider exterior community. Where once choice was limited to those who one knew locally, now due to contemporary global communication, the networks with which one can connect and the identities to which they are attached and one can identify with appear limitless. For James, the interviews with men he meets provide points of both similarity and difference in the way that their experience resonates with his own journey.

Similarly, Billie listens to the online stories of other teenagers whose parents have transitioned from female to male, to understand the process and reflect on her own situation. Early on Billie instructs the viewer: "Okay. Look at this". We see what seems to be a YouTube confessional of a young American woman whose father transitioned to a woman when she was 17. This young woman mourns the parent she lost but speaks of the "gift of knowing that her parent has chosen an authentic life". This story resonates strongly with Billie, and she listens to it several times throughout the film.

James and Billie's connection with global communities seems a very natural part of the narrative, but it was a highly conscious decision by the filmmakers. In addition to the advice offered by gender consultant Del Herbert Jane, the filmmakers drew upon the experience of LGBTQ communities in Adelaide, New York and San Francisco and include several short 'real life' testimonials in the film. It was through the magazine for transgender communities, *Original Plumbing*, that the filmmakers located and interviewed a number of transgender parents and their families including the young woman described above. The use of *Original Plumbing* as an intermediary articulated the filmmakers' intention to reflect the experiences and identities of gender diverse communities beyond Australia. Writer Cormack says the decision to include additional points of view was "really conscious". Commenting on the insular nature of *52 Tuesdays'* narrative he notes that, "it [was] important to hear other voices…and it was important for an audience to see a greater world". For Hyde, the trip to San Francisco was an important part of James' character journey but also represented an opportunity to provide a broader view of transgender experience: "We couldn't tell all trans stories or *the* trans story but we certainly felt that we needed to show that this isn't just a one off thing, that there [are] people in the world who live like this and have been for many years".

The Film: Networking Globally – Film Festivals as Intermediaries

52 Tuesdays premiered at the Adelaide Film Festival in 2013 where it received an enthusiastic local reception, perhaps as a result of its active local presence and vigorous social networking. Local support notwithstanding, writer Cormack stated the purpose behind making *52 Tuesdays* was always recognition at international film festivals.

International film festivals are one of the ways in which low-budget films can find attention and markets. Drawing on Pierre Bourdieu's term cultural capital, Liz Czach (2004) writes that films come to international festivals to accrue 'critical capital' in the form of awards and attention for the directors, producers and the films themselves. Success at one festival often results in success at another because while festivals are separate they are also connected. At the end of the festival circuit the accrued critical capital is monetarised as global sales. Festivals have now become immensely important players in global film distribution and sales for independent films such as *52 Tuesdays*. Traditionally, independent filmmakers value-add their films through progressive screenings at the A list festivals of Berlin, Cannes, Locarno, Venice, Toronto, London, Sundance and Rotterdam. As numbers and varieties of festivals have proliferated over the last 20 years, success at the traditional festivals is no longer the only route to global sales. The path taken by *52 Tuesdays* is a case in point.

As noted above *52 Tuesdays* was always conceived of as a festival film. The filmmakers decided early that the production process of filming once a week for 52 weeks would deliver a film with a different and unpredictable narrative structure, which could be exciting. It could also act as a 'cut-through' concept that could distinguish *52 Tuesdays* from other films on the crowded circuit. Before the shoot finished, producer Bec Summerton took a promotional cut of *52 Tuesdays* to the industry market 37° South at the Melbourne International Film Festival where Visit Films, an international sales agent, expressed interest. Film festivals function as intermediaries, enabling connections between filmmakers and sales agents. Sales agents use festivals to create a profile for their films that enhance their potential sale value to international territories. Agents often have close relationships with festival programmers so they are well informed as to what festivals are looking for. Nevertheless, wanting the film to be 'discovered' on its own merits the filmmakers chose to do a 'cold submit' for the 2014 Sundance Film Festival. The 'buzz' around the film began when Sophie Hyde was awarded the 2014 Best Director for World Dramatic followed by the Crystal Bear for Young People at the Berlinale. Shortly after the Sundance festival, *52 Tuesdays* signed with U.S. distributor Kino Lorber. *52 Tuesdays* is now available in over 50 countries, and in the 18 months following Sundance *52 Tuesdays* has been exhibited at more than 90 international festivals. At least 50 of these are LGBTQ festivals.

In his essay on European film festivals, film historian Thomas Elsaesser (2005) writes that since the 1970s film festivals have been sites of politically contested identity. Nowhere is this clearer than in the proliferation of LGBTQ film festivals. Since the early 1990s queer film festivals have been active in using themselves to identify and unite queer communities while queer communities have realised the political advantages of being highly visible on the international film festival circuit (Rhyne 2006, 618). The visibility and relative affluence of Western queer communities have provided a lucrative market for distributors of international queer films, and increasingly, too, queer cultural production is being seen as an essential part of how the queer community defines itself and expands within a global capitalist economy. Rhyne argues that economic channels of cultural exchange are "key modes through which gay and lesbian organisations imagine 'community' beyond geographic boundaries" (Rhyne 2006, 619). One such example is the San Francisco film festival Frameline, which over the last 30 years has become a global media organisation "with a strategic plan that includes providing content to international cable and satellite providers and, implicitly, accessing the global markets or developing nations" (Rhyne 2006, 619). Clearly times have changed since B. Ruby Rich asking "What happened to New Queer Cinema?" in *Village Voice* March 26, 2002 wrote: "there's no financial return for filmmakers and video artists – nobody's going to finance their next project off the queer festival circuit" (quoted in Rhyne 2006, 617).

52 Tuesdays screened at Frameline 38 in 2014. An examination of the film's reception at Frameline and at several other LGBTQ festivals reveals significant changes in the way LGBTQ films are reviewed and received by audiences. *52 Tuesdays* was reviewed twice at Frameline. After a brief synopsis focusing on Billie's story, each review drew attention to different aspects of the film. On June 7, 2014, on the "7 films to watch at Frameline 38" site, Living Low wrote: "This remarkable movie possesses the diversity that LGBT cinema much needs, and its groundbreaking work in filmmaking made it win big at both Berlin and Sundance". Filmbalaya, writing on July 6, 2014, on the "Frameline 38: here's what we're looking forward to" site was more interested in the process: *Why it's on my radar:* "Forget about the film's narrative, the appeal for me here lies in the concept. True to its title, the film was actually shot over 52 Tuesdays, and in chronological order, mind you. To ignore such an ambitious project would be a crime against the spirit of independent cinema, and I'm no criminal".

The Sydney Mardi Gras reviewing the film in February 2014 focused on the process also: "The fascinating aspect of this intimate story is the unique form of the story's chronology", as did the LA Outfest review writing in July, 2014: "an amazing film not just for its story of a woman transforming into a man who asks her daughter to live with her father during this change. It's also amazing in the way it was filmed: every Tuesday over a year's time". These reviews are a small sample of the 90-odd LGBTQ festivals *52 Tuesdays* attended, but the emphasis on the process over content suggests a far more relaxed audience approach than the common 1990s response of anger if a film's content deviated from separatist lines (see Rich 1999, 79–89).

A partial answer may lie in the role the international film festivals play in determining what is culturally accepted and what is not. As Czach notes, "Queer festivals help define what gay, lesbian, bi-sexual and trans-gendered cinema is; a festival such as Views from the Avant-Garde comments on the state of experimental cinema; and so on. The programming decisions amount to an argument about what defines that field, genre or national cinema" (2004, 85). Another answer may be that LGBTQ audiences feel sufficiently comfortable in their identity to watch a variety of stories. This seems to be the case in the recent response to transgender issues as represented in mainstream film or television projects: for example, United States sitcom *Transparent* won several 2015 Emmy awards, and medium-budget films such as *The Danish Girl* and *About Ray* starring Naomi Watts have had mainstream release in 2015.

My 52 Tuesdays: Creating a Global Network

The collaborative nature of *52 Tuesdays* always encouraged the film-makers to think in terms of engaging with an audience beyond the life-time of the film. This culminated in a social media project now known as *My 52 Tuesdays*, a web and smart phone-based companion project that invites users to be part of a "worldwide participatory project where people build and share a unique portrait of a year in their lives" (*My 52 Tuesdays* website, 2013).

Created by the filmmakers in collaboration with experience-design company Sandpit, *My 52 Tuesdays* poses a question on the project website every Tuesday. The questions are related to the feature film's themes such as bodily change, authenticity and secrets. For example: "What does it feel like to kiss?" (Week 1) or "What's something you look forward to each week?" (Week 3). Various crew or cast members appear in photos holding signs on which these questions appear giving the audience further contact with the personalities responsible for the film. Several cast and crew members including Hyde, Cormack and cinematographer/editor Bryan Mason are also registered as participants in the project, allowing other participants information about their 'real' lives. Participants respond to the questions by posting photographs of themselves and their written responses. These responses can be posted publicly or kept private, because, according to the site, "it is a project about you, set in time, distinctly personal and lovingly communal – but only if you choose it to be so, because ultimately it is a project about choice" (2013). Within this interactive platform users are invited to form a long-term relationship with an extension of *52 Tuesdays'* story world. Just as the feature film utilises a year-long production methodology to capture Billie and James' stories of personal growth and change, the website offers fans of the film and other registered participants the opportunity to involve themselves in a similar project of their own. For the filmmakers, the aim was to give the audience a chance to engage with the concept of committing to doing something on the same day every week for a year, just as they had done.

Technological constraints meant that while participants could view each other's postings they could not communicate with each other. That aside, the *My 52 Tuesdays* project displays many of the characteristics of social media in its displays of playfulness, self reflective and confessional behaviour. For example, Week 36 features a photograph of a question written on the back of a young woman's naked body. Although her face is not visible, her haircut suggests that it is *52 Tuesdays'* lead actress Tilda Cobham-Hervey. She asks "are you comfortable in the nude?" There are 106 photo responses to the question, some of which feature full frontal nudity. Actress Danica Moors (James' love interest in *52 Tuesdays*) is photographed standing naked, her body partially hidden behind a rack of children's clothing. She holds a sign that reads "yes, if the heat is on". Moors' presence as one of *My 52 Tuesdays'* participants, and the intimate access she grants to images of her body, builds on the seeming authenticity offered by the film. Further, the inclusion of Cobham-Hervey's image creates a direct connection between lead actress and online participant by suggesting that she is speaking directly to the user. In *52 Tuesdays*, Cobham-Hervey's character Billie creates a series of videos in which she speaks directly to the audience, so one can observe the same approach used to create further engagement.

My 52 Tuesdays also creates an imagined world-wide community that is defined by simultaneous participation. As Murray and Johanson (2015) observe, "the thrill of participating on a designated day of the week is partly due to the knowledge that this participation is matched by 2000 other subscribers across the world, if not at the same time then at least within the one Tuesday, and that their sometimes-intimate responses to the question are showcased alongside your own" (60). The week-by-week responses of individual participants fosters the creation of real-life 'characters' from around the globe, each with distinct lives and concerns that are revealed week by week; however, the responses when viewed en masse detail something greater: a poetic and insightful account of contemporary thought on issues such as bodily angst and sexuality. This is possible as the site allows for each week's responses to be viewed as a mosaic of photographs, with the larger image reflecting a global network of users.

At festivals such as Adelaide and Sundance *My 52 Tuesdays* had a physical presence in the form of a photo booth. Inside the booth, which contained a screen and a keyboard, an image of Tilda Cobham-Hervey explained the *52 Tuesdays* production process and invited participants to subscribe. The *My 52 Tuesdays* booth and site also contributed to the marketing of the film. At the booth, participants were given a photo strip showing the screening times of the film. The website shows user contributions but also the trailer and festival ticket links. It also connects with the film's Twitter and Facebook sites. The regularly updated stream of user-generated content keeps attention focused on the feature film or perhaps draws attention back to it. Discussing the *My 52 Tuesdays* project, Cormack said it was envisioned as a way of keeping a festival audience connected to the film until its cinema release perhaps a year later. Initially the filmmakers thought that *My 52 Tuesdays* as a stand-alone project might generate a life of its own, but the project has remained connected to the life of the film. The film generates interest in the project rather than the other way around.

Conclusion

The Oxford Dictionary defines 'community' as "a group of people living in the same place or having a particular characteristic in common'. Th" success of *52 Tuesdays* as an example of global community cinema lies in this definition of community and its relation to commonality. The film is about a group of people living in the same place, but the problems they face of how to live authentically are ones common to many other people throughout the Western world. Recognition of the global commonality of these issues forms part of the narrative as the characters reach beyond their own community to connect with communities across the world. Similarly, by tapping into both local and global networks, the filmmakers draw upon the knowledge, experience and resources of a range of individuals and community groups.

A further global commonality explored by the film is that of time. The process by which the film was made – filming only on Tuesdays for a year – invited the audience to experience temporality with the filmmakers. The process had many rules around time (see Figure 5.1 above), but a deliberate part of the process was to allow the passing of time to be a variable outside the filmmakers' control. The effect of a year-long shooting schedule on the film was unknowable, but this was part of the process. Further, the extension of a normal six-week shoot to a 52-week shoot allowed for greater participation from the community of the film (cast, crew and the online community both local and global) than would otherwise have been the case.

The opportunity to let their audience experience time in the same way as the filmmakers also lay behind *52 Tuesdays'* online companion project, *My 52 Tuesdays*. Using the same temporal structure as the film – every Tuesday for a year – participants became producers of their own media content. By watching the film, and interacting with the application/website, "viewers, too, gain access to a new type of power by internalizing the stories, redefining the issues and uniting to challenge old stereotypes and traditional power concepts" (Bery 2003, 103).

Ultimately the global relevance of *52 Tuesdays* can be summed up by its success at international film festivals both LGBTQ and mainstream. The film's subject matter meant it was always going to be popular with LGBTQ communities, but the fact that it is now available in over 50 countries is verification that local communities are increasingly global communities.

References

About Ray. 2015. Motion picture, U.S.: Gaby Dellai.

Bery, R. 2003. "Participatory Video that Empowers." In *Participatory Video: images that transform and empower*, edited by S. A. White, 102–121. New Delhi: Sage.

Butler, Judith. 1990. *Gender Trouble: feminism and the subversion of identity*. New York: Routledge.

Comunian, Roberta. 2012. "Exploring the Role of Networks in the Creative Economy of North East England: economic and cultural dynamics." In *Encounters and Engagement between Economic Cultural Geography*, edited by Barney Warf, 143–157. Berlin: Springer.

Cornish, Laura and Alison Dunn. 2009. "Creating Knowledge for Action: the case for participatory communication in research." *Development in Practice* 19 (4): 665–677.

Czach, Liz. 2004. "Film Festivals, Programming and the Building of a National Cinema." *The Moving Image* 4 (1): 76–88.

Dooley, Kath. 2014. "A Promise of Change: *52 Tuesdays* (2013)–a case study of collaborative, low-budget feature-filmmaking practice." *Studies in Australasian Cinema* 8, (2–3): 150–162.

Elsaesser, Thomas. 2005. "Film Festival Networks: the new topographies of cinema in Europe." In *European Cinema: face to face with Hollywood*, edited by Thomas Elsaesser, 82–107 Amsterdam: Amsterdam University Press.

Hines, Sally. 2006. "Intimate Transitions: transgender practices in partnering and parenting." *Sociology* 40 (2): 353–371.

Murray, Virginia. "Who Am I? 52 Tuesdays, Intimacy and the Search for an Authentic Life." *Sex Education*, DOI:10.1080/14651811.2015.1078785: 1–13.

Murray, Virginia and Katya Johanson. 2015. "The Cut-Through Concept: *52 Tuesdays*, festivals and the distribution of independent Australian films." *Studies in Australasian Cinema* 9 (1): 52–65.

"My52Tuesdays." http://my52tuesdays.com/my52tuesdays/about/, n.d.

"My52Tuesdays." n.d. *Question- Week 36*. http://my52tuesdays.com/my52tuesdays/question?q=8Ih20nd9tG.

Orbach, A., J. Rain and R. Contreras. 2015. "Community Filmmaking As Research: (re) considering knowledge production through the camera's lens." *Development in Practice* 25 (4): 478–489.

"Oxford Dictionary." n.d. https://www.google.com.au/search?q=oxford+dictionary+community+definition&ie=utf-8&oe=utf-8&gws_rd=cr&ei=Y6JjVqz_HKTVmgWH06TIAg.

Plummer, Ken. (1995) 1997. *Telling Sexual Stories: power, change and social worlds*. London: Routledge.

Rhyne, Ragan. 2006. "The Global Economy of Gay and Lesbian Film Festivals." *GLQ: Journal of Lesbian and Gay Studies* 12, (4): 617–619.

Rich, B. Ruby. 1999. "Collision, Catastrophe, Celebration: the relationship between gay and lesbian film festivals and their publics." *GLQ: Journal of Lesbian and Gay Studies* 5 (1): 79–89.

Stacey, Julia. 1996. *In the Name of the Family: rethinking families in the postmodern age*. Boston MA: Beacon Press.

The Danish Girl. 2015. Motion picture. U.K.: Tom Hooper.

Thomas, V. 2011. "Yumi Piksa' - Developing A Community-Responsive Way of Filmmaking in Melanesia." *Pacific Journalism Review* 17 (2): 27.

Transparent, 2014. Television series, U.S. Jill Soloway.

White, Patricia, B. Ruby Rich, Eric Clarke and Richard Fung. 1999. "Queer Publicity: a dossier on lesbian and gay film festivals." *GLQ: Journal of Lesbian and Gay Studies* 5 (1): 73–79.

White, S. A., 2003. Ed. *Participatory Video: images that transform and empower*. New Delhi: Sage.

6 The Collaborative Practices of the Colectivo Cine sin Autor (Authorless Cinema Collective)

Asier Aranzubia, Miguel Fernández Labayen and Aitor Iturriza

This chapter offers an analysis of the film and video practices of the Colectivo de Cine sin Autor (Authorless Cinema Collective, CsA hereafter), an emerging agent in local and national community filmmaking in Spain. The starting point of the CsA is, as stated by its name, to work without singling out a particular author. On the contrary, its main premise is to negate the hierarchical authority that prevails in traditional cinema and avoid the *auteurist* aspirations of cinema workers, in an attempt to reach 'authorless cinema'. According to CsA, authorless cinema should allow the redistribution of creative power and thus foment a horizontal structure to write and produce films. Therefore, the collective becomes an intermediary between Cinema as an Institution (with hegemonic and distinct modes of industrial production and cultural consumption) and any potential practitioner. In its own words, "the CsA is a real-socio-fiction to produce (films) with and from people or collectives alien to the dominant film production and enable (the production) of their own images and their surroundings" (Tudurí 2008, 8).

Since its founding in Madrid in 2007, CsA has participated in the production of eight films, a music video and a web series. During these years, the collective has collaborated with high schools, neighbourhood associations and adult education centres. Its proposal has called the attention of art institutions, such as Museo Nacional Centro de Arte Reina Sofía and Intermediae at Matadero, who have granted temporal and permanent residencies for the collective. Last but not least, other initiatives have grown out of the core collective, adapting the authorless methodology to other environments, such as Murcia and Toulouse. A Cinéma sans Auteur collective has been active in Toulouse since 2012, taking CsA's ideas into a different context and developing CsA's interest in working with local agents in specific places. CsA has shaped a transnational informal network formed by a wide range of organisations, spaces, facilities and individuals.

The aim of this chapter is two-fold: on the one hand, we describe and analyse the film practices of the CsA as a way to develop cultural networks that provide access to audiovisual means to communities and collectives. On the other, the article asks in what way CsA may be an example of a good cultural practice and, therefore, be used for the implementation of policies that promote cultural diversity. Therefore, we will first offer an overview of the theoretical and procedural perspectives of the collective. Then, we will highlight different examples of their work with local communities and state institutions. Finally, we will contrast these practices with current policies and research about cultural diversity.

All in all, the chapter delivers a detailed critical account of CsA's methodology and complements previous accounts that locate the work of the collective in a broad, global context of collaborative media (Sedeño 2012a, 2012b, 2013; Villaplana 2015). While this previous scholarship proves fruitful to vindicate and call attention to CsA's project from a general perspective, we wish to scrutinise the work of CsA in order to evaluate its qualities as well as its shortcomings in a specific context. By incorporating the accounts of the daily interactions of the collective, we challenge traditional narratives that tend to exalt the work of film collectives as harmonic, progressive endeavours, following recent debates about the political role of film collectives (Interview with Osborne, in Bauer and Kidner 2013). At the same time, we want to highlight the complex network of amateur and professional participants, grassroots organisations and national institutions that coalesce in CsA's projects.

This mixture of official and non-official actors is key to understanding the scope of CsA as a critical practice and as a collaborative enterprise. If "collaboration entails not only production and consumption of what media scholars call texts, but also design of infrastructures" (Löwgren and Reimer 2013, 4), it is then mandatory that we take a close look at the way these infrastructures develop and enhance different cultural practices. In these terms, our article calls for an analysis of cultural policies and strategies, in order to understand the scale and the relational nature of the cultural negotiations led by the CsA. We will thus understand the work of CsA as a part of a local and transnational network, which favours the creation of pedagogical opportunities in spaces of social change from different angles and by using diverse methodologies.

In order to reflect upon the flexibility of the cultural network and the political dimension of the community practices of the CsA, we situate ourselves at the crossroads of disciplines such as film studies and political economy, with the shared interest in media industries as a common denominator. In this chapter, we want to bring together the attention film scholars like Marijke de Valck (2007) have paid to Bruno Latour's Actor-Network Theory to explain how film festivals work and the close analysis that creative industries' researchers like Comunian (2012, 2016) have carried out in relation to the nodes and connections developed in cultural events and markets. The combination of the two approaches may account for the shifting interdependency that exists between actors and networks. In this case study, CsA illustrates the complex dynamics and interactions that shape the cultural, economic and social networks in which community filmmaking initiatives partake.

This chapter is the result of reflections and data collected during two research projects financed by the Spanish Ministry of Economy and Competitiveness and developed by Universidad Carlos III de Madrid. The first, "Diversidad de la industria audiovisual en la era digital (2015–2016)" (ref. CSO2014-52354-r; http://diversidadaudiovisual.org/) focuses on the challenges of cultural diversity in the media context. The project departs from a precise definition of what a good practice is and aims to identify 'good practices' within the Spanish audiovisual sector, such as those of CsA. The second research project, "Las relaciones trans-nacionales en el cine digital hispanoamericano: los ejes de España, México y Argentina" (CSO2014-52750-P), analyses the strategies of film production and circulation developed in Spain, Mexico and Argentina in the digital age. This project maps out and analyses the spaces and dynamics of the production and circulation of digital cinema, attending to the economic and cultural practices of the different actors involved (producers, distributors, film festivals, film critics and different communities). From the fusion of the two projects and the joint work with PhD student Aitor Iturriza, we have conducted semi-structured interviews with the founders of CsA (Gerardo Tudurí, Eva Fernández and Daniel Goldmann) as well as with other people involved in the project, such as Helena de Llanos and workers from institutions such as Intermediae, which have been collaborating with CsA.

CsA and the Politics of Collectivity: A Cultural Theory, a Cinematic Practice

From 2008 until the present, CsA has produced ten titles. As can be seen on Table 6.1, the diversity of the places, people and institutions that have intervened in the production of the films speak of the social and political intentionality of CsA, who aims to intervene through the creation of practices of media literacy, critical pedagogy and social empowerment. The multiplicity of productions, collectives and places collected in this filmography speaks of CsA's desire to intervene in different areas of the public sphere. At the same time, the time devoted to each project signals the longevity of the working processes, which will be discussed below.

Theoretically speaking, CsA wishes to implement a working method based on 'authorial suicide', which implies a systematic dismantling of the hierarchical structure that preserves the authority of the director and works against the division of labour that privileges the power of some positions within film production (screenwriter, producer, direc-tor of photography, editor). This Foucauldian reading of filmmaking would ideally lead to a horizontal, participatory and democratic mode

Table 6.1 CsA's production (own elaboration)

Year	Production	Collective	Place
2007–08	Recording of 3 general assemblies	Patio Maravillas, Kintopp collective	Patio Maravillas (Madrid)
2008–11	*De qué*	High school students	Humanes high school
2010–12	*Sinfonía de Tetuán*; *+101*	Neighbors; students of the adult education center	Adult education center Tetuán
2010–13	*Bourrasol*; *Le cahier de Kader*	Neighbors; children from a social center and a Maghrebi	Toulouse
2012–14	*Negrablanca*	Inhabitants of Blanca	Blanca (Murcia)
2012–14	*Entrenosotros*; *Vida fácil*; *Locura en el colegio*; *Más allá de la verdad*	Teenagers and students	Intermediae; Legado Crespo School
2014	*K de kalle*	Members of different associations of Carabanchel	Carabanchel
2012–	*Mátame si puedes*	Inmates of the Psychosocial Rehabilitation Center of Arganzuela	Centro de Rehabilitación Psicosocial de Arganzuela and the bank La Caixa

of production, one that could make true one of multiculturalism's objectives: the self-representation of minorities and disenfranchised communities. According to CsA, the work procedure should then follow a model based on a collective decision-making process, which would affect every phase of the cinematic process, including screenwriting, shooting, editing, distribution and exhibition. These politics of collectivity and collaboration try to find "a new way of organising the film production" and a "politics of social participation" (Tudurí 2013) that situate CsA's project in an undefined area in the midst of video activism, development cooperation, critical pedagogy and collective intelligence. Along these lines, CsA conceives itself as a theoretical and artistic construct with a social goal:

> *CsA was born as a cultural theory that encourages an artistic practice, more precisely a film shooting practice, that, together with a constant critical revision, forms a whole new model of film production. The authorless concept puts aside the authority and property*

inherent to authorship, in order to let producer collectivities emerge. The creation process – so far cinematographic – is horizontal, that is, all the decisions related to preproduction, script, shooting, editing, postproduction and distribution are taken in assemblies, in a progressive collectivization of both the work and productive process. Understanding culture as a faculty to inhabit and transform this world, AC wants to stir up where from, how and what for films are produced.

(Cine sin Autor 2016)

CsA emerged in 2007 in Madrid's Patio Maravillas, but its origins can be tracked back to 2005 in Valencia. It was there that Gerardo Tudurí and Miguel Ángel Baixauli developed a project called *Correspondencias* (Correspondences). *Correspondencias* consisted of recording video-letters in a high school in Valencia and sending them to the students in an indigenous community in Cuzco, Peru. The goal of these video-letters was to link two high school students' communities around the issue of migration. Throughout the project, Tudurí, who had ample experience in the area of cooperation and development, became aware that visual anthropology methodologies were not satisfactory in this context. Tudurí realised that the video letters, after being recorded, always went through his hands and Baixauli's (the organisers); therefore, even if indirectly, the students were being restricted, and their feelings and thoughts were being filtered. The letters of the teenagers were conditioned by Tudurí's and Baixauli's supervision of the shooting and the editing. Therefore, this intervention mediated between the teenagers and their final product. This experience triggered Tudurí's reflection about authorship, and he became concerned with erasing authorship.

In the following years, the authorless project grew out of an intense theoretical reflection. Digging in a genealogy of collective and community practices, Tudurí was hooked by the experiences of the Medvedkin Group, Jorge Sanjinés and the Ukamau Group, and Jean Rouch. These cinematic practices, as diverse as they are, also allowed for a relational reading, one in which cinema had been used with a political and social objective in order to connect with communal experiences in Third World countries.[1] Tudurí worked with Eva Fernández, co-founder of CsA, in order to create a theoretical corpus and test these ideas and concepts within a context of contemporary film production, where the digital became key in not only producing and distributing the films made at a low cost, but also circulating and promoting the ideas and writings of the collective. When in 2007 the CsA started working in Patio Maravillas, a self-managed multipurpose art and cultural space, these writings were put together as a manifesto. The manifesto not only vindicated a certain type of cinema, but also put forward a theory about film authorship and collective filmmaking that would be labelled 'authorless cinema'.

Tudurí and Fernández joined the Patio Maravillas a little after the building was squatted. In a personal interview with Gerardo Tudurí, 10 March 2015, he recalls the intense political atmosphere that could be felt in the Patio.[2] Tudurí and Fernández talked to the collective Kintopp, which at the time was running the audiovisual part of the Patio, to make the first practices of CsA. Upon agreement, CsA carried out their first three experiences as a collective, which consisted of recording three general assemblies of the Patio Maravillas between December 2007 and March 2008. The last recorded assembly was edited on DVD under the title *Guión. Esto NO es una película* (Screenplay. This is NOT a film). On the back cover of the DVD, CsA printed the following statement: "The Self-Managed Polyvalent Space 'Patio Maravillas' of the city of Madrid has allowed the launching of a self-managed cinematographic experience called Authorless Cinema: a film method that leads to collective creation, to the filmic self-representation of a social collective" (Cine sin Autor 2008). A few lines below, the statement continued, in this case regarding the cinematic style pursued by the CsA: "we consider that CINEMATIC REALISM only takes place when the subject (individual or collective) intervenes in every moment of the production and circulation of the work that represents him/her/them, and this creation opens ways of transformation for him/her/them and their surroundings" (Cine sin Autor 2008; capital letters in the original). During these first years, the quest for cinematic realism becomes one of CsA's main goals. This concern with a particular film style and the achievement of verisimilitude and honesty in the final 'object' through participation will progressively disappear in favour of an emphasis on the work process. After all, like Ella Shohat and Robert Stam wrote in the mid-1990s, "an obsession with 'realism' casts the question (of multicultural representation) as simply one of 'errors' and 'distortions', as if the 'truth' of a community were unproblematic, transparent, and easily accessible" (Shohat and Stam 1994, 178).

Although the distribution of CsA's DVD was limited to the social centre Patio Maravillas, its manufacturing already proves that CsA's project was in the process of consolidating itself. That same year, 2008, Gerardo Tudurí published the collective's first manifesto, under the title *Manifiesto del cine sin Autor. Realismo Social Extremo en el siglo XXI (versión 1.0)* (Manifesto of Authorless Cinema. Extreme Social Realism in the Twenty-first Century – version 1.0). The manifesto is 60 pages long and profusely defines the theoretical and methodological perspectives of CsA. Its length and rhetorical excess prove the ambition of the project. This written statement and public presentation follow the tradition of film manifestos, which "postulate ways in which to re-imagine the medium, how moving images intervene in the public sphere, and the ways film might function as a catalyst to change the world" (McKenzie 2014, 2).

The drive to write about and research film history and film production continued, and CsA opened a blog in which it published a post each Sunday of the following five years. All of these entries were published in 2012 in the volume *La política de la colectividad. Cine sin autor. blog. Ideas derramadas* (The politics of collectivity. Cine sin autor.blog. Scattered ideas). Its 593 pages exemplify the ideological development of CsA. At the same time, they are a sample of how the collective underwent a process of self-awareness, which culminated in the publication of the first manifesto and the departure from Patio Maravillas. According to Tudurí, "our operating mode was the classic militant outline: work in other things and put your time and money in the production of films with those who usually do not have that opportunity. Make movies with authorless methods and at the same time build a film theory based on all of this activity" (Tudurí 2013, 77).

Daniel Goldmann and David Arenal joined Tudurí and Fernández in what would constitute the core of the collective. However, a process of eviction of Patio Maravillas began, and work conditions changed. The urgency of the eviction forced CsA to move out of the Patio, but the influence of that experience remained. Patio Maravillas was not only a meeting point for the creators of CsA, but it was also one of the central nodes of the new political party, Podemos, currently the third political force in the Spanish parliament and the ruling party in Madrid. Some of the people who participated in the first experiences of CsA at the Patio Maravillas became (8 years later) councillors in Madrid City Hall. The nomadic period of the collective began, although the roots of that first experience would provide some stability and connections for CsA in the long run.

The Nomadic Years: Humanes and Tetuán

"How would a film about your life be?" This was the question that CsA asked a dozen students and ex-students of a high school in Humanes, in the South of Madrid. The question activated the authorless *dispositif* and led to the first production collective of CsA. The four founders of CsA had found a place to work in an unexpected space, far from the milieu where their project had come to life. Instead of working in a social centre or in the progressive circles of radical politics, CsA tested its principles in a high school in one of the humblest areas in the region of Madrid.

At the beginning, they came and went on a weekly basis. Humanes is a 40-minute drive from downtown Madrid. Little by little, they adapted the frequency of their visits to the needs of the project. The production of the film took two and a half years, and the film opened in Medialab Prado in April 2011 under the title *¿De qué?* (What of?).

The experience was satisfactory. Beyond the first tests in Patio Maravillas, this was the first time that CsA undertook a project autonomously. Out of the experience, the collective reflected upon the need to adapt the theoretical framework to a practical methodology, one that could function in a concrete context: for instance, in Humanes CsA confronted the resistance and attitude of a group of teenagers unfamiliar with assemblies and horizontal functioning. Unlike the social collectives that had been working with CsA until then, in this case the authorless methodology had to find ways to become familiar with the teenagers' experience, which was far removed from CsA's ways of working.

Besides, the collective faced the preconceptions the teenagers had about cinema as a narrative and economic medium. That is to say, the expectations of the community addressed by CsA regarding cinema were biased by the social perception of what could be loosely thought of as Hollywood narrative cinema. This was an obstacle faced in Humanes that CsA has tried to overcome in every single project; it affects the disposition of the participants in the experiment as well as the development of the whole authorless methodology. In other words, CsA has seen how the communities they have worked with think of films as genre narratives produced on a hierarchical basis: a director, a screenwriter and a star or two. These conventions also affect the economic dimension of the film being made, since cinema is inevitably identified with celebrity culture, red carpet screenings and a final product or art object, namely, the film itself. Of course, this social imaginary is what the collective is trying to fight against. Thus, CsA has coined different concepts that negate the hegemonic mode of production and consumption. If the author becomes a no-author, the film has NO-end, the film should have no screenplay and so on. In the case of the Humanes project, the collective came up with the sentence "This is not a film" in order to eliminate the students' horizons of expectations, which were paradoxically generated by the collective itself when it first announced the production of a film with a group of teenagers, neighbours or students. "This is not a film" wanted to make explicit the different approach that CsA has to cinema. The collective aims to work towards a pedagogy that eliminates the differences between workers in the production of cinema and helps create a participatory mode of film production. At the same time, this perspective broadens the assumptions of the different communities regarding cinema, familiarising them with narrative and aesthetic possibilities beyond hegemonic Western cinema.

Another challenge that the collective faced with the Humanes experience was the need to establish a permanent headquarters in a predetermined geographical location. CsA thought it was mandatory to establish a permanent and direct contact with the communities that were working within its logics and projects. Physical distance proved a burden, both from a material and a psychological perspective. CsA's allocation in Patio Maravillas had been easy, since the Patio itself was a bigger project and infrastructure in which CsA inserted itself. Once the collective moved out of the Patio, the CsA became a single independent project. Therefore, if the problem of working in Patio Maravillas consisted of the representational strategy of the Patio, where everyone was a part of the squatter community, the challenge in Humanes was how to make a movie and manage a teenage collective that was supposed to work as a production unit making a film about itself. CsA concluded that the process of making a film should become an ongoing meeting point, in which the cinematic experience would be a mainly social experience.

The first attempt to solve this problem took place in the Madrid neighbourhood of Tetuán. Daniel Goldmann was living in Tetuán, and Gerardo Tudurí rented an office in the area in order to establish the headquarters of the collective and experience the daily routines of the hood. It was then that they came up with the concept of *plató-mundo* (world-set), defined as "our surroundings, the scenery where we move around everyday and live (...). Our life places, these are the new sets of cinema of the 21 Century" (Tudurí 2013, 98).

In Tetuán the collective shot different projects. In 2009, they shot what would become *Sinfonía de Tetuán* (Tetuán's Symphony), an audiovisual piece that explored in the likes of the city symphonies the spaces and inhabitants of the district. CsA worked along with the neighbour association Asociación Ventilla, looking for the participation and involvement of the residents in the area.

After this first contact, CsA started other initiatives that explored three specific spaces in the quarter: the already mentioned Asociación Ventilla, the Bar Benito and the Adult Educational Centre of Tetuán. They used the first two places to shoot and screen their practices with the regulars. As for the third one, they produced the film *+101*, organised and shot by 15 members of the centre. The film opened at Museo Nacional Centro de Arte Reina Sofía in a film programme called "¡Para saber hay que imaginarse!" (To know one must imagine!), which included films by the Berwick Street Collective and other initiatives.[3] Again, CsA tested its ideas and found that they could improve their methodologies. However, the work with the district overwhelmed them. Despite the appeal of turning the neighbourhood into a set, they found that they did not have the means to control and realise their goals.

A Factory for an Authorless Cinema

One of the influences of CsA was Michel Gondry's project "L'usine de films amateur" (Amateur film factory). On a post in CsA's blog on 12 February 2012, Gondry's words echoed and framed the reflections of CsA about its own work: "with this project, people make their own film and enjoy it because they are in it. They have created it. It is a different experience from watching a product made by an artist or by an industry" (Gondry in Cine sin Autor 2012). In fact, Gondry's initiative, based on his own film *Be kind, rewind* (2008), included the circulation of the movies made in the factories through different arts centres and museums in New York, Sao Paulo or Paris, where in the Centre Pompidou 311 films of 4500 participants were made.

CsA wanted to implement what they initially called "Open studies of authorless cinema", something that was finally called "The factory of authorless cinema". Two ideas were highlighted: create production spaces and make amateur remakes of well-known films as a creative incentive. The concept of 'the factory' had been in the mind of the collective for some time, but in order to put it into practice they needed to contact different institutions and have a material space. As Tudurí recalls, "the goal was to achieve that a cultural institution incorporated the collective's film activity in its logic. This would give the collective three coordinates: a clear reference space for the people to know where the collective 'works,' a definite duration for our activities that would break the nomadic inertia and the uncertainty around a way of working based on using our free time and our homes, and an economic start in order to have the means to operate" (Tudurí 2013).

The first institution to open its doors to CsA was Medialab-Prado, a cultural centre of the Madrid city council conceived as a production and research laboratory in order to explore collaborative experimentation. After some months in Medialab-Prado, the nomadic years truly ended with the entrance of CsA into Intermediae, located in the Center for Contemporary Creation, Matadero-Madrid. Intermediae is a production space "thought as a production laboratory of social innovation, specialized in visual culture based on participation" (Intermediae 2016). In 2012, CsA joined Matadero Madrid and started working in Intermediae, establishing its first Authorless Cinema Industry. This was the first time that CsA had external financial backing and a space to settle. The factory worked from 4:00 to 9:00 pm and gave the collective a reference, a space that allowed whoever was interested in the project to connect with the collective in an immediate way. At the same time, the collective made use of its previous knowledge and went out around the neighbourhood of Legazpi, where Intermediae is located, in order to look for neighbours who wanted to make a film. This two-way mode of operating led to an increase of collaborators and bigger visibility for the project among professionals and amateurs alike. Gerardo Tudurí estimates that between 80 and 100 people visited the factory on a daily basis (2015). Between 2012 and 2014, CsA produced five films in its factory.

CsA's project grew enormously, and it started accomplishing one of its goals: opening new factories in other cities. Emmanuelle Trépagny and Lisa Chelle, CsA's collaborators, opened Cinéma sans Auteur in Toulouse in 2010. In 2012, the project consolidated and began developing two ways. One, more in line with CsA's procedures in Madrid, implied collaborating with social centres, cultural associations and art residencies. The other implied following a film tradition close to Medvedkin's Cinema-Train: a Cinéma sans Auteur-caravan that tours around Toulouse. The caravan is equipped with everything needed to make authorless films, from a camera to editing tools. In 2014, Cinéma sans Auteur screened its first film, *Le cahier de Kader* (Kader's notebook). Children from a social centre and an immigrant from the Maghreb were the main participants in the production of this film. At the same time, the neighbours from the Lalande quarter have been shooting a film since 2013 about the evolution of their neighbourhood.

Another initiative that grew beyond the headquarters in Madrid was *Negrablanca* (Blackwhite), a film shot in Blanca, a small town in Murcia, from 2012 to 2014. Helena de Llanos, a participant in CsA's projects, moved to Blanca in 2012 in order to produce a film collectively with the citizens of that town. Also known by the name *¿Hacemos una peli?* (Do we make a film?), it is the outcome of the artist residency program Centro Negra, run by the city council of Blanca.

After the experiences during its first five years of existence, CsA has improved its methodologies and modified some of its theoretical assumptions. The writing of the blog and the practical experience of collective filmmaking led to a new manifesto. *Cine XXI. La política de la colectividad. Manifiesto del cine sin autor 2.0* (Cinema 21. The politics of collectivity. Authorless cinema's manifesto 2.0) was included in the July 2013 issue of *Arte y Políticas de Identidad*, published by the Art School of the University of Murcia.

Also, CsA was included in other spaces and obtained institutional recognition. In 2013–2014 CsA was selected for a Research Residency at the Museo Nacional de Arte Reina Sofía, an initiative in collaboration with the Chancellor's Conference of Madrid's Public Universities and the Banco Santander Foundation. CsA also obtained funds from the Social Foundation of La Caixa. The collective has been invited to different conferences and workshops in universities and arts centres, an example of their impact in a social and cultural milieu that is reconsidering the ways of producing and consuming cultural artefacts. This frantic activity has helped the development and establishment of a network of different communities, museums and educators. However, in a personal interview, Tudurí was sceptical of the alliance with institutions and official organisations. In his own words, "there is no institution that is going to subject itself to the opinion of the people that participates in these processes. (…) The good thing about a CsA's assembly is that the institution must come down and face the members of the collective, who can then pose their criticism. Problems have come out after these encounters, they (the institutions) have not been able to take it".

The cultural and political activism of Patio Maravillas, the participation and collaboration with media professionals in the nomadic years and CsA's factory, the institutional connections with key cultural spaces in Madrid such as Matadero Madrid and the Museo Nacional Centro de Arte Reina Sofía, the economic support by financial entities such as the Fundación Social La Caixa, the educational link to universities such as Universidad Complutense de Madrid and the integration into the international film festival circuit are examples of the collective's wide connections. CsA's growth, reach and sustainability are linked to this amorphous network of institutional and collaborative relations with cultural agents and neighbours of the different places where CsA has developed its activities.

Conclusions: CsA and Cultural Diversity

In their genealogy of the concepts of 'good' and 'best' cultural practices, María Trinidad García Leiva and Ana Segovia foster "a new critical definition" that avoids the ambiguity and vagueness of these concepts as used in the UNESCO Convention on the Promotion and Protection of the Diversity of Cultural Expressions (García Leiva and Segovia 2014). García Leiva and Segovia put forward the need of talking about 'contextual practices', in order to move away from conceptions of good/best practices as "final, timeless and universal actions" and "clarify why, for whom and under what circumstances" these practices are good (García Leiva and Segovia 2014, 92).

Following Kenneth King's study of best practices, García Leiva and Segovia warn about the Taylorist origin of the concept of 'best practice' and its connection with industrial management and the agricultural industry. Thus, García Leiva and Segovia call for the need to redefine 'good practices' in the context of cultural diversity. For these authors, in order for an action to be considered a 'good practice', it should fulfil some requisites. First, it must be effective. That is to say, it must accomplish its goals showing a 'tangible impact' in the protection and/or promotion of cultural diversity in media industries. Second, the practice must last and prolong its action under similar circumstances throughout time. Third, it must be a transformative practice, since it should contribute to change in the conditions of promotion and/or protection of cultural diversity. Last, it must be transparent so that public access to the information regarding its formulation, implementation and impact is secured.

Two other factors, although not mandatory, are seen by García Leiva and Segovia as needed for practices to be considered excellent. These two requirements are that the practice be exemplary and that it be reflexive. It needs to be exemplary in the sense that it can be used as a source of inspiration for other agents and contexts. It should be reflexive so that the action can reconsider its own process and evaluate the way it works.

CsA, as far as we have seen, fulfils all the requisites to be included in a catalogue of "good cultural practices", as developed by fellow scholars in one of our research projects (Gallego and Segovia 2014). CsA is efficient because its works are evidence that its methodology enables a more diverse access to the means of production. It is a lasting action because over the last eight years it has succeeded in consolidating its methodology, which has been replicated in contexts different from the original. It is a transformative action because it intervenes in the communities where it has been put into practice, and it strengthens the social fabric of said communities. It is transparent because the audiovisual and written documentation for every project is available to every citizen. It is exemplary because it has already been used as a model for similar experiences. Finally, it is reflexive because it has led to a considerable quantity of texts in which the promoters of this idea have questioned and challenged their own process and the way the collective works, trying to overcome problems that have arisen.

CsA is not only a good practice. It is an initiative that connects with one of the most fruitful endeavours of UNESCO's Convention on the Protection and Promotion of the Diversity of Cultural: the audiovisual training of citizenship in order to favour the access of excluded communities or citizens to the means of audiovisual production. In CsA's own words: "(our goal is to) invest time and money in the production of films with those who usually do not have that opportunity" (Tudurí 2013, 77).

If we analyse the audiovisual initiatives that have been funded by the International Fund for Cultural Diversity (IFCD), we can conclude that one of the most important missions that the Convention has imposed upon itself is to increase access to audiovisual production in developing countries. Thus, among the initiatives that the IFCD supports (Albornoz 2015), we may find the project led by the Brasilian NGO Video nas Aldeias, which consists of the production of an educational audiovisual collection to be used in classrooms, made out of six films and a didactic unit. The collection was made by six towns (waiãpi, ikpeng, panará, ashaninka, mbya-guarani and kisêdjê) and aimed to promote cultural diversity and fight negative stereotypes of the indigenous groups. It is not a coincidence that CsA has used the experiences of Vídeo nas Aldeias as one of its main references; their influence can be tracked in the writings of Tudurí and the other members of the CsA collective.

Although the difficulties to access the means of production of the communities aided by the IFCD and those faced by the members of the CsA are very different, they both share at least two contact points. On the one hand, and as it has been explained, CsA shares with these initiatives the desire to open up the citizens' access to the tools and procedures of a cultural expression usually reserved for cultural and economic elites. On the other, both CsA and the initiatives promoted by the Convention are handicapped when it comes to reaching their audiences. Although digital technologies have allowed access to audiovisual media to almost every citizen (especially in the Northern hemisphere), content distribution is still in the hands of few intermediaries.

From the perspective of granting access to audiovisual production, CsA is an initiative that signifies an important advance in terms of diversity. The potential of the initiative as a promoter and agent of diversity is compromised by the difficulties that its creations (like all of those that consciously locate themselves in the margins of the audiovisual circuit) find in order to escape minor consumption. Be that as it may, it should be noted that CsA's experience finds its meaning not in the final product but in the process of making it. As stated in this chapter, CsA is, overall, a methodology.

Acknowledgements

The authors would like to thank Gerardo Tudurí, Eva Fernández, Daniel Goldmann and Helena de Llanos for sharing information about CsA and being always ready to answer our questions about the collective.

Asier Aranzubia wrote this chapter as part of the research project "Diversidad de la industria audiovisual en la era digital (2015–2016)" (ref. CSO2014-52354-r), financed by the Spanish Ministry of Economy and Competitiveness.

Miguel Fernández Labayen wrote this chapter as part of the research project "Las relaciones transnacionales en el cine digital hispano-americano: los ejes de España, México y Argentina" (CSO2014-52750-P), financed by the Spanish Ministry of Economy and Competitiveness.

Notes

1 Surprisingly, the CsA makes no reference to similar experiences in Spain, although the 1970s saw an eruption of film collectives and collaborative practices in the context of late Francoism militant and marginal cinemas (Fernández Labayen and Prieto Souto, 2012).
2 As of December 2015, the squatters in Patio Maravillas were evicted at 5:30 am, August 4, 2015. Some of the users and sympathizers of Patio Maravillas are current members of Ahora Madrid, the party that runs the Madrid government since 2015. Conservative newspapers like *ABC* have repeatedly pinpointed this connection between Ahora Madrid and the squatters in Patio Maravillas, most prominently in relation to the participation of some of the squatters of Patio Maravillas in the controversial activities of the 2016 carnival. See for example: http://www.abc.es/espana/madrid/abci-mayer-ficho-responsable-carnaval-entre-okupas-patio-maravillas-201602092305_noticia.html.
3 The whole program can be consulted here: http://www.museoreinasofia.es/actividades/saber-hay-que-imaginarse-0 The film can be seen here: https://vimeo.com/67080122.

References

AECID. 2009. *Manual para completar la ficha de análisis. Banco de buenas prácticas.* Madrid: AECID.

Albornoz, Luis A. 2015. "The International Fund of Cultural Diversity: a new tool for cooperation in the audiovisual field." *International Journal of Cultural Policy.*

Cine sin Autor. 2008. *Guión. Esto NO es una película.* DVD. Patio Maravillas.

Cine sin Autor. 2012. "Fábricas anónimas para una nueva Industria de cine. Nota sobre el sistema cinematográfico futuro." http://cinesinautor.blogspot.com.es/2012_02_01_archive.html.

Cine sin Autor. 2016. "What Is?" http://matamesipuedescsa.wix.com/csa-english#!qu-es/cycf.

Comunian Roberta. 2012. "Exploring the Role of Networks in the Creative Economy of North East England: economic and cultural dynamics." In *Encounters and Engagement between Economic Cultural Geography*, edited by Barney Warf, 143–157. New York: Springer.

Comunian, Roberta. 2016. "Temporary Clusters and Communities of Practice in the Creative Economy: festivals as temporary knowledge networks." *Space and Culture.* first published on July 25, 2016 doi:10.1177/120633121 6660318.

de Valck, Marijke. 2007. *Film Festivals: from European geopolitics to global cinephilia.* Amsterdam: Amsterdam University Press.

Fernández Labayen, Miguel and Xose Prieto Souto. 2012. "Film Workshops in Spain: oppositional practices, alternative film cultures and the transition to democracy." *Studies in European Cinema* 8 (3): 227–242.

Gallego, J. Ignacio and Ana I. Segovia. 2014. "Análisis de casos de buenas prácticas en las industrias culturales y creativas." In *Tendencias y buenas prácticas en las industrias culturales y creativas*, edited by Marga Fuentes and Ángel Badillo, 147–166. Salamanca: GRIC/Universidad de Salamanca.

García Leiva, Mª Trinidad and Ana I. Segovia. 2014. "Good Practices in Audiovisual Diversity. Hype or Hope?" *Observatorio (OBS*) Journal* 8 (4): 91–103.

Intermediae. 2016. "¿Qué es Intermediae?" http://intermediae.es/project/intermediae/page/que_es_intermedi.

King, Kenneth. 2007. "Engaging with Best Practice: history and current priorities." *Norrag News* 39: 9–15.

Löwgren, Jonas and Bo Reimer. 2013. *Collaborative Media: production, consumption, and design interventions.* Cambridge, MA: MIT Press.

McKenzie, Scott. 2014. *Film Manifestos and Global Cinema Cultures. A Critical Anthology.* Berkeley and Los Angeles: University of California Press.

"Peter Osborne in Conversation with Paul Willemen." 2013. In *Working Together: notes on British film collectives in the 1970s*, edited by Petra Bauer and Dan Kidner, 39–46. Essex: Focal Point Gallery.

Sedeño Valdellós, Ana. 2012a. "Cine social y autoría colectiva: prácticas de cine sin autor en España." *Razón y Palabra* 80: http://www.razonypalabra.org.mx/N/N80/M80/11_Sedeno_M80.pdf.

Sedeño Valdellós, Ana. 2012b. "Pedagogías visuales radicales: prácticas de cine colectivo, y cine sin autor como herramienta pedagógica." *Actas IV Congreso Internacional Latina de Comunicación Social.*

Sedeño Valdellós, Ana. 2013. "Cine sin Autor como pedagogía crítica audiovisual. Bases teóricas, antecedentes y postura crítica." *Communication Papers. Media Literacy & Gender Studies* 2: 91–97.

Shohat, Ella and Robert Stam. 1994. *Unthinking Eurocentrism. Multiculturalism and the Media.* New York and London: Routledge.

Tudurí, Gerardo. 2008. *Manifiesto del Cine sin Autor. Realismo social extremo en el siglo XXI.* Madrid: Centro de Documentación Crítica.

Tudurí, Gerardo. 2013. *The Politics of Collectivity. Authorless Cinema Manifesto 2.0:* http://media.wix.com/ugd/75e5b9_75f881855075472890 eff2c7630ba20f.pdf.

Villaplana, Virginia. 2015. "Documentalidad. Cine sin autoría, pedagogías visuales colectivas y valor afectivo." In *Revisitando el cine documental: de Flaherty al webdoc,* edited by Vanesa Fernández, 33–54. La Laguna: Cuadernos Artesanos de Comunicación. Sociedad Latina de Comunicación Social.

7 Community Media as Social Innovation

Transformation, Agency and Value

Jon Dovey, Shawn Sobers and Emma Agusita

Purpose and Platforms of Community Filmmaking

> There's all this talk of giving communities access: to be able to participate: to be given a platform. Access to what? Participation in what? A platform for what?
>
> —(Fox et al. 2006)

The above quote was delivered at a public forum[1] debating the responsibility of the arts and media to engage the public, particularly when the work is publicly funded. On the panel were (then) Labour Minister of Culture David Lammy MP, activist artist Simon Poulter, and Claire Fox – Director of The Institute of Ideas. Amongst a panel of largely supportive voices for the argument to encourage artists to engage communities, Fox presented a contrary agitation, from the standpoint of a cynic, stating that artists should just be allowed to get on with what they do best and not get distracted by 'trendy calls' of community participation and 'amateur collaborations'. This chapter argues that, even though we may disagree with many of Fox's views, this kind of fundamental critical questioning is essential if community filmmaking is to realise and articulate its value. Fox's questions focus the thesis of our chapter – what is the purpose of the community media intervention, what is the benefit, and for whom?

Implicit in this enquiry is the premise that community media practices strive towards some kind of personal and social transformation of participants and is carried out – in some way – to enhance the experiences, awareness and skills of the participant groups (Goldfarb 2002). This chapter discusses the *Creative Citizens* study, an extensive research project conducted (as part of a larger team through the AHRC's Connected Communities Programme) by the authors from 2013 to 2015, looking into the community media practices of the *South Blessed* collective, a self-motivated network of young creatives approximately 18 to 26 years old. The study is an on-the-spot analysis, witnessing the practices of the network as it attempts to negotiate the dynamics between inclusive community media ethos and neoliberal entrepreneurialism, in its various approaches to media making and dissemination. YouTube, Facebook and convergent digital media cultures were central to South Blessed's activities.

The perspective that structures our chapter offers the opportunity to explore the discursive formations and claims of community video practices in relation to the testimony or participants. We suggest that despite the appearance of digital media abundance the need for informal education aimed at critical media production practice is more important than ever in the constitution of twenty-first-century citizenship.

Context and Method

There's been a tendency in some high-tech circles to act as if participatory culture originated with YouTube or social networking with Facebook. Instead, we need to place these practices in a larger historical context.

(Jenkins et al. 2016, 11)

Our historical contextualisation draws attention to the kinds of claims that have been made for the societal impact of technologies that afford access to the means of media production. This context produces a historical backdrop against which we argue, from our evidence, that individual motivations and the mobilisation of participants' affective energies, rather than technology, are key drivers of the complex networks of agency that can produce wider societal outcomes.

Enthusiastic responses to the early miniaturisation of video technologies and their adoption by critical activists committed to a more participatory and democratic media led to the first wave of community media in the 1970s, summarised by Nigg & Wade (1980):

The two fundamental concepts informing this practice are *access* and *participation*. There is a conviction that the means of communication and expression should be placed in the hands of those people who clearly need to exercise greater control over their immediate environment, particularly in housing, schools, traffic schemes, play and recreational facilities. (7)

This wave included photography, video, newspapers, poster collectives, mural workshops and radio networks. The potential of this first wave of community-led media was understood not just at the level of grassroots activism but also by some of the leading critical theorists of the new left[2]. This foundational moment for community media saw its potential primarily as a movement that could mobilize both existing communications systems and new media technologies in order to transform the public sphere by making it more diverse, more accountable and more available to the everyday needs of ordinary people.

These rhetorics resurface 30 or so years later in the discursive formation of Web 2.0; in one Sunday supplement article from 2006 we find the founders of Wikipedia, Flickr and Wordpress all proclaiming that the means of media production are indeed now available to "everybody everyday". Jimmy Wales predicted, "*It's going to be a part of everyday life – creating and sharing media will be a thing that normal people will do all the time, every day, and it doesn't seem strange*", whilst Caterina Fake and Stewart Butterfield of Flickr observed "What's changed is expanding on that theme of communication and personal publishing and making it available to millions of people *who don't have technical skills*", a theme echoed by Wordpress' Matt Mullenweg "Now you see people *with no technical ability* creating really amazing sites reaching audiences they would never have imagined reaching" (all in Lanchester 2006).

The idea of the benefits and value of community-led media production has a long history of desire, forecast and organisation. The historic practice of community media occurred in project spaces designed and funded by third-sector organisations based in communities. These organisations have been rooted in youth work, community development, informal education, community arts and independent film networks. They were founded on didactic principles and rested upon the central idea that access to the means of media production (in an era when they were a scarce and centralised resource) will deliver a more democratic and representative public sphere. Even the Web 2.0 founders' comments are predicated on the amazement that media resources are *no longer* scarce, but will be in the hands of everyday people with no technical ability. This alleged condition of course begs some questions for the historical project of community-led media practices, what exactly is their function if the means of production have already been democratised? What are the values and benefits of community video in the era of media abundance?

South Blessed, the site for the Creative Citizens investigation was not a third-sector brokered initiative. It was a spontaneously organised creative network led and mobilised by young people themselves. Here the role of the third-sector organisation was a) in the background as a previous training resource for many of the young people involved and b) as an occasional source of employment, funding or mentoring.

The Creative Citizens case study explored how South Blessed, an informal youth network of creative citizens, generated value through its activities. South Blessed showcased a diversity of young, creative talent from South West England in music, fashion, poetry, skateboarding, street art, graffiti, film, comics, media activism and journalism. At the time of the research South Blessed was centred on a website with over 3000 music, comedy and news clips made in the South West of England. The study attempted to articulate the community or civic benefits of this informal network of people, struggling for success in the creative economy.

The Creative Citizens South Blessed study utilised four research methods, 1) Analysis of South Blessed social media activities and online content, 2) asset mapping focus groups with key South Blessed personnel, 3) participant observation of the co-creation process of a creative product, and 4) qualitative interviews of South Blessed participants and stakeholders. For the purposes of this chapter, we will discuss three key findings from this study, drawing primarily on qualitative interview data as the mode of discussion and participant observation notes from the co-creation process of the making of a graphic novel. We have chosen to build the chapter around a few long quotes from our interviewees as they a) are representative of our wider coding and b) offer an important texture of the experience of the young people at the heart of this investigation.

Transforming Subjects

We begin with evidence that suggests the notion that members of the South Blessed network were engaged in deeply transformative experiences driven by particular forms of socially constructed agency, with a deep sense of self and transformative agency. This transcended the creative space, changing the experience from a mere project or volunteer job to an extension of a world view and aspirational ideology. Viewing it as a form of pedagogy, educational theorist Frank Smith (cited in Ballard 2003) states, *"the way we identify ourselves is at the core of all learning because all learning pivots on who we think we are, and who we see ourselves as capable of becoming"* (12). South Blessed participants shared these personal motivations with a commitment to advocacy and a strong sense of public voice characterised by a drive to contribute to a wider shared culture. Theses voices are fuelled by private passions that become network assets through newly spreadable and shareable media (Jenkins, Ford and Green 2013). The core interview subjects all aspired to support themselves through their own self-determined creative effort. This informal creative economy is driven by dreams of success, where getting your record cut, your film made or your label launched are common aspirations. However, these dreams are rooted in histories, biographies and places. Our interviews revealed that the mesh of productive assets includes the network brand of South Blessed itself, family ties, mutualism, the rhetorics of hope and self-empowerment associated with some elements of hip hop music, positive feelings associated with the discourses and claims of 'creativity' and the ability to engage forms of DIY enterprise and civic funding in support of visions and activity.

A young rapper who recently experienced his first commercial music success while working with South Blessed, told us how his involvement connected with his life narrative and that he was using the opportunity as a strategic mode of self-actualisation fused with identity formation.

> I was raised in the church and I still go. [It's] inspiring for me, especially on the music side... Every time... it's just, like, worshipping as well as a concert. From my point of view [I'm here for South Blessed's] focus on rappers...
>
> However, [their] logo is like a mix between the Great British flag and the colours of the Jamaican flag, so I think it's just bringing both cultures together – black culture, white culture, however you want to put it – together through rap, which is a black cultural thing. Just getting everybody involved rather than just targeting one market. South Blessed just wants to see everybody succeed around [them....They don't just focus on youth. They focus on Bristol as a whole.
>
> (Young music performer, member of the
> South Blessed peer network)

He went on to talk about using this experience to go to university to study media and business, so he can gain knowledge about all aspects of the entertainment world. At the time of writing, a recent Twitter post from this respondent (16th May 2016), who is now London based and gaining national exposure, shows him in a photograph with Jamal Edwards MBE, the now 25-year-old millionaire founder of SBTV. London based, initially SBTV was a YouTube channel not that dissimilar to South Blessed,[3] starting off featuring up-and-coming UK rap and grime artists, and is now a multimillion pound organisation drawing some of the biggest names in contemporary music, fashion and media. For many, Edwards became a role model for this entrepreneurial self-actualised ideology,[4] which for their generation traces its roots to the DIY music scenes of reggae sound systems and particularly Hip Hop culture (Basu and Werbner 2001, 251). The adoption of business savvy in the application of community-minded social enterprise tendencies, fused with realities and acceptance of neo-liberal capitalist practices in their operations, will be discussed in the next section (Tricksters & entrepreneurs). However, entrepreneurial discourse cannot be wholly separated from the discussion of the transformational subject. Without full knowledge and access to the resources needed to have power over one's own process, any transformation would only be partial and, as Freire argues, would be a *"weak point of dependence"*, rather than true independence (1972, 42).

The most potent example of this praxis transformation in the South Blessed network is that of the young aspiring filmmaker who worked closely with the proprietor full time for approximately three years, to help with editing and other production processes. The apprentice was financially supported by his mother as an alternative route to gain experience in the media industry, rather than using the money to attend a formal filmmaking programme at a university. After becoming highly technically accomplished whilst working for South Blessed, he recently left and started up his own production company and is making a significant impact for local music artists. Although this is an extreme and unique case, the talent development aspect of South Blessed methodology to their relationship building with its network was seen to be engrained in everyday practices of allowing people opportunities, which was recognised by another member of the network, who discusses how South Blessed supports others in the practice of 'exploiting' talent,

> Bristol does have a culture of tryers, there are a lot of people trying but because there is lack of accessibility so it is in turn just filled with tryers… because they can't grab what they are trying for. That feeds the notion of South Blessed which is to exploit people who want to manifest, exploit tryers. It gives them that accessible thing; it is an equivalent of whatever they are trying for.
>
> (Young media producer, member of the South Blessed peer network)

The respondent's use of the term 'exploit' above is significant, for her this is not a negative; a platform that aggregates local talent to gain attention for its network brand is 'exploiting' "people who want to manifest" in the most positive way, offering them "an accessible thing".

In the final part of this section, we will discuss the transformational self, regarding the founder and proprietor of South Blessed, Vince Baidoo. To omit this would mean giving only a *partial* history and the impression that Vince is a *mere* manager of operations rather than an active agent and practitioner in the network. When we started this project, South Blessed was predominantly identified by its outputs of hip hop music videos with local young rappers and documentaries on the Tesco Riots[5] and other transferable and activist approaches to community media production. From the early stages of the research Vince articulated three prime new directions he wanted South Blessed's work to take: 1) To move away from music videos to instead produce more documentary and activist films, 2) to have a corporate and commercial department of South Blessed to produce media for conferences, events and weddings, etc., which would have the priority of making money and 3) to explore his love of anime and his (as yet under-developed[6]) interest in scriptwriting, possibly for animation.

These discussions led to the co-creation element of the research, a co-creation project in which we supported Vince's writing and publishing of his first graphic novel, *Indigo Babies*. He wrote the entire storyline and script himself, and the novel was illustrated by Silent Hobo, a high profile, locally based graffiti writer, whose work Vince had always admired. What we observed with the production of the graphic novel are the three ambitions as identified by Vince coming together in dynamic and unexpected ways. For the purposes of this section, we will concentrate on points 1 and 3; point 2 will be discussed later in this chapter. The content of the novel brings with it the community-themed concerns and activist-based ideas and narratives that we saw in his earlier documentary and music video work; most significantly the theme of the Tesco Riots is used as the backdrop of the comic story-world. From the perspective of a content and discourse analysis of the graphic novel, the text fits squarely within the themes of the majority of South Blessed's previous lens-based output, such as questioning state power, young people's (unrecognised) intelligence and ability, social rebellion, conspiracy theory, youth sub-culture, secret societies, alternative forms of education and alternative methods of acting ethically.[7] (The story follows a group of young people with special technological powers and an eco-activist culture who have to make some political choices about which side they are on in a violent insurrection.) Whilst themes such as these have been explored in Vince's previous outputs, a new skills level saw him express them in fictional written form, a new departure and development of his creative ability. The co-creation project that formed part of our research saw him develop an added layer of creative confidence to his already diverse creative arsenal. Subsequently Vince began to define himself as a transmedia producer, rather than simply a filmmaker. As Vince himself explains:

> Well, I think that whole process...right now I'm very clear that what I've been doing my whole life is transmedia storytelling, [yet] at that point it wasn't so clear that that's what it was...the fact that the idea could transfer from a film to a comic...meant there was a core idea waiting to bubble. So, in the end it was a blessing in disguise, because I would argue that comics is the ultimate form of story-telling because it's so simple in its form. ...But transferring from film to comic just gave me the clarification of what it was I was doing in the first place. So I think that's just where it helped me; it helped refine the idea...and then to refine what that actually is, and to now strengthen the possibilities of developing South Blessed into a transmedia production company.
>
> (Vince Baidoo – South Blessed proprietor)

In this case study the graphic novel has become the embodiment of the new subjectivities at play, with new pedagogies no less present and a significant shift for Vince himself, as he embraces a new creative identity. This shift has been significant to the extent that, at the time of writing (two years after *Indigo Babies* was published), Vince has now set up a publishing company (Crown Root) and released 12 more graphic novels, working with various emerging writers and illustrators, in keeping with his socially engaged talent development ethos and entrepreneurial business practices.

As observed by a member of the South Blessed network:

> They acknowledge who they are and they just want to manifest themselves. I think that is what makes South Blessed interesting because you know you are seeing genuine people that are just manifesting themselves.
>
> (Young media producer, member of the
> South Blessed peer network)

Tricksters & Entrepreneurs

The second research finding under discussion is the notion of the members of the network operating as dynamic trickster entrepreneurs. The young people in our research sample were finding new ways of enacting forms of community media activism whilst traversing the tensions among creative, commercial and community benefit. The socialist politics of benevolent intervention that informed traditional community media approaches based in third-sector organisations were here challenged by the entrepreneurial dynamics of a 'digital start up meets DIY' culture. Subjects' commercial aspirations indicate that media access and public voice alone are no longer enough (Sobers 2010, 197). Social enterprise here supports both an aspiration to make money *and* engage in creative activity that produces citizenship benefits.

For instance, many young people in the network are interested in starting-up enterprises that capitalise on and develop their own and other young people's creative skills and talent.

> The music videos that we did were for people that were in the same year as us at school, and people that they knew...Obviously we're just getting started, and we've got a little bit of experience, but we'll do these ones for free, then after a certain number of videos we'll start charging them, and see how far we go. Because obviously we have to make a living off of it. We can't just put all of our time into it and then we have nothing to fund our equipment, and that kind of thing.
>
> (Young Media Producer, member of South
> Blessed peer network)

Vince himself started off as a participant in traditional community filmmaking educational projects when he was 12 years old, with Sobers (co-author of this chapter) being one of his first project facilitators in 2001 and one of his most recent in 2011. Vince continued participating in community projects over a period of more than ten years, and South Blessed itself was formed whilst he was participating in his final community media project, the Second Light scheme in 2011. Whilst much of South Blessed's output speak to many of the interests of traditional community media as we have come to know it, in terms of giving people a voice and debating local issues (Nigg and Wade 1980, Dowmunt 1980, Alvarado, Gutch and Wollen 1987, 37, Dewdney and Lister 1988, Harding 2005, 15, and Lewis 2006, 18), the business models he wants to employ to take his work forward are very different and more commercial, without the apparent awkwardness that many of us who worked in community media felt when discussing making money, much of it being not for profit, publically funded and precarious. According to Dunford 2007):

> Funding for community-based media work is limited, and what little there is available is highly competitive. Community media practitioners have been forced to think outside conventional media circles to develop sustainable projects. (315)

Through the process of production of the *Indigo Babies* graphic novel we have seen Vince's second aspiration come into play, *"to have a more corporate and commercial department of South Blessed to produce media for conferences, events and weddings etc. – which would have the priority of making money"*, (as described in the previous section). This saw Vince using the opportunity to reimagine what was possible as a community media output and squarely position it as a transmedia commercial enterprise to make money. He built his business awareness throughout the process, with the priority of creating a saleable asset that both academic and non-academic partners agreed would become the business module to allow South Blessed to become more financially sustainable. This self-determining agency is how the notion of trickster is conceptualised in this chapter, not as one who cannot be trusted, but rather as one who creates alternative solutions and carves their own path to reach a desired goal, eschewing traditional models. According to Hyde (2008):

> Trickster starts out hungry, but before long he is the master of the kind of creative deception that, according to a long tradition, is a prerequisite of art. (17)

What we witnessed observing the South Blessed network was a swift-thinking innovative entrepreneurial spirit of seeking new business solutions, often based on a gift economy (Mauss 1954), finding methods of maximising what little (and precarious) resources they had.

The storyworld of the *Indigo Babies* graphic novel itself mirrors trickster behaviour, following a group of young people who, when observed from the surface could appear to be acting in a questionable manner, but when observed in a broader context appear to be operating in a clever, forward-thinking and ethical way. The Indigo characters embody the notion of a misunderstood and demonised demographic, who, rather than being judged for doing things their own way rather than the 'norm', would reveal new paradigms. Hyde (2008) explains it thus:

> Where someone's sense of honourable behaviour has left him unable to act, trickster will appear to suggest amoral action, something right/wrong that will get life moving again....The trickster is a boundary-crosser, [though there are also] cases in which the trickster creates a boundary, or brings to the surface a distinction previously hidden from sight. (7)

In many ways, the emphasis on the output being saleable was the point at which this process stopped being a community media project and became a set of commercial economic-labour relationships. Up-and-coming, young collaborators were paid, and they became contractors; the transferable process pedagogies, traditionally prized by community media operations, were marginalised for the benefit of getting the product produced efficiently on time to get to market. Therefore, we need to reflect: in this transaction of actions and motivations from community to commercial, what has been gained and lost?

Figure 7.1 Page from the *Indigo Babies* graphic novel, specially adapted by Vince Baidoo for a conference presentation about the project and posted on his social media sites, referencing the begins of character trickster thinking within a social network. Original copyright remains.

We may have lost the nurturing pedagogies we have seen present in previous community media relationships, where the scaffold of the project framework is to build and identify the transferable skills of participants and where process is paramount over production in terms of an assumed ethical practice (Goldfarb 2002, 58). Critics of this emphasis of process in participatory education have questioned the un-realistic '*big tent*' safe bubbles that these projects create around participants (Cummings, Dyson and Millward 2003, 63), and we have spoken elsewhere about the blocked ceiling participants of some community projects have faced, where their aspirations to work in mainstream media might not be met by the small scale of the projects they are involved in (Sobers 2010, 191).

As a research team we would venture to say what has been gained has been new subjectivities within community media discourse – and a maturing of the old traditional models. The Creative Citizen as trickster navigates tight spaces, shifting identities to achieve civic and creative aims. This co-production process has seen Vince adopt a trickster role to navigate from an activist and music-based filmmaking practice to a commercial platform, which has deep-seated foundations and long-held aspirational goals. The up-and-coming talented young people that have collaborated with him during this process will not have had a third-sector 'sanctioned' learning experience but will have had direct creative and entrepreneurial experiences that are arguably no less valuable. Therefore, work-based learning is argued to have benefit, not only academic courses.

In this case study the graphic novel has become the embodiment of the new subjectivities at play, with developmental pedagogies of social enterprise no less present.

Citizenship Benefit

The final research finding we will discuss from the Creative Citizens project is that of the wider citizen benefit accruing from the South Blessed operation. The processes we have been observing produce a range of benefits that expand beyond that of the individual transformed participant. These community assets begin with the motivation of particular kinds of individuals but, through the operation of the particular milieu, produce identifiable benefits for a range of actors in the network. We summarise these benefits as:

- individual engagement and social productivity,
- informal and formal learning opportunities,
- training and employment in creative economies,
- community cohesion and
- alternative sources of news for local media.

Importantly we identified these benefits as arising from the particular milieu of the informal spaces of the creative economy where specific kinds of values are enacted. We use the idea of milieu to try to express that mix of space and place, particular cultural forms and histories and identifiable products, services and networks that create a scene.[8] These informal creative economy milieu are made up of people who perform music, DJ, write, tell stories, use video and photography, paint, draw (in this case graffiti) and consume and customize fashion. It's a milieu rarely motivated by just money, drawing on all kinds of support, but it nevertheless has an identifiable (though difficult to measure) economic impact by constituting a night-time economy and the cultural conditions for a very wide range of entrepreneurial enterprise (cafes, bookshops, workshops, studios, bars, venues.) These spaces are characterised by cultures of aspiration entrepreneurialism and community solidarity. The asset map produced in one of our workshops with respondents produced lots of emphasis on Bristol Talent, Bristol Community and just Bristol as a place. This also attached to Nightlife (night-time economy), Live Shows, word of mouth, a Young Entrepreneurs group, a business development training agency, political groups and music labels to create a strong sense of this network of young people embedded within a very rich milieu. We also know from their asset mapping talk and from our previous interviews that their descriptions of this milieu are characterised by very powerful bonds of solidarity and mutualism. Their sociality is here understood as a route to personal development, 'manifestation' and actualisation of an authentic expressive self, truth telling, mutual support, optimism, hope and empowerment. Within this milieu, offline activities, sites and relationships were more important than a primary reliance on online platforms. While the function and form of South Blessed would not be possible without social media, offline networks and relationships with the physical Bristol milieu were the main drivers of their creative endeavours and modes of communication.

So whilst South Blessed did not start out as a community media organisation in the historical definition of the process, it did nevertheless produce community benefit. South Blessed produced informal education and training for young people to engage with the world of work, to develop skills and confidence and to earn money. Whilst the entire network was highly precarious – dependent on a mix of street bucket collections, freelance work, higher education loans, training, internships and job seekers allowance – it was held together by very strong affective ties towards the South Blessed brand, by friendship, shared histories, family ties and aspirational beliefs. We might also be inclined to read this as evidence of new forms of subjectivity, creativity and resistance that are the paradoxical formations of precarity described by Gill & Pratt, "This *double meaning* is central to understanding the idea and politics associated with precarity; the new moment of capitalism that engenders precariousness is seen not only as oppressive but also as offering the potential for new subjectivities, new socialities and new kinds of politics" (2008, 3). Here the "new socialities" produce traditional benefits like training and engagement but also surprising new assets that are enabled by the newly socialised forms of media sharing,

> I feel it's a little bit like the Google of Bristol sometimes. If you want to know the real Bristol, none of the stuff you see in the tourist books, what's being recommended, if you just want to know what the people of Bristol are about, the youth of Bristol, everything Bristol really, I would just say go to South Blessed. They've got so many different videos, so many different bits of information.
>
> (Peer media producer)

The development of these assets through YouTube and Facebook sites had some surprising outcomes in terms of, for instance, community cohesion, when local community police team asked the South Blessed proprietor to sit on the local police community liaison committee, a highly charged space for the predominantly African-Caribbean community. During particular moments of community tension, the network also became a news source for mainstream journalists who were interested in accessing footage only available within the network and using it a source of information and corroboration. Finally, South Blessed was acknowledged by regional community video operators to have created genuine innovation in the field by enacting a 'digital native' version of community media, "That is something that we have long needed in the sector. We have never been able to prove it. We have never been able to make it work, getting access to local audiences" (Local community media producer).

The South Blessed case study demonstrates many of the same motivational patterns arising from the apparently spontaneously self-organising network that is a product of the participatory cultures afforded by digital technologies. Jenkins et al. (2006) argued that this new 'Participatory Culture' is characterised by:

- 'affiliation', elective group formation in online community around enthusiasms, issues or common cultures;
- 'expression', music, video and design tools in the hands of far more users than ever before for every kind of human mode of communication;
- 'collaborative problem-solving' mobilising collective intelligence, crowdfunding, online petition making, alternate reality gaming, wiki based shared knowledge practices and
- 'circulations' playing an active role in directing media dynamics through the new flows of viral media driven by Twitter, Facebook and YouTube.

South Blessed clearly demonstrated each of these characteristics; it was bonded by affiliation to place, taste and milieu; it was constituted by sharing expressive video clips made on the cheap by a wide range of aspirant musicians and MCs; it used collaborative problem solving through its Facebook page that was a constant site of question and answer, from availability of equipment through to the ethics of sitting on the police committee; and of course its members were forever 'circulating' their favourite music tracks or manga recommendations via YouTube comments and Facebook status updates.

However, whilst South Blessed may have been afforded by technology, it was not determined by it. In fact, the ethos and the values that constitute the network can be tracked back through a number of sites and practices. The *Kuumba Afrikan Arts Centre* in the St Paul's area was for instance cited as a key early informal learning space for the proprietor, as was the Watershed, a the long-established cultural cinema and media arts centre in the middle of Bristol, which was also an important site for his non-school learning. Several key members of the network had initially met one another and received their initial training at a British Film Institute-funded programme that offered BBC internships. Ethos and value have histories and sites; they are not the product of technologies but of culture, organisation, education and activism.

Before we conclude, we wish to return to one of our opening questions: what are the values and benefits of community video in the era of media abundance? The simple response to this question from our evidence is that the idea of abundant media production tools and infrastructure is just plain wrong; a perception produced by professionals who often have more computing power in their homes than the average aspirant creative worker can muster. The South Blessed respondents stressed that access to the network's single desktop iMac (for editing) and a halfway decent video camera was a major asset; the attachment here to a single powerful computer is in marked contrast to the flipping open of Apple laptops that characterises every gathering of the digital commentariat.

The video camera was bought for the South Blessed proprietor by a close member of his family as a personal investment in his future. The other kit has been bought through the income made by street bucket collections (which are frequently managed by another close family member). Young people associated with the network were invited to undertake street collections for "Young People's Creative and Media" training; their recruitment was based on their affective attachment to the South Blessed brand; however, the collections were unlicensed and borderline legal. A tiny amount of corporate sponsorship for new talent brings in the occasional bit of new software for testing and opportunities to network with other young digital creatives at showcase and development events. This is anything but a picture of media abundance – it turns out that in this context at least access to the means of production is still a significant motivating force.

Conclusion

The values enacted in the accounts above show how creative aspiration, public sphere intervention and personal transformation have the potential to combine in new forms at the contemporary sites of community video production and exchange. The evidence from our case studies suggests that young people involved in community media activities enact values of self-actualisation, representation and participation, informal education and training. By enacting these values in their networks, they produce significant assets for their communities and milieu. Access to technology for production has remained a key attractor of activity; however, the motivations and values enacted by the participants have been a far more significant driver of impact.

Our findings show that despite ready access to social media platforms and, to a more limited extent, media production tools, human relationships, interactions and peer support are most valued by members of community video networks. Phil Shepherd, the former chair of UK's Community Media Association, stated in 2008 that the practice of community media should be viewed as "80% community and 20% media".[9] The human interaction dynamics of community video remain its unique selling point, produce value for communities at large and are most valued by participant networks.

Notes

1 The forum took place in January 2006 at the offices of Child Poverty Action Group (CPAG), London, hosted by Kate Green, then CEO of CPAG, later a Labour MP.
2 For example, Hans Magnus Enzensberger's 1970 essay *Constituents of a Theory of Media* (Enzensberger 1988) and Raymond Williams in the visionary section on "Alternative Technology" at the end of his 1974 book *Television Technology and Cultural Form.*
3 SBTV was founded in 2006, and South Blessed in 2011.
4 See – '*Jamal Edwards: 'don't start a business to make money; start it with a passion.'* by Emma Featherstone, The Guardian, 8th April 2016.
5 On Apr 21 2011 a police operation to evict squatters prompted what became known as the Explain the Tesco Riot, where protests against the opening of a new Tesco Express supermarket conflated with support for the squatters to produce a night of violent civil disturbance. South Blessed acquired some of the best footage of the events by being already embedded in the local community.
6 Under-developed primarily due to his dyslexia and hesitancy to express himself in the written word, relying instead on the spoken word and use of lens

based media as his mode of expression. This in turn has subsequently seen him become a highly articulate and impressive public speaker.

7 South Blessed's YouTube channel is - https://www.youtube.com/user/southblessed - (Last accessed 14 May 2016).

8 Webb's study (2007) of the networked worlds of popular music, including Bristol Music Culture, provided useful concepts for understanding the South Blessed network, which we identified has a nested set of cultures operating, characterized by connections, commonalities and cultural tastes (30). Webb uses three lenses of abstraction to examine music culture: at the micro level of social practices that occur in individual's 'life worlds', at the meso level in terms of how these cluster in relevant 'fields' of cultural production and at the macro level concerning how the milieu becomes extended through dialectical local, national and global connections (often facilitated by technologies).

9 Spoken at the Community Media Association Annual General Meeting – 23 February 2008, Sheffield, UK.

References

Alvarado, Manuel, Robin Gutch and Tana Wollen. 1987. *Learning the Media: an introduction to media teaching*, London: MacMillan Education Ltd.

Ballard, Keith. 2003. "Including Ourselves: teaching, trust, identity and community." In *Inclusion, Participation and Democracy: what is the purpose?* edited by Julie Allan, 11–32. Netherlands: Kluwer Academic Publishers.

Basu, Dipannita and Pnina Werbner. 2001. "Bootstrap Capitalism and the Culture Industries: a critique of invidious comparisons in the study of ethnic entrepreneurship." *Ethnic and Racial Studies* 24 (2): 236–262.

Couldry, Nick. 2012. *Media, Society, World: social theory and digital media practice*. Cambridge: Polity Books.

Cummings, Colleen, Alan Dyson and Alan Millward. 2003. "Participation and Democracy: what's inclusion got to do with it?" In *Inclusion, Participation and Democracy: what is the purpose?*, edited by Julie Allan, 49–65. Netherlands: Kluwer Academic Publishers.

Dewdney, Andrew and Martin Lister. 1998. *Youth, Culture and Photography*. London: Macmillan Education.

Dowmunt, Tony. 1980. *Video with Young People*. London: Inter-Action Community Arts Series.

Dunford, Mark. 2007. "Successful Fundraising in the UK." In *The Alternative Media Handbook*, edited by Kate Coyer, Tony Dowmunt and Alan Fountain, 309–315. Oxon: Routledge.

Enzensberger, Hans-Magnus. 1988. "Constituents of a Theory of Media." In *Dreamers of the Absolute* by Hans-Magnus Enzensberger, 20–53. London: Radius.

Fox, Clare, Kate Green, David Lammy and Simon Poulter. "Art and Social Benefit." Panel Discussion. Child Poverty Action Group, London, January 2006.

Freire, Paulo. 1972. *Pedagogy of the Oppressed*. London: Penguin Books.

Gill, Rosalind and Andy Pratt. 2008. "In the Social Factory?: immaterial labour, precariousness and cultural work." *Theory, Culture and Society* 25(7–8): 1–30.

Goldfarb, Brian. 2002. *Visual Pedagogy: media cultures in and beyond the classroom*. Durham: Duke University Press.

Harding, Anna. 2005. *Magic Moments: collaborations between artists and young people*. London: Black Dog Publishing.

Hartley, John. 2015. "A Problem of Knowledge – Solved?" In *The Creative Citizen Unbound*, edited by Ian Hargreaves and John Hartley, 25–48. Bristol: Policy Press.

Hyde, Lewise. 2008. *Trickster Makes This World: how disruptive imagination creates culture*. New York: CanonGate Books.

Jenkins, Henry, Sam Ford and Joshua Green, J. 2013. *Spreadable Media: creating value and meaning in a networked culture*. New York: New York University Press.

Jenkins, Henry, Mizuko Ito and danah boyd. 2016. *Participatory Culture in a Networked Era: a conversation on youth, learning, commerce and politics*. Cambridge: Polity Press.

Jenkins, Henry with Ravi Purushotma, Katie Clinton, Margaret Weigel and Alice. Robison. 2006. *Confronting the Challenges of Participatory Culture: media education for the 21st century*. http://www.newmedialiteracies.org/files/working/NMLWhitePaper.pdf.

Lanchester, John. 2006. "A Bigger Bang" *Guardian Weekend* (4.11.06): 17–36.

Lewis, Peter. 2006. "*Community Media: giving "a voice to the voiceless."* In *From the Margins to the Cutting Edge: community media and empowerment*, edited by Peter Lewis and Susan Jones, 13–39. IAMCR: Hampton Press, USA.

Mauss, Marcel. 1954. *The Gift: forms and functions of exchange in archaic societies*. Illinois: Martino Publishing.

Nigg, Heinz and Graham Wade. 1980. *Community Media: community communication in the uk: video, local TV, film and photography*. Zurich: Regenbogen-Verlag.

Sobers, Shawn. 2010. "Positioning Education within Community Media." In *Understanding Community Media*, edited by Kevin Howley, 188–199. Los Angeles: Sage.

Webb, Peter. 2007. *Exploring the Networked Worlds of Popular Music: milieu cultures*. New York: Routledge.

Williams, Raymond. 1974. *Television Technology & Cultural Form*. London: Fontana.

Part III

Community Filmmaking

Practice in Places and for Places – a Short Introduction

Caroline Chapain

Community film making is part of the wider practices of community media and tends to be a site of enquiry about place dynamic, identity and local development (Howley 2010). This short introduction sets the theoretical debates around these issues, which are then explored in more depth in the three chapters included in this part. These chapters discuss how community filmmaking has been practiced by filmmakers through projects in different local and national contexts. More specifically, they explore the professional challenges that filmmakers encountered when practicing community filmmaking and the potentials it offers to support the development of peoples and/or places in Britain and Germany (Daniel Mutibwa), in Ireland (Eileen Leahy) and in Canada (Sharon Karsten).

Community media and filmmaking emerged in the 1960s as a counteracting practice aiming to facilitate the production of cultural content often ignored in mainstream media. Howley (2010) defines community media as the "range of community-based activities intended to supplement, challenge or change the operating principles, structures, financing and cultural forms and practices associated with dominant media" (2). One key element of these activities has been to democratise the means of media production by making them more participatory, giving every citizen access to media production to better 'tell' stories through self-representation (Sandoval and Fuchs 2010). By definition, community filmmaking process is characterised by a certain degree of community participation in the filming process and thus has been associated with both amateur and professional practices encompassing a wide range of cultural, social, political and economic objectives and motivations. As discussed by Mutibwa, reconciling these various objectives can be challenging for filmmakers. However, community film making also offers them more freedom, as they can more easily play with rules of production and experiment with communities (Fox 2004, Shand 2008). As such, practices take place along a continuum between professional and community activities leading to some boundary work between the two realms. As noticed by Meyer (2008), these boundaries can only be revealed "through temporal, spatial and material processes. These are, in fact, many places where boundary-work takes place; boundary-work is interconnected with objects, tools, bodies, and specific spaces and places" (8). As a consequence, it is important to analyse community filmmaking within its national and local contexts and to understand how it unfolds in various places.

The Role of National Cultural, Social and Policy Frameworks

Jiménez and Scifo (2010) emphasise that community media are dependent on the social, cultural and policy frameworks within which they are embedded. In particular, support from public policies may target various objectives such as promotion of pluralism, social inclusion, local empowerment and cross-cultural dialogue; this will be dependent on their recognition of the role that community media can play in supporting these agendas (ibid.). This, in turn, will affect the availability of public funding towards community media and filmmaking. Both Mutibwa and Karsten discuss the long tradition of community media and filmmaking in, respectively, Britain and Germany (Mutibwa) and Canada (Karsten).

In Britain, as discussed by Mutibwa, the 1970s and 1980s saw an important movement of film workshops whose production was sponsored by public funding and characterised by films with a social and oppositional functions portraying 'less represented' communities (see Long et al. 2013 for a discussion of the Birmingham film and video workshop in the UK). However, the movement decreased when public funding disappeared in the 1990s. Alternatively, in Germany, Mutibwa highlights that the focus was more on developing community media and open-access channels that served as a 'social laboratory' for community engagement. These have grown in strength since the reunification of Germany in the 1990s. In contrast, in her chapter, Karsten notes that the community video movement in Canada developed in the 1970s at a time where the country struggled to make sense of its diverse identities and as such played a reflective role in the construction of the Canadian identity. On the one hand, it took the form of artist-run centres offering easier access to film production and exploring ways to make new uses of video within a community context. On the other hand, the Canadian government sponsored a national initiative to unearth and put forward the needs and agendas of various Canadian communities.

Building on this tradition, Karsten argues for the use of community filmmaking in supporting a more complex cultural mapping of local communities in Canadian cities today – taking into account communities' intangible cultural assets – to feed into local planning processes. Similarly, in her chapter, Leahy suggests that community filmmaking can play a key role in giving a voice to and empowering communities living in areas undergoing urban regeneration processes by bringing them together and helping them regroup and rebuild themselves in times of change.

Community Filmmaking Practices within Local Contexts

There is a wide literature discussing how creative processes, practices and outcomes – filmmaking within them – are embedded within places (Scott 1999, Hall 2004). Despite global influences, creative workers and producers tend to be embedded in particular local cultural frameworks (e.g. inter-personal norms, methods and language) reinforced in day-to-day transactions with other creative producers with complementary expertise and skills (Scott 1999). They may draw heavily on local cultural assets such as natural landscapes, way of life, street scenes, heritage, etc., as visual raw material and stimuli for aesthetic creativity and inspiration (Scott 1999, Drake 2003). Given the way community filmmaking works and operates i.e. by being about and/or undertaken in partnerships with communities, these localised cultural and social elements will be even more important. As a result, community filmmaking is influenced by local cultural representations and contributes to new cultural representations of the places within which these communities are located.

The film content produced tends to reflect how the communities in question relate to these places, both in terms of current perceptions and images and their hopes and desires as illustrated by Leahy and Karsten. This content, nevertheless, tends to be mediated both through the creative vision of filmmakers and the way communities are involved in the filming process. The latter will be dependent on community filmmakers' degree of understanding and participation in the filming process and thus of existing local communities' resources and capacities. As discussed by Mutibwa, Leahy and Karsten, various processes of community involvement can be put in place by filmmakers depending on the purpose of the community filmmaking projects.

In our research, we also found that the methods used by filmmakers were linked to projects' objectives, filmmakers' ethos in terms of community participation and existing communities' resources and enthusiasm with regards to filmmaking (Malik, Chapain and Comunian 2015). Filmmakers' practices were highly dependent on the mediation and technical skills they had developed throughout both community films and commercial film projects even though they were open to experimentation and new learning (ibid). In addition, local creative policies and supporting infrastructure play an important role in supporting the development of community filmmaking (ibid.). Filmmakers are embedded in particular local and regional creative ecosystems, which can enable but also inhibit their practices (Chapain and Comunian 2010).

Community Filmmaking in Support of Local Development

More widely, the three chapters included in this part touch upon the role of community filmmaking as a tool to support community development by helping local population and/or disenfranchised communities to re-think and reinvent their neighbourhoods or better express their views and also allowing communities to participate in and engage with creative practices. There is a wide literature discussing the cultural, well-being and social impacts that participating in the arts and creative activities can generate for people and communities (Matarosso 1997, Lowe 2000, Reeves 2002, Evans and Shaw 2004, Arts Council 2008, Devlin 2009, Cebr 2013, Fleming 2015). Overall, participating in creative activities can improve people's cultural capital i.e. "shared cultural networks and relationships, however, defined, that facilitate cultural, social and eco-nomic interaction between members of the group" (Throsby 2003, 169). The general assumption is thus that the arts can be used to support per-sonal development, learning and skill development and help bring people together, increasing social cohesion, pride and sense of identities within communities and can foster positive environmental outcomes in terms of regeneration and attractivity of places (see Chapain and Hargreaves 2016 for a review).

Obviously, these impacts are going to vary depending on the nature of the creative projects in question, their objectives and the participation processes put in place by filmmakers. Building on the co-creation model from Frow et al. (2011), we can say that collaboration within community filmmaking can take place at different stages along the film value chain from co-conception and co-design to co-production, co-promotion, co-distribution, etc. More importantly, this collaboration tends to in-clude both co-creation of meaning and co-experience between film-makers and communities in interactive processes based on the utilisation and mobilisation of their respective capabilities and resources (ibid.).

The chapters by Mutibwa, Leahy and Karsten touch on this dimen-sion. They examine the collaboration and co-creation processes put in place by filmmakers within various projects and the cultural and social impacts these projects have had on people and places in terms of cul-tural and social capital. As a result, both Leahy and Karsten call for the use of community filmmaking in supporting local cultural and urban development. It is important to note though that investing in creative activities to foster non-economic outcomes is not exempt of pitfalls and can be subject to a process of instrumentalisation of creative activities for non-cultural goals as reviewed by Leahy in her chapter. In addition, as highlighted by Mutibwa, the civic goals of community filmmaking can be difficult to reconcile with the more economic and professional goals that filmmakers need to pursue as well. In her chapter, Karsten also highlights the important role that filmmakers have in balancing power relationships between communities and other actors such as local planners and local authorities when using community filmmaking to support local development.

References

Arts Council 2008. *What People Want from the Arts*. London: Arts Council England.
Cebr 2013. *The Contribution of the Arts and Culture to the National Economy*. A Report for Arts Council England and the National Museum Directors' Council. London: Centre for Economics and Business Research.
Chapain, Caroline and Roberta Comunian. 2010. "Enabling or Inhibiting the Creative Economy: the role of the local and regional dimensions in England." *Regional Studies* 44 (6): 717–734.
Chapain, Caroline and Ian Hargreaves. 2016. "Citizenship in the Creative Economy." In *The Creative Citizen Unbound: how social media and DIY culture contribute to democracy, communities and the creative economy*, edited by Ian Hargreaves and John Hartley, Bristol, UK: Policy Press.
Devlin, Paul. 2009. *Restoring the Balance. The Effects of Arts Participation on Well-being and Health*. Newcastle upon Tyne: Voluntary Arts.
Drake Graham. 2003. "'This Place Gives Me Space': place and creativity in the creative industries." *Geoforum* 34: 511–524.
Evans, Graeme and Phyllida Shaw. 2004. *The Contribution of Culture Regeneration in the UK: a review of evidence*. A report to the Department for Culture Media and Sport. London: London Metropolitan University.
Fleming T. 2015. Cultural and Creative Spillovers in Europe. Report on a preliminary evidence review. Fleming Tom Creative Consultancy, http://www.artscouncil.org.uk/advice-and-guidance/browse-advice-and-guidance/cultural-and-creative-spillovers-europe accessed on 16th February 2016.
Fox, Broderick. 2004 "Rethinking the Amateur: acts of media production in the digital age." *Spectator* 24(1): 5–16.
Frow, Pennie, Adrian Payne and Kaj Storbacka. 2011. "Co-creation: a typology and conceptual framework." In *Proceedings of ANZMAC 2011*, 1–6, ANZMAC, Perth, Australia, 1st November 2011.
Hall, Peter. 2004. "Creativity, Culture, Knowledge and the City." *Built Environment* 30: 256–258.
Howley, Kevin, ed. 2010. *Understanding Community Media*. London: Sage.
Jiménez Nuriá-Reguerro and Salvatore Scifo. 2010. "Community Media in the Context of European Media Policies." *Telematics and Informatics* 27: 131–140.
Kay, Alan. 2000. "Art and Community Development: the role the arts have in regenerating communities." *Community Development Journal* 35(4): 414–424.
Long, Paul, Yasmeen Baig-Clifford and Roger Shannon. 2013. "What We're Trying to Do Is Make Popular Politics: The Birmingham Film and Video Workshop." *Historical Journal of Film, Radio and Television* 33(3): 377–395.
Lowe, Seana. 2000. "Creating Community: art for community development." *Journal of Contemporary Ethnography* 29(3): 357–386.

Malik, Sarita, Caroline Chapain and Roberta Comunian. 2014. *Spotlight on Community Filmmaking: a report on community film making and cultural diversity.* London and Birmingham, UK: Brunel University, the University of Birmingham and Kings College.

Matarosso, Francois. 1997. *Use or Ornament? The Social Impact of Participation in the Arts.* Stroud, UK: Comedia.

Meyer, Morgan. 2008. "On the Boundaries and Partial Connections between Amateurs and Professionals." *Museum and Society* 6(1): 38–53.

Reeves, Michelle. 2002. *Measuring the Economic and Social Impacts of the Arts: a review.* London: Arts Council England.

Sandoval, Marisol and Christian Fuchs. 2010. "Towards a Critical Theory of Alternative Media." *Telematics and Informatics* 27: 141–150.

Scott, Allen. 1999. "The Cultural Economy: geography and the creative field." *Media, Culture and Society* 21(6): 807–817.

Shand, Ryan. 2008. "Theorizing Amateur Cinema: limitations and possibilities." *The Moving Image* 8(2): 36–60.

Throsby, David. 2003 "Cultural Capital." In *A Handbook of Cultural Economics,* edited by Ruth Towse. Cheltenham: Edward Elgar.

8 Surfing Multiple Tides

Opportunities and Challenges for Contemporary British and German Community Filmmakers

Daniel H. Mutibwa

Introduction

Emerging out of the oppositional political and cultural movement in Europe from May 1968 onwards and often referred to interchangeably as 'avant-garde', 'independent', 'revolutionary', 'experimental' or simply 'non-commercial' (Dickinson 1999, Harvey 1978, Rees 1999), community filmmaking has tended to be associated exclusively with a civic function. Such a function comprises using (documentary) film both as a form of social and political expression and as a platform through which structural systemic failings are exposed, interrogated and critiqued. From the outset, community filmmaking has been seen to position itself against perceived dominant mainstream politics and culture as well as hegemonic artistic and filmic traditions and associated organisational forms and practices by engaging in the making of (documentary) films and videos that serve specific communities and audiences. The ultimate goal has been to highlight 'alternative representations' (Dickinson 1999) and to engage with pressing issues in community and public life for which mainstream media either fail to or are unwilling to provide an outlet (Blanchard and Harvey 1983, Negt and Kluge 1993).

However, evolving socio-political and socio-economic circumstances have meant that nascent imperatives of a particularly professional, artistic and commercial nature now play an increasingly influential role in contemporary community filmmaking. The interplay between these divergent imperatives and the civic function can sometimes be at odds, posing huge problems for community filmmakers. Moreover, these filmmakers can be subjected to systemic pressures such as demands from subsidy and politics, all of which have an impact on their work. Drawing on relevant literature and ethnographic field research, I address three key issues in this chapter. First, I discuss the ways in which community filmmakers respond to the interaction of professional, artistic and commercial imperatives alongside the core civic function. Where this interplay is ridden with tensions and contradictions, I highlight how community filmmakers negotiate these. Second, I present the response of community filmmakers to systemic pressures. Third, I evaluate how these filmmakers perceive their work following competing imperatives and systemic pressures.

Based on carefully selected case studies drawn from British and German contexts, my core argument is two-fold: a) the environment in which contemporary community filmmakers operate sometimes compels them to prioritise commercial, artistic and professional imperatives over the civic function and to give in to systemic pressures, and b) such practice provides crucial insights into the current dynamics impacting community filmmaking in a way that is only beginning to draw scholarly attention. The chapter is structured as follows. I specify how I deployed ethnography as a method of data collection, discuss the origins and development of community filmmaking in both Britain and Germany based on relevant scholarship and policy discourse, explain the different imperatives shaping the sector, then present community filmmakers' responses to the interaction between the different imperatives and to constraints from subsidy and politics followed by filmmakers' perceptions of their work before providing concluding remarks.

Methodology

This research set out to explore how contemporary community filmmaking in Britain and Germany has evolved since the countercultural era with a particular focus on principles, organisation, practice and practitioners' perceptions of their work. This required studying community filmmakers' experiences, interactions and communication, all of which – to varying extents – linked to their biographical life histories as well as everyday personal and professional practices. A robust and detailed engagement with these aspects among many other things called for an ethnographic approach to fieldwork to help gather and unpick data that illuminated how the community filmmakers under study conceived of and constructed the world around them and what they saw as their role in it, something that was realised and yielded rich insight. The research questions at the heart of this ethnographic enquiry conducted between 2009 and 2012 read as follows:

1 In what ways do contemporary community filmmakers respond to the interaction among professional, artistic and commercial imperatives alongside their core civic function?
2 How do these filmmakers respond to challenges posed by systemic pressures?
3 How do these filmmakers perceive their work following competing imperatives and systemic pressures?

In response to these questions, I identified and studied four community filmmaking organisations that constituted *Amber Films* and *Stratham*

Productions in Britain and *Fotolabor* and *Dahlberg Productions* in Germany, respectively. Throughout this chapter, pseudonyms are used to refer to the last three named case study companies, their respective productions and other work in accordance with the ethical terms (anonymity and confidentiality) under which 'preferential' access to pursue ethnographic fieldwork at those companies was given. In contrast, real names and titles are used for *Amber Films*, its productions and other work because I solely studied publicly accessible documentary evidence (during the summer of 2015), 'pseudonymising' of which would have presented ethical challenges. This derived from the fact that, because of timing issues, access at *Amber Films* did not materialise, unfortunately, but this was counterbalanced by the fact that it is the most widely studied case study in the sector in Britain, owing to its pioneering status.

I spent four weeks each at *Stratham Productions*, *Fotolabor* and *Dahlberg Productions*, during which I studied documents and artefacts, conducted semi-structured qualitative interviews and recorded everyday interactions and practices as a participant observer. All the companies under study in this chapter were selected based on longevity, a strong commitment to the civic function and the receipt of subsidy and/or broadcaster commissions. Britain and Germany were chosen for this piece of research because both countries share a common history of the oppositional political and cultural movement of the countercultural period, exhibit a relatively similar social democratic culture and are characterised by considerable structural inequities that lend themselves to being addressed by community filmmaking in ways that mainstream media, film and cinema may be unable or unwilling to.

Community Filmmaking: History and Theoretical Overview

Under the workshop movement especially from late 1970s onwards, community film production utilised documentary film as a means of recording and communicating the real-life experiences of ordinary people and as such served a clearly defined social purpose (Nigg and Wade 1980). In order to try and achieve a significant impact, many community filmmakers in Britain and Germany strove to make films cheaply and independently, which they toured in a bid to reach out to working-class and minority audiences in non-conventional venues across the country and to engage in discussions with such audiences after the showings (Dickinson 1999, Medienzentren und Videogruppen in der BRD 1984).

To this end, community filmmakers made effective use of 'alternative' production and distribution networks to break free from conventional circuits of cultural production and circulation (Higgins 1999) and from perceived constrictive public funding whenever possible (Hobson 2007). Generally, receipt of public subsidy was a bone of contention because of the fear of appropriation into the establishment (Higgins 1999). In Britain, those community filmmakers who received public subsidy "saw no contradiction involved in making films about social reform within the context of state patronage" (Dickinson 1999, 129). In Germany, community filmmakers were entitled to state funding if they could prove that their work had value in terms of cultural enrichment (Hollander 1992, Negt and Kluge 1993). This was especially the case where such work drew on, engaged with and represented local culture, heritage and place, among other things, using film as a medium, something that speaks to one of the overarching themes in this edited collection.

In terms of organisation, community filmmakers favoured a horizontal way of working, characterised by a commitment to equality and non-specialisation of tasks. Moreover, such filmmakers were keen to facilitate the involvement of ordinary people in all aspects of production. For example, ordinary people were allowed to look at and contribute to an unfinished film (Blanchard and Harvey 1983, 231). Although this tended to prolong the production process, it granted ordinary people the opportunity to shape the meaning-making process significantly in line with the core civic function. Arguably, this can be viewed as the origin of the development of networks and/or communities of practice, another key theme of this edited collection.

Further still, although many community filmmakers were very passionate about their work, "few managed to make a living out of their film work [which explains why many] worked at other jobs to earn money..." (231). Nevertheless (and with a spirit reminiscent of pre-Second World War documentarists before them), community filmmakers "remained faithful to their [...] cause and presented a picture of a group of dedicated and idealistic filmmakers subjected to 'hard work' [...] long hours and low wages" (Swann 1979, 26). In Britain, the 1980s witnessed a significant growth of the community filmmaking movement (Catterall 1999, Hobson 2007). Gradually, this generated stiff competition among filmmakers in the sector for both subsidy and Channel Four broadcasting slots. While some commentators saw this development as a distraction from the initial causes of the oppositional film movement as a whole (Dickinson 1999), others noted the inadvertent need for the sector to 'professionalise' and 'enterprise' (Newsinger 2009). This not only meant conforming to television conventions and making money in order to become self-sustaining in alignment with professional and commercial imperatives, but it was also largely a response to the Thatcherite 'enterprise culture' that favoured entrepreneurialism over the reliance on subsidy (Catterall 1999).

Community filmmaking in Germany between the 1970s and 1990s developed slightly differently owing primarily to political circumstances. Whereas the socialist government in the former German Democratic Republic favoured and invested heavily in local community and municipal print media, which were perceived to be far easier to control than audio-visual media (Huettner and Nitz 2009), then West Germany experimented with community communication initiatives already from the late 1970s onwards (Hooffacker and Lokk 2009). The most prominent among these were open-access channels that enabled interested local communities to engage in the production of audio-visual programmes (as long as these were non-commercial and non-professional in nature) as part of the effort to enhance broader democratic communication (Hollander 1992, Negt and Kluge 1993). Ole Prehn (1992) observed that these experiments went above and beyond merely providing a media platform for expression and representation to serving as "social laboratories for testing the degree of participatory potential in the respective communities" (252). Community filmmaking in the reunified Germany has significantly benefitted from this development ever since and has gone from strength to strength, albeit with some significant challenges along the way.

By contrast, when Channel Four and the other public institutions in Britain withdrew their funding from the sector by the early 1990s (Newsinger 2009, 158), many community filmmakers either left the sector out of frustration (Dickinson 1999) or moved to work for diverse production companies that made documentaries under traditional commissioning arrangements with diverse broadcasters. These developments may explain why many community filmmaking organisations did not survive beyond the 1990s (Newsinger 2009). In the 2000s, the interaction among the ascendant artistic, professional and commercial imperatives in co-existence with the core civic function can place huge demands on community filmmakers in both countries. Before looking at community filmmakers' responses, it is helpful to explain the different imperatives in a little more detail.

Divergent Imperatives in Contemporary Community Filmmaking

As specified above, contemporary community filmmaking is steered by a number of imperatives that may not always be compatible. Its perceived core civic function, we saw, makes use of (documentary) film as a form of social and political expression in the interests of diverse communities and audiences. To borrow Corner's (2000, 2) words, this function promotes "publicity for citizenship", "journalistic inquiry and exposition" and "radical interrogation and alternative perspective".

Furthermore, the core civic function – to use Nichols' words – facilitates the making of work that aims "to explain aspects of the world to us [...] to analyse problems and propose solutions [to] invite us to understand aspects of the world more fully [to] observe, describe, or poetically evoke situations and interactions [and] to enrich our understanding of aspects of the historical world by means of their representations" (2001, 165). In marked contrast to mainstream public service and commercial media, community filmmakers strive to work with communities and publics to construct images and meanings that are evidently of relevance to people therein in an effort to present the 'alternative' lived experiences outside of what may generally be viewed as the norm (Nigg and Wade 1980).

Professional imperatives in cultural production orient community filmmakers to make good use of key attributes such as skill, competence, judgement and a devotion to a calling (McIntyre 2012) in putting together ideas and material in what Kilborn and Izod (1997, 4) call "documentary discourse". Alongside skillsets in other areas of professional work like research, budgeting, project management, administration, marketing and distribution, an integral component of professional imperatives in filmmaking more generally is the adherence to ethical considerations that take into account the intention of documentary work and the obligation to all the stakeholders of such work (Katz 2003, 334).

Community filmmaking can be said to be guided by artistic imperatives that have multiple dimensions owing to the understanding that "everyone will have their own response to [artistic] work [and will] make different judgements of [such work]" (Matarasso 2000, 53). In an interview response to what artistic qualities constitute, for example, a practitioner noted that, "making [film] is all about creativity. It's not just about technology. It's about coming up with ideas, it's about telling stories and doing it in a way that makes people [want to watch]" (Shaw 2001, 52). To DiMaggio (n.d., 41), artistic quality is about "craft skill, daring or disturbing content, innovative production technique [...]". Parker and Sefton-Green view artistic imperatives as facilitating "the ability to question, make connections, innovate, problem-solve, communicate, collaborate and [...] reflect critically" (Oakley 2009, 4). Overall, artistic imperatives can be said to constitute novelty and the ability to put across key ideas in a manner that is accessible and addresses day-to-day issues and challenges (Matarasso 2000, McIntyre 2012).

Commercial imperatives can potentially coerce community filmmakers into making market-driven production decisions that seek the greatest degree of profitability, something that invariably dictates the nature and content of documentary work (Berra 2008). Critical theorists of cultural production take this further and argue that if there is no audience to which a particular cultural product can be sold profitably or if the audience does actually exist but may not possess the purchasing power to deliver swift profits and cover production costs, then that cultural product is highly unlikely to be made (Miege 1989, Peterson 1982). For many community filmmaking companies intent on providing socially relevant cultural products that tend to be commercially unviable, aligning commercial imperatives with the civic function puts producers in a very difficult position.

Additionally, although public subsidy is intended to support the creation of work that embodies civic values but may not be financially viable, it often comes with strings attached. In certain cases, such strings may be at variance with the core civic function that is understood to make community filmmaking distinctive. This begs the question of how community filmmakers are able to undertake their work in this net of constricting imperatives.

Case Studies: Interplay of Divergent Imperatives and Community Filmmakers' Responses

From the outset, the companies under study in this chapter demonstrated a strong commitment to civic values. For example, *Amber Films* – which was founded as a limited company in London but later moved to Newcastle upon Tyne – documented changes in working-class life and work in the region. Established in 1976, *Stratham Productions* served predominantly three local communities in London. *Fotolabor*, initially formed as an umbrella organisation for diverse alternative publications in 1976/1977, is a Berlin-based community filmmaking entity specialising in photography and documentary. Similarly located in Berlin is *Dalberg Productions* founded formally in 1981. The company makes documentaries and news directed primarily at German-Jewish audiences in Berlin and across Germany and Europe. Each of the case study companies is now presented in more detail.

Amber Films

We have seen that *Amber Films* portrayed alternative working-class representations in ways in which these had not hitherto been widely known (Newbury 2002). Comments by Murray Martin, a founding member, appear to affirm this from the very beginning

> I mean, there was a discussion about what we should do [...] I was already engaged in documenting working-class life, and that's what interested me, and I think, ultimately that evolved into Amber's mission statement [...] What was important to me was that the individuals who you then attracted and who stayed felt passionate in the same way, and that very quickly became the basis of the evolution of the group, I think [...] So, in a way, I was always dragging everybody towards us documenting a working-class life, although as a creative collective.
>
> (Martin 2002)

An illustrative example of a documentary film that reflected a skilful negotiation of *Amber Films*' civic ambition with the different imperatives is entitled *High Row (1973)*. Recorded in a small drift mine near Alston, in Cumbria, the film documents a working day in the life of seven miners who had given up better-paying jobs in exchange for a more independent working life (Dickinson 1999, 258). The civic value of *High Row* is three-fold: First, *Amber Films* "let the men direct the vision" of the film (254), something that gave the miners an opportunity to provide insights into their working conditions based on the authority of their experiential knowledge. Second, the documentary provided a visual representation of a form of employment or trade that is nearly defunct in contemporary European society. Third, the production facilitated discussions relating to miners' working lives and broader working-class culture when toured to different audiences.[1]

Professional imperatives were manifested in the amount of background research undertaken to understand the mining trade from which "a much harsher script" had been written and to which the miners had responded saying that "[i]f you think that you wouldn't work down the mine" (254). What is more, *Amber Films* made use of a range of documentary filmmaking conventions to "weld various components (words, images and sound effects) into an artefact that can have both functional and aesthetic appeal" (Kilborn and Izod 1997, 12). From an ethical perspective, *Amber Films* built a working and community relationship with the miners, remarkably remunerated the miners for their involvement and collaborated with academics who supported the documentary with expertise.

From an artistic vantage point, *High Row* made an effort to "communicate something of the men's own vision of their lives in a rich texture of sounds and images [whereby the omission of commentary and dramatic climax enabled reliving] the pace and rhythm of their working day, while creating a cinematic prose poem from the surreal, yet harmonious co-existence of grinding archaic machinery and unperturbed wildlife".[2] Financially, the documentary attracted large audiences, implying that it was commercially successful. *High Row* benefitted from subsidy too in its production. There is no evidence to suggest that such public support posed any problems or constraints. Virtually all *Amber Films'* productions I have reviewed to date appear to have followed a more or less similar pattern. We now turn to the second British case study, namely, *Stratham Productions*.

Stratham Productions

Ethnographic research at *Stratham Productions* showed that from its inception, the company has worked primarily with community groups across London. In the production of documentaries and news content, the four core filmmakers at the company attach great importance to building a 'mutually beneficial' relationship with community groups, as one of the core staff called Debbie comments:

> We respond to individuals - not solely issues - and take the time to develop a relationship that is mutually beneficial with participants [...] There is a focus on access and participation across [our] work, which covers themes of urbanism, regeneration, gentrification, displacement etc. and social conscience [...] *Stratham Productions* is often commissioned to work in partnership with a number of community-led projects as a media partner. Although this does not always end in a film, it's still worthwhile because offshoots emerge from which many films have been made.
>
> (Debbie)

During my fieldwork at the company I assisted on one of the 'offshoots' called *Nature before Olympics,* which comprised a series of short documentaries. Following up on how the idea for this documentary emerged to ascertain whether socio-political goals were identifiable, I learnt that the selection of the subject matter treated in this serial documentary stemmed from ideas and actual experiences gained while *Stratham Productions* worked on a commissioned five-year partnership programme with community-led projects around London.

Work on *Nature before Olympics* began in 2005 after it transpired that several natural spaces were to make way for the construction of some of the facilities for the London 2012 Olympics games. The short film series documented the resistance of a number of communities to these plans both before and during the construction phase, helping them to express their emotional situation (Grigsby 1995, 8–9 *cf.* Kilborn and Izod 1997, 7). Some participants took a leading role in the making of this documentary in line with civic values, but professional imperatives emphasised that the direction and power needed to be in the hands of a film director or production crew (Rosenthal 2007). Chapman (2007), for example, contends that relinquishing too much authorship and power on the part of the director or production crew "amounts to a gamble with creative vision" (15). In my role as a participant observer at *Stratham Productions*, I became aware that the company's core filmmaking team was very much aware of this conundrum.

Indeed, in an effort to maintain the 'creative vision' of *Nature before Olympics* and to observe the conventions of 'documentary discourse', the core team assumed a more creative and directorial role at times, and at others they let community groups lead the creative vision. On many occasions when *Stratham Productions'* filmmakers dictated the vision, I witnessed that "events [were] specially orchestrated to make them more amenable to capture by the camera [while] [i]n other cases subjects [were] directed in

such a way that their 'contributions' fit[ted] in with the film-makers' pre-
conceived notions of what [was] required" (Kilborn and Izod 1997, 199).
Whatever its limitations, this participatory approach points to a mostly
skilful negotiation between socio-political and professional imperatives.
We now look at *Fotolabor* – the first of the two German case studies.

Fotolabor

Fotolabor similarly works in partnership to help local communities in
Berlin in – as Hans, one of *Fotolabor's* two founding members put it –
"finding and expressing their voice in their own way and on things that
mean something to them", an expression that can take the form of "an
exhibition or a slide show on the Internet or as a book or poster or film...".
A review of documentary evidence at *Fotolabor* – in conjunction with data
from interview accounts – demonstrates that a recurring theme in the company's work over the decades concerns urbanisation and related issues.

A documentary that exemplifies this is *The Victims of Urbanisation
(2004)*, which tells a story of how local government initiatives aimed at
redeveloping the inner city since the early 1980s have fostered a two-fold
pattern. On the one hand, increasing urbanisation has reshaped Berlin into
one of the most prominent metropolitan cities in Europe, which is beneficial in a number of ways. For example, many old housing estates have been
refurbished or demolished, giving way to new corporate blocks that have
attracted businesses and investments. In turn, these have contributed to
the city's economic growth in terms of employment and tax income.

On the other hand, however, this development has fostered a shortage
of reasonably affordable residential units, rendering the rent prices in
these blocks extremely high. Working-class tenants, the unemployed and
immigrants with habitually low disposable income find it especially hard
to afford such exorbitant prices; they have been hit hardest. The documentary observed that many have not only lost their homes but are being
pushed out of the inner city and out of sight of the general public and
foreign tourists. Indeed, a look at the photographic record assembled by
Sven – the second co-founding member of the company – over the decades shows many disadvantaged individuals retreating to the "numerous backyards of the city", which are themselves "being clamped down
on". Not only have such individuals "been thrown out of these places",
according to Sven, but "a huge portion of the city's history has also
been destroyed". Having recorded these developments for years through
social photography and documentary film, Sven is very critical of the
unresponsiveness of politics and mainstream media to these injustices.
Of this grim scenario, Sven remarks:

> We keep making the general public aware of the fact that [this]
> leaves many people on the fringes of society who no longer quite fit

into the mould [of the city] due to social and political problems and are [therefore] displaced. They are driven out of areas... areas where a given image of the city has to be cultivated and in this image, a certain and increasingly large group of people does not fit in. That is the dark side of this city.

(Sven)

From a civic perspective, *The Victims of Urbanisation* engages "with aspects of the real world that [have] some drama and perhaps importance – that we might do something about a particular situation or at least should be aware of it" (Chapman 2007, 2). In doing so, it demonstrates "special relevance to the socio-political world [in the sense that it] help[s] us to gain a better sense of the place which we as individual citizens might occupy within the larger order [and reminds us] that what we are witnessing can, potentially at least, spill over into the world which we or others like us inhabit" (Kilborn and Izod 1997, 231).

My ethnographic fieldwork revealed that professionalism in the production of *The Victims of Urbanisation* was reflected in the prolonged years of observation, research, holding conversations with victims, conducting interviews with local authorities and studying archival records on the subject. As such, aspects of real-life experiences were merged with other material gathered through imagery from social photography and skilfully crafted into the documentary. From an artistic perspective, filmmakers at *Fotolabor* utilised the documentary to explain the process of increasing urbanisation by making connections with its associated problems in an imaginative and compelling way. Although the documentary was unable to secure public subsidy because it was "too disturbing for [the local authorities]", it was well received at screenings where it made good sales and was even purchased by a broadcaster. I now discuss *Dahlberg Productions*.

Dahlberg Productions

Founded by Bianca and a colleague in 1981, *Dahlberg Productions* has predominantly engaged with themes concerning the German-Jewish community in Berlin, across Germany and in Europe as reflected below:

> In essence, our work is all about Jewish life. It's not primarily about the past but we do obviously allude to the historical circumstances and how we think they relate to certain aspects of life today. If you watch public service television, you will notice that [Jewish life] is reported in terms of the Holocaust [...] or in terms of the rich or the Middle East crisis. Such reporting is usually laden with stereotypes that are always reproduced. We try to counter [these] and lots of other misperceptions [...] with testimonies of contemporary

witnesses [...] If at the end of it all, people can relate with and think about what they've seen and heard, I can't think of a better way that reflects what the real situation is, [portraying] ordinary [Jewish] people who like everyone else have problems and may be rich or poor.

(Bianca)

The company thrived on commissions from diverse broadcasters until the mid-1990s to make documentary films covering Jewish community and public life in former East Germany that Bianca noted "was not well known in the West". A documentary that typifies the company's work is titled *Vivid Memories (1987)*. It tells a story of a high-ranking Secret Service officer in the Nazi regime military who is tried in court decades after the Holocaust ended for war crimes against humanity.

The documentary makes use of the verbatim aesthetic by drawing on extensive research and on edited scripts from the court trial to engage with subject matter, and in doing so, comes across as powerfully persuasive, authentic and informative, mainly because it provides a unique forum for protagonists to speak for themselves. *Vivid Memories* was financially successful, and it is used as an educational resource as are a number of the company's documentaries that I studied. Strikingly, a number of the documentaries I reviewed, including the most recent ones, appeared to follow a similar formula.

However, the scaling back of commissions following structural developments in the German broadcasting landscape since the early 1990s has gradually compelled *Dahlberg Productions* to turn to alternative sources of income to sustain its work. My ethnographic research indicated that the company has since coped in two main ways: producing commissioned industrial films and maintaining a regular broadcast news bulletin via Berlin's iconic open-access channel, which tends not to interfere with filmmakers' work provided such work fulfils the basic technical and ethical (and sometimes artistic) standards of the station. The former has involved mostly non-corporate films that have featured in anniversary events, commemorative rituals, exhibitions, presentations, public-service announcements and artistic installations. Examples include exhibition films for memorial centres and sites, as well as associated educational programmes and information events that aim to preserve a verbal and visual record of the causes, process and consequences of the Holocaust.

A closer engagement with the audio-visual news bulletin showed that it engages with the contemporary lived experiences of Jewish people across Europe. Often, contributions utilise the past to provide context and relevance in illuminating such experiences. Additionally, the news bulletin plays a kind of 'community-building' role that requires the facilitation of and engagement with consensus building around Jewish collective memory and its construction, interpretation and representation. The prolonged, in-depth engagement with multiple views on key issues around concepts, historical narratives, authorial voice and terms of reference among many other things has meant that *Dahlberg Productions* has established itself as an authority on Jewish issues. This may be viewed as the company's greatest strength, but Bianca has indicated that oscillating between the community-building role and working to professional news-making standards that may require adhering to objectivity and its associated norms of balance and impartiality can be very challenging.

The Question of Autonomy and Perceptions of Work

Like all cultural production, community filmmaking is not always insulated from the art-commerce/subsidy dialectic, which positions the relationship between creativity and commerce as one that is highly 'polarised' and ridden with 'conflict and struggle' (Hesmondhalgh 2007, 70). This means that the capacity of filmmakers to shape their work and exercise freedom from particular demands can be severely constrained by various factors, thereby generating difficulties. Community filmmakers under study in this chapter have tended to respond in four different but interrelated ways: diversifying their income base; compromising between their autonomy and receipt of subsidy; embracing low-cost production strategies; and branching out into other content dissemination formats. For example, *Amber Films* strategically widened their income base right from the outset by investing and reinvesting in property to safeguard their autonomy (Dickinson 1999, 251).

Filmmakers at *Fotolabor* strive to achieve a balance between retaining independence and receiving subsidy as the following example demonstrates. In 2006, producers made *What Now for Johanna?*, a documentary that tells a story of Johanna, a 67-year-old unemployed, disabled woman. The documentary responded to a series of government reforms, which became known as *Agenda 2010,* that were introduced by the Social Democratic/Green coalition government in 2003. *Agenda 2010* aimed to boost the weak economy by reducing health-care and welfare benefits, restructuring labour regulations and reforming the pension system. *What Now for Johanna?* set out to highlight the adverse effects these reforms would have on disadvantaged groups across the country, particularly the unemployed, the ill, the disabled and the poor. According to Hans, although it was widely believed that *Agenda 2010* would spark economic growth and reduce unemployment, it was at the expense of the disadvantaged.

However, authorities declined to fund *What Now for Johanna?* noting that it was "too polemic and biased". It received funding only after producers addressed these concerns "by rework[ing] a few scenes", pointing to a compromise between autonomy and demands from subsidy. Filmmakers at *Stratham Productions* have averted this kind of compromising by incorporating workshops into their core work, adopting "low budget tactics for producing stuff [such as] getting the best out of last year's technology rather than keeping buying new stuff", "recycling stuff" and acquiring subsidies from Europe without strings attached. All these serve as strategies to diversify the company's funding base. *Stratham Productions* also makes effective use of social media and film screening festivals to disseminate its work, a strategy that is instrumental in helping the company to circumvent commercial pressures exerted by mainstream broadcasters and cinemas.

Owing to declining broadcast commissions, *Dahlberg Productions* gradually broadened its repertoire by creating a regular broadcast news bulletin and undertaking non-commercial industrial productions, as we have seen. The sponsored films that earn *Dahlberg Productions* a significant additional income tend to publicise services offered by a range of Jewish community organisations, particularly in the areas of family and social care and health as well as entertainment and leisure. A number of sponsored films I studied recorded rare footage of Jewish heritage in former Eastern Germany and as such were featured in exhibitions in memory institutions and used as learning resources in education.

A collation of insights drawn from interviews, reviews of documentary evidence and my field notes taken as a participant observer indicated that the community filmmakers under study perceived their work following conflicting imperatives and constraints from public support along four main lines: professionalism, autonomy, impact and passionate attachment to work. In terms of professionalism, Murray Martin of *Amber Films* spoke about how "they've always argued for professionalism [meaning] you're only a film-maker if you live off film-making..." (Dickinson 1999, 250). He underlined the need to professionalise without compromising *Amber Films'* ideals by selling members' skills as crew to television in order to develop their craft but wouldn't make mainstream television films (Newsinger 2009, 132).

Charles at *Stratham Productions* identified accreditation problems the company faced when he noted that "there's been numerous situations where we've gone on a shoot and we've been told: 'Oh no, you can't come in or you can't film this or that because you're not officially accredited...' Well it's not about some kind of special recognition of a profession. It's about information and control". All the filmmakers under study emphasised the versatility of community filmmaking, which they noted constituted a range of professional tasks spanning research, making grant applications, doing accounts and project managing, among many others.

Community filmmakers also stressed the significance of freedom in being able to determine the terms of their creative engagement, noting the desire "to work independently", to be able "to work outside of [mainstream] television" and "outside of the mainstream film industry". Autonomy meant being able "to try out things", to "fail without being blamed for it" and "not to allow funding to dictate the nature and content of work". Closely linked to this is the aspect of impact, which manifested itself predominantly through being able to "influence public discussions", "discovering stories that need to be told" and "helping to give a voice to those that are not heard or outright ignored". In turn, passionate attachment to work was fostered and displayed in the gratification derived from the enjoyment and enrichment of working with communities, despite the sometimes very challenging working conditions.

Conclusion

This chapter has explored three interrelated aspects, namely, a) how British and German community filmmakers respond to the interplay among professional, artistic and commercial imperatives alongside their core civic function, b) how such community filmmakers respond to systemic pressures and c) how they perceive their work following conflicting imperatives and systemic pressures. The case study companies make the most of their long-term involvement in and knowledge of the communities they serve to facilitate the expression and representation of multiple lived experiences by documenting the impact of pressing issues affecting community and public life, something that chimes in with recent research in England (Malik, Chapain and Comunian 2014). With the exception of *Amber Films*, the rest are struggling and have had to adopt pragmatism to endure. What Willemen (1989, 10) once argued for Third Cinema, I argue for contemporary community filmmaking: for it to be seen as a flexible sphere characterised by research and experimentation, one that adapts to shifting dynamics at work in social struggles and speaks to a socially pertinent discourse that both the mainstream and the authorial cinemas exclude from their regimes of signification.

Socially pertinent discourse here is reflected in the use of (documentary) film as a medium for expression and representation of issues of concern, interest and relevance to local communities in a way that is meaningful to them. Key to this is the role of community filmmakers as 'media partners' in community projects as we have seen and as research elsewhere has shown (Cumming and Norwood 2012). Shifting dynamics at work embody the need for professionalisation and enterprise, not only to highlight the importance of being seen to be professional as the accreditation problems at *Stratham Productions* and news-making values at *Dahlberg Productions* indicate, but also the need to develop strategies to attract income in order to survive and sustain work. It is here that research and experimentation have been instrumental in helping to move beyond (documentary) film to devise other modes of representation and communication that have taken the form of news and informational content provision as is the case with *Stratham Productions* and *Dalberg Productions* and of (social) photography and exhibitions as demonstrated by *Amber Films* and *Fotolabor*. These developments can be said to speak to issues of content and process innovation, something that has presented both opportunities and challenges in which the civic function remains discernible, albeit to varying degrees.

Notes

1 See further details on *Amber Film's* website - http://www.amber-online.com/archives/high-row.
2 Amber Online. "High Row." Accessed July 28, 2015, http://www.amber-online.com/archives/high-row.

References

Berra, John. 2008. *Declarations of Independence: American cinema and the partiality of independent production.* Bristol, UK: Intellect.
Blanchard, Simon. 2001. "A Third Tier of Television: the growth of 'restricted service licence' TV in the UK – Trends and Prospects." Accessed March 5. http://www.bftv.ac.uk/projects/thirdtier.htm.
Blanchard, Simon and Sylvia Harvey. 1983. "The Post-war Independent Cinema – Structure and Organisation." In *British Cinema History*, edited by James Curran and Vincent Porter, 226–242. Totowa, NJ: Barnes & Noble Books.
Catterall, Peter. 1999. *The Making of Channel 4.* London: Cass.
Chapman, Jane. 2007. *Documentary in Practice: filmmakers and production choices.* Cambridge: Polity.
Corner, John. 2000. "Documentary in a Post-documentary Culture? A Note on Forms and their Functions." Accessed July 24. http://www.lboro.ac.uk/research/changing.media/John%20Corner%20paper.htm.
Cumming, Gabriel and Carla Norwood. 2012. "The Community Voice Method: using participatory research and filmmaking to foster dialog about changing landscapes." *Landscape and Urban Planning* 105(4): 434–444.
Dickinson, Margaret. 1999. *Rogue Reels: oppositional film in Britain, 1945–90.* London: British Film Institute.
Harvey, Sylvia. 1978. *May '68 and Film Culture.* London: British Film Institute.
Hesmondhalgh, David. 2007. *The Cultural Industries.* 2nd Edition. Los Angeles: Sage.
Higgins, John W. 1999. "Community Television and the Vision of Media Literacy, Social Action, and Empowerment." *Journal of Broadcasting and Electronic Media* 43(4): 624–644.
Hobson, Dorothy. 2007. *Channel 4: the early years and the Jeremy Isaacs legacy.* London: I.B. Tauris.
Hollander, Ed. 1992. "The Emergence of Small Scale Media." In *The People's Voice: local radio and television in Europe*, edited by Nick Jankowski, Ole Prehn and James Stappers, 7–15. London: John Libbey.
Home Office. 1988. *Broadcasting in the 90s: competition, choice and quality: the government's plans for broadcasting legislation.* London: Her Majesty's Stationery Office.

Hooffacker, Gabriele and Peter Lokk. 2009. "Kurze Geschichte der 'Presse von Unten." In *Buergermedien, Neue Medien, Medienalternativen*, edited by Gabriele Hooffacker, 9–32. Munich: Verlag Dr Gabriele Hooffacker.

Huettner, Bernd and Christoph Nitz. 2009. "Linke Medien Vor and Nach der Internetrevolution." In *Buergermedien, Neue Medien, Medienalternativen*, edited by Gabriele Hooffacker, 33–50. Munich: Verlag Dr Gabriele Hooffacker.

Katz, John S. 2003. "Family Film: ethical implications for consent." In *Image Ethics in the Digital Age*, edited by Larry P. Gross, John S. Katz and Jay Ruby, 327–342. Minneapolis, MN: University of Minnesota Press.

Kilborn, Richard and John Izod. 1997. *An Introduction to Television Documentary: confronting reality*. Manchester: Manchester University Press.

Malik, Sarita, Caroline Chapain and Roberta Comunian. 2014. *Spotlight on Community Filmmaking: a report on community filmmaking and cultural diversity research*. London and Birmingham: Brunel University, the University of Birmingham and King's College London.

Martin, Murray. 2002. "An Oral History of British Photography." *British Library Sound Archive*. (Catalogue Number-F10984-F10988).

Matarasso, Francois. 2000. *Did It Make a Difference? Evaluating Community-Based Arts and Business Partnerships*. London: Arts & Business.

McIntyre, Philip. 2012. *Creativity and Cultural Production: issues for media practice*. Basingstoke: Palgrave Macmillan.

Medienzentren und Videogruppen in der BRD. 1984, "'Das andere Video' Zehn Jahre politische Medienarbeit. Ein gemeinsamer Verleihkatalog von Medienzentren und Videogruppen." Freiburg/Frankfurt/M: Medienwerkstatt Freiburg/EDN video.

Miége, Bernard. 1989. *The Capitalisation of Production*. New York: International General.

Negt, Oskar and Alexander Kluge. 1993. *Public Sphere and Experience: Toward an Analysis of the Bourgeois and Proletarian Public Sphere*. Minneapolis: University of Minnesota Press.

Newbury, Darren. 2002. "Documentary Practices and Working Class-Culture: an interview with Murray Martin (Amber Films and Side Photographic Gallery)." *Visual Studies* 17(2): 113–128.

Newsinger, Jack. 2009. "From the Grassroots: regional film policy and practice in England." PhD diss., University of Nottingham.

Nichols, Bill. 2001. *Introduction to Documentary*. Bloomington, IN: Indiana University Press.

Nigg, Heinz and Graham Wade.1980. *Community Media: community communication in the UK: video, local TV, film and photography*. Zurich: Regenbogen Verlag.

Oakley, Kate. 2009. "'Art Works' – Cultural Labour Markets: A Literature Review." *Creativity, Culture and Education Series*. Accessed October 17. http://www.creativitycultureeducation.org/research-impact/literature-reviews.

Peterson, Richard A. 1982. "Five Constraints on the Production of Culture: law, technology, market, organizational structure and occupational careers." *Journal of Popular Culture* 16(2): 143–153.

Prehn, Ole. 1992. "From Small Scale Utopianism to Large Scale Pragmatism: trend and prospects for community oriented local radio and television."

In *The People's Voice: local radio and television in Europe*, edited by Nick Jankowski, Ole Prehn and James Stappers, 247–268. London: John Libbey.

Rees, Alan L. 1999. *A History of Experimental Film and Video: from the canonical avant-garde to contemporary British practice.* London: British Film Institute.

Rosenthal, Alan. 2007. *Writing, Directing, and Producing Documentary Films and Videos.* 4th Edition. Carbondale: Southern Illinois University Press.

Shaw, Phyllida. 2001. *Creative Connections: business and the arts working together to create a more inclusive society.* London: Arts & Business.

Swann, Paul. 1979. "The British Documentary Film Movement, 1926–1946." PhD diss., University of Leeds.

Willemen, Paul. 1989. "The Third Cinema Question: notes and reflections." In *Questions of Third Cinema*, edited by Jim Pines and Paul Willemen, 1–29. London: British Film Institute.

9 Participatory Production Processes in Community Filmmaking During Urban Regeneration in Dublin

Eileen Leahy

Introduction

This chapter contrasts the participatory production processes of three community filmmaking projects from Dublin to discuss how cultural production can support communities through the difficult process of urban regeneration. It highlights the practices and objectives of community filmmaking during a period of intense change for communities and shows how participation in cultural activity helps groups maintain their identity under the threat of change. This chapter also cautions against the danger of allowing community filmmaking to be co-opted for commercial gain, as globalism has generated intense competition between cities and prioritised the commercial motivation of cultural development over the social justice focus of community development.

This chapter approaches film as a social and cultural practice, in which culture is defined as a process, involving interconnected systems of meaning, that constructs a society's way of life. The analysis of the production processes of community films made in Dublin, Ireland, uses an interdisciplinary methodological approach, which looks at participatory filmmaking in its cultural and social environment. This necessitates an examination of the theoretical underpinning of notions such as urban regeneration, participation and social exclusion. The chapter is based on a qualitative research analysis bringing together findings from five semi-interviews, round-table discussions and participant-observation with the filmmakers and communities involved over the period of 2009 to 2012. The filmmaking process is explored as a cultural activity in which members of a community participate, and this approach is reinforced by textual analysis to examine how the production processes are reflected in the texts. The films addressed vary in terms of form, with artist cinema, drama and experimental film examined as examples of community filmmaking in a particular context of urban regeneration.

The rest of the chapter is structured as follows:

- a discussion of the relevant theoretical literature, focusing on urban regeneration, theories of participation and critiques of current cultural policy;

- an analysis of the community filmmaking practices encountered in Dublin, with examples from Fatima Mansions, a social housing estate in Dublin city;
- a discussion of how participatory film production allowed the Fatima community to rebuild its identity and its relation to place and
- To conclude, some comments on the implications for community and for urban development.

Theoretical Background

Urban regeneration has been important in economies' transition from industrialism to post-industrialism, with competition between cities intensifying under globalism. Urban regeneration involving the redevelopment of residential areas in cities is part of this process and typically involves an attempt to solve the social issues associated with deindustrialisation. In Ireland, urban regeneration usually refers to the regeneration of social housing estates in disadvantaged areas of the city and is undertaken through public-private partnerships. Described as a means for local authorities to fund the upgrade of its decaying social housing as well as a solution for the social exclusion experienced by residents of such estates, urban regeneration has also provided private property developers with opportunities to develop local authority-owned sites in the city, through policies that ultimately promote gentrification and favour profit over social gain (Hearne 2009).

Urban regeneration poses a threat to community in very practical ways: residents are relocated while housing is being demolished and rebuilt. This means a reconfiguration of the community when some residents do not return and new residents arrive in the newly privatised parts of the estates (Tenants First 2005, 1–3). These intense changes destabilise the community's identity. According to social anthropologist Anthony P. Cohen (1985) communities use culture to reassert themselves when faced with this kind of major social change. He argues that there is an apparent homogeneity of social forms under modern capitalism but that this is merely superficial, masking real and significant differences between groups. Crucially, he argues that the more pressure there is to conform, the more communities assert their boundaries symbolically through culture (70), and cultural activity becomes more important when the community is undergoing change (36–38). At the same time, the community development aspect of urban regeneration encourages participation in culture as a way for the community to deal with their changing circumstances and to promote the participation of the community in the regeneration process.

Advocates of community development argue that by participating in cultural activity disadvantaged communities can engage in the process of understanding and challenging their oppression. Through their active participation in social, political and cultural processes of change, marginalised groups can promote democracy, as much by challenge and resistance as by consent. Collaborative and participatory community media and cultural practices are considered to be an important element of this process (Gillan 2010, 132–136, Howley 2010, 184, De Michiel 2008, Meade and Shaw 2007, 413, 417–419).

However, a number of weaknesses in these approaches have been identified. Community development often seeks to promote participation as positive in its own right, separate from the social, political and economic contexts of inequality (Gillan 2010, 133, Carpentier 2009, 411–412). While much of the literature on community arts and media argues that participation is in itself empowering for the individuals and groups involved, it has been noted that notions of empowerment are often inadequately defined, without any evidence of its benefits to groups and with vague methodologies for measuring its achievement (Carpentier 2011, 14, Gillan 2010, 133, Belfiore 2009, 99–101). According to Nico Carpentier (2011) the concept of participation itself has been used in such a wide variety of settings that the term has come to mean 'everything and nothing', with its political import unacknowledged. He argues for the centrality of participation to democracy but shows how the conflation of access, interaction and participation has obscured the link between participation and power and obstructed the equalising objectives of participatory approaches in media (13–28). In this way, a veneer of participation can be attached to initiatives that merely provide access or interaction rather than full participation with equalised decision-making.

A number of further critiques demonstrate how recent cultural policies have co-opted ideas of participation in the service of regressive public policies or for commercial gain, especially in relation to recent discourses on the creative economy (Lysgård 2013, Stevenson, Rowe and McKay 2010, Gray 2007, Hesmondlagh and Pratt 2005). In this regard, Eleonora Belfiore (2009) provides a damning indictment of recent public discourse on the subsidised cultural sector, in which she argues that intentionally impenetrable writing and a lack of concern for clarity or truth obscures numerous, unquestioned assumptions about the arts and obstructs the empirical measurement of the effect of arts and culture on people. This is relevant in the context of urban regeneration because the cultural industries are central to current ideas of urban development, in which clusters of creative industries are thought to enhance the quality of life in cities and to boost economic growth (for examples, see Mould 2015, Landry 2012, Landry and Bianchini 1995). Cultural development involves a range of planning and development approaches to making cities more 'creative', ranging from the provision of cultural facilities to attracting and facilitating creative industries and personnel (Lysgård 2013). Film production can be considered a central player, cited

repeatedly as a creative industry, used as a model for flexible speciali-
sation, or providing an example of creative clusters of small businesses
that drive economic growth in urban contexts (Dahlstrom and Hermelin
2007, Scott 2006). Film has also been considered of importance in urban
regeneration strategies of place making and remaking, where the gloss
attached to the film and television industries allows the commodification
of redeveloped locales (Mathews 2010). Therefore, film and television
production are considered important in implementing cultural development policies. This leads to the question of whether community filmmaking, said to be based on and guided by community development's social
justice principles, has actually been co-opted in the service of the more
commercially focused aims of cultural development (Pratt 2010, 16).

At the same time, community filmmaking is itself open to critique.
Ruby (1992), for example, points to the lack of documentation on the
extent and depth of involvement of community groups in filmmaking
and argues that if the collaboration were truly based on parity, then
the community would not need outsiders to mediate or facilitate the
production (51–54). Another criticism concerns the implicit and explicit
objectives of community filmmaking. Janine Marchessault (1995), for
example, shows how the hugely influential Canadian National Film
Board's Challenge for Change (CFC) programme of the 1960s and
1970s was largely aimed at integrating the margins into the mainstream
of Canadian life, without transforming the power relations between the
two (134). She also argues that the formal properties of CFC's participatory films and videos involved the rejection of style in favour of direct
speech, an anti-aesthetic trope that characterised most of the CFC films.
The non-professional look of these films suggested authenticity, honesty
and directness, which obscured their mediated, government-sponsored
context and created political ambiguity by giving the impression of
the camera as a faithful recording apparatus servicing the community.
She further argues that the production of films through the CFC programmes worked to defuse direct action, containing and neutralising
difference and stifling resistance (137–143). These are arguments that
could also apply to community filmmaking in Ireland during the Celtic
Tiger era when the primary aims were to promote social inclusion for
disadvantaged groups.

Social exclusion has recently become the dominant discourse of public
policy in relation to disadvantage. According to Marie Moran (2006),
the rhetoric of 'social exclusion' has substituted discourses of inequality
and obscured the structural causes and material conditions of poverty,
constructing exclusion as an individual problem and locating responsibility at the individual and community levels, thereby releasing the state
and mainstream population from accountability. She argues that 'social
exclusion' as a term is used to signify a wide and diverse range of social
and political issues unproblematically and uncritically. Difficulties with

definitions and conceptual understandings of social exclusion mean that a consensus on what constitutes 'social exclusion' may be impossible to achieve, and critics contend that this is particularly relevant in the current era of partnership approaches to alleviating disadvantage, where a wide variety of institutions, organisations and groups with disparate objectives and interests work together (181–187). Due to this lack of critical engagement, policies and strategies to tackle social exclusion confuse social inclusion with integration and seek to normalise disadvantaged groups without challenging the status quo. For example, Moran (2006) argues that Irish social policy dealing with social exclusion focuses on participation of disadvantaged groups "in sports, arts, culture, education, 'the information society' and the community" or in the labour market, without any attempts to increase their participation in governance or decision-making. She points out that replacing the language of equality and poverty in Irish policy with the language of social inclusion "allows for retention of political kudos associated with a concern for social change, without the compunction to carry out the structural and redistributive reform necessary to achieve this" (190–191). In light of the conflation of cultural development with community development, of participation with access and of social inclusion with integration, we can see how community filmmaking can present itself as an attractive panacea for participation in urban development or even for participation in culture itself. Examples of participatory filmmaking in a Dublin context raise some interesting questions in this respect.

Community Filmmaking Practices in Fatima Mansions, Dublin

Fatima Mansions was a small, inner-city social housing complex, built in the late 1950s in a south central district of Dublin. This complex of apartments or 'flats' housed a small community of less than 400 households and had become a victim of the residualisation of social housing over the 1980s in Dublin. Grassroots community activism initially drove the urban regeneration of this estate, but during the economic boom of the late 1990s plans for regeneration were handed over to a Public Private Partnership by Dublin City Council, perhaps because as land values escalated over the Celtic Tiger period this became a valuable location. The local community fought hard to remain involved in the regeneration, which was completed in 2009, just as the economy collapsed, so that much of the community development component that the local community fought to retain was abandoned due to budget cuts.

Media was a key component of community development in Fatima, through interventions in mainstream media representation (Conway, Corcoran and Cahill 2012, Donohue and Dorman 2006), production of participatory media (Ananny, Strokhecker and Biddick 2004), arts and cultural projects, communications strategies and digital media education (Donohue and Dorman 2006), to name a few. The three film projects from Fatima that are examined in this chapter were made as part of the community development process in the area. They emerge from three very different initiatives, an oral history through drama project, film production training and an art project. Each of these three projects had very different aims, and each film differs greatly from the others, although all three were made in a very small community in this compact inner-city location.

Women with Balls (Fatima History Project 2006), a dramatised mockumentary, tells the story of a football match between two opposing teams and developed as a film from experimental community theatre in which a local group looked at Fatima Mansions' history through the personal stories of participants. The Fatima History Project was formed as a community development initiative to find the lost history that would explain the disadvantage experienced by residents of the estate (Whyte 2012). The group included local community development worker Joanie Whyte and local artist Kieran Doyle O'Brien, who facilitated and recorded the group's stories and improvisational drama. The use of film developed when the documentation of the project evolved from audio recording to video. The goal was to use personal and family histories to develop a social analysis of the circumstances of this community's oppression. Workshops were based on the process of "dig where you stand", derived from Paulo Freire's work, which aims to delve into the lived experience of ordinary people in order to uncover the hidden past of a community, or group, that has been omitted from historical records.

Thus the justification for community filmmaking in Fatima came from the history of oppression, particularly internalised oppression, and attempts to place the conditions of Fatima in the wider social context in which national and local government policies, as well as social change, contributed to the degradation of the Fatima Mansions estate. Role-playing was an important part of the workshop process, and this led to the group's performing dramatic productions to share the learning with other communities. Making a film allowed the dissemination of this learning as DVD copies of the film could be exhibited widely (Whyte 2012). *Women with Balls* dramatizes the oral history of the community by fictionalising a range of complex interpersonal, community and social relationships as a match between opposing football teams, drawing on the friendly rivalry that has historically existed between Fatima Mansions and a neighbouring estate, Dolphin House, to symbolically define the community.

After completing this first film, the Fatima History Project decided to form Fatima Film Productions and get some professional training in order to make a series of ten short films. A group trained with actor-director Vinny Murphy for over a year. Although Murphy's community filmmaking practice is embedded in community development and community arts, his approach uses the conventional structures and processes of the film industry with strictly defined roles and methods, rather than a collective production process or experimental methods. Murphy contends that participants in community filmmaking can learn a great deal from being treated in exactly the same way as a professional team. He suggests that this hierarchical approach facilitates critical media literacy, with practical skills, teamwork and collaborative practices central to the learning in film, because filmmaking is, by necessity, a collaborative endeavour. He believes that working together in such a structured way has a transformative impact on individuals through the mutual dependency, cooperation and bonding that is a by-product of collaboration and that personal and community development is facilitated by the framework this collaboration provides. Participants are assigned, or choose, specific roles, from script-writing, directing, sound recording or camera operating, lighting, wardrobe or assistant directing and so on. These roles are adhered to strictly, just as in the film industry. Murphy believes that this allows the group to develop a variety of personal as well as professional skills. (Murphy 2012). *Dolls House* (Murphy 2010) was the first film made by Fatima Film Productions, and, although funding has been cut so that the planned series of films has not been realised, film production training continues to be provided in the community.

In contrast, *The Day in Question* (What's the Story Collective, 2010) was an art film, and therefore its aims and approach were very different than each of the other two films. This film emerged from a long-term initiative, in which relationships were built up over a number of years and a project developed involving youth workers, young people and artist Fiona Whelan who worked collectively on personal stories dealing with issues of power. The group was initiated in 2007 by Whelan, who invited youth workers and young people to collaborate on sharing personal stories of power in a collaborative art project. They began by examining their own personal experiences of power and powerlessness. Each member of the collective shared a personal story anonymously, which was audio recorded and transcribed. These were read aloud in the group, and an event was staged in which they were read to an invited audience. At this point it was noted that many of the stories from the young people involved their negative experience of policing locally. As a result, the collective developed a collaboration with An Garda Síochána (the Irish police force), with officers reading the young people's stories aloud at a public event called *The Day in Question* at the Irish Museum of Modern Art (IMMA) in 2009. This event was documented on film, and this film, although originally intended as a record of the event, was edited as an artist film installation and screened as part of a wider installation during the collective's artist residency, Policing Dialogues, at The Lab in Foley Street, Dublin in 2010 (What's the Story? Collective 2010).

The objectives of each film project in Fatima varied considerably, and each project also adopted very different approaches, only *Dolls House* was made as a result of a specific filmmaking initiative, with a professional film industry approach throughout. For the other two projects the filming came after extensive development of the projects themselves, and the filmmaking approach developed organically in line with each of the projects. *Women with Balls* was completely amateur in terms of technical skills and participants learned by doing; however, local visual artist and illustrator Kieran Doyle O'Brien, who filmed the action and edited the film, played an important part in shaping the film visually. *The Day in Question* relied on professional camera work from local photographer and filmmaker Enda O'Brien and was directed by artist Fiona Whelan, with professional editing from Fast Forward Productions. The film is collectively produced but has a sole author-director with a combination of amateur, artist and professional filmmaking input contributing to the final film.

Thus, we see very different participatory processes at work, with a variety of developmental and educational outcomes. The films themselves also function as tools for sharing learning and experiences with other communities and with the wider public. The participatory processes through which these films were made vary from collective to collaborative, so that the filmmaking process can involve a diversity of community film approaches to achieve a multiplicity of objectives. There are a number of questions around whether those objectives can be achieved through participation.

One question concerns whether participation in community filmmaking in the contexts of urban regeneration is in the interests of the community or mainly serves to homogenise the communities involved. It can also be argued that community film in Fatima has facilitated the integration of this marginalised community into mainstream Dublin, rather than transforming the unequal power relationships that caused their marginalisation. Although some of the films question the basis of oppression and involve the contextualisation of disadvantage within the wider social and economic environments, on the whole they do not provide solutions beyond allowing the community to take a place within the mainstream. This is not to suggest that participation in cultural production is not of value, but that participation in itself can function as consolation for adversity without seeking to change the circumstances of that adversity. Most community filmmaking is mediated through a middle class lens, in the form of professional filmmaker or artist 'facilitators' who help the community to realise film projects or train members in filmmaking. It is difficult to assess the extent to which this mediation impacts on the participation of individual community members, and on the content of the films, without long-term participant observation of participatory production processes. In those few instances where there is no professional mediation the films, as cultural products, can be marginalised for a variety of reasons, not least the lack of resources, knowledge or access on the part of the filmmaking group. *Women with Balls* is a case in point; the film is not available online or on DVD, and even information about the film is scant and hard to come by. Films made through professional facilitation, regardless of their original objectives, are more likely to be extensively documented, exhibited or screened at festivals or other events and valued as cultural productions in themselves.

It is noteworthy that the non-professionally produced community films can also be undervalued by the communities themselves. Again, *Women with Balls* is a case in point. This film has been very popular at local screenings and has been considered more "interesting to watch" than its professionally mediated counterparts (Murphy 2012). However, the community decided after making this film that it needed professional expertise and launched Fatima Film Productions with professional training and facilitation to make further films. The community underestimates the significance of their achievement in producing a film with little experience, minimal, piecemeal funding and no real infrastructure. At the same time, professional intervention has not achieved the objectives aimed for, ostensibly due to funding cuts, but arguably also due to the demands that professionalisation might make on the community with a switch of focus from the creative process to industry standards in the final product.

Nevertheless, in spite of these reservations, I would suggest that the community filmmaking process is useful for the communities involved in several ways, primarily through building and sustaining the community involved as well as through reaffirming the community at times of intense change. In addition, in the context of urban regeneration the community can be expected to change. Cultural production allows communities to experiment with changing roles and relationships within the community itself and in the wider social world. The filmmaking production process can also allow the community to reaffirm its existing relationships and values, competencies, norms and rules. The following discussion demonstrates some of the ways in which participation in filmmaking allows the community to sustain itself.

Discussion

One of the ways in which the film production context creates community for the participants is through a resistance to the domination of space by capitalism. Filmmaking allows the community to physically claim the space when they film in it, thereby resisting their exclusion via the construction of place by capitalism, while also offering an alternative construction or imagining, not only of the place inhabited but also of the community, as David Harvey (1993) describes (6–23). This is particularly relevant in the context of urban regeneration, where private developers and building contractors have visibly and disruptively occupied the physical places of the community, demolishing buildings and putting up barriers around building sites, along with the very obvious and tangible presence of a large number of construction workers and the noise, dust and traffic disruptions that are caused.

By forming, or working with, a film production crew the community can physically and visibly occupy those places while filming in them, thus reclaiming and creating them anew, a feature of the filmmaking process that is referred to in the texts. For example, *Women with Balls* opens on the community members wandering around the boundary of the construction site and boarding a Luas tram, which is significant in claiming the Luas for the community because it had recently been launched as a new transport system in Dublin during 2004. Another scene provides a lengthy focus on the football team retrieving their ball after Winnie kicks it over the fence, topped with barbed wire, separating the construction site from the football pitch. The team reacts to the recovery of the ball as though it is a victory. In another occupation of place, *The Day in Question* allowed young people from the Rialto community to lay claim to the museum and gallery spaces of IMMA and The Lab, the kind of spaces from which they are typically excluded. Their occupation of IMMA was significant because this is a cultural facility very close to the neighbourhood in distance but remote in terms of cultural engagement. The collective was in the museum neither as producers nor consumers of high art but as participants in a dialogue about power so that for the duration of the event the space itself was transformed from that of a bastion of high culture to one of engagement and community. In addition, there was a parallel occupation occurring where the group occupied the same space as their nemeses, the Gardaí, simultaneously and on an equal footing, so that power relations were reconstructed during the event. The collective's residency at the Lab, an art space near the city centre, was also important in terms of the community's claiming the gallery space over a period of time as the artists and cultural producers, rather than as the subjects of cultural production.

The film *Dolls House* also involved the occupation of place, in this case the film was mostly set in an interior location in one of the newly built apartments, into which Fatima residents were about to be moved. The filming could be said to offer the community the opportunity to physically occupy this space and to define it before individuals and families moved in and therefore to lay a prior claim to that of the newer tenants and purchasers who would also be moving in on completion.

Michel de Certeau's (1984) understanding that dominant, controlling interests order society through place, whereas ordinary people evade this control by operationalising place as space (117) is pertinent in this regard. Thus it can be argued that the community film production context is a tactic that subverts the disciplining order of demolition and construction norms and procedures during urban regeneration. During demolition and construction, the community will have been denied access to the spaces it previously inhabited; film production allows community members to retake these places and recreate them as spaces. It might conversely be argued that this opposition of the community to the domination of space by capital reaffirms the community without altering the status quo, as Harvey (1993) describes in relation to regional resistance to capitalism's control of space (24–25). In the case of Fatima the community integrates itself into the regenerated place, or the dominant hegemonic order, without changing the existing power relations. Thus, we see in *Dolls House* that the characters' movement through the city centre shopping area allowed the space of capitalism to be claimed by the community as consumers, instead of as working class, production-line workers who had become excluded from consumerism through unemployment, poverty, drug-use and crime. During the film production process the community members could occupy these spaces of capitalism in a particular way, privileged as cultural producers rather than merely as the consumers the film constructs them as, so that their distinct relation to the production-consumption paradigm is remade.

In addition, the film production process involves a transformation of identity for individual members as well as the community itself. During the liminal period of urban regeneration, the boundaries of the community are fluid and can be remade. As de Certeau (1984) describes, boundaries are established at intersections between communities (124–128), thus the film production context serves as an important intersection of one group, the community, and others, the professional filmmakers or community development organisations for example, where the community's boundary, and therefore its identity, as Cohen (1985) argues, can be re-established. Filmmaking in itself can be ritualistic, and the community film production context can also be understood in terms of a ritual that affirms and reaffirms the community in a liminal space in which the normal rules of social life are suspended and a period of transition operates (Peterson 2003, 241). In the context of urban regeneration, the filmmaking process can be an important means of transforming the community identity in order to facilitate new conditions, such as the arrival and integration of new communities through tenure mixing or the displacement of some individuals from the community, for example.

Conclusion

This chapter has demonstrated that there are various approaches to the community filmmaking process, ranging from dialogue to collaboration to complete collective participation. It explored the diversity of approaches to community filmmaking by communities from Fatima Mansions, including a Freirean oral history project, a film industry approach and a community arts approach. This examination showed that the participatory processes of community filmmaking in Fatima Mansions have been central to community development initiatives, often emerging from projects that have non-film or non-communicative aims.

A critique of the rationale for community filmmaking, involving ideas such as participation, empowerment and social inclusion, was outlined in this chapter, showing a lack of clarity, under theorisation and inadequate documentation. As a result there is a danger of the concept of participation being co-opted in the promotion of the creative economy without any substantive aim to address issues of inequality. Although community film production cannot be shown to achieve all of the aims of social inclusion and empowerment that are promised, it does serve important functions for disadvantaged communities. Community film production allows groups to redefine themselves in the face of change and thus preserve, build or maintain community. This is achieved through filmmaking as a tactic that reclaims commodified places and remakes them as spaces of community. The symbolic boundaries of community are re-established through a ritual of film production as a rite of passage from one identity to another, changing social relationships within the community and constructing community beyond the group for other groups and organisations involved in the process.

This exploration of participatory culture and urban regeneration, despite being limited to a specific Dublin context, points to the tensions between cultural development's appropriation of participatory and collaborative processes in the globalising creative cities endeavour. At the same time, the discussion of community filmmaking's potential for remaking places and spaces also shows how community development can in turn appropriate the creative industries for community, in order to allow local groups to regroup and rebuild themselves during the intense social change engendered by urban regeneration.

References

Ananny, Mike, Carol Strokhecker and Kathleen Biddick. 2004. "Shifting Scales on Common Ground: developing personal expressions and public opinions." *International Journal of Continuing Engineering Education and Life Long Learning* 14 (6): 484–505.

Belfiore, Eleonora. 2009. "On Bullshit in cultural Policy Practice and Research: notes from the British case." *International Journal of Cultural Policy* 15 (3): 343–359.

Carpentier, Nico. 2009. "Participation Is Not Enough: the conditions of possibility of mediated participatory practices." *European Journal of Communication* 24 (4): 407–420.

Carpentier, Nico. 2011. "The Concept of Participation: if they have access and interact, do they really participate?" *CM - časopis za upravljanje komuniciranjem* 6 (21): 13–36.

Certeau, Michel de. 1984. *The Practice of Everyday Life.* Berkeley, CA: University of California Press.

Cohen, Anthony P. 1985. *The Symbolic Construction of Community.* London: Ellis Horwood, Tavistock.

Conway, Brian, Mary P. Corcoran, and Lynne M. Cahill. 2012. "The 'Miracle' of Fatima: media framing and the regeneration of a Dublin housing estate." *Journalism* 13 (5): 551–571.

Dahlstrom, Margareta and Brita Hermelin. 2007. "Creative Industries, Spatiality and Flexibility: the example of film production." *Norsk Geografisk Tidsskrift - Norwegian Journal of Geography* 61 (3): 111–121.

De Michiel, Helen. 2008. "A Mosaic of Practices: public media and participatory culture." *Afterimage* 35 (6): Unpaginated.

Dolls House. 2010. Directed by Vinny Murphy.

Donohue, Joe and Peter Dorman. 2006. *Dream/Dare/Do: a regeneration learning manual.* Dublin: Fatima Groups United.

Foord, Jo. 2009. "Strategies for Creative Industries: an international review." *Creative Industries Journal* 1 (2): 91–113.

Gibson, Lisanne and Debborah Stevenson. 2004. "Urban Space and the Uses of Culture." *International Journal of Cultural Policy* 10 (1): 1–4.

Gillan, Margaret. 2010. "Class and Voice: challenges for grassroots community activists using media in 21st century Ireland." *Interface: A Journal for and about Social Movements* 2 (2): 126–148.

Gray, Clive. 2007. "Commodification and Instrumentality in Cultural Policy." *International Journal of Cultural Policy* 13 (2): 203–215.

Harvey, David. 1993. "From Space to Place and Back Again: reflections on the condition of postmodernity." In *Mapping the futures: local cultures, global change,* by J. Bird, B. Curtis, T. Putnam, G. Robertson and L. Tickner, 3–29. London: Routledge.

Hearne, Rory. 2009. *Origins, Development and Outcomes of Public Private Partnerships in Ireland: the case of PPPs in social housing regeneration.* Dublin: Combat Poverty Agency.

Hesmondlagh, David and Andy C. Pratt. 2005. "Cultural Industries and Cultural Policy." *International Journal of Cultural Policy* 11 (1): 1–13.

Howley, Kevin. 2010. *Understanding Community Media.* London: Sage.

Kovacs, Jason. 2011. "Cultural Planning in Ontario, Canada: arts policy or more?" *International Journal of Cultural Policy* 17 (3): 321–340.

Landry, Charles. 2012. *The Creative City: a toolkit for urban innovators.* London: Earthscan Publications.

Landry, Charles and Franco Bianchini. 1995. *The Creative City.* London: Demos.

Lysgård, Hans Kjetil. 2012. "Creativity, Culture and Urban Strategies: a fallacy in cultural urban strategies." *European Planning Studies* 20 (8): 1281–1300.

Lysgård, Hans Kjetil. 2013. "The Definition of Culture in Culture-Based Urban Development Strategies: antagonisms in the construction of a culture-based development discourse." *International Journal of Cultural Policy* 19 (2): 182–200.

Marchessault, Janine. 1995. "Reflections on the Dispossessed: video and the 'Challenge for Change' experiment." *Screen* 36 (2): 131–146.

Mathews, Vanessa. 2010. "Set Appeal: film space and urban redevelopment." *Social & Cultural Geography* 11 (2): 171–190.

Meade, Rosie and Mae Shaw. 2007. "Community Development and the Arts: reviving the democratic imagination." *Community Development Journal* 42 (4): 413–421.

Moran, Marie. 2006. "Social Inclusion and the Limits of Pragmatic Liberalism: the Irish case." *Irish Political Studies* 21 (2): 181–201.

Mould, Oli. 2015. *Urban Subversion and the Creative City.* Oxon: Routledge.

Murphy, Vinny, interview by Author. 2012. *Community Filmmaking* (30 March).

Peterson, Mark Allan. 2003. *Anthropology and Mass Communication: media and myth in the new millenium.* New York: Bergahn Books.

Pratt, Andy. 2010. "Creative Cities: tensions within and between social, cultural and economic development: a critical reading of the UK experience." *City, Culture and Society* 1 (1): 13–20.

Redmond, Declan and Paula Russell. 2008. "Social Housing Regeneration and the Creation of Sustainable Communities in Dublin." *Local Economy* 23 (3): 169–179.

Ruby, Jay. 1992. "Speaking for, Speaking about, Speaking with, or Speaking alongside: an anthropological and documentary dilemma." *Journal of Film and Video* 44 (1/2): 42–66.

Scott, Allen J. 2006. "Creative Cities: conceptual issues and policy questions." *Journal of Urban Affairs* 28 (1): 1–17.

Stevenson, Deborah, David Rowe, and Kieryn McKay. 2010. "Convergence in British Cultural Policy: the social, the cultural, and the economic." *The Journal of Arts Management, Law, and Society* 40 (4): 248–265.

Tenants First. 2005. *The Real Guide to Regeneration.* Dublin: Tenants First.

The Day in Question. 2010. Directed by What's the Story? Collective.

What's the Story? Collective. 2010. "What's the Story? Collective." *Section 8.* Accessed February 23, 2013. http://section8.ie/wordpress/.

Whyte, Joanie, interview by Author. 2012. *Fatima Community Filmmaking* (04 April).

Women with Balls. 2006. Directed by Fatima History Project.

10 Rewalking the Path

Community Video, Deep Cultural Mapping and Sustainable Canadian Cities

Sharon Karsten

> It is within the shifting ground of questioning, experimentation, and engaging with non-artists that we might come together to create models that further challenge current forms of power.... We as cultural workers need to start at places of *not knowing* in order to build up knowledge together.
>
> —Dana Claxton and Tania Willard (2012, Para 3)

Introduction

Cultural Mapping is an emerging and interdisciplinary field of inquiry that explores and uncovers layers of cultural significance embedded within place. The practice, defined by Stewart and the Creative City Network of Canada as "a process of recording, analyzing and synthesizing information in order to describe the cultural resources, networks, links and patterns of usage of a given community or group" (Stewart 2007, 70), has been applied to numerous and varied circumstances – from the exploration of indigenous peoples' history and territory to the recognition of heritage and arts assets to the contestation of political boundaries. UNESCO has endorsed cultural mapping as "a crucial tool and technique in preserving the worlds intangible and tangible cultural assets" (UNESCO nd, para 3) and has promoted its use within a wide range of development contexts. As communication technologies have evolved over the past decade, new forms of cultural mapping have been pioneered that tap into alternate (including both tangible and intangible) dimensions of place through dynamic platforms such as video and interactive/immersive online environments.

Canadian cities have, throughout the past decade, signed on to the concept of cultural mapping – the practice having been proliferated amongst municipalities of all sizes (Jeannotte 2015, 109). This widespread engagement can be attributed, in part, to a federal incentive enacted in 2005 through the Paul Martin Liberal Government, in which the Government allocated gas-tax revenue to municipalities compliant in the creation of an Integrated Community Sustainability

Plan (ICSP). As culture was positioned within the ICSP process as a key dimension of sustainable cities, the development of these plans in turn generated a focus on cultural planning and on cultural mapping in particular (109–110).

While numerous Canadian cities have taken up cultural mapping, focus within these maps tends to be placed on the tangible rather than intangible qualities of place. The majority of Canada's municipal cultural maps provide a basic inventory of established cultural assets – identifying and making widely accessible, for instance, cultural facilities such as museums, libraries, galleries, etc. Intangible assets such as community stories, legends, cultural expressions, collective change-ideas, visual histories, etc., are rarely included. This situation is notable given the value (and legitimisation) accorded in recent years to such 'intangible' data within twenty-first-century governance frameworks – particularly within sustainability frameworks (Duxbury and Jeannote, 2010, Landry 2012, xxxiii).

Canada's community video movement, developed through a unique set of socio-political conditions beginning in the 1970s, is particularly well positioned, I argue, to open doors of inquiry, concerning the intangible dimensions at play within Canadian cities. Given the movement's long-standing commitment to community activation and engagement, its history of grassroots narrative formation and its concern for media democratisation, its integration into cultural mapping projects might help to both 'deepen' the place-based understandings generated through cultural mapping practices and spur radical evolutions of this practice. Community video processes might bring to bear new democratic possibilities within cultural mapping projects – cultivating multi-layered, inclusive and localised manifestations of the public sphere.

This chapter begins with an overview of cultural mapping as a governance practice – including a critical discussion of its power and potential within a public sphere context. It then hones in on the Canadian community video movement – looking at the set of circumstances through which this movement emerged – starting in the late 1960s/early 1970s and evolving into the present. Here is shown the alignment had by this movement with a bottom-up democratisation project – seen in some circles as socially innovative and in others as playing into a bio-political governance agenda. The history and current potential of Canada's community video movement is considered within the practice of Canadian municipal cultural mapping – through a case study (the *Where Is Here* project) in which community video is used to elicit colloquial expressions of place. In referencing this project, I ask how community video practices might be used within municipal governance contexts to empower citizens in the making of collectively owned futures.

1 Cultural Mapping - an Overview

The rise of the knowledge economy as a dominant framework has brought about a key shift in the relationship between municipalities and their constituent populations. This shift, described by David Harvey (1989, 3–17) as a move from managerialism to entrepreneurialism, has governments attempting to work with and through their constituent populations to "productively activate" them. Within this paradigm, cultural mapping becomes a vehicle by which governments both engage with and propel forward constituent bases and by which they create, within essentially diverse populations, shared goals and identities (Moore and Borrup 2015). Within this new governance relationship, the link between cultural mapping and local identity is particularly relevant – with the cultural questions "who are we?" and "what might we become?" becoming increasingly valued within municipal contexts as starting-points for engagement and development (Hawkes 2001). By exploring these fundamental questions, municipal developers tap into the "lifeblood of the community and the mainstream of the creative economy" (Mercer quoted in Jeannotte 2015, 99) and can approach development from a position of core values and beliefs.

The emergence of deep cultural mapping has enabled developers to tap into this lifeblood in new and potentially revolutionary ways and has, in fact, challenged the status and definition of 'developer' by bringing development tools and processes into the hands of communities. Deep mapping is described by Kathleen Scherf (2015) as "an inherently interdisciplinary practice, [facilitated by] digital technology [that enables mapping to] get beyond the brochure and provide rich content across disciplines, cultures and time". In practice, deep mapping presents "as a geographical map" but utilises "rich content to 'volatize' and convey spirit of place" (341). In the process of moving 'beyond' traditional cartographic representation, deep mapping holds, according to Scherf, a kind of liberating potential – allowing us "to tell much more than any map traced by a cartographer ever could" (343) and allowing communities to take ownership of their own stories and trajectories. The integration of deep maps into municipally led cultural mapping processes has only just started to occur.

1.1 Critical Positioning

Cultural mapping, including deep mapping, can on one hand be understood as a technology complicit in the construction of a more dynamic and robust public sphere. This concept, whose roots harken back to the agora of ancient Greece, refers to an arena conceptually distinct from, and yet integrally connected to, the state and market – "through which political participation is enacted through the medium of talk... a theatre for debating and deliberating" (Fraser 1990, 57). First popularised in the western world by Habermas, the public sphere construct references a particular set of social/political conditions in seventeenth-century Britain and France in which the foundations for a culture of public deliberation were purportedly laid – through such mechanisms as literary salons (Habermas 1989, 32), "public assemblies, pubs and coffee houses, meeting halls", etc.… as well as "organs of public information and political debate" such as newspapers and journals (xii). These domains constituted arenas in which "the mind was no longer in the service of a patron" (33) and in which opinion became, through exchange and deliberation, freed from the bonds of economic dependence.

Habermas' theory has been critiqued as essentialist (Griffin 1996) and chided for its subscription to a reality of unification (van Dijk 1999, 164). Still, many theorists see within it a starting point for a kind of politics in which democracy from below can be systemically nurtured and enacted. Laclau and Mouffe, for instance, refer to the public sphere as a "radical alternative to an aggregative model of democracy" that reduces the democratic and cultural process to the expression of predefined interests and preferences (i.e. those registered in a vote). The concept acknowledges, in their view, the ways in which political and cultural identities are not given but "constituted and reconstituted through debate" (Laclau and Mouffe 2001, xvii). The public sphere, in this view, ascribes to participants a position of agency and serves as a catalyst to allow world-making capacities to emerge within populations (Arendt 1958, 51–56). Habermas shows us that the creation of meaning, and of democratic subjectivities, occurs through processes that are, at the core, cultural.

The communicative framework offered by deep cultural mapping can be seen as a kind of public sphere platform – the practice providing a space for dialogue and exchange that allows for a plethora of agendas and perspectives to be publicly expressed and negotiated. Here, a quality of experience is shared that potentially transcends the experience achieved within formalised public discourse. By allowing local populations to delve deeply into their life-worlds, to convey these worlds through text, imagery, sound, video and 'experiential' or 'cultural' reasoning (McGuigan 2005, 427–443), another realm of interchange is made possible. In this exchange, citizens become meaningfully engaged in the construction and reconstruction of their collective futures.

While on one hand deep cultural mapping is seen to hold a revolutionary democratising potential, the process has been seen in some lights as having the opposite effect. Positioned within a Foucaultian analytical framework premised on the notion of bio-power, deep cultural mapping can be seen to reinforce dominant hierarchies while maintaining a semblance of localised agency. Bio-power serves, in this framework, as a form of contemporary control concerned first with the discipline of the human body, where the body is understood as a machine: economically useful, productive, etc. (Foucault 1978, Part 5). This form of power is manifest in an array of cultural establishments, such as education, the military, the workplace, etc., and seeks to create a more disciplined and effective population. Here, 'soft-power' governance tactics are enacted by the ruling elite upon their constituent populations, in which beliefs and behaviours are moulded in particular ways – and in which certain kinds of subjectivities are actively produced. Tony Bennett (2002) shows how the museum as a contemporary institute reinforces certain behavioural norms and expectations and thereby serves as an instrument of bio-power – reproducing desired characteristics within a population:

> Rather than embodying and alien and coercive principle of power which aimed to cow the people into submission, the museum – addressing the people as a public, as citizens – aimed to inveigle the general populace into complicity with power by placing them on this side of a power which it represented to it as its own. (184)

By the same argument, the cultural mapping process can be conceived as an apparatus for behavioural alteration and control. Here, populations are brought to behave in certain ways – and to feel ownership over their behaviour. Deep cultural mapping is, in this light, positioned as a tool for governments to structure subjectivities at will – allowing citizens all the while to feel a sense of agency in inscribing their destinies.

Alongside this view, however, is an argument that shows this same force (bio-power) as being reclaimed within bottom-up power-subversion agendas. Hardt and Negri (2005) show such reclamation as stemming from the 'multitude' – that is, from an "internally different, multiple, social subject whose constitution and action is not based on identity, or unity (or much less, indifference), but on what it has in common" (100). They see 'biological productivity' within the multitude – claiming within this construct an inherent decision-making and leadership capacity. Bio-power can, in this view, be accomplished both 'from above' – enacted by governments upon populations – and 'from below' – used as a tool of 'the people' in the enactment of collective resistance and the construction of new narratives (Negri 2003, 263). This view of bio-power is affirmed by Blencowe (2012), who attributes to the concept a 'productive potential' through which can be created new, embodied experiences.

In determining how we look at deep cultural mapping projects in relation to the construct of bio-power and contemporary neoliberal governance, we might do well to heed Purcell (2008), who cautions against an overly structuralist or reductionist analytical approach: "there is a danger that as we develop a robust critique of the various injustices of neoliberalization, we will focus only on the doors it is closing". Purcell advocates, rather, for an approach that recognises the "contradictions of, and the emerging resistance to, neoliberalization [and neoliberal governance frameworks]" and for a view of these frameworks as 'historicized' (3).

In this light, cultural mapping can be seen as produced within and through the unique circumstances of its actualisation. Of paramount importance in this equation is the government/ artist as technologist/ community relationship and the willingness of governance agents to allow and support community-driven deep mapping approaches as part of a public sphere agenda – drawing upon and making way for the wisdom embedded within established and emerging forms of community activation and creative practice to drive radical new approaches to space and community.

2 Community Video

Here we return to the central argument of this article – that community video can, in certain instances, be used by municipalities as a tool, epistemology and community development approach to go 'beyond' standardised and tangible representations of place and community and towards representations that delve deeper into (and that productively activate) the multiplicity of histories, identities and desires (i.e. intangible assets) housed within place. I make this argument within the context of Canadian municipalities – recognising the current plight of these entities to invent new cultural and community development approaches given the advent of the ICSP. Before launching into an exploration of the agendas embedded within the Canadian community video movement, however, it is necessary to first present a broader context for this phenomenon by tying it to its 'parent' movement – community media.

Howley (2005) defines community media as: "grassroots or locally oriented media access initiatives predicated on a profound sense of dissatisfaction with mainstream media form and content, dedicated to the principles of free expression and participatory democracy, and committed to enhancing community relations and promoting community solidarity" (2). This movement includes a set of practices that, while rejecting 'tight definition' and embodying a polymorphic array of disciplines and communicative philosophies, offers a useful framework by which to describe the "complex interaction between people's attempts to democratize the mediascape and their contextual circumstances" (Meadows et al. 2009, 167). Through citizen-owned communication tools such as "zines and other print media, film and video documentation, controversial visual arts installations, street theater and other forms of culture jamming, and any of the many other forms of delivery" (Dreher 2010, 152), the community media movement provokes bottom-up challenges to dominant power-formations – enabling citizens to creatively and critically reconstruct their collective political, social and economic realities.

Not all communities using media as a platform for resistance are seen as part of the 'community media movement'. Many examples exist of grassroots community-led media mobilisations premised upon repressive, hostile and violent ideological positions. In contrast to these, the community media movement stakes its claim in the necessity of plurality and in a commitment to citizen participation as a fundamental pillar of democracy (Howley 2010, 341). While we recognise the movement's progressive stance and strong social-democratic assertions, we should also acknowledge that the terms 'progressive' and 'democratic' are defined differently within different contexts and that a significant degree of tension (and critical discord) exists within the movement as related to its emancipatory claims.

Community video exists as a branch of community media that grew to prominence in numerous industrialised nations during the '60s – in times rife with political turmoil and amidst a rapidly evolving technological landscape. With the introduction of the Sony Portapak in 1965 – one of the first film cameras made widely available to consumers (Boyle 1992, Para 1) – activists and artists throughout the globe began banding together to use this technology to explore and expose perceived injustice and to enable communities to self-represent and present counternarratives to those commonly being propagated by the film industry.

3 Community Video in Canada

Community video took on a unique set of qualities within Canada starting in the 1970s. Pluralist governance practice was at its peak – the Pierre Trudeau Liberal government passed an internationally regarded multiculturalism policy in 1971 and cemented within the nation's collective imagination a metaphor of Canada as a 'mosaic', juxtaposed sharply against the U.S. metaphor of 'melting pot' (Canadian Museum of Immigration n.d.). Canada was struggling to define itself as a distinct and autonomous (yet diverse) nation – an entity culturally different from its southern superpower neighbour (emitting unprecedented waves of media and cultural content) and its French and British colonial influences (Dowell 2013, 214).

Canadian media theorist Marshall McLuhan, along with Herald Innis, George Grant and others, were to develop throughout this period a distinctly Canadian critical line of inquiry and intellectual tradition – characterised by a discourse on technology in which it was positioned "as constitutive of social and psychic space" (Marchessault 2005, 74). In McLuhan's view, great artists as technologists and symbolists created "insights into the modern world and its relationships with the past … by presenting the observer with fragmentary images of reality and forcing him to become a participant in the process of piecing them together in a pattern of significance" (Morrison n.d.). Artists were seen, in other words, as translators or 'seers' – able to synthesise and 'make sense of' (or map) an array of essentially disparate fragments.

This critical media tradition was not confined to the halls of the academy but was popularised within larger Canadian society. McLuhan, for instance, having a "genuinely distinctive personality... [and] an effusive scholarly sociability" was to rise in the ranks in the 1960s and continuing into the '70s as a wildly popular academic superstar (Deetz 2012). Many of the themes, epistemologies and pedagogical/critical debates housed within his theories (including his understanding of the artist's role as 'mapping' agent) can be seen played out within the country's emerging community video movement.

3.1 Community Video & the 1970s Art Scene

One of the key factors shaping Canada's community video movement in the '70s (in addition to the situational factors already mentioned), was the dramatic evolution of the country's arts scene. Canada's artist-run culture came into existence in the early '70s – in part due to funding provided by the Canada Council for the Arts to an emerging network of Artist-Run Centres (Robertson 2006, 124, VanFossen 2007, 3). This network played a role in facilitating, disseminating and presenting work produced outside established and conservative frameworks offered by public and commercial galleries (Burgess 2011, 13) and was concerned with the self-determination and experimentation of artists. The network bore strong ties to various social movements (5) and provided a seedbed for the emergence of a particular kind of community video that was profoundly connected to place and community (Snider 2015, 60).

AA Bronson (1983), an artist, curator, cultural administrator and publisher working within the network throughout the '70s and into the present speaks about the ways in which the emergence of film and video practice through these centres was tied in with a larger national project of self-awareness and identity formation:

> [in] Canada in the late Sixties there was no way to see ourselves, no way to know we existed. Certain media had a magnetic importance. Video had a magnetic importance. We all knew the importance of seeing ourselves. In 1971, A Space started its video programme with Lisa Steele and Tom Sherman. In 1972 Video Inn opened its doors in Vancouver...In 1974 Art Metropole began video distribution. And then suddenly everyone everywhere in Canada was making video and this was a Canadian thing. So video is a connective tissue (Para 20).

Bronson's comments convey a cultural renaissance occurring within the country throughout the '70s in which the principle of community engagement featured prominently and in which community video was seen to play a catalytic role.

This role was accomplished through a series of services offered by Artist-Run Centres that included the provision of access to, and support for, production – offering up at below-market rates such tools as editing equipment and software, animation equipment and software, film cameras, film processing facilities, etc.; support for exhibition – some centres taking on a 'screening' and/or a distribution mandate and the provision of programming aimed to offer professional development to members, such as workshops, seminars, training opportunities and artist talks. Many centres were, as well, to advance contemporary art discourse through critical publications and critical art dialogues (Burgess and DeRosa 2011, 6). Through this slate of services, and through an overall structure premised upon self-organisation, the Artist-Run Centre network grew to innovate new ideas around the ways in which video could be used in the context of communities.

At the same time as the Council began funding this network, the National Film Board produced its now well-known community engagement program – *Challenge for Change* – an initiative that sent video activists into a wide array of small/rural communities throughout the country to 'tell their stories' and engage local groups in a national poverty-reduction agenda. This was, by all accounts, "an ambitious initiative that brought together the unlikely partners of government bureaucrats, documentary filmmakers, community activists, and 'ordinary' citizens" and that used video as a vehicle for the articulation of a diverse set of agendas and needs within these communities. The program, which encouraged filmmakers to collaborate with subjects instead of merely documenting them, shone light on numerous social-justice issues – ranging from "women's rights to housing to First Nations struggles to agriculture" (Baker, Waugh and Winton 2010, 4). *Challenge for Change* invoked international attention for its approach to art-based community narrative building, and served as a site of democratic innovation – a place where new ways of thinking about the democratic process in relation to narrative and technology were played out.

It is important to note that these initiatives were not welcomed unanimously and were at times the subject of significant controversy. Critics of *Challenge for Change* positioned the program as a vehicle by which to further a bio-political governance agenda. Under then Prime Minister Pierre Trudeau's brand of 'technocratic liberalism', which included the pursuit of "democracy through McLuhenesque technological modernity" (Stewart 2007, 50), *Challenge for Change* was to be labelled "one of the many educational and promotional processes used to convey the new role of the state in administering people's lives" (Druick 2010, 343).

The program's concern with localised issues surrounding poverty reduction and the pursuit of social justice was said to be used by the federal government as an "advocacy tool for federalism itself" (344) – a way to show a new relationship at play between federal powers and localised problems and to thereby accomplish a form of bio-social engineering and control. Critiques of the Artist-Run Centre network tend to focus on its development from an organic, vibrant change-initiative in the early '70s to an entity infused with a bureaucratic logic – a network constrained by the limitations imposed by its own operating infrastructure (Snider 2015, 46).

Acknowledging these critiques, it is important to avoid underplaying the 'from below' bio-political force emanating from these initiatives. The '70s afforded, as Naomi Klein (2010) observes, "a moment of looseness with creativity within the public sector [at the time]" (xxiv) in which was allowed to emerge another way of thinking about governance entities and their role in supporting/nourishing the public sphere. Here, artists were positioned as agents responsible to activate populations in order to 'make sense' of an increasingly fragmented socio-political landscape. Artists coming from the community video movement tradition with its concern for self-governance, social justice and localised forms of expression and exchange were well positioned to catalyse and evolve, through narrative and technology, a new kind of public sphere.

Challenge for Change was disbanded in 1975 (the program's last film was released in 1980) (Weisner 2010, 73) alongside the rise of a new managerial approach to federal governance in Canada that left little room for art-based experimentation within development and policy-formation domains. The program left its mark, however. Videos produced through this initiative continue to be distributed and viewed today, and the program continues to be referenced as an example of innovative, community-based production.

3.2 Community Video: The Present

Canada's community video movement today has evolved in a multitude of ways – responding to shifts in technology and political climate and to the prevailing winds of change brought about by forces of globalisation. Canada's artist-run video network now consists of over 80 centres – including over 20 media-specific centres (Artspace n.d.). These centres continue to play a vital role in the Canadian arts ecology – supporting the "production and critical advancement of emergent artistic practices and contributing to the development of the careers of artists and arts administrators" (Burgess and De Rosa 2011, 5). Many of these centres, having matured and in some cases become 'bureaucratised', continue nonetheless to cultivate strong links with communities – serving as conduits for culturally informed forms of democratic participation.

The intersection of community engagement practices with emerging forms of technological communication has formed a key nexus of experimentation within such centres as Oboro (Montreal) (n.d.), the Grunt Gallery (Vancouver) (n.d.), and Urban Shaman (Winnipeg) (n.d.). Numerous artists have spearheaded, through these and other centres, cutting-edge community-based technological interventions – testing out and activating the 'story-telling' potential at play within new and emerging communication technologies.

The National Film Board, as well, continues to cultivate community-based, technology-infused forms of expression and experimentation. Of note is the organisation's *Interactive* series – an online collection of "innovative, interactive stories exploring the world – and our place in it – from uniquely Canadian points of view" (n.d.). This program combines video with a range of new-media and gaming technologies to create immersive 'story-based' experiences for participants that go beyond linear narratives to map connections among places, people and themes. Video is used alongside photography, photo essays, sound clips, interactive maps, etc., to bring participants into experiential engagement with particular sets of ideas, places and identities. Along the same lines, the creative laboratories operated by such centres as the Banff Centre for the Arts (n.d.), and by various post-secondary institutions throughout the country (including, for instance, Emily Carr University of Art and Design), have proliferated projects that explore the role of arts, media and technology in enabling democratic (i.e. public sphere) participation. Within these spaces, artists 'try out' ideas as related to the construction and activation of culturally informed public spheres – often delving deeper into the poetic and symbolic dimensions of the public sphere than is possible in municipally led public consultation processes.

Recognising that technological, political and social changes occurring globally throughout the last 30 years have in many ways resulted in a broadened scope and definition of community video, lines can still be drawn that link Canada's contemporary community video movement to that of the 1970s. The dedication shown through many of the above-mentioned production venues to a wider social change agenda, deep and meaningful community connectivity and local citizen activation, reveals a persistent vision of Canadian community video as a vehicle for public sphere activation.

4 *Where Is Here*: A Case Study

In what follows, I draw attention to a particular community video/citizen activation project currently underway on the west coast of Canada – *Where Is Here: Small cities, deep mapping, sustainable futures* (Karsten et al. 2016). I point, in particular, to the nature of the community media/municipal government partnership at play in this project and unpack the question of how such partnerships and projects might be developed in ways that are meaningful, artful and respectful of a local community's existing and emergent identities.

4.1 Context

Where Is here is a Social Sciences and Humanities Research Council-funded project initiated in January 2016 by four researchers, including a community media practitioner and theorist through Vancouver Island University. The project began in recognition of an urgent identity crisis faced by numerous small cities on the west coast and takes as its research subject three small cities located therein: Nanaimo, Courtenay and Port Alberni. These cities have faced significant economic and social changes in recent decades necessitating a return to the drawing board in terms of development and strategic planning. The closure of key resource extraction establishments in recent years, in forestry, mining, fishing and other sectors, has resulted in the evaporation of jobs and opportunities, the out-migration of young people and a proliferation of social problems (City of Port Alberni 2007, 7). At the same time, these cities have witnessed an influx in retirees, artists and 'lifestyle escapees', as their mild climates and rural/remote destination status draw those wishing to pursue 'non-mainstream' forms of living (Meyer 2009, Para 8).

Each of these cities has, in recent years, committed to a diversification of its economic base. The City of Courtenay's official community plan shows its commitment to "support community economic development strategies that focus on locally owned and operated businesses and recognize educational and cultural/arts initiatives as having significant growth potential" (2016, 15). The City of Nanaimo's (2008) plan speaks to the interconnectedness of social, ecological and economic paradigms – advocating that planners "build upon the strengths of the city and work to improve those areas where changes in economic, social, environmental conditions would create a stronger, more effective, sustainable city" (15). Port Alberni's plan advocates for a continued "diversification of the local economy" as a way to "increase the number and stability of higher paying jobs" (2007, 14).

Within these plans is recognised the need for these municipalities to augment their core economic bases – diversifying these through a holistic approach to community and development. Featuring prominently in these three plans is the recognition of environment, lifestyle and quality of life as key factors underlying resident retention and growth and that economic growth occurs, in part, through ties of connection with place. Acknowledging and tapping into local/endogenous cultures and economic/social assets is seen, within these plans, as a necessary step in creating authentic and locally owned growth strategies.

The *Where Is Here* project explores local resident connections with place – specifically resident connections with the downtown cores of these three focus cities. Acknowledging downtowns as centre points of community pride and collective representation, the project team set out to illuminate the cultural dimensions of these places and, in particular, the social/cultural factors that attract and connect people to them. Residents were encouraged, via a widely disseminated call, to speak on video and in place to the spots within their downtown cores where they felt most connected to community. Videos, which were non-edited and each less than 1.5 minutes in duration, were produced by the project team (including the 4 lead researchers and 9 students) over the course of three months. Videos were then uploaded to an online map of each downtown and made available to the wider public (see www.whereisherecultural-mapping.com).

The video collection phase of the project was seen as successful – generating significant interest amongst residents in each of these three communities (over 80 videos were produced) and sparking new ideas and insights surrounding place. The stories that emerged are varied and diverse – some speaking to the role of cultural establishments in the downtown core; others highlighting forgotten histories or unique characteristics of the landscape; still others delving into personal stories of connection that illustrate deep emotional ties within physical and cultural landscapes. As a compilation, these stories provide access to new understandings surrounding each downtown's 'sense of place' and draw attention to the 'intangible' cultural networks and assets at play.

The project is now launching into a Phase 2, which involves making the map accessible to the wider community as an engagement platform. Residents within these cities are encouraged and enabled to make their own videos (using iphones, etc.) for upload onto the map. This second phase, which makes this platform dynamic, is seen as a key aspect in the activation of a story- and place-based 'public sphere'. Here, in the activation of community-made stories and visions for planning purposes, the line between 'planning' and 'community development' becomes blurred.

4.2 Potentials

One of the key opportunities arising from this project pertains to its potential to create meaningful relationships between planners and marginalised communities. The medium of community video, in its tendency towards the visual, the narrative and the colloquial, might provide an alternative venue through which marginalised communities, and in particular those not normally inclined to participate in formal/bureaucratic municipal planning conversations, 'tell their stories' – and thereby take up and/or strengthen their role in community visioning processes. Targeted and community-rooted cultural mapping projects that actively include marginalised populations embody the possibility, it seems, of involving such populations meaningfully in decisions that affect them.

Community media, in its collaborative and creative dimensions, requires municipal planners to meet such communities within their own lived domains – and on their own terms.

4.3 The Role of Government

Within this process of community development/planning, the role of government requires consideration. *Where Is Here* was constructed in consultation with the municipal governments in each of these cities (the City of Courtenay, of Nanaimo and Port Alberni) – each of which came onto the project in a partnership role that involved disseminating and championing the project within its respective citizen populations. The solicitation of videos was aligned with two of the municipalities' 'revitalization' initiatives and was embraced by these municipalities as a way to tap into new, and 'hard to grasp' (within a planning and development context), understandings of place. Yet, while municipal partnerships were key to the project's success, project leadership was and is housed in the project team – working through an academic institution. This team, which hails from and brings to bear a range of knowledge domains – including planning, small city economic development, media production and community media theory and practice, took on the task of overseeing and managing the project – making possible a form of community engagement that is both 'relevant to', and 'removed from', local government. Given the concerns expressed earlier in this piece around the role of government in 'productively managing' populations in alignment with predefined purposes, such an 'arms-length' relationship between municipal cultural mapping projects and their respective government strategists is, in this researcher's view, desirable.

4.4 Benefits to Municipalities

Taking inspiration from the *Where Is Here?* process, I would like to posit a number of potentials to be found in community video-infused approaches to municipal cultural mapping. This practice embodies within it the propensity, I argue, to:

- challenge top-down power imbalances at play within municipal governance frameworks;
- give power to artists as interpreters and to 'civic society' – i.e. non-profits, community members – in engineering their own communities' futures;
- incorporate into municipal planning processes elements of plurality – accommodating and championing voices of resistance;
- provide access to places, peoples and ideas normally not accessible within traditional participatory planning processes;

- provide access to narratives and stories that are rich and complex and
- tap into the emotional/cultural landscapes of populations in ways that traditional bureaucratic planning processes cannot.

Conclusion

Having made an argument for the greater inclusion of community video practices and epistemologies in Canada's municipal cultural mapping projects, we should emphasise that the effectiveness of this inclusion is dependent upon the openness of local governing bodies to the introduction of new epistemological approaches. Municipal cultural mapping proponents wishing to use community media must, it seems, divest themselves of top-down agendas and engage authentically with community video practitioners. This involves inviting participation from video and community activists from the start of mapping processes through their completion. It involves listening to and actively soliciting the input of video practitioners and responding to suggestions presented in an authentically dialogic way. In short, it involves activating community video interventions as a 'lens' within a holistic process of endogenously driven development, rather than as a tool to achieve narrowly defined socio-economic growth agendas.

Such an approach to cultural mapping, accomplished with a spirit of reflexivity, respects the 'unknownness' of the results produced within and through this process. By forfeiting the power to unilaterally frame and articulate issues and relationships – drawing instead upon the narrative power held by artists, activists and communities to see and 'map' the world and of a diverse range of citizens to share and communicate their views – a municipal cultural mapping process might become infused with radical potential, taking on the qualities of a dynamic and inclusive public sphere. Within Canada's municipal development landscape, such an approach to cultural mapping – drawing upon the insights and knowledges gained throughout the past 50+ years through the country's robust community video movement – might spark a new way of doing governance, bringing to bear a role for community video practitioners not only as observers, translators and storytellers, but as visionaries, leaders and keepers of the public sphere.

References

Arendt, Hannah. 1958. *The Human Condition, Second Edition*. Chicago: University of Chicago Press.

Artspace. n.d. Accessed December 1, 2015. http://artspace-arc.org/resources/links/.

Baker, Michael Brendan, Thomas Waugh and Ezra Winton. 2010. "Introduction: Forty Years Later... A Space for Challenge for Change/Societe nouvelle." In *Challenge for Change: activist documentary at the National Film Board of*

Canada, edited by Michael Brendan Baker, Thomas Waugh and Ezra Winton. Montreal, Canada: McGill Queen's University Press.

Banff Centre for the Arts. "Visual and Digital Arts". n.d. Accessed January 13, 2016. https://www.banffcentre.ca/visual-digital-arts.

Bennett, Tony. 2002. "The Political Rationality of the Museum." In *Critical Cultural Policy Studies: a reader*, edited by Justin Lewis and Tony Miller. *Hoboken, NJ*: Blackwell Publishing Ltd.

Blencowe, Claire. 2012. *Biopolitical Experience: Foucault, power and positive critique*. London: Palgrave Macmillan.

Boyle, Dierdre. 1992. "From Portapak to Camcorder: a brief history of guerilla television." *Journal of Film and Video* V44: 1–2. accessed December 1, 2015, http://www.experimentaltvcenter.org/portapak-camcorder-brief-history-guerrilla-television.

Bronson, A. A. 1983. "The Humiliation of the Bureaucrat: artist-run centres as museums by artists." In *Museums by Artists*, edited by AA Bronson and Peggy Gale. Art Metropole, 1983, 29–37. Accessed December 1, 2015. http://goodreads.timothycomeau.com/aabronson/.

Burgess, Marilyn and Maria De Rosa. 2011. *The Distinct Role of Artist-Run Centres in the Canadian Visual Arts Ecology*. MDR Burgess Consultants and Canada Council for the Arts. Accessed December 1, 2015. http://canadacouncil.ca/council/research/find-research/2012/artist-run-centres.

Canada Council for the Arts. n.d. "The Evolution of the Canada Council's Support of the Arts." Accessed December 1, 2015. http://canadacouncil.ca/council/about-the-council/the-evolution.

Canadian Museum of Immigration – Pier 21. nd. "Canadian Multiculturalism Policy, 1971." Accessed December 1, 2015. http://www.pier21.ca/research/immigration-history/canadian-multiculturalism-policy-1971.

City of Courtenay. 2016. "Official Community Plan: a blueprint for Courtenay, 2016." Accessed May 15, 2016. http://www.courtenay.ca/assets/Departments/Development~Services/Bylaw_2387_OCP.pdf.pdf.

City of Nanaimo. 2008. "planNanaimo: official community plan, 2008." Accessed May 15, 2016. http://www.nanaimo.ca/assets/Departments/Community~Planning/Offical~Community~Plan~-~10~Year~Review/OfficialCommuni-tyPlan2008.pdf.

City of Port Alberni. 2007. "Official Community Plan, 2007." Accessed May 15, 2016. http://www.portalberni.ca/content/official-community-plan.

Claxton, Dana and Tanya Willard. 2012. "Imperfect Compliance: a trajectory of transformation." In *Institutions by Artists: Volume Two*. Vancouver: Fillip Editions/Pacific Association of Artist Run Centres. Accessed December 1, 2015. http://arcpost.ca/articles/imperfect-compliance.

Deetz, Stanley A. 2012. Ed. *Communication Yearbook 15*. London: Routledge.

Dowell, Kristin L. 2012. *Sovereign Screens: aboriginal media on the Canadian west coast*. Lincoln: U of Nebraska Press.

Dreher, Tanja. 2010. "Media Interventions in Radicalized Communities." In *Understanding Community Media*. Edited by Kevin Howley. Los Angeles: Sage.

Druick, Zoe. 2010. "Meeting at the Poverty Line: government policy, social work, and media activism in the challenge for change program." In *Challenge for Change: activist documentary at the National Film Board of Canada*, edited by Thomas Waugh, Michael Brendan Baker and Ezra Winton. Montreal: McGill Queen's University Press.

Duxbury, Nancy and Sharon Jeannotte. 2010. *Culture, Sustainability and Communities: exploring the myths.* 353/15. In Centro de Estudos Sociais, University of Coimbra, 2010, N.353. Accessed December 1, 2015, https://www.ces.uc.pt/myces/UserFiles/livros/614_CES%20Oficina_353.pdf.

Foucault, Michel. 1978. *The History of Sexuality Volume 1.* New York: Random House Inc. Part 5.

Fraser, Nancy. 1990. "Rethinking the Public Sphere: a contribution to the critique of actually existing democracy." In *Social Text* 25/26: 56–80.

Griffin, Cindy L. 1996. "The Essentialist Roots Of The Public Sphere: a feminist critique." *Western Journal of Communication* 60/1.

Grunt Gallery. "Media Lab." n.d. Accessed April 20, 2016. http://www.grunt.ca/media-lab.html.

Habermas, Jurgen. 1989. *The Structural Transformation of the Public Sphere: an inquiry into a category of bourgeois society.* Translated by Thomas Berger & Frederick Lawrence. Cambridge: MIT Press.

Hardt, Michael and Antonio Negri. 2005. *Multitude: war and democracy in the age of empire* New York: Penguin Books.

Harvey, David. 1989. "From Managerialism to Entrepreneurialism: the transformation in urban governance in late capitalism." *Series B, Human Geography* 71(1): 3–17.

Hawkes, J. 2001. *The Fourth Pillar of Sustainability: culture's essential role in public planning.* Vic: Cultural Development Network. Accessed December 1, 2015. http://www.culturaldevelopment.net.au/community/Downloads/HawkesJon%282001%29TheFourthPillarOfSustainability.pdf.

Howley, Kevin. 2005. *Community Media: people, places and communication technologies.* Cambridge: Cambridge University Press.

Howley, Kevin. 2010. "Local Media, Global Struggles." In *Understanding Community Media*, edited by Kevin Howley. Los Angeles: Sage Publications Inc.

Jeannotte, Sharon. 2015. "Cultural Mapping in Ontario." In *Cultural Mapping as Cultural Inquiry*, edited by Nancy Duxbury, W.F. Garrett-Petts and David MacLennan. New York: Routledge.

Karsten, Sharon, Pam Shaw, Alanna Williams and Nicole Vangeois. 2016. *Where Is Here: small cities, deep mapping, sustainable futures.* Accessed December 1, 2015. www.whereishereculturalmapping.com.

Klein, Naomi. 2010. "Forward - Putting Ideas into the World. A Conversation with Naomi. Klein about Starting Conversations with Film." In *Challenge for Change: activist documentary at the National Film Board of Canada*, edited by Thomas Waugh, Michael Brendan Baker, Ezra Winton. Montreal: McGill Queen's University Press.

Laclau, Ernesto and Chantal Mouffe. 2001. *Hegemony and Socialist Strategy: towards a radical democratic politics.* Second Edition. Verso, 2001.

Landry, Charles. 2012. *The Creative City: a toolkit for urban innovators.* Earthscan.

Marchessault, Janine. 2005. *Marshall McLuhan.* Los Angeles: Sage.

McGuigan, Jim. 2005. "The Cultural Public Sphere." *European Journal of Cultural Studies* 8/4: 427–443.

Meadows, Michael, Susan Ford, Jacqui Ewart and Kerrie Foxesll. 2009. "Making Spaces: community media and formation of the democratic public sphere in Australia." In *Making Our Media – Global Initiatives towards a*

186 *Sharon Karsten*

Democratic Public Sphere, edited by Clemencia Rodriguez, Dorothy Kidd and Laura Stein. Charlottesville, VA: Hampton Press.

Meyer, Hans Peter. 2009. "Challenging the Settlement Challenge on East Coast Vancouver Island." In *Sustainability and Quality of Life in BC's Rural and Small Town Communities*. Accessed December 1, 2015 http://waterbucket.ca/gi/files/2009/10/Hans-Peter-Meyer_Challenging-the-Settlement-Challenge_Oct-2009.pdf.

Moore, Stephanie and Tom Borrup. 2015. "Introduction, Cultural Mapping" (Create Community Connections, 2015). Accessed December 1, 2015, http://artsengaged.com/bcnasamples/chapter-nine-cultural-mapping.

Morrison, James C. n.d. *Marshall McLuhan: no prophet without honor.* Cambridge, MA: Institute of Techology. Accessed November 27, 2015, http://www.mit.edu/~saleem/ivory/ch2.htm.

National Film Board. n.d. "Interactive". Accessed December 1, 2015. https://www.nfb.ca/interactive/.

Negri, Antonio. 2003. *Time for Revolution*. London: Bloomsbury.

Oboro. n.d. "Services and Mandate." Accessed March 15, 2016. http://www.oboro.net/en/page/services-and-mandate.

Purcell, Mark. 2008. *Recapturing Democracy: neoliberalization and the struggle for alternative urban futures.* London: Routledge.

Robertson, Clive. 2006. *Policy Matters: administrations of art and culture.* Ontario, Canada: YYZ Books.

Scherf, Kathleen. 2015. "Beyond the Brochure: an unmapped journey into deep mapping." In *Cultural Mapping as Cultural Inquiry*, edited by Nancy Duxbury, W.F. Garrett-Petts and David MacLennan. New York: Routledge.

Snider, Jennifer. 2015. *Art Administration as Performative Practice / Organizing Art as Institutional Critique*. MA thesis, OCAD University, 2015. Accessed December 1. http://openresearch.ocadu.ca/295/1/Snider_Jennifer_2015_MA_CADN_THESIS.pdf.

Stewart, Michelle. 2007. "The Indian Film Crews of Challenge for Change: representation and the state." *Canadian Journal of Film Studies* 16(2): 49–81.

Stewart, Sue. 2007. *Cultural Mapping Toolkit*. Vancouver: Creative City Network of Canada and 2010 Legacies Now. Accessed November 15, 2015. http://www.creativecity.ca/database/files/library/cultural_mapping_toolkit.pdf.

UNESCO. n.d. *Tools for Safeguarding Culture*. UNESCO Bangkok, Accessed. December 1, 2015, http://www.unescobkk.org/culture/tools-and-resources/tools-for-safeguarding-culture/culturalmapping/.

Urban Shaman. n.d. "About Urban Shaman." Accessed April 15, 2016. http://www.urbanshaman.org/.

van Dijk, Jan. 1999. *The Network Society: social aspects of new media*. Translated by Leontine Spoorenberg. London: Sage.

VanFossen, Rachael. 2007. *Opening up Space: towards an expansive vision for Multidisciplinary Arts in Canada – Research report prepared for the Multidisciplinary Work Group of the Canada Council for the Arts*. Canada Council for the Arts. Accessed December 1, 2015. http://canadacouncil.ca/council/research/find-research/2007/opening-up-space.

Weisner, Peter K. 2010. "Media for the People: the Canadian experiments with film and video in community development." In *Challenge for Change: activist documentary at the National Film Board of Canada*, edited by Thomas Waugh, Michael Brendan Baker and Ezra Winton. Montreal: McGill Queen's University Press.

Part IV

Engagement and Participation in Community Filmmaking – a Short Introduction

Sarita Malik, Caroline Chapain
and Roberta Comunian

This final section of the book puts the spotlight on issues of community engagement and participation, which policy interventions have positioned film as having the power to facilitate. There is limited research on that and what this implies for artists as well as audiences involved. The chapters presented here highlight the challenges and rewards of engaging communities with film by considering how various communities, for example, children, youth, Lesbian Gay Bisexual and Transsexual (LGBT) and radical film activists, engage and participate in the making, distribution and exhibition of community-led cinema.

Community Participation as a Form of Cultural Democracy

In the postwar years, the United Nations (UN) defined community development as "a process designed to create conditions of economic and social progress for the whole community with its active participation" (1955). The idea that active participation is socially progressive has framed cultural policymaking and strategies since then, and community film has often been utilised as a key medium to implement this. Community participation has routinely been aligned with notions of cultural democracy and, more recently, discourses of social inclusion, a dominant policy frame around which cultural policy has been based. As previously outlined in the book, community arts across a range of arts forms, from theatre to dance to film, have often been based around active participation and dialogue and geared towards notions of cultural democracy, community development and social transformation (Mayo 2000).

Critiques of the Rhetoric of Engagement

There are those who have observed that even alongside these social and cultural objectives, community arts and media can be utilised as a tool for 'top-down', expert-led initiatives rather than 'bottom up' community-led strategies for social inclusion. Thus a common example of community arts and media is where the experts go in to communities in order to develop communities' cultural knowledge and skills, rather than those communities themselves leading the process; the critique here is that these initiatives are "geared to the needs of the commissioners, funders and organizers rather than the participants" (Price 2015, 7). Price argues that participation has been positioned as innately virtuous; an "automatic methodological virtue" (2015, 3). He calls for a more active critique of the policies and practices that claim 'participation' and an interrogation of the assumption of shared interests (between communities and other stakeholders). Central to this problematisation of participation is the issue of power relations, something that has been most notably addressed in the sociology of development and in the wider critical literature on community development. It has been usefully noted that differing development agendas can co-exist, ranging from "top-down initiatives to change peoples' attitudes and behaviours, and conversely, as participatory strategies for cultural and political transformation, from the bottom-up" (Braden and Mayo 1999, 191).

These issues are addressed in Chapter 13 as Alicia Blum-Ross reflects on the assumption and frameworks generally used in youth community media projects through her extensive ethnographic work with them in London. She argues that the common 'deficit' view adopted by intermediaries and project leaders that sees youth as 'disengaged' while 'digitally enabled' often drives many of the projects, without an honest assessment of the kind of youth and individuals involved.

Another element that drives these interventions for engagement seems top-down policy initiatives, rather than bottom-up exploration of communities and their needs (Besch and Minson 2001). This generally can be contextualised in the broader instrumental use of the arts for community objectives, criticised by many academics (Belfiore 2002). Therefore, as the chapters in this section highlight, it is important to distinguish the discourse of engagement and positive impact rhetoric, from more realistic accounts of what can be achieved by engaging a range of diverse communities and audiences and the challenges as well as the rewards of this kind of work.

Community Filmmaking as an Example of Community-led Engagement

The significance of film for these opportunities and threats in terms of what community filmmaking actually 'does', is something that is addressed in this final section on engagement and participation. The chapters provide a focus on the more bottom up, community-led, interactive approach as an example of the participative mode of community filmmaking. Whilst the four chapters in this section address some of these intricacies around the social function of community filmmaking, they also resist positioning community filmmaking as a simple tool for engagement and participation. They do provide a set of valuable observations of how film (for example video used in community contexts) can actually function as a tool for community participation and, indeed, empowerment within sometimes quite fragile contexts. Important within these analyses is a critically reflexive acknowledgement of issues of precarity and the complexities at work and also a foregrounding of the cultural dimension in how community development is understood.

For example, Pahl and Pool identify "the digital capture of the moving image" as "everyday cultural practice" and suggest that this changes the possibilities and implications of its use. They explore this "rich yet muddled field" by using film as a participatory method that involves engagement processes in order to analyse the cultural practices and experiences of children and young people. Importantly, and following on from the background of concern about the ethical integrity involved in the gap between rhetoric and practices of engagement and participation, Pahl and Pool suggest a need for the academic world to be aware of, "the dangers of constructing the field of film outside the realms of young people's agency". Steve Presence, in his close insight into the world of radical film networks in the UK, notes how the condition of precarity is now a standardised feature of employment in advanced capitalist economies and considers this in relation to radical filmmakers and the exhibition of these films in local, community contexts. The significance of Presence's analysis for questions of engagement and participation is that he offers a first-hand analysis of the complexities of engaging communities in radical, politically engaged cinema today. This is pertinent given the role of counter-cinema and the politicised dimension of so much of the early community film (for example, workshop movement) of the 1970s and 1980s.

Community Filmmaking as a Reflective Practice

One way community filmmakers can address the issues around the rhetoric of community engagement and the power imbalances potentially arising from community filmmaking projects is by engaging in more reflective practices. Raelin (2002, 66) characterises reflective practice as stepping back to question ourselves on the "social, political, and emotional data that arise from direct experience with one another. [...] It typically is concerned with forms of learning that seek to inquire about the most fundamental assumptions and premises behind our practices". Being reflective is usually an important aspect of artists' skills and practices. Indeed, research shows that they tend to bring this individual practice to activities they undertake with 'non-artist' learners (Pringle 2009). However, reflective practices can have various forms, structures and depth and be either personal or collective (Amulya 2004).

The chapter by Mock, Parker and Way offers an example of how filmmakers can engage in reflective practice about their work as well as how they can support reflective practice regarding the communities with which they work. This reflection is done at various levels and using different media, highlighting as well the potential of transmedia projects. First, their chapter critically reflects on and analyses the objectives, methods and the unfolding of their community film project *Heaven Is a Place*, a short dance film they produced with the LGBT community in Plymouth. Second, they discuss how they have used poetic dance and film to help participants reflect on their identity within the city of Plymouth. Third, they reflect on the role that geography and place can play within the construction and reflection of such identities. Finally, they explore participation in both dance and film and how *Heaven Is a Place* as an output of the project was perceived by project participants. As with other contributions within this section on engagement and participation, such reflective exercises on the practice of community filmmaking contribute to the building of knowledge about community filmmaking, its potential and its challenges.

References

Amulya, Joy. 2004. *What Is Reflective Practice?* Cambridge: Centre for Community Reflective Practice, Massachusetts Institute of Technology.

Braden, Su and Marhorie Mayo. 1999. "Culture, Community Development and Representation" *Community Development Journal* 34(3): 191–204.

Belfiore, Eleonora. 2002. "Art as a Means of Alleviating Social Exclusion: does it really work? A critique of instrumental cultural policies and social impact studies in the UK." *International Journal of Cultural Policy* 8: 91–106.

Besch, Janice and Jeffrey Minson. 2001. "Participatory Policy Making, Ethics and the Arts." In *Citizenship and Cultural Policy,* edited by Denise Meredyth and Jeffrey Minson. London: Sage Publications.

Mayo, Marjorie. 2000. *Cultures, Communities, Identities: cultural strategies for participation and empowerment.* Basingstoke: Palgrave Macmillan.

Price, Jonathan. 2015. "Contesting Agendas of Participation in the Arts." *Journal of Arts and Communities* 7(1–2): 17–31.

Pringle, Emily. 2009. "The Artist as Educator: examining relationships between art practice and pedagogy in the gallery context." *Tate Papers* 11, http://www.tate.org.uk/research/publications/tate-papers/11/artist-as-educator-examining-relationships-between-art-practice-and-pedagogy-in-gallery-context.

Raelin, Joseph. A. 2002. "'I Don't Have Time to Think!' versus the Art of Reflective Practice." *Reflections* 4(1): 66–79.

United Nations. 1955 Secretary-General. *Social Progress through Community Development.* New York: United Nations Bureau of Social Affairs.

11 Heaven Is a Place

The Politics and Poetics of LGBT Location in a Community Dance Film

Roberta Mock, Kayla Parker and Ruth Way

Introduction

Through a discussion of a local, movement-based performance for and through digital video, this chapter draws upon a range of scholarly disciplines (including performance studies, film studies, somatics, queer studies, urban studies and human geography) from the perspective of practitioner-researchers to reflect upon the implications and potentials of a community filmmaking practice that is simultaneously aesthetic, political, spatial and social. In particular, it considers how the process-driven triangulation of thinking bodies, sexual subjectivities and emplacement within such a practice might enable us to acknowledge, consolidate and reimagine a community that had been either erased or marginalised in dominant accounts of its city.

Heaven Is a Place is a short dance film,[1] made in 2014 by the authors of this chapter in collaboration with members of the lesbian, gay, bisexual and trans (LGBT) community in Plymouth in South West England. Filmed in some of Plymouth's most visually spectacular, evocative and liminal waterside locations – its docksides, marinas, look-out points, cruising spots, clubs and bathing areas – it explores becoming, melancholy and the erotics of place through the human geography of an 'ocean city'.[2] In addition to choreography arising from site-responsive physical vocabularies, the film features scenarios and movement scores that reflect personal memories and queer histories of the city, developed in the first instance through a series of movement workshops that were co-organised with the LGBT advocacy organisation, Pride in Plymouth.

The project integrated a cast of seven emergent professional performers, working in a range of movement-based disciplines (including dance, physical theatre and aerial performance), and 16 members of Plymouth's LGBT community to produce a film that was intended for moving image art and dance film audiences.[3] Although this dynamic produced a range of challenges (not least to terminology and categorisation), which will be discussed below, we consider *Heaven Is a Place* to be community filmmaking because it was made with and for a community of non-professional performers who participated in its creative process and established their own roles and representation therein. However, it is probably more accurately described as a hybrid form of screendance, socially engaged practice and documentary film: that is, as a moving image work in which motion and aesthetic movement are the primary expressive elements of that particular community. The film attempts to capture the development and moment of dance performance within a filmic portrait of an actual place recorded at a particular time. Although its loose storyline can certainly be read metaphorically, the work is primarily non-representational, aligning to Stella Bruzzi's central tenet of documentaries that they 'are performative acts, inherently fluid and unstable [...] whose truth comes into being only at the moment of filming' (Bruzzi 2006, 1 and 10).

Heaven Is a Place arose from a EU-funded Cultural Co-operation programme (with partners in Greece, Spain and Turkey), the overarching focus of which was the legacy of the French writer, playwright, filmmaker and activist, Jean Genet (1910–1986). Thirty years after his death, Genet continues to exert a huge influence on queer writing, theatre and film practices, and yet his position on homosexuality as an identity position was always complex. Originally our two creative 'work packages' within this programme were meant to run parallel to, but separate from, each other; these were the making of a site-responsive dancefilm and the running of somatic movement workshops for non-performers from Plymouth's LGBT community. Each was to respond specifically, but in different ways, to Genet's insistence on actively recognising and confronting the oppression of minority cultures and the ways in which he made difficult, subtle and challenging political statements in the creative spaces that exist between actuality and illusion. It was only after we completed the first series of workshops with members of Plymouth's LGBT community that we extended the invitation to help us envision and participate in the film, transforming it into a community filmmaking project. In retrospect, this can only be described as an organic process, arising from both the vitality and creativity of the workshop participants and our increasing discomfort with both representing – or worse, appropriating or simply using – the lived experience of others and being othered.

Caoimhe McAvinchey (2013) has noted a number of ways of framing the intersection of performance and community; one of the most significant revolves around *where* the work takes place. To these geographic (and often institutional) 'communities of location' she suggests adding "communities of identity" and "communities of interest", in order to reveal "a wide range of fluid, nuanced and responsive social processes" through performance making. The non-professional performance community that came together to make *Heaven Is a Place* with us – a community of 'queer' Plymothians who were interested in an open-ended creative exploration – embraced all three framings.[4] This aligns with Kirsten Macleod's observation that 'community media' is often both a *form* of "participatory practice which allows people to mediate their own identities' and also a *process* that 'is deeply connected to ideas of place" (in Malik, Chapain and Comunian 2014, 24).

Points of Departure

There were three co-determining departure points for *Heaven Is a Place*: the inspiration of Jean Genet as artist and activist; the experiences of Plymouth's LGBT communities past and present and the mythogeography of the city itself. At least superficially, there was good reason these resonated conceptually and thematically. For instance, Genet's 1947 novel, *Querelle de Brest*, revolves around the themes of doubling, homosexual desire and violence, its setting reflecting his adolescent fascination with ports (White 1994, 334). In Genet's poems, such as "Le Pecheur du Suquet", "La Parade" and "Un Chant d'Amour", one finds malicious children who make water shiver, bodies hanging by a single foot from the mizzen-mast and "feet uncurling the sea" (Genet, 1950). These are images that resonate deeply in Plymouth, a city – like Brest – defined by its maritime location, its status as a port and its severe bombing during WWII, which destroyed most of its centre. It is the location from which the Pilgrim Fathers supposedly set sail to colonise America and one still dominated by its dockyards and the Royal Navy.

The Plymouth of *Heaven Is a Place* is at once generic, metaphoric and specific in its materiality – a city in which it has never been easy to be gay or lesbian or bisexual or trans. Much of our historical understanding was drawn from the work of Alan Butler, who – in addition to being co-director of Pride in Plymouth with his partner, Mark Ayres – was then completing his doctoral thesis, based on dozens of oral history interviews, about the performance of LGBT pride in Plymouth from the middle of the twentieth century onwards. These interviews form the basis of an award-winning LGBT archive, deposited with the Plymouth and West Devon Record Office, with much of the material now available online. Alan was our community liaison and dramaturg, in the European sense of the role, and we reflected many of his research findings in the film. One is the extent to which queer culture in Plymouth has been shaped historically by the sexual flexibility of sailors and matelots. Another is that many gay people paradoxically have felt less certain of their community and even less safe since homosexuality was legalised and openly gay people could serve in the military. As long as LGBT culture remained 'hidden' in dockside bars and dancehalls, it was vibrant and silently accepted in the city at large.

Plymouth is often characterised as being 'on the periphery', its massive granite walls and fortresses facing the sea built to stave off an invasion by Napoleon. Some, of course, were also built to stave off an invasion by the sea itself. Its strength and our vulnerability in the face of its power was made explicit less than two months before we began filming, when a storm cut the city off from the rest of the country for weeks on end and battered much of its seafront. We had to climb over barricades, erected during the long repair process, to film many of the scenes. Sometimes, however, it was simply not possible for our three points of departure to coalesce as we might have hoped. Although we were welcomed on several site visits to *HMS Drake*, for instance, we were unable to secure permission to film within our schedule on either the military base or the adjacent dockyards controlled by the Ministry of Defence.[5]

Nonetheless, arising from Plymouth's specific historical and material landscape, *Heaven Is a Place* embraces many of Genet's themes and tropes: the lonely youth full of longing; how the costume one wears allows a shift from one persona to another, leading to adventure with others; the performance of self in a continuing process of change; the juxtaposition of the transient physicality of the human body with the materiality of natural phenomena; the drifting of bodies through spaces of dynamic potential. The film's eventual narrative trajectory is a receptacle: a travelling woman – a *vagabonde*, performed by the aerialist, Laura Murphy – arrives at Plymouth's Bretonside bus station and, following the promise of encounter, journeys through various locations before setting sail through Plymouth Sound, and to the ocean beyond, with an older sailor she has met at one of the city's waterfront gay bars (who, it is hinted, might stand in for Genet himself).

Genet's last explicitly aesthetic work dealing with homosexuality was his only film, *Un Chant d'Amour* (1950, 25 minutes). Like many of his early works, it is set in the homoerotic environment of a prison where, prevented from speaking to each other, the prisoners use their bodies to communicate. Elizabeth Stephens suggests that, for Genet, dancing constitutes a "corporeography, a bodily writing through which erotic desire is expressed" and that "[t]he body that writes itself through the language of dance in Genet's work is not a stable, essential one, secure within its own boundaries, but rather one that is both constituted and opened through the process of self-representation" (2006, 160 and 166). This accurately describes our approach to both choreography and performing presence in *Heaven Is a Place*.

Pre-production: Somatic Preparation for Contingency and Encounter

The film's creative research and development period with community participants started with a series of movement workshops, five months before filming began. Led by the film's choreographer, Ruth Way, and her assistant, Claire Summers, they were designed for people with no previous movement or performance experience and informed by Shin Somatic® processes and principles. In accordance with many community dance practices, the workshop delivery focused on nurturing self-worth, building self-confidence and accepting difference in order to promote inclusion and trust between participants (Bartlett 2008, 41). As Mark Ayres told us, "Many members of the LGBT communities lack confidence as adults due to bad experiences at school and some have even been rejected by their own families". This awareness shaped the principal aims of these workshops for participants: to focus on re-sourcing their creativity; to develop opportunities to be in dialogue with others; and to enable them to contribute their distinctive voices to the overarching artistic project.

Exemplary of the processes explored is 'matching through touch', which develops tactile kinaesthetic rapport between participants, focusing on the quality of touch in order to support individuals through a movement pattern. As Miranda Tufnell and Chris Crickmay note,

> What touches us, and what we ourselves reach out to touch, shapes every aspect of who we are. We are formed by touch, our sense of ourselves growing from the feel of contact between our bodies and what is around us. (2004, 122)

The practice of touch, and the openness and empathy it can engender, was central to the movement and choreographic direction on site, emphasising a heightened level of tactility through various modes of contact with surfaces and structures. Other workshop exercises included witnessing each other's movement explorations and either 'dancing back' or describing the images and how they made us feel. This practice resists the urge to claim to know or interpret someone else's experience. Rather, the aim is to open up the potential for bodily knowing and learning from each other, taking responsibility for what we see and feel and supporting clarity in verbal and non-verbal communication. As a result, one of the emerging themes that arose from this practice in the workshops was the importance of visibility, of 'being seen'.

Community workshop participants who wanted to continue working with us (and almost all of them did if they were available to do so) were involved in further ensemble work in one of the pivotal scenes of the film; some (including Cornelius van Rijckvorsel, who is the only person seen speaking and sails the boat in the closing shots)[6] eventually performed in other scenes as well. Perhaps as significantly, however, the workshops inspired and taught us much more about the issues, themes and movement vocabularies that needed to be expressed and developed through choreographic processes on site. Evoking an imaginative interplay of oppositions that resonated closely with Genet's work, these included appearing and disappearing, ascending and descending, arriving and leaving, advancing and retreating, filling and emptying, expanding and contracting, including and excluding, imprisoned and released, grounded and airborne.

Primarily, however, in preparation for filming, we concentrated on training both professional and community performers to be responsive, generous, empathic and as physically prepared as possible to encounter each other and the environment. As a conscious strategy focusing on the moment of such contingent encounters, we had no storyboard or synopsis or set choreography at the start of our three-week production period. We had only our creative departure points and a shooting schedule, listing filming locations and which performers we wanted to be there and in what clothing.

Although we had chosen 12 sites in consultation with our dramaturg and community participants (we were only able to explore two with the professional performers through guided improvisation over the previous month), more than half had not yet been confirmed or were subject to last-minute uncertainty due to structural damage, unexpected commercial development, insurance queries or access problems. Almost all locations were weather dependent. As is the case for many community films made in the UK, the limited availability of a diverse group of non-professional performers within a specific filming window meant that the principal scene featuring all of the community participants was firmly scheduled in our only indoor location: a gay club on Plymouth's Barbican (Figure 11.1).

Figure 11.1 Cast and crew briefing meeting prior to filming at OMG on Plymouth's Barbican.

Production Strategies: Documenting the Derive through Actualitié

Because our choreographic and filmmaking processes were inevitably conjoined through the availability and accessibility of people and places in a given moment, the journey of the performers is aligned to the moving image timeline; the sequences were shot almost entirely in the order in which they are seen in the film. The film therefore represents the organic development of its production process and documents the dialogical encounter between reality and image through screen performance. This chronology is entwined with a looping spatio-temporality, in that places are revisited and renewed, scenarios are replayed and performances are re-enacted.

This mirrors the cinematic strategies found in both Genet's film and his writing: the use of parallel plotlines, close-ups of gestures, flashbacks and temporal disjunction. There are many other ways, however, in which Genet haunts our film. Hélène Cixous has reflected upon his "erotic and nostalgic vagabondage, his wandering around cities", noting that Genet is "one of those ghosts in search of a stage, a place to make an appearance. There's a close relationship between the secret forces of a place and the likelihood of a spectral crystallisation" (2012, 33). As a revenant in *Heaven Is a Place*, he puts words in mouths. He places phone calls. He is conjured by the performers, attracted by the secret forces of specific places.

Our vagabond, played by the only performer in the film who did not live in Plymouth, guides and is guided by the spirit of Genet. She is lured to the sea, a sea that both delivers her beyond and is itself beyond, and finds her stage in the sky (as an aerialist who performs on a rope hanging from a crane, high above a Plymouth boatyard (See Figure 11.2)). Her movement through the city can be best understood in terms of the situationist tactic known as the dérive. In his seminal 1958 text, Guy Debord described the dérive as "a technique of rapid passage through varied ambiences", which is quite different from a journey or a stroll. Dérives involve "playful-constructive behaviour" and usually take place in urban environments. Their spatial fields depend on significant points of departure, like a bus station. From there, dérivistes disregard all the usual motives for movement and action, and instead let themselves be "drawn by the attractions of the terrain and the encounters they find there". This chimes uncannily with Genet's understanding of community and identification: "You can select a particular community other than that of your birth, whereas you are born into a people; this selection is based on an irrational affinity, [...] an emotional – perhaps intuitive, sensual – attraction" (1983). *Heaven Is a Place* not only produces and is produced by such a community, it also documents the search for one.

Figure 11.2 Still from *Heaven is a Place* (2014) featuring Laura Murphy.

The film draws on the *actualitié* style of early filmmakers such as the Lumière brothers, which depicted ordinary people and everyday events and led to genres of documentary, as well as special effects, staged narratives and fictional reconstructions. The principal camera acts as a reflective witness, observing and recording the semi-choreographed performance of dance unfolding in response to a specific location. Informed by 'direct cinema', in which the audience participates in observing 'reality' unfold on the screen, the cinematographer used a tripod to capture a wide viewpoint of the performers' bodies moving in a real environment. This creative documentation of *actualitié* – what occurred in front of the camera – also reflects the formal stylistic elements of Genet's work for stage and cinema.

The observational mode of filming created space on the screen for the dance sequences; framed by the camera, the viewer can see the performers' bodies moving in relation to place. Sometimes the camera was released from its fixed position and held in the hand, its lens moving gently in response to the action of the performers' bodies, allowing a more subjective viewing experience through a dance between the camera and the performers-in-place. The second handheld camera was integrated within the choreographed visual dance as a 'performer' in order to capture embodied views, responding to series of intimate encounters between the participants' bodies, as life's moments to be shared with 'friends' on social media. The use of lightweight recording equipment and a small crew allowed us to be open to improvisation and to interweave chance elements, such as the performance by the two bar staff, on duty at our only indoor location, who were keen to participate in the project.

Moving in Place: Looking Out and In

Our approach as a filmmaking team to working in a specific site was influenced by the geographer, Edward Relph (1976). In line with his research methodology – which he described as "a phenomenology of place" – we allowed each location to reveal itself to us over a series of visits, improvisations, rehearsals and the moment of filming itself. The development of the screenplay and the evolving processes of production were informed by the filmmakers' and performers' bodily experiences of these places, allowing our senses to connect with what lay unseen beneath the visible landscape. By framing selected areas of the visual field, the choice of shot and so on, our decisions in creating moving images can create audience awareness of a performer's 'existential insideness', described by Relph as a deep unselfconscious immersion in place (1976, 55).

These production choices mirrored our choreographic processes in external locations, during which the movement vocabularies and themes developed in the community workshops acted as substrata. The act of producing space through the body and reclaiming self-agency informed how the professional performers began to generate choreographic material through the distinct architectural structures and material properties of specific sites. In this section, due to space limitations, we will focus on the first location we explored and filmed in this way, although the method was the same for all. Its choice reflects the lure of the sea and evoked for us the diverse transient community of Plymouth's waterfront areas, comprising the homeless, asylum seekers, drug addicts, those seeking transgressive sexual liaisons, dog-walkers, fishermen and -women, picnickers, ship-spotters, swimmers, beach-combers.

The scene involved all of the professional performers and, in moments such as these, working as an ensemble, we came to see them as the embodied spirits of a specific site, although they could just as easily be a group of clubbers avoiding home in the early morning. Because we see them from the vantage point of the vagabond, who glimpses their bodies through one of the small windows in the WWII defensive structure, we named the location Vagabonde's Lookout East.

This site, at Devil's Point, comprised an upper space framed by a metal balcony, a place to lean on and look out to sea and beyond to the horizon. Later in the film, the dancers occupy these positions; the two women, in their military uniforms, dance romantically in the sunshine on the top level, as they emerge figuratively and literally from restrictions into the freedom to conform. But in this scene, they inhabit the neglected space beneath, one that, to us, smelled of suffering; dampness saturated the walls and ground. It felt devoid of human contact and warmth, lacking in purpose. A central supporting column dominated the space, which was dug into the earth with one side facing the sea, and a series of cold metal benches hugged the back wall.

The dancers explored its internal structures, surfaces and spatial dimensions, improvising on the theme of 'appearing and disappearing'. The moment when one unconsciously mimicked the central pillar, the space was suddenly imbued with a structurally integrative power and emotional resonance. He could barely sustain the contact with the floor, balancing on his toes and pressing the palm of his hand upwards into the ceiling. In this moment, we experienced the manifestation of the struggle to find a connection and the resolve to live through that difficulty. These oppositional forces became the anchoring points and spatial coordinates for a performance score. In contact with the surface of the ground – lying and crawling on it and touching its crevices and textures – the performers were able to support themselves and each other and find their way to the portals through which they could potentially pass and be seen.

The camera captured and exposed the oppositional elements inherent in this unfolding score: the near and far proximities of bodies, individually and together, in space; the exploration of in and out, above and below, ground and ceiling, benches and walls. On one of those walls was a small scrawl of graffiti, which never quite was in frame. It was only after the cameras were finally packed away that we realised what this graffiti was trying to communicate: No to Europe.

Financed by the European Union, in a programme that aimed to foster cultural co-operation between European partners, we made *Heaven Is a Place* against the backdrop of a European election in which the largest political gains in both England and France were made by nationalist parties that preyed on fear of difference, of invasion.[7] We deliberately made a European film – and this is one of the reasons almost all of the (albeit limited) spoken text in the film is in French. Jean Genet reminded us that borders are always instruments of control, sites where inclusion and exclusion are made manifest; that the sea connects us to the world and that we can be both on the margin and at the centre of a complex network of relations.

Heaven Is a Place is an attempt to make meaning of and with and for a specific city that is more than itself – that is, it is also its passageways and its underground spaces; it is Europe and its sea. Suggested by Cixous in her writing about Genet (2012, 32), we imagined a Plymouth that suddenly unfurled and turned itself out from a single vantage point: "Bienvenue à Bretonside", announces the voice from the bus station loudspeaker in the opening scene. It is a place that is constructed, dialectically, through what it has excluded, kept hidden, pushed to its borders, where the land drops away.

Filming a Queer Counter-public Cartography

The spaces connected through the vagabond's journey in *Heaven Is a Place* are those that Michel Foucault would describe as 'heterotopic' (1967/1984). They are marginalised yet paradoxically perform important and complex social and cultural roles. We might also understand them as 'queer spaces' that exist in the shadows of heteronormative comings and goings. For the architectural historian Aaron Betsky, a 'queer space' is "a space of difference", an arena of doubt, self-criticism, and "the possibility of liberation" (in Gandy 2012, 730).

Queer, like dérive, is both a verb and a noun. It is also an adjective that deliberately both means and doesn't mean the same thing, and so it is a word that many find both troublesome and slippery. Michael Gandy, for instance, prefers the term 'queering space', which seems to avoid theories of identity formation based on sexual difference as well as subsequent political action, but not quite. Gandy's formulation is based on the use or appropriation of space. As he notes, "Activities such as cruising" – that is, the practice of visiting public spaces for the purpose of meeting people for anonymous same sex encounters – are a "form of site-specific spatial insurgency", a socio-cultural practice in "which human creativity and the sexual imagination are radically combined" (Gandy 2012, 734).

One of Plymouth's most enduring cruising spots (although less so now) is the Lion's Den cove on the Hoe. Reached via steep steps from the promenade above, it is a small, curved, now-dishevelled amphitheatre, facing the sea. The Lion's Den had been a men's only nude bathing area throughout the 1950s. In the 1960s, its original glass roof was ruined in a storm and not replaced; as it became less acceptable to sunbathe nude during the day, the site became increasingly associated with the gay male community. It was suggested as a filming location through Alan Butler's research as well as by a number of project participants.

Choreographer Carol Brown draws our attention to how dancers produce "a set of relationships between body, space and architecture". The resulting matrixial field offers "a transgressive threshold of co-emergence for the dancing subject and the unfolding of spaces within choreography as encounter" (Brown 2010, 59). The Lion's Den featured in several scenes in *Heaven Is a Place*; at the centre of the film is a duet between two of the professional performers (See Figure 11.3). The choreography, arising from the themes and movement vocabulary developed in the community workshops, as well as through the dancers' guided

Figure 11.3 Still from *Heaven is a Place* (2014) featuring Adam Whiting and Erik Koky at the Lion's Den.

improvisations in this specific site, explored the dynamic opposition of ground and sky, dropping and falling, fullness and emptiness, expansion and contraction, power and vulnerability, hunting and being prey. Just beyond them, arms draped around each other's shoulders, their gaze shifting in unison from the sparkling sea to the two young men dancing together in and out of the shadows, are Alan Butler and Mark Ayres who co-direct Pride in Plymouth.

Something that became increasingly evident to us while making *Heaven Is a Place* is that very few members of Plymouth's LGBT community then referred to themselves individually or collectively as 'queer'.[8] Rather, queer seems to be our way, as filmmakers, of understanding a scenario that embraces Genet and Plymouth and some of the members of its LGBT community, as well what the film is trying to represent and achieve aesthetically and politically. It is not possible in the space available here to rehearse the numerous intersecting theoretical formations, arguments and manoeuvres that have transformed this single word – queer – into such a rich terrain over the past two decades. However, the working definition that served as the backbone of the critical exploration in the film is that queer is the politics of the liberation of desire and is expressed in terms of erotic potential. It involves viewing the world and one's place in it through a previously neglected homosexual matrix with all the historical awareness that entails. Pragmatically utopian – if we can ever describe the utopian as pragmatic – queer has built in its own obsolescence.

When we enter the public domain – in this case, through the making of an artwork – we are speaking both on behalf of and to a group of people we can barely imagine but whom we wish to affect. Indeed, this is at the heart of the constitution of such a group, what Michael Warner describes as 'a public'. Publics are always "mediated by cultural forms" and exist "only by virtue of address" (2002, 419). They are social spaces created through discourses that are temporal and reflexive. Indeed, for Warner, the "addressee of public discourse is always yet to be realized", and for this reason, such discourse involves "open-endedness, reflexive framing" and "accessibility" (2002, 416). These terms also describe our strategy for *Heaven Is a Place*, a strategy that understands 'publicness' as a form of embodied creativity and world making.

There are some publics, however, that comprise those who have been excluded, or exclude themselves from, hegemonic norms or expectations. These, as Warner points out, are not simply subsets but are actually defined by "a conflictual relation to the dominant public" (2002, 423). Warner calls them counter-publics, and they are always at "some level, conscious or not", aware of their 'subordinate status'. 'Within a gay or queer counter-public,' he writes, "No one is in the closet" and "presumptive heterosexuality … is suspended" (2002, 424). As a result, the circulation of this counter-public discourse always eventually meets intense resistance. Warner notes that "the expansive nature of public address will seek to keep moving that frontier for a queer public, to seek more and more places to circulate where people will recognize themselves in its address" (2002, 424).

In August 2014, *Heaven Is a Place* was shown on the big screen in the centre of Plymouth's shopping district during the city's first formal Pride Parade, which passed directly under it. One of the film's participants told us that he felt the film offered the march's onlookers "a sense of our community". Mark Ayres believes that:

> Whilst most people that took part in the parade only saw a small piece of the film, it enhanced the sense of pride. Parading under the big screen with images of same sex couples dancing in iconic Plymouth locations was a very poignant moment. The imagery and video footage of the parade including the film on the big screen has been shared far and wide – creating a positive image of Plymouth.

As Barbara Abrash and David Whiteman observe, "the making and circulation of an independent film can create venues and platforms for the discussion of vital and controversial social issues, in environments that link personal and community experience and foster action" (1999, 97).

The insistence on reflexive locatedness as a guiding principle in *Heaven Is a Place* begins to model how community film might celebrate and extend diversity through the construction of a collectively shared counter-public cartography.

Some Findings: Community Filmmaking as a Nexus of Located Relationships

Since the end of the 1960s, community filmmaking has "enabled groups and individuals to use the media often used to misrepresent them to engage in new forms of collective self-representation" (Webb-Ingall 2014). Whilst there was no opportunity in our project to provide the training necessary for the community to devise, film and edit the professionally realised moving image artwork the commission required, we tried to evolve strategies for ensuring the widest and most meaningful possible participation by LGB and T community members from the outset within the limited time most had available to work with us. There are, however, inevitably tensions that arise from making a community film that is simultaneously intended to be an art product, especially one that needed to be completed within a limited timeframe to fulfil the obligations of funding.

Among Plymouth's wider LGBT community, there were some who thought the film was too 'arty'; without a conventional storyline or narrative positioning, they found it difficult to understand or to see 'the point' (one audience member described it, we presume metaphorically, as a "porno flick but without the money shot"). On the other hand, many expressed surprise and delight that it was a 'proper', 'professional' film. Pride in Plymouth, which originally became involved in the project as an activity with the potential to "bring members of the LGBTQ communities together", noted that they hadn't at first realised "what an immediate, tangible outcome a film can be for people. Participants can view it back and see it as the fruit of their labours and the fact that it looked so amazing made the process feel very worthwhile".

The making of *Heaven Is a Place* required continual renegotiation in order to balance the shifting expectations of diverse organisations, individuals and groups of people. As a result, we came to understand our roles as community filmmakers in this situation as cultural and aesthetic intermediaries between the LGBT performers and the commissioning body, constantly weighing up both creative imperatives (for example, to be original, innovative, technically precise) and the ethical implications of socially engaged practice, each with varying degrees of success. Occupying a position of trust, we attempted to best interpret and mediate the visions of and communications of the various axes of the network of relationships.

Whilst *Heaven Is a Place* does not set out to represent 'LGBT Plymouth' as a political entity or uniform collective – indeed, the authors would argue that a homogenous body such as this cannot exist – the LGBT community in Plymouth did consolidate through the process of developing, performing, making and showing the film. The experiences and perspectives of the group who were actively involved in the film directly inform both its screenplay and mise-en-scène, as do the documented lives of those individuals who had recently contributed to the Plymouth LGBT Archive. Indeed, Alan Butler has noted that he sees "the film as now part of the archive and watching it provides a doorway into the stories that are in there". He has screened it within presentations and conferences about LGBT oral history and archives and feels it offers "a version of Plymouth that might not chime" with widespread assumptions about the city. When he watches it in these contexts, Alan says that "it always makes me feel strangely homesick but for the place that the film portrays. A place that is very much the Plymouth we all know but strangely not at the same time".

The community participants chose the locations of *Heaven Is a Place,* and their narratives inform what we see on screen. The nightclub scene, which features all the performers as a cohesive community, is set in the gay club OMG, then newly opened on Plymouth's Barbican, and may be understood to represent the interior spaces of the city's pubs and bars where LGBT people could 'be themselves'. The choreographed duet at the heart of the film is performed at The Lion's Den, a site of personal significance to one of our key contributors: as a young teenager, alone and isolated in feeling and knowing he was gay, but not being able to make contact with anyone 'like him', this place by the sea was where he could see others 'like him'. It was important to our contributors that these places be featured before they are effaced by gentrification. To perform a politics of location, as we attempted to do in our film, is to create what Rosi Braidotti calls materially embedded, "embodied accounts" that "illuminate and transform our knowledge of ourselves and of the world" (2004, 133).

At the very heart of this process, for us, were the workshops grounded in somatic movement principles. These were designed to foster an inclusive and non-hierarchical working environment and to enable individual contributions to be seen and valued. Somatic bodywork is able to assist "people in experiencing and transforming the self through awareness relative to the living world, the environment, and others" (Fraleigh 2015, 5) by suspending judgement, not fixing, finding pleasure in movement, exploring openings, evoking embodied memory and trusting in intuition. When participants refer to the 'emotional' experience of filmmaking, the confidence they gained or the 'authenticity' engendered through it, they tend to refer specifically to these workshops. The moments of release and transgression these sessions produced began to reveal the unique qualities of each performer, his or her physicality and a renewed capacity to produce and reclaim space in the moment.

The transition, however, from workshop space to film location was not altogether smooth. Some participants expressed disappointment that, having explored and developed their individual stories via movement, these were reduced to abstractions or group work in the film. One participant noted that while this was a "pragmatic and understandable" decision, he felt it was "sad that more of the material from the workshops could not have been translated into the film more fully". Paradoxically, although we discussed the daunting prospect of 'not knowing' and dealing with ambiguity in a creative process, another participant would have preferred to have a firmer structure and sense of direction once the filming started. As community filmmakers, however, this was fundamental to our approach, practiced and rehearsed in the workshops. By sharing a collective sense of vulnerability and accruing value to performance and filming processes that were not mapped in advance, we hoped to inspire a more creative and open dialogue among all involved.

Perhaps the most significant legacy of *Heaven Is a Place* is the strengthening of bonds among those who were involved in its making. Two years after its completion, participants continue to speak of the ensuing 'comraderie', as well as long-lasting friendships and relationships that the film consolidated. There is a sense of collective ownership in the film, a feeling of pleasure in its professional aesthetic and technical realisation, that it is made in Plymouth and about being in Plymouth. In the words of one of its community participants,

> The film looks beautiful and other worldly and feels like an enhanced snapshot into a subculture that had been kept out of sight. It shone a spotlight onto a previously unseen stage. It celebrates places and lives that have often been considered by some to be shameful and those of us who took part are clearly proud of the film and their participation in it.

According to Mark Ayres, participating in the making of *Heaven Is a Place* helped Pride in Plymouth "to build the 'Pride Family' and its social status" as an organisation, growing in confidence as a cultural and political force in the city and beyond.

The 'heaven' of our collaboratively filmed encounter is the dynamic, multiple, shifting intersection of the temporal, the spatial and the experiential, combining emotional, corporeal, cognitive and memory registers. By focusing on embodied process and what Bruzzi describes as the "perpetual negotiation between the real event and its representation" (2006, 13), we believe it went some way towards shedding light on the "personal and community histories that [give] people a new sense of themselves and the political and social realities which shape their lives" (Abrash and Whiteman 1999, 96). Importantly, for us, it is a film that could only emerge through collaborative interactions in which the bodies of the present were prepared to meet the places of Plymouth's queer past on their own terms.

Notes

1 At the time of writing, *Heaven Is a Place* (16 minutes, 30 seconds) has been screened at Plymouth and Warwick Arts Centres, the Trans(m)it International Film Festival (Philadelphia, USA), within the International Competition of Kino der Kunst 2015 (Munich and Nürnberg, Germany) and at the Dances with Camera competition at the Short Waves Festival 2016 (Poznań, Poland), in addition to touring with the original EU-funded programme, 'Heaven on Earth?', to Piraeus (Greece), Zaragoza (Spain) and Istanbul in 2014. It is also a Cornwall Film Festival Competition Winner (2014). Credits: Kayla Parker (director); Ruth Way (choreographer), assisted by Claire Summers; Roberta Mock (executive producer); Roberta Mock, Kayla Parker and Ruth Way (screenplay); Stuart Moore (cinematographer) and Siobhán Mckeown (editor). For further production details, including cast list, please visit: http://www.kaylaparker.co.uk/other_films/other_films/heaven_is_a_place.html.
2 Plymouth adopted the motto 'Spirit of Discovery' in 1996, alluding to its rich heritage of naval exploration, Charles Darwin and Scott having both embarked on their global voyages from moorings close to its seaward border. However, signs welcoming visitors were frequently vandalised to read 'Plymouth – Spirit of Disco,' reflecting its lively club culture (*Plymouth Herald*, 2013). After a brief period as 'Positively Plymouth' (2010–2013), the city rebranded itself as 'Britain's Ocean City,' its visual motif being Smeaton's decommissioned lighthouse on the Eddystone Rocks rebuilt on Plymouth Hoe.
3 The professional performers were contracted and paid for 30 days (including training/rehearsals); community performers, who volunteered to be in the film following the workshop phase, were required to commit for about three days in total (including at least two workshops), although some chose to participate more than this. For the latter, we reimbursed all direct expenditure incurred in their participation. The authors of this chapter, all of whom are full-time academics, were *not* remunerated; however, all other members of the production team were.
4 The call to participate went out to over 2,000 individuals who follow Pride in Plymouth on social media. The 24 people who eventually worked with us included lesbians, gay men, bisexual men and women, and trans women; the majority of them had engaged with the organisation in the past. As one participant noted: 'It was the more activist/creative section of the community that took part so not perhaps the whole community but it included a wide variety of members from different generations'.
5 Similarly, while three of our professional performers (including the two women) appear in naval uniforms at various points in the film, of all the participants, only our assistant choreographer was acting or former military personnel.
6 Interestingly, Cornelius was the only participant who expressed to us dissatisfaction with the film. In particular, he was disappointed that it was not more like Genet's work.

7 Two years later, as this chapter was being revised for publication, Britain voted to leave the European Union, something that we wouldn't have believed when we were making the film.
8 The use of the term 'queer' has subsequently begun to emerge, for instance, in social media postings about the 2016 Plymouth Pride event.

References

Abrash, Barbara and David Whiteman. 1999. "The Uprising of '34: Filmmaking as Community Engagement." *Wide Angle* 21(2): 87–99.

Ayers, Mark. Email to authors.

Bartlett, Ken. 2008. 'Love Difference: why is diversity important in community dance?' In *An Introduction to Community Dance Practice*, edited by Diane Amans, 39–42. Basingstoke: Palgrave Macmillan.

Braidotti, Rosi. 2004. "Gender and Power in a Post-Nationalist European Union.' *NORA: Nordic Journal of Women's Studies* 12(3): 130–142.

Brown, Carol. 2010. 'Making Space, Speaking Spaces.' In *The Routledge Dance Studies Reader* 2nd edition, edited by Alexandra Carter and Janet O'Shea. Abingdon: Routledge.

Bruzzi, Stella. 2006. New Documentary: a critical introduction. Abingdon and New York: Routledge.

Cixous, Hélène. 2012. *Poetry in Painting: writings on contemporary arts and aesthetics*. Edited by Marta Segarra and Joana Masó. Edinburgh: Edinburgh University Press.

Debord, Guy. 1958. "Theory of the Dérive." Translated by Ken Knab (2006) and republished by the Bureau of Public Secrets [online] http://www.bopsecrets. org/SI/2.derive.htm.

Foucault, Michel. 1967/1984. "Of Other Spaces: utopias and heterotopias." Translated by Jay Miskowiec [online] http://web.mit.edu/allanmc/www/ foucault1.pdf.

Fraleigh, Sondra. 2015. "Part One: somatic movement arts." In *Moving Consciously: somatic transformations through dance, yoga, and touch*, edited by Sondra Fraleigh, 1–74. Champaign, IL: University of Illinois Press.

Gandy, Michael. 2012. "Queer Ecology: nature, sexuality, and heterotopic alliances.' *Environment and Planning D: Society and Space* 30: 727–747.

Genet, Jean. 1983. "Four Hours at Chatila." Translated by Daniel R. Dupecher and Martha Perrigaud [online] http://www.abbc.net/solus/JGchatilaEngl.html.

Genet, Jean. 1920. "Love Song." Translated by Marc Spitzer [online] http:// fablog.ehrensteinland.com/2015/03/04/dr-bens-just-a-prisoner-of-love/.

Malik, Sarita, Caroline Chapain and Roberta Comunian. 2014. *Spotlight on Community Filmmaking: a report on community filmmaking and cultural diversity research*. London and Birmingham: Brunel University, the University of Birmingham and King's College London.

McAvinchey, Caoimhe. 2013. "Introduction: Right Here, Right Now." In *Performance and Community: commentary and case studies*, edited by Caoimhe McAvinchey. London: Bloomsbury. Kindle Edition.

Relph, Edward. 1976. *Place and Placelessness*. London: Pion.

Stephens, Elizabeth. 2006. "Corporeographies: the dancing body in *'adame Miroir* and *Un chant d'amour*." In *Jean Genet: performance and politics*, edited by Clare Finburgh, Carl Lavery and Maria Shevtsova, 159–168. Basingstoke: Palgrave Macmillan.

Tufnell, Miranda and Chris Crickmay. 2004. *A Widening Field: journeys into the body and the imagination*. Hampshire: Dance Books.

Warner, Michael. 2002. "Publics and Counterpublics (abbreviated version)." *Quarterly Journal of Speech* 88(4): 413–425.

Webb-Ingall, Ed. 2014. "Community Video Then and Now: looking backwards to look forwards." [online] http://www.focaalblog.com/2014/12/18/ed-webb-ingall-community-video-then-and-now-looking-backward-to-look-forward/.

White, Edmund. 1994. *Genet*. London and Basingstoke: Picador.

12 'One screening away from disaster'

Precarity and Commitment in the Radical Film Network's Community Exhibition Sector

Steve Presence

Introduction

The Radical Film Network (RFN, www.radicalfilmnetwork.com) is an international network of individuals and organisations engaged in the production of political film culture. Convened in London in 2013, the RFN now consists of more than 100 organisations across 20 countries and ranges from production companies, archives and distribution platforms to film clubs, co-operatives (co-ops) and festivals. This diverse range of organisations is united by two things: a medium-specific focus on the moving image and a political identity marked by an affiliation with the politics of the left and the ideologies traditionally at its core, especially socialism, anarchism and radical environmentalism.[1] The community film culture in question here, then, is an overtly political one, distinguished in part by the overriding concern of those involved to use film to engender social and political engagement, participation and change.

This chapter explores the RFN's exhibition sector in the UK. Unfortunately for those involved both in exhibition and other sectors of radical film culture, another characteristic shared by the vast majority of organisations involved is a complete lack of funding and a corresponding paucity of time and resources. As a result, although the large number of organisations active in the network suggests that this film culture is alive and well, most radical film organisations also exist in a state of precarity, or 'existence without security' (Murray and Gollmitzer 2012, 419). The concept of precarity has been explored at length, both in macro socio-economic terms as a symptom of twenty-first-century capitalism (Neilson and Rossiter 2008, Standing 2011 and 2014) and as a condition that is particularly prevalent in the creative industries (Gill and Pratt 2008, Banks and Hesmondhalgh 2009, Ross 2010). Income instability, free labour, self-exploitation and associated pathologies such as alienation and anxiety are all markers of 'the precariat': a new international class of workers that lacks stable income, employment benefits and any meaningful control over labour and leisure time. Precarity is now a standardised feature of employment in advanced capitalist economies (Brault cited in Bain and McLean 2013, 96) and is so embedded in the cultural industries that most cultural workers in the UK actually depend on another job outside of the cultural field (Arts Council England 2010). In this context, we might think of radical film exhibition – and radical film activists more generally – as doubly precarious: a form of cultural work that is rarely (if ever) remunerated and carried out in their spare time by people that already rely on a second or third job to survive. How do organisations involved in radical film exhibition negotiate such precarious conditions, and how do these conditions shape their approach to exhibition?

In what follows I focus my attention on two radical film exhibitors: Liverpool Radical Film Festival (LRFF) and Birmingham Co-operative Film Society, or Birmingham Film Co-op (BFC). These organisations have been selected because they offer both contrasting examples and instructive similarities to other groups in the sector. Both organisations encounter similar challenges and share comparable aims but differ in terms of the nature of the events they organise, their internal structures and identities and the kinds of film they show. LRFF is an annual event – although it also hosts ad hoc screenings throughout the year – organised by a loosely decentralised team that operates horizontally and explores a range of approaches to radical film. BFC, by contrast, organises a year-round series of monthly screenings, is coordinated by an elected committee with fixed roles and selects films democratically via a ballot box. One must therefore be wary of generalising analysis of one organisation to another. As Lucy Küng-Shankleman has argued (albeit in relation to two very different organisations – the BBC and CNN), all organisations and cultures are unique, with unique strengths and weaknesses that are 'context-dependent' (2000, 202). Yet detailed analysis of these two organisations does yield insights that illuminate the sector more generally, and this chapter seeks to be of equal use both to scholars interested in this community film culture and to those groups that comprise it.

A broader aim of the chapter is more general. In the UK as elsewhere, radical film culture is a large and diverse – albeit precarious – facet of contemporary film culture but remains a significantly under-researched area. Academic work in the field has grown in recent years but is still relatively sparse, rarely focused on the UK and, with a few notable exceptions – Turnin and Winton (2014), Mazierska and Kristensen (2015); Tzioumakis and Molloy (2016) – predominantly focused on periods long since passed. In the UK, much of the more recent work on political film culture has concentrated on the 1970s and 1980s,[2] just as scholars involved with the resurgence of radical film culture in the 1970s and 1980s were preoccupied with rediscovering the radical film cultures of the 1920s and 1930s.[3] Documenting these histories is essential but must not be at the expense of our understanding of contemporary movements, of the organisations involved and of how and why they do what they do. Indeed, for the most part these earlier histories *are* well documented – see Dickinson (1999) for a thorough account of radical film in Britain from 1945 to 1990, for example – while the past 20 years of committed film culture in the UK is practically unaccounted for.[4]

Within the RFN's exhibition sector alone, for instance, many other organisations are deserving of further investigation. In the UK, for example, self-titled radical film festivals exist in cities, towns and villages such as Bristol, Brighton, Norwich and Tolpuddle (Dorset). RFN-affiliated festivals in the capital include the London Feminist Film Festival and London Labour Film Festival, while myriad other groups organise events up and down the country throughout the year. Such groups include Autonomy Films (Bridport), Full Unemployment Cinema (London), Manchester Film Co-op and Take One Action (Edinburgh). Outside the UK, festivals and exhibition groups affiliated to the RFN include the Brazilian International Labour Film Festival (São Paulo), Cinema Politica (Montréal), Guerrilla Cinema (Marrakesh), Subversive Festival (Zagreb) and Workers Unite Film Festival (New York City). While some excellent research into activist film festivals has taken place within the wider field of film festival studies, notably by scholars such as Iordanova and Torchin (2012), few of the organisations above have featured in this growing body of work thus far (partly because the field has tended to prioritise festivals to the neglect of other kinds of exhibition organisation, such as film clubs or co-operatives). Focusing on just two organisations here thus both fills a gap and illustrates the wealth of work that remains to be done in this large and heterogeneous field.

Research on activist film festivals has nevertheless generated a number of insights into how such organisations operate. For example, Iordanova (2012) has noted that the inclusion of discussion time after the screening event, in which the films and the issues they raise can be interrogated by the audience, is probably "the single most important feature that makes a festival activist" (16). Skadi Loist and Ger Zielinski's (2012) overview of queer film festivals notes the role of these festivals in the creation of counter-public spheres and that such "community-oriented, identity-based film festivals" differ in their organisational structures and funding patterns (51). Miriam Ross has explored how the "material and embodied" aspects of community exhibition – introductions, interruptions, the proximity of the projection equipment to the audience and so on – distinguish it from the lack of interaction and strictly delineated spaces of commercial exhibition (2013, 449–450). Winton and Turnin, meanwhile, distinguish 'community programming', in which films are selected with the interests of the audience in mind, from 'capital programming', in which the profit motive is the guiding principle (2013, 25).

These characteristics apply to the above groups and are evidenced in the case studies below, but different groups articulate these shared characteristics in different ways and for different reasons. Detailed scrutiny of individual case studies enables us to explore how and why behaviours common among radical exhibitors contribute to the rich diversity of organisations active in the sector. With a view to unpicking this intersection of commonalities and distinctions, in what follows, each organisation is framed in the same way – formation, objectives, internal organisation and external relationships – a structure that facilitates comparison and brings into relief their unique organisational identities.

Methodology (and Full Disclosure)

My relationship to this field is neither objective nor dispassionate. As a founder member of the Bristol Radical Film Festival collective and convener of the RFN, I am a committed participant in this culture as much as an observer of it. While this relationship inevitably colours the analysis that follows, it is also perhaps appropriate given that one of the distinguishing features of contemporary radical film culture (in the West, at least) is the strong links that many such organisations have with Higher Education Institutions. Indeed, the RFN received development support from my institution, the University of the West of England (UWE) Bristol and has more recently benefitted from an international research networking grant from the government's Arts and Humanities Research Council (AHRC) in the UK: 'Sustaining Alternative Film Cultures' (2015–2017).[5] The interviews that inform this chapter have taken place as part of that AHRC-funded project. Because of the nature of the organisations in question, there are very few, if any, secondary sources on which to draw. The methodology I have adopted is therefore a qualitative one, with analyses drawn from empirical data based on extended interviews with participants and participant-observation at selected events. Interviews are, of course, an unreliable form of data – interviewees inevitably present a particular version of themselves and assign their own set of values to the subjects they discuss – and participant observation is similarly shaped by the researcher's presence and her or his belief in what is relevant or important. These caveats aside, both methods can also produce valuable material for interpretation, as the following pages demonstrate.

1 Liverpool Radical Film Festival

Formation and Objectives

LRFF was established in 2012 by Brian Ashton, a retired car worker and trade unionist, and David Jacques, a trade unionist and established artist in the city. In 2011, Ashton and Jacques organised a series of screenings for "Liverpool: City of Radicals", a city-wide celebration of political activism in the city (Belchem and Biggs 2011). That event was so successful that they decided to organise an annual festival beginning the following year. Ashton, Jacques and Steve Eye, an activist with a social centre associated with Liverpool's long-standing radical book-shop, News from Nowhere, led the first edition of the festival in 2012, and two audience members – Hayley Trowbridge, then studying for a PhD in Film Studies, and Grace Harrison, an independent artist and researcher – joined the team to produce the festival the following year. LRFF is currently run by a team of seven: Eye remains, though Ashton left in 2014, and Jacques is now in an advisory role. Current members range from PhD students and independent artists and writers to a com-munity media producer and a cashier in a bookmakers. Crucially, all members of LRFF's organising team are volunteers, and the organisa-tion is unfunded. This is typical of radical film organisations and has wide-ranging ramifications for the LRFF's approach to programming, its organisational structure and the networks of organisations with which it works.

One of the most visible consequences of the volunteer-run nature of LRFF is its shifting approach to programming. As the team changes, so too does the kinds of events it organises as volunteers with different ideas and backgrounds get involved. The first edition of LRFF consisted of classic oppositional cinema and addressed key periods in the history of the left. Screenings ranged from classic oppositional films such as *The Battle of Algiers* (1966) and *The Spanish Earth* (1937) to sessions on video-activism with films by Cinema Action (1968–1989), Under-currents (1994–), and "Reel News" (2006–).[6] The second edition of LRFF also comprised both historical and contemporary work but, re-flecting the influence and interests of the new members of the festival team, displayed a broader, more questioning approach to radical film that, as Trowbridge argues in an interview with her, "doesn't have to be politically-motivated documentaries shot in a certain way ... 'radical' means much more than that".[7]

Alongside conventional political documentaries (*Gasland* [2010]; *Year of the Beaver* [1985]), the second edition of the festival thus screened films more radical in style than subject (*The Film That Buys the Cinema* [2013]), work by politically engaged artist filmmakers (Luke Fowler, Karen Mirza, Brad Butler) and sessions explicitly designed to explore multiple approaches to the concept of radicalism on film. That Trowbridge and Harrison were – with the support of the rest of the team – able to influence the conceptual approach of the festival illus-trates the speed and extent to which new members of volunteer-led festi-vals can influence the organisations they join. This level of agency makes such festivals satisfying organisations to work within and is an import-ant counter-weight to the precariousness of unfunded, volunteer-led or-ganisations (Bain and McLean 2013).

LRFF may have developed a more open, inquisitive approach to the concept of radicalism, but the core objectives of the festival remain staunchly political. As Anthony Killick, a PhD student that joined LRFF in 2014, unequivocally stated: "The festival is about instigating fundamental or systemic social change, and the screenings are intended to connect with protest movements and encourage direct action".[8] Nevertheless, the group has also debated the merits of labelling the festival 'radical', aware that it might suggest a vanguardist elitism on their part or that the negative connotations of the word – its association with ultra-left dogma or Islamic fundamentalism – could discourage potential audiences from attending. Yet rather than rename the festival and appeal to a broader audience, the group resolved to try to challenge the negative connotations of radicalism, emphasise the festival's inquisitive approach to the concept and promote the values of left-wing libertarianism to which they are committed.

Internal Organisation and External Relationships

LRFF's political values structure its internal relationships: the team operates collectively, all decisions are taken as a group and it actively avoids adopting a formal hierarchy in which members perform fixed roles and responsibilities. LRFF's internal structure – and its network of relationships with other groups – has emerged partly in response to its precarious existence and is an important means of negotiating that, but it is also the group's preferred way of being, not something that is resented-but-tolerated in light of the organisation's insecurity. However, a number of challenges also derive from this kind of organisation.

Decision-making and communication, for example, can take more time and are often fraught – 'massive chaos' was the phrase used by Trowbridge – which is especially draining for an unfunded community organisation run in volunteers' spare time. This structure can also result in some members of the team taking on more of the organisational labour than others, which can make those individuals dangerously valuable to the organisation and increase the likelihood of their becoming exhausted or 'burning out' – a doubly risky scenario. Also, this kind of informal horizontalism is susceptible to certain people's adopting leading roles unofficially and therefore without formal responsibility or accountability – what Jo Freeman famously referred to as the "tyranny of structurelessness" (1970).

The festival's collective, non-hierarchical structure, and the challenges involved in managing that structure, is an essential part of the organisation. Because LRFF has so little resources, those involved in the festival must want to be involved. As Trowbridge goes on to say, "ultimately we all do it because we want to do it, and if it became something we didn't want to do then we'd have no festival anyway". Organising in this way means that the group practices the kind of politics it promotes at its events, and being part of a democratic, non-hierarchical organisation and dealing with the difficulties that entails, is a key source of satisfaction for those involved.

Protecting the LRFF's ability to operate and organise in this way means maintaining its financial insecurity. The festival generates the small amount of money it requires by running a bar and selling food at their events, in addition to occasionally charging a small admission fee. These low-key moneymaking activities, combined with LRFF's mutually supportive relationships with other organisations in the city (explored below), enable the festival to sustain itself without funding. LRFF has chosen not to apply for the core funding that enables most other festivals to survive because of the potential consequences this could have on the group:

> We've talked about being a formal organisation and applying for money but if you get funding from the Arts Council or wherever then it's a job [and] that might change it … we operate on a degree of mindfulness and ethics, not processes, procedures, and documents. So I think we can do it without money. It's more the will of the group. That's what's important, having a group of people who want to do it and will make it happen.
>
> (Trowbridge 2015)

Given the relationship between LRFF's organisational structure and the group's political identity, the decision to remain financially precarious is understandable. Funding would inevitably entail a different organisational structure and set of relationships that would jeopardise its existence in the first place. For LRFF, volunteer labour is more important than funds, so arguably the biggest danger the festival faces is 'volunteer churn' and maintaining the organisation as the team of volunteers running it inevitably changes. As Trowbridge says, "the challenge is making sure that the group stays together. I don't necessarily mean the group of people who it is now, but having new people come in as other people are going, because people move cities, people's lives move on".

LRFF's external relationships with other grassroots, political or community-based organisations are both important to its organisational identity and key means by which it negotiates precarity. The organisations with which LRFF works provide the venues for its screenings, which is essential for an organisation unable to pay hire fees. Yet showing films at a variety of locations across the city is also central to the cultural and political motivations of the festival: it exists to support and strengthen the communities in which it operates, and touring the festival around a range of venues is thus a means of outreach and engagement. As Killick says:

> The purpose of using multiple venues is so we screen in various different parts of the city, getting to people who might not feel totally

comfortable in more mainstream 'cultural' spaces, which are mostly populated by middle class white people. Insofar as the purpose of the festival is to raise political consciousness, that's quite important. There's a phrase that says if the working class don't have access to it then it's not radical.

LRFF screenings have taken place in community halls, artists' studios, unemployed workers' centres, asylum support spaces and more recently in the Liverpool Small Cinema, a volunteer-run venue that some LRFF members were involved in building – but not in FACT, Liverpool's main arthouse cinema. Operating in these spaces is an attempt to reach the marginalised groups LRFF wants to attract and enables LRFF to run its events as it pleases, providing a bar and refreshments, hosting discussions and providing a partisan space for "communities to come together" to address the issues that affect them (LRFF 2016).

These intentions of LRFF are imbued into the ethos and atmosphere of its screenings and embody much of what Miriam Ross has described as the 'interstitial' – somewhere between the multiplex and home viewing experience – nature of community film exhibition (2013, 446). In 2015, LRFF took place at two venues in the city centre: Pagoda Arts, a Chinese community and youth centre, and a large, 'pop up' artists' studio space. Pagoda Arts was the main venue, a large two-storey building with one main room downstairs and a small kitchen to one side. An impressively large screen, comprised of a wooden frame with bed sheets pinned across it, had been assembled at the rear of the building. In contrast to the standards of commercial film exhibition, with its strict separation of auditorium and projection room, at LRFF a projector and laptop were present in front of the audience. A makeshift bar was assembled by the entrance to the kitchen, which sold cups of tea and coffee at morning screenings and beer, wine and single-pot dinners prior to the evening films. Screenings frequently started late as organisers dealt with technical hitches or delayed for late comers – rather than elicit complaints, these were the subject of jokes between audience and organisers. Each screening was introduced and subject to a discussion afterwards, and every event was free of charge. These elements are at the heart of LRFF's identity and encapsulate the ethos of the festival: welcoming and friendly but fiercely determined, familiarity and irreverence masking the steely political commitment that drives its organisers.

2 Birmingham Film Co-op

Formation and Objectives

The relationship between the co-operative movement and film is as old as cinema itself (Burton 2005). Today, three UK-based exhibition groups in the RFN operate as co-operatives: Birmingham Film Co-op (BFC),

Manchester Film Co-op (MFC) and the London Socialist Film Co-op (LSFC). Of these, BFC is the most recent – it began in 2010 while LSFC dates from 1992 and MFC from 2008 – and has the closest relationship with the UK's co-operative movement and the federated family of retail businesses that are its most visible facet. Indeed, this relationship was crucial to the formation of the group and the unique structure and approach to community exhibition it subsequently developed.

The BFC's beginnings can be traced back to 2008, when two friends and members of the Cooperative Party (the political arm of the co-operative movement), Richard Bickle and Bernard Parry, organised a screening of *Black Gold* (2006), Nick and Marc Francis' documentary about exploitation in the coffee industry. The event was a success, and in 2010, with another mutual friend, John Cooper, they began to think about forming a more long-term organisation to address the dearth of alternative, socially engaged film screenings in Birmingham.[9] A fourth member of the group, Phil Burrows, a film enthusiast and activist with Friends of the Earth, joined the group, and they approached the regional consumer co-op, the Central England Co-operative (CEC), for support.[10] The CEC agreed to provide a venue free of charge at the Birmingham and Midlands Institute, a public building in the centre of the city to which it is affiliated. With an initial team and venue in place, the group began to consider how it would operate and what its role in the community could be.

As the youngest of the political film co-operatives operating in the UK, BFC's organisers looked for inspiration from both the LSFC and MFC and chose to distinguish themselves in two key ways. Unlike the LSFC, Bickle, Parry, Cooper and Burrows chose not to reference a specific left-wing ideology in the title of the group. According to Bickle, this was "not because most of us wouldn't describe ourselves as socialists, but because we thought that might put off part of an audience that we wanted to engage".[11] Instead, they opted for a more neutral name and a catch phrase that gently alluded to the co-operative-influenced socialism of the group: Just Film, for a Fairer World. BFC also distinguished itself from MFC, which at that time organised its screenings into thematic seasons. BFC felt that this would risk attracting only particular audiences to each season and thus serve to maintain what they saw as existing divisions across different community activist groups. According to Bickle, in addition to a more general ambition to "grow the audience for progressive cinema in Birmingham", one of the main objectives of the organisation was to encourage people to make connections between different issues and to situate them within the context of a wider, integrated socio-economic totality:

> Our vision was that, in the economic and political culture in which we live, there is a lot of energy and participation in a whole range of single-issue organisations. ... So if you can start building up a

vision which is a bit bigger than one issue on its own, you can start to articulate what a fairer society might look like.

At first, then, like other radical exhibitors, building relationships with external organisations was at the heart of BFC's identity, and BFC decided to vary the subject of the films screened each month in the hope that a diverse programme of different films would bring people back more regularly and help build links across the various activist groups in the city that tended to focus on distinct issues.

Internal Organisation and External Relationships

Initially, BFC's approach was to build the co-operative in collaboration with these so-called 'single issue' organisations,[12] and it developed an organisational membership structure that allocated each organisation a proportion of free tickets for their members. However, this proved unsuccessful when only a few groups expressed interest, so the BFC organisers decided to base the organisation on an individual membership structure: let individual members vote on which films to show, and then invite local campaign groups to the screening when the chosen title overlapped with the group's work. BFC's democratic approach to programming is unique among radical exhibition groups in the UK – most of which are run along the more ad hoc lines of LRFF – and has wide-ranging ramifications for the organisation and the way in which it negotiates its precarious position.

Administrating BFC's democratic, co-operative approach to exhibition requires a complex internal structure and clearly defined roles and responsibilities. BFC is currently run by a committee of seven volunteers with designated roles: secretary, chair, treasurer and so on. To cement the relationship with the CEC, BFC also allows one of its members to sit on the board. These roles are performed by BFC members that are elected each year at the BFC's AGM. Although this organisational structure is more rigid than most other radical exhibition organisations, it is also more time-efficient once established. After meeting monthly for the first year, BFC committee meetings now take place just four times per year, with occasional meetings when needed. This is in stark contrast to the monthly meetings of MFC or the weekly meetings in the lead-up to LRFF's festival, for example.

BFC's membership structure also ensures a steady income stream. Membership costs £12 per year and, for the past two years, has been stable at around 45 members. Members receive reduced admission to each monthly event (£3 instead of £5), as well as voting privileges to participate in the selection of films and to elect committee members at BFC's AGM. BFC's income is also bolstered by an annual CEC grant of £400. Audience numbers can fluctuate significantly but typically range between

20 and 40 people, so BFC can expect to generate around £1500 per annum from membership fees, box office takings and the grant.

However, the security provided by this guaranteed income is offset by the higher costs of BFC's screening programme. Film selection consists of nominating short-lists of films three times a year, which are then subject to a ballot that opens at each screening and runs for one week afterwards. The winning films are then shaped into a programme for the coming season. Because the films the members select tend to be contemporary titles that already have a public profile, they often require significant screening fees (between £100 and £300) to be paid to distributors such as Film Bank or Dogwoof. Therefore, despite its income being higher and more stable than most other radical film exhibitors, BFC also exists in a state of precarity, the potential risk of a high-cost screening fee combining with a poor audience turnout means that the BFC is, as Bickle puts it, always "only one screening away from disaster". Yet for the BFC's organisers, this precarious but independent existence is preferable to one in which the organisation relied on external organisations for grant funding to survive: "autonomy and independence", says Bickle, form "one of the seven co-op principles, [and are] really important to us'. In a similar vein to LRFF, then, the BFC's organisers are committed to co-operatives as a mode of organisation, and this commitment keeps the organisation going.

Like LRFF, the atmosphere of BFC's screenings embodies the identity of the organisation. As noted, screenings take place in the same place each month: the CEC's Members' Hall in the Birmingham and Midlands Institute, a mid-nineteenth-century public building in the middle of the city centre. The Members' Hall is a spacious, conventional and sedate space, well equipped with soft chairs and inoffensive meeting-room furniture. While the space is thus able to cater to the variety of co-operative groups that use it, its purpose – to provide a space for co-operatives in the region – is unmistakeable from the large banners on the wall advertising the CEC and the values of co-operation.

As the audience enters the space, two members take their admission fees, and people congregate around the refreshments table. Like LRFF, a significant element of the BFC's events is the homemade flapjack, cakes, tea and biscuits (available for donation rather than a price). These refreshments are made by the BFC committee and brought by members of the audience, and thus both exemplify the care that has gone into the organisation of the event and serve as a reminder of the shared responsibility and collective spirit on which the event depends. Screenings begin with introductions and are followed by discussions, but the latter are usually very informal and are often held in the local pub rather than conducted in the Members' Hall. BFC events are thus tidier, more low-key affairs than those of the LRFF. In part, this derives from the fact that they are monthly events that do not need and could not sustain, on a regular basis, the effort that goes into shaping the annual LRFF events. Yet these understated, practically run screenings also reflect the gentle, homely, socialist spirit that pervades the BFC and ensures that the organisation can continue with the challenging task of exhibiting political films.

Conclusion

This chapter has analysed two very different radical film exhibitors and their respective strategies for negotiating precarity. As noted at the outset, one must be careful not to draw too general conclusions from analyses of unique organisations given that differences are invariably 'context dependent': what is a strength in one organisation may well be a weakness in another. Indeed, as we have seen, the decentralised, non-hierarchical, consensus-based approach of LRFF is a strength in the context of an anarchist-oriented festival run by volunteers that want to be part of an organisation with those politics. Similarly, the more concrete roles of BFC's committee are a strength in the context of a festival with socialist leanings, run by volunteers that prefer an acknowledged hierarchy and formal democratic processes. Yet to transpose their respective strengths across these organisations would be to transform them into weaknesses.

As this suggests, the single most important factor that enables these organisations to survive is the commitment of the volunteers involved and their shared belief in the ability of politically engaged cinema to make a positive contribution to the communities in which they work. Theirs is thus a dual commitment: to the politics of the organisation and to the films it shows as a cultural means of engaging with those politics, and their engagement with film is therefore always as much political as it is cultural; the films they show are always, in part, cultural means to political ends. Of course, the audiences for these films might be described as equally committed – to a mode of film viewing and consumption that emphasises post-screening discussion, shared experience and community solidarity. Exploring audience perspectives on the value and role of activist film festivals is an important avenue for future research.

From the organisers' perspective, the combination of a cultural commitment to film and a political commitment to community activism is at the heart of their organisations' ability to negotiate the precarious conditions in which they exist and is the reason their respective strategies for dealing with precarity are so often also simply their preferred way of being. LRFF hosts its events in several venues across the city not just because these are the spaces it can use for free but because the organisers are interested in building networks of solidarity among different groups involved in movements for social change. BFC selects its programme democratically and co-ordinates its activities via an elected committee not just because this generates membership fees but because its organisers are passionate about independent and autonomous, participatory, democratic control. From this perspective, it is unsurprising that both groups have decided to remain independent of funding structures that would risk changing the nature of the organisations and therefore the commitment of those involved.

Yet this also means that organisations such as LRFF and BFC remain precarious: as people move on or jobs and families make volunteer labour untenable, the danger is of course that such groups may dwindle and die out. Perhaps it was ever thus, but maybe it is also possible for community film policies to be instituted that enable such organisations to persist without changing (but that is a topic for another time). In any case, there are reasons to be hopeful. Beneath the welcoming surface of these organisations is a deep commitment to equality and social justice and a passionate belief in the power of film to contribute to those ends. That commitment will not dissipate any time soon. Moreover, the LRFF team and their audiences are growing, and while BFC's membership has remained constant over the past few years, a recent screening I attended, on a rainy Thursday evening, attracted nearly 100 people.

This chapter has shown radical film culture to be both alive and well and extremely diverse. I have focused on just two organisations, but this culture is comprised of many more hundreds of others, each with its own politics and organisational identities and interpretations of what 'radical film culture' means. Stuart Hall argued that identity is a process that is both constructed through recognition of shared origins, values and ideals and, as a discursive construction, constituted through a never-ending play of difference (1996). In bringing together a multitude of unique organisations that, though grounded in different political and geographic contexts, nevertheless share a certain broad set of ideals, I hope the RFN will equally help radical film culture maintain its identity and continue to change.

Notes

1 Radical environmentalism typically connects approaches to the environment to socio-economic critiques of capitalism, patriarchy and globalisation. See, for instance, Mies and Shiva (1993), Wall (1999) and Jensen (2006).

2 Events and publications include *Visions, Divisions and Revisions: political film and film theory in the 1970s and 80s*, a series of screenings and discussions at Raven Row gallery, 2010; *Reaching Audiences: distribution and promotion of alternative moving image* (Knight and Thomas, 2012; see also Knight, 2013); *Working Together: notes on British Film Collectives in the 1970s* (Kidner and Bauer, 2013); and *Reactivating the 1970s: radical film and video culture in theory and practice*, a seminar at Open School East, 2016.

3 See, for example, Donald MacPherson's *Traditions of Independence: British cinema in the thirties* (1980); Bert Hogenkamp's *Deadly Parallels: film and the left in Britain, 1929–39* (1986); or numerous related articles in journals such as *Screen*, *Afterimage* and *Undercut*.

4 See Presence (2013 and 2014) for an attempt to recover some of this more recent radical film history.

5 The project is being led by Professor Mike Wayne (Brunel), Dr Jack Newsinger (Leicester) and me and consists of a series of events at various industry and counter-culture film festivals in the UK and US. More information about the network and the research project is available at www.radicalfilmnetwork.com.

6 For more information on Cinema Action, see Dickinson, 1999, 263–288. For more information on Undercurrents and "Reel News" see Presence, 2015 and 2016 respectively.

7 All quotations from an interview with Trowbridge conducted on 11/06/2015.

8 All quotations from an interview with Killick conducted on 05/05/2015.

9 Film festival scholar Marijke de Valck has noted that many 'specialised' film festivals emerge in this way, in response to gaps or omissions elsewhere (2012, 35). Although Jeffrey Ruoff claims in the same volume that 'programming festivals is as different from year-round programming as night is from day' (2012, 17), this is one of many areas (in activist circles, at least) where monthly groups and annual festivals overlap, and another reason that film festival studies should to begin to explore other kinds of exhibition organisation alongside annual events.

10 The Central England Co-operative is the second largest independent retail co-operative in the UK and runs over four hundred businesses in the region, primarily in the food retail and funeral sectors.

11 All quotations from an interview with Bickle conducted on 20/05/2015.

12 Many activist organisations do ostensibly focus on single issues, and while it is important to build relationships between them it is also worth noting that struggles for change rarely address a single issue. For example, a recently successful campaign against a new MacDonald's fast food drive-thru opening in my neighbourhood–despite being commonly (and correctly) referred to as an anti-MacDonald's campaign–was in fact about a plethora of issues: food education, child advertising, physical and environmental health, traffic safety, urban planning, and democratic control over the communities in which we live.

References

Arts Council England. 2010. *Annual Equality Report 2009/10*. Accessed April 18 2016. http://webarchive.nationalarchives.gov.uk/20160204101926/http://www.artscouncil.org.uk/media/uploads/Final_annual_equality_report.pdf.

Bain, Alison and Heather McLean. 2013. "The Artistic Precariat." *Cambridge Journal of Regions, Economy and Society* 6: 93–111. doi: 10.1093/cjes/rss020.

Banks, Mark and David Hesmondhalgh. 2009. "Looking for Work in Creative Industries Policy." *International Journal of Cultural Policy* 15 (4): 415–430. doi:10.1080/10286630902923323.

Bauer, Petra and Dan Kidner. 2013. Eds. *Working Together: notes on British film collectives in the 1970s*. Southend-on-Sea: Focal Point Gallery.

Belchem, John and Bryan Biggs. 2011. Eds. *Liverpool: city of radicals*. Liverpool: Liverpool University Press.

British Film Institute. 2012. *Film Forever: supporting UK film, BFI Plan, 2012–2017*. http://www.bfi.org.uk/sites/bfi.org.uk/files/downloads/bfi-film-forever-2012-17.pdf.

Burton, Alan G. 2005. *The British Consumer Co-operative Movement and Film, 1890s-1960s*. Manchester: Manchester University Press.

de Valck, Marijke. 2012. "Finding Audiences for Films: programming in historical perspective." In *Coming Soon to a Festival Near You: Programming Film Festivals*, edited by Jeffrey Ruoff, 25–40. St Andrews: St Andrews Film Studies.

Dickinson, Margaret. 1999. *Rogue Reels: oppositional film in Britain, 1945–90*. London: BFI.

Freeman, Jo. 1970. "The Tyranny of Structurelessness." *Berkeley Journal of Sociology* 17: 151–165.

Gill, Rosalind and Andy Pratt. 2008. "In the Social Factory? Immaterial Labour, Precariousness and Cultural Work." *Theory, Culture & Society* 25 (7–8): 1–30. doi: 10.1177/0263276408097794.

Hall, Stuart. 1996. "Who Needs Identity?" In *Questions of Cultural Identity*, edited by Stuart Hall and Paul du Gay, 1–17. London: Sage.

Hogenkamp, Bert. 1986. *Deadly Parallels: film and the left in Britain, 1929–39*. London: Lawrence and Wishart.

Iordanova, Dina. 2012. "Film Festivals and Dissent: can film change the world?" In *Film Festival Yearbook 4: Film Festivals and Activism*, edited by Dina Iordanova and Leshu Torchin, 13–30. St Andrews: St Andrews Film Studies.

Iordanova, Dina and Leshu Torchin. 2012. *Film Festival Yearbook 4: Film festivals and activism*. St. Andrews: St Andrews Film Studies.

Jensen, Derek. 2006. *Endgame, Volume 1: The problem of civilization*. New York, NY: Seven Stories Press.

Knight, Julia. 2013. "Getting to See Women's Cinema." In *Watching Films: new perspectives on movie-going, exhibition and reception*, edited by Karina Aveyard and Albert Moran, 295–314. Bristol: Intellect.

Knight, Julia and Peter Thomas. 2012. *Reaching Audiences: distribution and promotion of alternative moving image*. Bristol: Intellect.

Küng-Shankleman, Lucy. 2000. Inside the BBC and CNN: managing media organisations. London and New York: Routledge.

Loist, Skadi and Ger Zielinski. 2012. "On the Development of Queer Film Festivals and Their Media Activism." In *Film Festival Yearbook 4: film festivals and activism*, edited by Dina Iordanova and Leshu Torchin, 49–62. St Andrews: St Andrews Film Studies.

LRFF. 2016. "About Us." Accessed January 28 2016. http://www.liverpoolradical filmfestival.org.uk/about-us/.

MacPherson, Donald. 1980. Ed. *Traditions of Independence: British cinema in the thirties*. London: BFI.

Mazierska, Ewa and Lars Kristensen. 2015. Eds. *Marxism and Film Activism: screening alternative worlds*. Oxford: Berghahn Books.

Mies, Maria and Vandana Shiva. 1993. *Ecofeminism*. London: Zed Books.

Murray, Catherine and Mirjam Gollmitzer. 2012. Escaping the Precarity Trap: a call for creative labour policy. *International Journal of Cultural Policy*, 18: 4, 419–438.

Neilson, Brett and Ned Rossiter. 2008. "Precarity as a Political Concept, or, Fordism as Exception." *Theory, Culture & Society* 25 (7–8): 51–72. doi: 10.1177/0263276408097796.

Presence, Steve. 2015. "The Contemporary Landscape of Video-Activism in Britain." In *Marxism and Film Activism: screening alternative worlds*, edited by Ewa Mazierska and Lars Kristensen, 186–212. Oxford: Berghahn Books.

Presence, Steve. 2016. Reel News in the Digital Age: Britain's radical video-activists." In *The Routledge Companion to Film and Politics*, edited by Yannis Tzioumakis and Claire Molloy, 103–111. London: Routledge.

Presence, Steve. 2013a. "Maintaining a Critical Eye: oppositional documentary on Channel 4 in the 1990s." In *Cinema, Television and History: new approaches*, edited by Laura Mee and Johnny Walker, 85–101. Newcastle upon Tyne: Cambridge Scholars Press.

Presence, Steve. 2013b. "The Political Avant-Garde: oppositional documentary in Britain since 1990." PhD diss., University of the West of England (UWE) Bristol.

Ross, Andrew. 2010. *Nice Work If You Can Get It: life and labor in precarious times*. New York: New York University Press.

Ross, Miriam. 2013. "Interstitial Film Viewing: community exhibition in the twenty-first century." *Continuum*, 27 (3): 446–457.

Standing, Guy. 2014. "Understanding the Precariat through Labour and Work." *Development and Change* 45 (5): 963–980.

Standing, Guy. 2011. *The Precariat: the new dangerous class*. London: Bloomsbury.

Turnin, Svetla and Ezra Winton. 2014. "Introduction: encounters with documentary activism." In *Screening Truth to Power: a reader on documentary activism*, edited by Svetla Turnin and Ezra Winton, 17–27. Montreal: Cinema Politica.

Tzioumakis, Yannis and Claire Molloy. 2016. *The Routledge Companion to Film and Politics*. London: Routledge.

Wall, Derek. 1999. *Earth First! and the Anti-Roads Movement: radical environmentalism and comparative social movements*. London: Routledge.

13 The Filmmakers of Tomorrow or the Problems of Today

Creativity, Skills and Cultural Identity in British Youth Filmmaking

Alicia Blum-Ross

Introduction

The UK has been at the forefront of support for and developments in youth filmmaking. From the Media Studies curriculum in schools, which includes a production element (Bazalgette 2000) to the dedicated resources for out-of-school youth production projects (Mediabox 2010, First Light 2009, Sefton-Green and Soep 2007) to the recent introduction of the nationwide BFI Film Academies (British Film Institute 2014a), teaching young people how to produce films has gained traction in the UK as not only a youth but also a creative-industries policy. In addition to formal educational and cultural-policy interventions, youth filmmaking in Britain also draws substantially from the legacy of community media initiatives, which have sprung up to engage with diverse communities in order to encourage a wide spectrum of people to "tell their stories" (Rowbotham and Beynon 2001, Fountain 2001, Thumim 2012).

In this chapter I discuss the history of youth filmmaking in the UK and analyse in detail some of the central discourses that underpin youth filmmaking as an educational intervention. Through empirical case studies I show that youth filmmaking is justified in one of three ways: enabling young people to feel a sense of belonging to physical and virtual communities, giving young people the opportunity to 'express themselves' as civic participants and giving young people essential technical and communicative skills for the future. These assumptions belie a set of narratives about young people that, though essentializing, are paradoxically opposite. These include the negative assumption that young people are politically apathetic (Coleman 2007), problematically relate to their local communities (Kintrea et al. 2008) and lack opportunities for future advancement (House of Lords: Select Committee on Digital Skills 2015). These 'deficit' narratives (te Riele 2006) are counterbalanced by the no-less troublesome view that young people are inherently creative "digital natives" (Prensky 2001) who will be intrinsically attracted by the appeal of technology to participate in youth filmmaking in order to learn skills to secure future employment (Chandler and Dunford 2012). The aims of this chapter are therefore to examine how these discourses produce images of youth that are problematic both in terms of positioning youth as 'deficit' and as naturally 'creative' and show how abstract discourses relate to the on-the-ground practice of youth filmmaking.

Methods

For 18 months in total, spread out over a period of two-and-a-half years between 2006 and 2009 I conducted ethnographic fieldwork with youth filmmaking sites in London (Hammersley and Atkinson 2007). This included extensive participant-observation, semi-structured interviews with both young people and adults and in some field sites I was able to incorporate participatory methods including video diaries and photo-elicitation (Gubrium and Harper 2013), where it was possible as part of the filmmaking process (e.g. making 'making of' films Blum-Ross 2012a). I also conducted textual analysis of the final films created by the young people, considering their visual, auditory and textual elements, along with the initial funding bids and other materials produced by the organisations themselves. This research is inspired by critical projects researching media production at the intersection of social anthropology (e.g. Bird 2010, Bräuchler and Postill 2010), education studies (e.g. Dahya and Jenson 2015, Thomson and Sefton-Green 2011), and media and communications studies (e.g. Fisherkeller 2011).

During my fieldwork I identified these 11 case study sites – projects I followed from initial funding bid through to final screening and sometimes beyond – through a combination of snowball sampling and purposive sampling in reading the announcements of awards available from public sector funders (Palys 2008). As is characteristic in the UK, all of these projects were funded at least in part by state bodies, local government up to national funders. Therefore, I was able to sit in on funding award discussions and conduct interviews with funders since they are by law open to public oversight. I conducted follow-up interviews with organisations in London where I had conducted my original intensive fieldwork sporadically during 2010 to 2012. Contact with filmmaking organisations was also facilitated by professional networks as then-Education Manager of the London Film Festival at the British Film Institute. Since the initial fieldwork period I have also occasionally acted as an external evaluation consultant for youth filmmaking organisations, and while these experiences are not reflected in the empirical case studies here, this professional experience undoubtedly influences my analysis.

For each case study I conducted roughly 30 to 100 hours of fieldwork, as some projects met for full days for short periods (e.g. during a school holiday), whereas others met sporadically for up to a year. Although the age of participants varied from site to site, all worked with adolescents (aged 12–21) and outside of the formal curriculum, although some projects took part physically in schools. All projects had between six and 20 participants. The fieldwork was conducted iteratively; as transcription, coding and analysis took place throughout the period later fieldwork were influenced by insights and experiences from earlier case studies. The corpus of fieldwork (interview transcripts, transcribed field notes, photo, video, audio, print and hand-drawn artefacts from case studies) were then hand-coded using a bespoke analysis process developed by inductively coding fieldwork themes and then synthesizing them as the fieldwork progressed.

All of the projects I studied were film*making* projects, as opposed to initiatives where the young people simply acted in or wrote scripts for films. This was key as I was interested in studying the full spectrum of activities involved in *making* a film, proposing that filmmaking is a unique activity in simultaneously involving technical, social and creative skills. In comparison with photography, for example, filmmaking often involves a more substantive teamwork element and therefore opportunities to develop social ties within a team and with adults (photography can involve this process, but less automatically so than filmmaking as many photography projects are run for individuals). Equally, technical skills from using a camera to learning editing software sit alongside creative choices about storyline, locations, shooting angles and beyond. Finally, the filmic 'product' has the potential to be seen by a far greater audience than, say, a theatre or dance production, meaning filmmaking projects also must consider dissemination routes, audiences and outlets as a central part of their work with young people.

History of UK Youth Filmmaking

With the launch of the Sony Portapak in the UK in 1969, creative activists began working with local residents in 'communities' across the country to document daily life. These early projects were premised largely on the concept of access; the media itself was seen as "the means of expression of the community, rather than for the community" (Berrigan 1979 quoted in Carpentier 2003, 426). The utopianism of early community and youth media was evident not only in the projects themselves but also in the way in which they were resourced. One educator described how it was "much less evidence-based than it is now, you didn't have to say 'I'm going to get X number of bums on seats'". The choice to work with young people was often opportunistic as, in his words, "they were the people who came forward to be worked with".

The 1980s saw the launch of Channel Four, which provided a wider platform for underrepresented groups on mainstream television (Harvey 1989). A central remit of Channel Four was to "enabl[e] people who would never normally have had that possibility to be involved in the process of representation" (Fountain 2001, 203). Despite the civic emphasis on empowerment in the early days of youth and community media, into the 1980s there was a shift away from ad hoc arts funding based on a model of empowerment (Dickinson 1999) towards an institutionalisation of the sector (Swinson 2001). Particularly for organisations that worked with young people, there was a growing emphasis on vocationalism (McCulloch 1986). Learning media production skills was seen as a method for growing the workforce of the future, rather than an intrinsic good in the here-and-now (Blum-Ross and Livingstone Forthcoming).

The 1990s saw a decline in support for youth and community media by public broadcasters, partly as television audiences became increasingly seen as consumers (Ang 1991) rather than publics (Couldry, Livingstone, and Markham 2010). Eventually, these became replaced by wider institutional interests in participation wherein "ordinary people" could "speak for themselves" (Thumim 2012). For example, in 2001 the youth filmmaking funder First Light was launched, with money from the UK Film Council amounting to £1million/year. First Light was focused on youth *creativity*, by providing a "new generation of young filmmakers" access to the tools and opportunity to make their own films (First Light 2009). The funders wanted to see, as a senior staff member reported in an interview, not just films about "stereotypical subjects… [First Light] is very much about creative stories and ideas" and not just "what happens on our estate at the weekend". This senior staffer emphasised that the organisation was not primarily concerned with academic achievement, as none of the projects was tied to the curriculum, but focused "very much on soft skills. But [these are] very hard to measure". She described the initiative as also oriented towards widening access to the film industry and that "what we should be undoing this terrible focus on the industry that it depends on who you know and how much money you have, rather than what your talent might be".

A few years later, in 2006, a related but distinct funding source called Mediabox was created, focused on encouraging youth civic participation and engagement. Mediabox was part of a wider New Labour interest in gaining input from publics into policy and involving young people in formal politics (Newman 2001). Technology was seen as a key way of engaging young people and overcoming 'apathy' (Bennett 2008, Loader 2007), although arguably less attention was paid to listening to what young people actually had to say (Blum-Ross 2012b, Lister 2008, Biesta and Lawy 2006). Even though Mediabox was funded initially at £6million for the first year, the fund was significantly oversubscribed so the actual rate of successful applications in London was only about 5%. Unlike First Light, Mediabox had an explicit remit to enable young people to use their 'voices' on 'issues' of importance to them (Mediabox 2010). In an interview, the then Executive Director of

Mediabox (who had previously worked for First Light) explained that First Light had been about:

> Getting young people together, whoever they are, to make a film. And they'll see it on the big screen and they'll think that's an interesting film, whatever it was about, like plasticine monsters. ... It was about learning the process they'd done it all themselves, it was very much their story but it was a film initiative. Whereas Mediabox has very much been about voices and platforms and opportunities to *have a say* so its very much using the media as a tool to enable that to happen, for young people to be able to express themselves.

Concurrent with Mediabox and First Light was also the national Positive Activities for Young People (PAYP) scheme, which ran from 2003 to 2006 and provided government funding for young people to take part in activities in order to support young people aged eight to 19 who were "most at risk of social exclusion, committing a crime or being a victim of a crime" (CRG Research Limited 2006). The arts, including filmmaking, were seen as uniquely able to deliver on the aim for young people to make a 'positive contribution' (a key target of the concurrent government-wide initiative Every Child Matters), as through their creative participation they would be able to "develop their skills, talents and interests" (Museums Libraries and Archives and Arts Council England 2009, 9).

While the New Labour period has since been characterised as a 'golden age' in terms of investment in the arts, this dovetailed problematically with commercialisation and a host of wider social objectives the arts were not always well-placed to address (Hewison 2015). When the Conservative/Liberal Democrat coalition came to power in 2010, many of the funders that had previously supported youth filmmaking constricted or ceased operations. Mediabox was defunded, and First Light has since been integrated with the national film education organisation Film Club to form Into Film, which emphasises film viewing and discussion in schools more than filmmaking, although does include some of the latter. The British Film Institute (newly reincorporating the duties of the UK Film Council, see Doyle et al. 2015) launched a filmmaking initiative called the BFI Film Academy, aimed at identifying and supporting "new and emerging filmmakers" who are "passionate about film" and "want a career in the film industry" (British Film Institute 2016). Select graduates from regional film academies take part in a two-week residential "talent campus" at the National Film and Television School in the summer.

Both Into Film and the Film Academies are part of the BFI's education strategy, which renews its focus on fostering "impact, relevance and excellence" in film education (British Film Institute 2014b). The BFI is explicit in balancing older "media literacy" oriented approaches from educators and the reality that the increasing "visibility around the creative industries, and the skills they require" (ibid) are drivers both of government policy and of young peoples' interest in film and filmmaking. The strategy writers lament that the "policy initiative of the creative industries has been seized by the computer and video games sector" (see Livingstone and Hope 2011), but they reassert that film education can also be instrumental in contributing to the growth of the creative industries.

This overview illustrates both how the landscape of funding and policy that undergirds youth filmmaking practice has changed, and how youth filmmaking organisations adapted to these changes. However, an overarching trajectory throughout this period has been an increased interest in sustainability, an attempt to make what were once ad hoc organisations run on the enthusiasm of activists who were happy to "live on the dole" to support their work, in the words of one of my informants, into "sustainable organisations that [have] proper employment packages and all that sort of stuff." As these youth filmmaking projects have fought for survival, with long-standing organisations closing their doors while new generations of initiatives have sprung up, the field has both shifted and remained remarkably unaltered at the practice level. Yet, as I argue below, policy and funding language does influence the actual practice of youth filmmaking. In the following sections I analyse some of the justifications for youth filmmaking, as described above, and demonstrate how these policy decisions and the way they are manifested on a practical level influence the articulations of social and cultural diversity in youth filmmaking.

Youth Filmmaking Discourses

Youth filmmaking is justified as both an intrinsically valuable and an instrumental activity. By describing youth filmmaking as being an 'intrinsically' beneficial activity I mean that advocates highlight the experience of taking part in the project itself, rather than the 'instrumental' impact that the project may later have on wider social or economic objectives (Belfiore 2012). As Gray (2002) described, many arts and cultural activities are 'instrumentalised' in order to gain access to resources, a process he called "policy attachment". Most recently, under new Labour, this practice became *de rigeur* for small arts organisations, who are generally now expected to deliver a host of social aims as a "return on the investment" of the funder. Yet, as this discussion of youth filmmaking indicates, this process is not without consequence. In each of the examples I discuss here there are ramifications for how young people are discursively positioned. It is not just that youth filmmaking projects *are* instrumentalised, but *why* and *how* this happens that influences the ways in which young people's social and cultural identities are represented, by themselves or others.

Something to Do, Someplace to Belong

From the early days of filmmaking on social housing estates to current projects that focus on addressing issues of youth unemployment, youth filmmaking has long been justified under the rubric of 'positive' activities (HM Treasury and Department for Children Schools and Families 2007) and giving young people 'somewhere to go'. Of equal importance is helping young people feel they 'belong to' their neighbourhoods as part of a condition of 'active citizenship' (Besch and Minson 2001). Yet at the same time, young people, especially young people of colour, are often pathologized for 'hanging about' in public spaces without permission (Corrigan 1979, Kehily 2007, France 2007), a growing problem as interstitial spaces become increasingly commercialised (Chatterton and Hollands 2003). Concerns regarding young peoples' occupation of public space reached a fever pitch in recent years when the popular press disseminated a narrative of "feral youth" (Narey 2008).

Of the many youth filmmaking projects I encountered during my fieldwork, several specifically attempted to intervene in young peoples' supposedly problematic relationships to their local, regional and national communities. This included addressing not only what was sometimes characterised as "problematic territoriality" (for example "postcode gangs" as discussed in Kintrea et al. 2008), but more prosaically the fact that many young people in London from disadvantaged communities had only very rarely, if ever, reported travelling outside their immediate local areas. One educator I interviewed described this to me as an example of a circumscribed "village mentality" wherein the young people stayed only within the confines of their neighbourhood. Another educator described this openly offensively, as the young people being "territorial animals". Yet this contrasted dramatically with the global scales of migration that some of these young people had experienced – for example, while they may never have been into central London they may have visited family in rural Bangladesh or the Caribbean during school holidays.

Many youth filmmaking projects were thus conceived of as an intervention into young peoples' sense of space and place (Blum-Ross 2013). For example, I studied a filmmaking project for young people in East London to study the River Lea, a formerly industrial river that wound through the site of the London Olympics in 2012. In 2008, a group of 16 young people made a series of films about the river, both from a historical perspective researching the industrial past and history of migration in the area and a contemporary look at a nature reserve that was to be affected by the upcoming start of major construction for the Olympics. The young people came mainly from the local Bangladeshi community, but additional students had been selected for participation by the partnering secondary school because they were recent migrants from the

Sudan, Nigeria and China, or because they needed additional support for social reasons (e.g. having been bullied in school).

The project was explicitly framed in the funding application as being about the instrumental aims of "neighbourhood renewal" and "community cohesion" but by the facilitator of the project in terms of the intrinsic goal of helping the young people "see the beauty in the world around [them] those little glimpses... which might not otherwise be accessed but which are really inspiring". For both the funder and the adult facilitators the initiative was oriented towards giving the young people something 'constructive' to do outside of school, particularly for the young men who were more likely to be described as 'disengaged' (by their own and the teachers' reports). The project was also aimed at enabling a new relationship to the surrounding area (and by extension, to both familiar and unfamiliar places), and in common with the "citizenship curriculum" helping foster a "sense of belonging – of identity – with the community around them" (Qualifications and Curriculum Authority 1998, 61).

At the conclusion of the project, some of the young people reported that they had experienced this aesthetically oriented approach to their local area as changing how they felt about their neighbourhood. One young woman noted that she felt she could now see that the people "help each other from young to old, they help the neighborhood in a way that they treat people like their own member of a family". Another told me "you know with this film, it made our eyes get a bit bigger, like we can see things a bit more". In this sense the project was an intervention into their 'practice' as citizens (Osler and Starkey 2003), deemed necessary because of the perception that they experienced few opportunities in the area and had a problematic relationship to venturing outside of it. Although the project can be said to have been successful in achieving the aim of engaging the young people with the community, the setup of the project did not privilege their already-existing local competencies or experiences. There was little effort made to establish what the young people *did* know or how they currently experienced their area, before it was intervened on.

Youth Voice & Participation

Another central justification for youth filmmaking is that it enables young people to have a 'voice' on issues of concern to them, and to 'participate' in public spheres – something young people are limited in many ways from doing (Weller 2007). The emphasis on expression has long accompanied youth and community media as many projects specifically orient towards giving "voice to the voiceless" (Marchessault 1995). Youth media is seen as particularly able to deliver on the goal of 'youth voice' (Poyntz 2013, Soep 2006) as teaching filmmaking becomes about helping young people "tell their own stories in their own voice" (Into Film 2014). The emphasis on youth 'voice' is tied to a wider movement in recent decades towards privileging expression as a means of civic engagement and participation, even if there is little critical interrogation about whether and how voices enter into public spheres, who is invited to speak and whether the person is listened to (Couldry 2010).

Many youth media projects, and indeed funding sources, are linked to the process of fostering youth voice and to the goal of youth civic participation (Blum-Ross 2016). For example, the Department for Communities and Local Government (DCLG) funded a project around political engagement for young British Muslims (Blum-Ross 2012b). The initiative, called *Reelhood*, was run by an organisation providing support and advocacy for Muslim young people from a variety of ethnic backgrounds. The aim of the project, as described in the initial proposal to DCLG, was to use film to "discuss and debate a wide variety of social issues" and make a documentary highlight "the concerns of British Muslims in order to effect a positive social change and have an active effect on the political agenda". The project was funded under the DCLG "Prevent" remit aimed at targeting extremism amongst British Muslims. The project organisers hoped that the young people would gain 'hard' technical skills in relationship to filmmaking (and had hired a professional filmmaking team with high-quality equipment to co-facilitate the sessions), alongside 'soft' interpersonal and communication skills and specific skills relating to political organising and lobbying on issues of importance to them.

The project ran over weekends and during school holidays for several months and in the end involved eight young people aged 16 to 22. The young people worked in three teams of a director, a producer and a cameraperson to make three separate documentary films exploring: youth gangs, the 'stop and search' policing statute and the variety of forms of protest against the Iraq War. These relatively hard-hitting topics were in keeping with the remit of the project, which had an instrumental aim to help support young people to engage with 'politics'. Notably, however, there was a mismatch between the conception of 'the political' as understood by the funders (formal/state political structures) and by the young people who emphasised the informal or 'personal' politics of practice rather than formal institutions (Mouffe 1993, Lister et al. 2003). In this project, as in many others, the final product was packaged in a specific vernacular form – the font used by the organisation resembled a graffiti 'tag', and all three films featured a hip hop soundtrack. As Fleetwood (2005a) has analysed, this use of supposedly youthful vernacular attempts to underline the 'authenticity' of the young peoples' stories, an attempt made most visible in the choice to name the project "Reelhood" in the first place.

In actuality, young people used the films, in particular the second two, as a way of questioning political decision-making itself. When I asked one of the young female participants, who was previously active in youth organising, about whether she thought of "going into politics" she told me "when I think of politics, I think of a bunch of old guys sitting around a table having their cigars and cups of tea or coffee or whatever and saying 'eeny meeny miny mo what shall we talk about today?'" The young people also took exception to the premise of the funding source itself; one young woman described "Prevent" as "quite insulting really, it suggests that you don't have your own mind to make your own decisions and they have to put in measures to prevent you from becoming brainwashed… just because you're young and you're Muslim [it doesn't mean] that you're going to turn to that side".

The young people, thus, acted as "justice-oriented citizens" (Westheimer and Kahne 2004) in questioning structures of power, despite how they had been framed by the funder. Yet the premise of youth voice was important to the young people as well, for example, when a young man told me that what was most important to him was not making the film itself but the "outcome, the result. If it's going to make any change or if it's a waste of time. I mean, obviously it's not a waste of time because I [will learn] quite a lot of skills but is anyone else going to get any aspect from it or anything?" They demonstrated their own sophisticated awareness of the ways in which the premise of the funding and the organisational mandate had circumscribed them and proposed their own critique.

Skills for the Future

A third way in which youth filmmaking is seen as influencing young people is helping develop a host of skills for future employment or even adulthood in general. In this sense, young people are described in terms of what they are in the *process* of becoming or in terms of what they *cannot yet* do or comprehend (Buckingham 2000). The discourse of 'growing up' itself belies the emphasis on an imagined future (Lesko 2001), positioning children and young people in a state of "becoming rather than as a legitimate state of being-in-and-for-the-world" (Scheper-Hughes and Sargent 1998, 13). Filmmaking is seen as 'preparing' young people for the future in two overlapping but distinct ways – by providing practical training and experience should they seek a career in the creative industries (or encouraging them to do so) or by honing their 'soft' interpersonal or communicative skills in order to prepare them for employment or 'the future' more broadly (Chandler and Dunford 2012).

In my research I found many organisations that had anecdotal evidence of instances where young people, especially those otherwise unconfident or quiet, had risen to the opportunity occasioned by the film project and had performed well. For example, one project organiser told me about a student she had encouraged to think of a future as a film-maker, even though the student had been excluded from school. She described how he had been ask to sort out the food for the film and how:

> He was going to MacDonald's and blagging free burgers and stuff... we said that's really important, that's what a producer does on a film is blag stuff! And he said I thought I was just doing whatever, you know, because they see it almost as a negative thing to go and blag stuff whereas we're saying no it's a skill!

The 'skills' proposed by youth filmmaking organisations are thus considered to be essential for professional life, writ large, but also are conveyed to young people as being important for potential careers in the film and creative industries. Throughout my fieldwork, there were similar exhortations to young people that they could "be a Director/Producer/Writer/Cameraperson" and beyond. Although many facilitators used this language simply as a way of attempting to support young people in broadening their horizons, rather than a specific hope that they would seek actual employment in the film or creative industries, for some projects this was one of the explicit goals. With a new generation of youth media organisations came some distancing of the initial strongly social justice-oriented beliefs of the first generation, which privileged participation over 'quality', and a move towards identifying and supporting 'excellence' that belies the new orientation of funders as well (Blum-Ross 2015). This interest does not just come from adult intermediaries, however, but also from young people who may frame their participation explicitly around gaining skills and work experience to help them achieve their future goals, rather than simply having something to do.

Another case study from my research was the OUT initiative, which brought together young people who identified as Lesbian, Gay, Bisexual or Transgender (LGBT) and was sponsored by a major cultural institution in London in collaboration with a youth media production company. OUT consisted of a weeklong series of events as part of a film festival where the young people attended talks and master classes led by professional filmmakers (several who had films concurrently appearing in the festival), including directors, screen-writers and producers. Although the workshop had been quickly booked by 20 participants, 11 to 14 young people (aged 16–20) showed up each day. In contrast to other groups I studied, this group was mainly white (of the participants approximately six identified as being from black, Asian or Minority Ethnic communities) and skewed slightly older, which influenced the level of investment in filmmaking the young people described. At the end of the film festival, the young people made a short film in collaboration with a youth filmmaking organisation, which was produced on Saturdays over a period of several months after intensive brainstorming and writing sessions, filming on location and an extended edit with a smaller sub-group of participants.

The project balanced the intrinsic aim of finding like-minded young people (in terms of interest in film and in terms of their identification as LGBT) and the instrumental aim of future employment. The latter came as much from the young people as from the organisation, for example when one young woman described "its just that I have characters in my head that I make stories up with and its that I want to let other people into them instead of just keeping them in". The creativity discourse was coupled with the skills discourse for the young people as well as for the project organisers, for instance when one young woman described how "if you really like films you'll want to make them yourself, so [coming here] is motivated by creativity and wanting to do better". Some of the young people worried about the conflation of their sexuality with the products of their creativity, noting that while they benefitted from being part of the LGBT community as part of the festival the filmmakers were "not seen as filmmakers, they are seen as *gay* filmmakers. But on the plus side there's film festivals [like this one] where you'll almost certainly find an audience". Ultimately, the film they made as part of the OUT project was screened at the festival the following year, and several of the young people (although by no means all) went stayed involved with the cultural organisation and pursued their own film careers using the film on their show reels. The project had not only taught the young people practical skills, but in many ways had also allowed them to join a community of practice (LGBT filmmakers) and thus learn from professionals how to leverage connections and identity to help access support.

Discussion

Seeking to understand the ways in which youth filmmaking, and the discourses that underpin it, activates or constrains wider social and cultural identities is undoubtedly complex. In outlining a history of the sector in the UK and detailing three of the many central justifications for youth filmmaking, I have attempted to demonstrate the recurrent assumptions about young people that underlie these projects. Ultimately, two dominant narratives are presented in each of the cases above, and while they contrast they also, paradoxically, overlap. The first narrative is of youth 'deficit', wherein young people are rhetorically constructed as a problem in need of a solution (te Riele 2006). This perspective locates the problem with the young people, rather than with society writ large. For example, discussions around young people having problematic relationships to their local area, demonstrating a lack of knowledge about or loyalty towards their neighbourhood often do not account for the systematic lack of investment in youth services and education or the increased privatisation that actively prohibits young people from occupying public space.

For all the rhetoric around youth 'voice' there is little investment in listening to what young people have to say (Macnamara 2013). The final screening of the *Reelhood* project was only sparsely attended by the MPs and political figures who had supported it initially, and those that did come told me in interviews that the films had largely just confirmed what they believed they knew already. Even Mediabox, a well-resourced government funder, also fell victim to the overwhelmingly negative portrayal of young people in the mainstream press. The Executive Director reported that the organisation consistently tried to get the films created by the young people more widely disseminated but that when "a kid stabs another kid in the street and it always makes the news unfortunately, because that's the way of the world". There are thus two possible explanations in this example as to why young peoples' voices may be marginalised: the first is that the dominant narrative of young people is already established in the mainstream press (and thus attempts to undermine it fall on deaf ears) but surprisingly, that even youth filmmaking organisations and young people themselves often mirror these same forms of representation.

For example, although the Mediabox guidance read "don't forget that an 'issue' is not necessarily a 'problem' and that the young people may choose to highlight things in their community that they are proud of" (Mediabox 2009), the vast majority of funded projects highlighted negative issues. Of the many projects I encountered, a strikingly high number (almost two-thirds) dealt substantially with issues around gang crime and youth violence (Blum-Ross 2016). The reasons for this are myriad, but one possible explanation is that both project organisers and young people themselves subtly accept, and echo, the conception that projects about young people must present themselves in specific ways in order to be considered 'authentic' (Fleetwood 2005b). The ubiquity of specific tropes associated with young (especially minority male) urban lives in youth filmmaking products, from the use of graffiti-like fonts to the omnipresent hip hop soundtrack, is difficult to resist. These tropes are led by both adult facilitators and young people but in my fieldwork were little discussed or interrogated. Thus while the ideal of youth 'voice' and participation remained a promise, young people were not often supported in developing critical reflexivity around these issues, and the particular mechanics of funding did not encourage the adult facilitators or funders to do so either.

The second, more positive but no less problematic, view of young people revealed in this rhetoric is that of intrinsic creativity and technological *nous*. One facilitator described to me how when you get a group of young people "in a room, they can literally have leaps of imagination that are incredible and part of it is helping them manage that process".

This discourse of youth potential is echoed by Halleck, who assumes that young people are better able to fight the "duped acceptance of mass media" because children and young people have "natural curiosity and vigorous imaginations [that] can still function" (Halleck 2002, 50). Though the terms have changed, there are echoes of this depoliti-cised, untethered 'creativity' discourse (Malik 2013, Banaji, Burn, and Buckingham 2010) found also in the hyper-inflated language of 'digital natives' (Prensky 2001). This language assumes that young people are intrinsically attracted to digital technologies, and like the problematic language of "telling your own stories" erases the importance of diver-sity amongst young people and differential issues of access and of his-tories of representation (Helsper and Eynon 2010). Constructing young people as intrinsically creative and therefore able to produce a host of ground-breaking films that can energise not only the film industry but also the adults who work with them (young people being a "shot in the arm" according to one facilitator I interviewed) ignores the fact that young people are, like old people, both creative and uncreative, digitally able and digitally afraid. The emphasis on future creative employment also potentially misleads young people, given that the film and creative industries are severely competitive for new entrants, especially those from minority or low-income backgrounds (O'Brien et al. 2016). Equally, as project facilitators themselves might be able to attest if pressed, the sec-tor is often characterised by precarious employment and can place signi-ficant pressures on creative workers (Morgan, Wood and Nelligan 2013).

Conclusion

This discussion of youth filmmaking has demonstrated the variety of ways in which projects are discursively positioned and how these dis-courses influence the ways in which youth filmmaking comes into being in practice. I have argued that three of the most oft-referenced justifi-cations for youth media – as offering a positive source of belonging, as providing young people with a means of self-expression and as a means to gain skills for the future – all rest on problematic foundations. These discourses demonstrate the assumption of youth deficits and intrinsic aptitudes that both undermine the capacity for young people to be rep-resented and to represent themselves as fully socially and culturally di-verse. While many youth filmmaking organisations do nuanced work on the ground, these discourses must nonetheless be examined in order to understand the possibilities afforded by youth filmmaking. Establishing youth as a period of 'otherness' by highlighting an imagined universal ability does little to counteract hegemonic depictions of youth or pro-vide evidence for more nuanced and responsive youth provision. Finally, the element of futurity with which the creativity or digital-abilities discourses are couched constructs young people as simply 'people becoming' (Christensen and Prout 2002), of interest because of their potential rather than intrinsic benefits in the here-and-now. This future orientation neither interrogates what kinds of futures are actually being achieved (for instance, whether there are jobs in the creative industries, who can access them or what they might offer), nor does it address what young people might gain from participating in youth filmmaking as a process rather than as an outcome.

References

Ang, Ien. 1991. *Desperately Seeking the Audience*. London: Routledge.
Banaji, Shakuntala, Andrew Burn and David Buckingham. 2010. The Rhetorics of Creativity: a literature review, 2nd Edition. In *Creativity, Culture and Education Series*. London: Creativity, Culture and Education.
Bazalgette, Cary. 2000. *Moving Images in the Classroom: a secondary teachers' guide to using film & television*. London: British Film Institute.
Belfiore, Eleonora. 2012. ""Defensive Instrumentalism" and the Legacy of New Labour's Cultural Policies." *Cultural Trends* 21 (2): 103–111.
Bennett, W. L. 2008. "Changing Citizenship in the Digital Age." In *Civic Life Online: learning how digital media can engageyYouth*, edited by W. Lance Bennett, 1–24. Cambridge: MIT Press.
Besch, Janice and Jeffrey Minson. 2001. "Participatory Policy Making, Ethics and the Arts." In *Citizenship and Cultural Policy*, edited by Denise Meredyth and Jeffrey Minson. London: Sage Publications.
Biesta, Gert and Robert Lawy. 2006. "Citizenship-as-Practice: the educational implications of an inclusive and relational understanding of citizenship." *British Journal of Educational Studies* 54, 1 (March 2006): 34–50.
Bird, S. Elizabeth. 2010. Ed. *The Anthropology of News and Journalism: Global Perspectives*. Bloomington, IN: Indiana University Press.
Blum-Ross, Alicia. 2012a. "Authentic Representations? Ethical Quandaries in Participatory Filmmaking with Young People." In *Negotiating Ethical Challenges in Youth Research*, edited by Kitty te Riele and Rachel Brooks, 55–68. Abingdon: Routledge.
Blum-Ross, Alicia. 2012b. "Youth Filmmaking and 'Justice-Oriented Citizenship'." *Nordic Journal of Digital Literacy* 7 (4): 270–283.
Blum-Ross, Alicia. 2013. "'It Made Our Eyes Get Bigger': youth filmmaking and place-making in East London." *Visual Anthropology Review* 29 (2): 89–106.
Blum-Ross, Alicia. 2015. "Filmmakers/Educators/Facilitators? Understanding the Role of Adult Intermediaries in Youth Media Production in the UK and the USA." *Journal of Children and Media* 9 (3): 308–324.
Blum-Ross, Alicia. 2016. "Voice, Empowerment and Youth-Produced Films about 'Gangs'." *Learning, Media and Technology* (Special Issue 'Voice and Representation in Youth Media Production in Educational Settings: transnational dialogues'). doi: 10.1080/17439884.2016.1111240.
Blum-Ross, Alicia and Sonia Livingstone. Forthcoming. "From Voice to Entrepreneurship: the individualization of digital media and learning." *Journal of Digital Media Literacy*.

Bräuchler, Birgit and John Postill. 2010. Eds. *Theorising Media and Practice (Anthropology of Media)*. Oxford: Bergahn Books.

British Film Institute. 2014a. "BFI Film Academy." Accessed 21 September. http:// www.bfi.org.uk/education-research/5-19-film-education-scheme-2013-2017/ bfi-film-academy-scheme-2013-4.

British Film Institute. 2014b. Impact, Relevance and Excellence: a new stage for film education. London: British Film Institute.

British Film Institute. 2016. "BFI Film Academy." Accessed 30 January. http:// www.bfi.org.uk/education-research/5-19-film-education-scheme-2013-2017/ bfi-film-academy-scheme.

Buckingham, D. 2000. *After the Death of Childhood: growing up in the age of electronic media*. Cambridge: Polity Press.

Carpentier, Nico. 2003. "The BBC's Video Nation as a Participatory Media Practice: signifying everyday life, cultural diversity and participation in an online community." *International Journal of Cultural Studies* 6 (4): 425–447. doi: 10.1177/136787790364003.

Chandler, Chris and Mark Dunford. 2012. The Power of Youth Media to Change Lives. Media Trust.

Chatterton, Paul and Robert Hollands. 2003. *Urban Nightscapes: youth cultures, pleasure spaces and corporate power, critical geographies*. London: Routledge.

Christensen, Pia and Alan Prout. 2002. "Working with Ethical Symmetry in Social Research with Children." *Childhood* 9 (4): 477–497. doi: 10.1177/ 0907568202009004007.

Coleman, Stephen. 2007. "How Democracies Have Disengaged from Young People." In *Young Citizens in the Digital Age: political engagement, young people and new media*, edited by Brian D. Loader, 166–185. London and New York: Routledge.

Corrigan, Paul. 1979. *Schooling the Smash Street Kids, Crisis Points*. London: Macmillan.

Couldry, N. 2010. *Why Voice Matters: culture and politics after neoliberalism*. London: Sage.

Couldry, N., S. Livingstone and T. Markham. 2010. *Media Consumption and Public Engagement: beyond the presumption of attention*. 2nd ed. Basingstoke: Palgrave Macmillan.

CRG Research Limited. 2006. Positive Activities for Young People National Evaluation: Final Report. Department for Education and Skills.

Dahya, Negin and Jennifer Jenson. 2015. "Mis/Representations in School-Based Digital Media Production: an ethnographic exploration with Muslim girls." *Diaspora, Indigenous, and Minority Education: studies of migration, integration, equity, and cultural survival* 9 (2): 108–123.

Dickinson, Margaret. 1999. *Rogue Reels: oppositional film making in Britain, 1945–90*. London: British Film Institute.

Doyle, Gillian, Philip Schlesinger, Raymond Boyle and Lisa Kelly. 2015. *The Rise and Fall of the UK Film Council*. Edinburgh: Edinburgh University Press.

First Light. 2009. "About Us." Accessed 11 December 2009. http://www. firstlightonline.co.uk/about-us/board-of-directors/.

Fisherkeller, JoEllen, ed. 2011. *International Perspectives on Youth Media: cultures of production and education, mediated youth*. New York: Peter Lang.

Fleetwood, Nicole R. 2005a. "Authenticating Practices: producing realness, performing 'youth'." In *Youthscapes: the popular, the national, the global,* edited by Sunaira Maira and Elisabeth Soep, 155–172. Philadelphia: University of Pennsylvania Press.

Fleetwood, Nicole R. 2005b. "Mediating Youth: community-based video production and the politics of Race and Authenticity." *Social Text* 82 (1): 83–109.

Fountain, Alan. 2001. "Opening Channels: Channel 4 and after." In *Looking at Class: Film, Television and the Working Class in Britain,* edited by Sheila Rowbotham and Huw Beynon. London: Rivers Oram Press.

France, A. 2007. *Understanding youth in late modernity.* Maidenhead: Open University Press.

Gray, Clive. 2002. "Local Government and the Arts." *Local Government Studies* 28 (1): 77–90.

Gubrium, Aline and Krista Harper. 2013. *Participatory Visual and Digital Methods.* Walnut Creek, CA: Left Coast Press.

Halleck, DeeDee. 2002. *Hand-Held Visions: the impossible possibilities of community media, communications and media studies series.* New York: Fordham University Press.

Hammersley, Martyn and Paul Atkinson. 2007. *Ethnography: principles in practice.* 3rd ed. London: Routledge.

Harvey, Sylvia. 1989. "Deregulation, Innovation and Channel Four." *Screen* 30 (1): 60–78. doi: 10.1093/screen/30.1-2.60.

Helsper, E. and R. Eynon. 2010. "Digital Natives: where is the evidence?" *British Educational Research Journal* 36 (3): 502–520.

Hewison, Robert. 2015. *Cultural Capital: the rise and fall of creative Britain.* London: Verso.

HM Treasury and Department for Children Schools and Families. 2007. Aiming High for Young People: a ten year strategy for positive activities. HM Treasury and Department for Children Schools and Families.

House of Lords: Select Committee on Digital Skills. 2015. Make or Break: the UK's digital future. London, UK: House of Lords.

Into Film. 2014. "Our Story." Accessed 26 March. http://www.intofilm.org/our-story.

Kehily, Mary Jane. 2007. *Understanding Youth: perspectives, identities and practices.* London: Sage.

Kintrea, Keith, Jon Bannister, Jon Pickering, Maggi Reid and Naofumi Suzuki. 2008. Young People and Territoriality in British Cities. Joseph Rountree Foundation.

Lesko, Nancy. 2001. *Act your Age!: a cultural construction of adolescence, critical social thought.* New York; London: Routledge.

Lister, Ruth. 2008. "Unpacking Children's Citizenship." In *Children and Citizenship,* edited by Antonella Invernizzi and Jane Williams. London: Sage Publications.

Lister, R., N. Smith, S. Middleton, and L. Cox. 2003. "Young People Talk about Citizenship: empirical perspectives on theoretical and political debates." *Citizenship Studies* 7 (2): 235–253.

Livingstone, Ian and Alex Hope. 2011. Next Gen: transforming the UK into the world's leading talent hub for the video games and visual effects industries. London.

Loader, Brian. 2007. "Young Citizens in the Digital Age: political engagement, young people and new media." 1–213.
MacNamara, Jim. 2013. "Beyond Voice: audience-making and the work and architecture of listening as new media literacies." *Continuum: Journal of Media & Cultural Studies* 27 (1): 160–175.
Malik, Sarita. 2013. "'Creative Diversity': UK Public Service Broadcasting after multiculturalism." *Popular Communication* 11 (3): 227–241.
Marchessault, Janine 1995. "Reflections on the Dispossessed: video and the 'Challenge for Change' experiment." *Screen* 36 (2): 131–146.
McCulloch, Gary. 1986. "Policy, Politics and Education: the technical and vocational education initiative." *Journal of Education Policy* 1 (2): 35–52.
Mediabox. 2009. Big Mediabox: Stage 1 application guidelines.
Mediabox. 2010. Accessed 23 April 2010. http://www.media-box.co.uk/about/what-is-mediabox.
Morgan, George, Julian Wood, and Pariece Nelligan. 2013. "Beyond the Vocational Fragments: creative work, precarious labour and the idea of 'Flex-ploitation'." *The Economic and Labour Relations Review* 24 (3): 397–415. doi: 10.1177/1035304613500601.
Mouffe, Chantal. 1993. *Return of the Political*. London: Verso.
Museums Libraries and Archives, and Arts Council England. 2009. Using the Arts and Culture to Deliver Positive Activities for Young People. Museums Libraries and Archives, Arts Council England.
Narey, Martin. 2008. "Most Adults Think Children 'are Feral and a *Danger to Society*'." Last Modified 17 November 2008 Accessed 5 March 2009. http://www.timesonline.co.uk/tol/life_and_style/education/article5167811.ece.
Newman, Janet. 2001. *Modernising Governance: new labour, policy and society*. London: Sage.
O'Brien, Dave, Daniel Laurison, Andrew Milesc, and Sam Friedman. 2016. "Are the Creative Industries Meritocratic? An Analysis of the 2014 British Labour Force Survey." *Cultural Trends*. doi: 10.1080/09548963.2016.1170943.
Osler, Audrey and Hugh Starkey. 2003. "Learning for Cosmopolitan Citizenship: theoretical debates and young people's experiences." *Educational Review* 55 (3): 243–254.
Palys, T. 2008. "Purposive Sampling." In *The Sage Encyclopedia of Qualitative Research Methods*, edited by L.M. Given, 697–698. Los Angeles: Sage.
Poyntz, Stuart R. 2013. "Public Space and Media Education in the City." In *Current Perspectives in Media Education: beyond the manifesto*, edited by Pete Fraser and Jonathan Wardle, 91–109. Basingstoke: Palgrave Macmillan.
Prensky, M. 2001. "Digital Natives, Digital Immigrants." *On the Horizon* 9 (5): 1–2.
Qualifications and Curriculum Authority. 1998. *Education for Citizenship and the Teaching of Democracy in Schools: final report of the Advisory Group on Citizenship, Qualifications and Curriculum Authority*. London: Qualifications and Curriculum Authority.
Rowbotham, Sheila and Huw Beynon. 2001. *Looking at Class: film, television and the working class in Britain*. London: Rivers Oram Press.
Scheper-Hughes, Nancy and Carolyn Fishel Sargent. 1998. *Small Wars: the cultural politics of childhood*. Berkeley: University of California Press.

Sefton-Green, Julian and Elisabeth Soep. 2007. "Creative Media Cultures: making and learning beyond the school." In *International Handbook of Research in Arts Education*, edited by L. Bresler, 835–854. New York: Springer.

Soep, Elisabeth 2006. "Beyond Literacy and Voice in Youth Media Production." *McGill Journal of Education* 41 (3): 197–214.

Swinson, James. 2001. "Putting Life into Theory." In *Looking at Class: film, television and the working class in Britain*, edited by Sheila Rowbotham and Huw Beynon. London: Rivers Oram Press.

te Riele, Kitty. 2006. "Youth 'at Risk': further marginalizing the marginalized?" *Journal of Education Policy* 21 (2): 129–145. doi: 10.1080/026809 30500499968.

Thomson, Pat and Julian Sefton-Green 2011. Eds. *Researching Creative Learning: methods and issues*. Abingdon and New York: Routledge.

Thumim, Nancy. 2012. *Self-Representation and Digital Culture*. Houndmills, Basingstoke, Hampshire; New York: Palgrave Macmillan.

Weller, Susie. 2007. *Teenagers' Citizenship: experiences and education*. London: Routledge.

Westheimer, Joel and Joseph Kahne. 2004. "What Kind of Citizen? The Politics of Educating for Democracy." *American Educational Research Journal* 41 (2): 237–269.

14 "Can we fast forward to the good bits?"

Working with Film: Revisiting the Field of Practice

Kate Pahl and Steve Pool

In this chapter, we explore the uses of film in community-oriented research and how they relate to power inequalities both within and beyond projects with a particular focus on engagement and participation. Neither author primarily identifies him-/herself as a filmmaker. However, we use film in our respective fields of ethnography and visual arts practice. We suggest that film is a valuable tool that affords opportunities to view the world differently, to make meaning with young people and to carry strong messages across domains. Our field of practice includes New Literacy Studies and cultural studies (Kate) and arts practice, with a focus on visual art and participation (Steve). We draw on the respective fields of ethnographic research and engaged critical art practice. These then intersect with the field of participatory film. In our experience, we identify this coming together as the point that each method (ethnography, arts practice, film) offers the possibility to materialise lived experience through surfacing hidden texts and situated literacy practices. Pahl's work has described the way in which identities and practices sediment into texts, in her work with Jennifer Rowsell (2007). She has explored this in her work (2014a) in relation to power and post-colonial perspectives over many years as an ethnographer. Steve likewise brings a long experience of working with film with children and young people. Here, we explore our genealogies with a focus on participatory film and focus on unpacking our relationship to that field, drawing on the reflexive turn within ethnographic research from Bourdieu and Waquant (1992) to explore our field of practice.

Increasing access to equipment and familiarity with manipulating digital footage and platforms for sharing the moving image have resulted in a plethora of film production processes within research. These are often used within engagement and participation contexts. We suggest that much of this work remains marginal within traditional research outcomes, such as the UK's Research Excellence Framework and journal articles. These tend to ignore the emancipatory potential of digital media as a platform young people can use to speak and be heard, as is highlighted by Potter (2012). We review the relationship between the production of film and its consumption, suggesting that it is necessary to consider the context of how film outputs are viewed and how this relates to a consideration of its productions. This is particularly important in community co-production contexts, where filmmaking can provide the most accessible and meaningful research outcome for participants and be seen as a form of community engagement yet become marginalised in the context of knowledge production and transfer in an academic discourse.

It is increasingly clear that the digital capture of the moving image has become an everyday cultural practice, and this has changed the possibilities and implications of its use within research as described by Parry (2013). In the context of the everyday, video is no longer special or extraordinary for many young people; the distinction between the production and consumption of video as a textual artefact has become blurred. Our research engages with this reality and aims to surface experience at the cusp of everyday life. We aspire to generate collaborative spaces within the world of schools and young people and allow new dialogues to emerge. We share an experience of making films with children and young people as described in previous articles and chapters, for example, Pool and Pahl (2015) and Pahl and Pool (2011). We are interested in working alongside young people to make sense of collective meanings that are situated and relational. We describe these objects of meaning making as 'literacy artefacts' from Rowsell and Pahl (2010), that is, material and digital objects that carry meaning and are interested in the multiple meanings generated within different contexts. Film has become intertwined with our practice, arising naturally from an interest in children's everyday meaning making. The work spans a period of significant change in the relationship of the moving image to everyday literacy practices, paralleled by a shift in young people's access to multiple digital platforms where they can be seen and heard.

Our methodologies stem from ethnography and arts practice. Kate takes from Campbell and Lassiter (2015) a focus on collaborative ethnography as a mode of enquiry, whereby participants work with the research team in a shared endeavour to uncover meanings and ways of knowing in community contexts. This might involve developing shared repertoires of practice (such as writing field notes or research reflections together) and ultimately co-authoring research papers and outputs (e.g. blogs, exhibitions, seminars and films). Steve has identified that his practice stems from the idea of the bricoleur from Rogers (2012) and is often dependent on what is 'to hand' and what comes readily in a situation. Our methods are therefore intuitive, arts based and focused on relationships and situated ways of knowing.

We argue that the complexity of film production and consumption entangled within community research projects creates a rich yet muddled field, as Parry (2015) articulates. In the past, programmes of work were often built on the belief that filmmaking enables children and young people to have a 'voice', an assumption that has been troubled within the research literature, for example in the work of Wood (2015) or Blum-Ross (2015a, 2015b). Here, we question how this voice is potentially diverted through the intervention and agendas of adults. In a previous book chapter, Hall, Pahl and Pool (2015) we have explored the different ways in which young people have been using film or represented within film. Here, we describe our approaches to community film production, its historical foundations and its relationship as a site of agency for young people in the context of the social digital space. To do this we look back with some distance to explore how three community films we were in-volved with were listened to and understood in different contexts.

We are particularly concerned as to the potential impact of *context* for watching community films. Often, 'impact' is unproblematically de-fined as something that is about 'showing' things that have happened, sometimes in film, but without critique. The sense of filmmaking as it is embedded deeply in the everyday process of making, recording, editing and showing may be urgent and sometimes very compelling for those involved. It is sometimes the case that the resulting film does not carry its message or power into a more removed context. In some cases, it is rarely shown or more worryingly, it is edited into fragments, often uti-lised to show snapshots of what is considered 'authenticity' at academic conferences. Audience, purpose and intentionality can become blurred, even more when research aims, research institutions and project com-missioners are folded into the mix.

Below, we draw on the detail of our research projects that employed film as a participatory method and involved engagement processes in order to analyse what is going on when children and young people, to-gether with artists, filmmakers, ethnographers and everyday life, are tangled up together on screen.

Community Meets Film: Examples from our Practice

In this section, we write from our individual perspectives about some ex-amples of filmmaking practices with young people. We explore through these narratives what we learned when academic research and our per-sonal expectations got tangled up in the process, drawing on the work of Goodman and Cocca (2013). We use these experiences to question and address issues of audience and representation in community filmmaking practices. We begin with a discursive account of a community filmmak-ing project in which Kate first began to question the affordances and po-tential problems of using film. She gives an account of a project in which participants produced a film to ask questions about the types of provi-sion available for young people within a community library. Although very successful in the specific and supported context of a local consul-tation, Kate's subsequent showing of the film at an academic conference led to concerns about the relational aspect of the films produced in community filmmaking. We then discuss the making of a film with young people in collaboration with the youth service based in a community hall on a housing estate. This filmmaking project formed part of a policy review for government called "Making Meaning Differently". We use these exemplars to tease out the complexity of making films in locations such as schools and youth centres, and the ways in which, through the production and sharing process, meanings can shift and intentions be compromised. (See also Soep (2014) for a discussion of the benefits of a youth-driven radio station.)

1 Shifting Contexts: a Film about Rotherham Libraries

Kate Pahl writes: In 2009, I was commissioned by Yorkshire Forward to conduct an evaluation of a literacy initiative called Inspire Rotherham. (For more on this project, see Pahl and Allan (2011)). The brief was to explore ways in which structures and processes were supporting, or not supporting, literacy development for young people, particularly in communities where the statistics showed low educational attainment. I was interested in the role of libraries in facilitating literacy for children, drawing on Neuman and Celano's work in Philadelphia (2001, 2006). In these studies, particular individuals were found to be key in influencing or changing the ways in which young people related to libraries. Literacy development was linked to a raft of community support. I was very interested, at that time, in participatory video making with children and young people, drawing on my recent project with Steve Pool (2011) where a group of young people had co-analysed the ways in which artists had worked in a school in a coal-mining area. This work was primarily about giving young children agency over the modes and delivery of research. Rather than provide a pre-set repertoire of methods, we decided to create opportunities for children and young people to experiment with modal choice and decide how they participated in research. This was drawing on increasingly powerful work in the field of the New Sociology of Childhood, for example, in the work of James and Prout (2004) and Emma Uprichard (2008). Heartened by young people's positive response, I began working informally in a community library in Rotherham, with a broad intention of finding out how young people used the library and what they needed to happen to support their literacy development.

My research assistant, Chloe Allan, and I began a number of interventions in the library, which was in a building that used to be a community swimming pool situated in a designated 'deprived area'. It was the informal meeting place of a number of young people in the area, who congregated there after school. A supportive community librarian and outreach worker enabled the group to stay within the library and encouraged us to work with the group.

The group of children and young people included those who had been described by a librarian at a different library as 'running wild'. We wanted to work with this group to develop insights about how they saw literacy and what they wanted from their community library. The group of young people was happy to meet weekly, and provided with buns and juice, they devised a programme with us called 'Research Rebels'. We were able to construct a timetable for a research project that would ask questions about what the library meant to the young people. Within this plan, the young people devised questions to ask members of the public and decided to draw on our plethora of equipment (flip cameras, still cameras and audio recording equipment) to make a film about what the library meant to them. The process was jumpy and not without problems. Not all the same young people turned up every week. We conducted a community walk around and a set of interviews with some filming by the young people about their impressions of the library. Slowly, we amassed a collection of short clips, audio recordings and still photographs. We began to edit these with the young people on site but were defeated by crashing software and the slowness of our editing process. In the end, we edited the film ourselves but were aided by the young people in deciding what clips to use and how to present the material. We presented edited drafts of the film for discussion in our weekly meetings.

The film included commentaries on library usage by the young people (including commentaries on dual language books and access for people with disabilities) along with more provocative questions, including discussions about who used the libraries and why. The young people also asked members of the public, "why don't you give more people respect?", which upset one of the interviewees. A short clip of the community walk around highlighted the presence of drug dealers in the area. Within the film lay stories of loss and devastation; one of the adult interviewees has died since the film was made, and some of the young people have gone in and out of the public care system.

The final film was shown in the library. The children and young people selected their audience – their parents, carers, siblings, members of the library staff and one key person – the deputy Head of Libraries for Rotherham. This person was invited to hear their message – that the children valued the library but would like to be valued and respected themselves. They also wanted more drama workshops and activities based in the site. This message was clear; they also acknowledged the way in which the library was useful for different purposes (Facebook, job applications, reading to children, access for disabled people and support for people who spoke multiple languages). The film also highlighted the way in which the library was important in an area where the street literacies were less strong. The idea of the 'literacy rich area' came from Neuman and Celano (2006) but was also taken up in the final Inspire

Rotherham policy, which was translated by Deborah Bullivant, director, into a community story shop, Grimm and Co, located in the town centre. The showing of the film was effective in that it inspired the children and young people to articulate their ideas to the head of libraries. Subsequently, I (Kate) gave a presentation on the ecologies of literacy in London, at the Institute of Education, and showed the film. To my dismay, the audience laughed. Part of this could have been the children's ironic joking about library staff and their provocative question, "Why Don't You Show More People Respect?" While the children were not intentionally funny, they did speak with noticeable Northern accents. This led to a further project, funded by the AHRC Language as Talisman project,[1] about the importance and value of regional dialects. This highlighted the ways in which the specific regional dialect of the area was not approved of by Ofsted, and through this a repositioning of local linguistic practices and a revaluing of local languages was part of the project.

Reflecting on this project today, I realize the film's reach was very limited. When I asked the young people where it could be shown, they said "not Rotherham", which spoke of the needs of the young people to retain privacy. However, when I showed the film in "not Rotherham", the trope of the 'other' that is, the children with regional accents, made it difficult to show to a Southern English audience. Thus, the production of the film was compromised. I have since seen this moment as one in which I rethought how film production, tangled in research agendas, could itself shift research agendas and ideas.

2 Telling it Slant: Making Meaning Differently

Steve Pool writes: In 2012 as part of a project to explore representation in the context of a decentralised planning and localism agenda[2] I was commissioned as an artist filmmaker to produce a video with a number of community-based organisations to 'Carry a message to government'. The short title of the project was "Making Meaning Differently". The brief had a clear focus on empowering participants to find a voice through film as a route to greater participation. In partnership with a youth group leader we decided to work with a group of young people that had only recently started to meet in a youth club based at a community centre. The area was considered to have a lack of provisions for young people and a perceived problem with groups hanging out together in public places. The youth worker was very experienced, had worked on a number of projects with the University of Sheffield and was keen to provide opportunities for the group to participate in broader discussions. The project offered the potential for the voices of young people to be heard within a national forum. We aimed to open discussions and debates around the politics and lived experience of young people as a way to build connections within the group. Politically, the British National

Party (BNP) had made significant inroads in the area; turnouts for local elections were low, yet many of the young people were well informed and concerned with local issues. Changes within local authority funding associated with the coalition government's austerity program were having a direct impact on the lives of families on the estate, and these changes provided interesting starting points for conversation.

Within this focused group context, it was necessary for the research team to consider the wider project's scope. Across the project, we were working in six areas to gain snapshots of the potential of the Arts and Humanities to explore ideas of representation. The project brief was specifically to explore what the arts and humanities could offer the field of community governance and representation. Partners included Sheffield City Council, Rotherham Youth Services and the Department of Communities and Local Government (DCLG) and Sheffield University's Department of Town and Regional Planning. Initially the project brief requested a single short film spanning all the projects; this would provide a backdrop and context for a more traditional report. It was intended that this report would take the form of 'slide pack' presentations in which statistical information and ideas are presented in detailed PowerPoint slides, a way of reporting familiar to government departments.

Working in close partnership with the research team we collectively tried to find a common theme and approach to provide a core message for a single film. This included a day of practical filmmaking workshops and individual interviews with each member of the project team. It soon became apparent that the breadth of the project and divergent epistemological and methodological framings were not compatible with a single short video. At the film training session, I presented the power of film in a research context. I stressed the idea that film was good at getting across clear and straightforward ideas and provided the potential to open a space for people to speak honestly about issues that concerned them and the importance of brevity, of refining and editing down ideas so the film carries a clear and importantly situated message. In this project, the strength of film as a medium seemed incompatible with a complex academic argument, discourse and multiple sets of expectations. A muddle of emotions and histories collided with short timescales and the need to bridge the gulfs between very different academic fields (the arts and humanities), the Research Councils, community organisations and individual participants. On some projects, the need to look for simplicity and consensus can make film a perfect tool for drawing people together and opening up areas of shared ground. On this project, however, film provided a contested space, and the conversations became circular and introspective. It was apparent that producing a single film that could effectively hold all the viewpoints simultaneously was impossible, so the team decided to make multiple films including interviews and more narrative community videos. All films are hosted on a project website

(http://spsheff.wix.com/makingrepresentation), and they were given to
the Department of Communities and Local Government (DCLG) on
an interactive DVD; however, the extent to which they were watched
or shared and their impact remain limited. This experience was also
described and analysed by Steve Connelly and colleagues (2015). The
ease of fast forwarding or ignoring video and its low status compared to
written or statistical research raise many questions about video's default
use as a way to share ideas from marginalised or ignored voices within
communities.

This experience raised some key questions for the project team. For
film to be an effective tool of empowerment, everyone involved in the research projects need to consider the forum where the film will be shown
and the context of this showing. Space and time are important considerations in order to listen to the voices that emerge. There needs to be
a clear understanding of the contract between community filmmakers
and their intended audiences. We now retrospectively explore two films
made in the Making Meaning Differently project in order to look at
some of our concerns when a film gets out of our control.

The focus of our joint work was to make a film with a group of young
people who felt distant from the government. With the support of youth
worker Marcus Hurcombe, we worked with group of ten young people, who had been identified as not engaging with youth work provision
and who met up in an ex-miners centre on an estate. The group was
self-organizing: dancing, talking and sheltering from the weather, they
demonstrated strong and supportive emotional connections, and a sense
that they were looking out for each other. We were concerned about
centralising the ideas and agencies of the young people, to start where
they were rather than engaging them directly in our research questions.
We spent time together trying to encourage brainstorming. After a number of visits with the group, it became ever clearer that they would only
engage with us on their own terms. It is important to view this in the
context of a project exploring voice. We had to leave our very specific
research questions and objectives at the door if we were to have any
opportunities to gain an insight into young people's lived realities. So
often, we develop projects that attempt to listen yet do not allow space
for collective ideas to emerge. This often results in all participants taking
part in a performance that is to large extent already scripted through a
set of implicit and explicit expectations.

The young people were not happy with the format of a conventional
film or documentary: nobody wanted to appear on camera, nobody
wanted to take an active role in developing a message or constructing
narrative, nobody was very interested in the equipment. The group as a
whole was happy to talk informally but was resistant to getting involved
in any activities that felt structured by adults. In conversation, they had
much to say to government, and although feeling very removed from the

national political process they were aware that changes in local authority provision were impacting their day-to-day lives. Guided by the youth
workers' patience and experience a sustained and emergent process began. We recognised that what we initially considered resistance was actually a form of empowered participation. Over a number of sessions,
without cameras or even the basic idea that we were making a film the
group began to focus on narratives. Drawing on his personal experience
one young person suggested using shadow puppets as a way to tell the
story. The youth worker facilitated a storytelling session. Through this
joint exploration, a clear narrative emerged of a real life incident in a
local shop where a man carrying a snake threatened the group with a
knife. The young people felt that the intervention of a local police officer was inadequate, and this led to their feeling unsafe in their familiar
hangouts; they felt ignored and in danger.

The story presented important aspects of the group's personal relationships to the state and their concern that the structures of authority
did not extend to them. They felt that they were considered outsiders
and a problem. The narrative held a clear message about the feelings
and lived experience they wished to share with government. It was a
complex and difficult message and would not conveniently slip into a
slide-pack or make sense outside of the context from which it emerged.
Over the following weeks through dance, shadow puppetry, theatre
and storytelling, we tried to capture a message to send to government
that in some way represented the young people's concerns and allowed
for multiple messages within a number of different modes. We drew on
the idea of modal choice from Jennifer Rowsell (2013), that is, the idea
that different messages could be articulated within different modes,

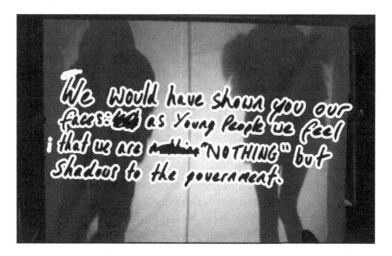

Figure 14.1 Shadow dance. Source: Image from Steve Pool.

so linguistic modes offered argument, visual modes offered still or moving image. The final film emerged from process; it was messy and chaotic. In some ways, it captures the space of the youth club: spontaneous dancing, fag breaks, leaders and followers, adults trying to make adult sense in a space controlled by young people. Ironically the film is full of politics: a deep, ingrained politics of growing up tough, the importance of friends, the importance of building space that makes sense and taking control of the things that you can still control. We sat together and edited a three-minute film to be shown alongside other material at a sharing of findings event at a conference in London for the DCLG.

On initial viewing, the research team felt that the film didn't carry a clear message so we inscribed the young people's messages onto the screen through layering young people's written thoughts onto the image. We screened the finished film at the end of a session, and the young people and youth worker were positive. The process had been engaging, and although many of the young people had dipped in and out, they shared ownership of the result, agreeing it was a 'nice film' that they felt represented them well. The group had been supported in the technical production, and I had demonstrated how to manipulate materials and technologies. The final cut of the film represented some of their ideas through a complex visual narrative. In some ways, the film did represent their ideas differently in that the young people chose how they wanted to be represented and came up with a scripted play and written slogans to convey their ideas to government.

The 'Making Meaning Differently' project was complex and multi-layered. I knew that the project's moment in the spotlight would be short lived and the opportunity to inform policy limited. However, I felt that it was ethically necessary to find a relevant forum to share the Rotherham film with its intended audience. This would require making a space in terms of time and environment for the film to breathe. The film does not represent high art or good cinema; it lacks narrative and finish, yet it carries a significant amount of voice and holds concern about a very human need to feel safe in your own community. In planning the presentation to the DCLG it was decided to cut the film from three minutes to one and a half minutes; other films were shown or partially shown.

When the time came to show the Rotherham film, the program of events had overrun. The television provided had poor sound; the slide packs were assumed to be the most important contribution to policy. They were familiar, they contained information that would be useful, they were easy to act on or ignore. During the time we were making the film, many things have happened in Rotherham, and much of it revolved around young people from marginalised groups not being heard or not being able to find a voice. I don't think the film of shadow puppets and violence against young people, dancing, a man with both a snake and a knife and police turning a blind eye would ever have made a difference in the scheme of things. However, perhaps an emphasis on making places for people to speak and people to listen that don't get 'fast forwarded to the good bits' (a quote from an academic keen to limit a long film showing) would be a step towards making different types of representations and encouraging a closer form of listening.

3 Making Change Happen Through Film: Trainers

Kate Pahl writes: In my work, I try to develop what I describe as an embedded way of researching with young people. For example, if I'm working in schools, I meet with a group of young people every week for a period of time to listen and talk without a clear research question or specific focus. I aim to generate a space where their concerns, stories and lived experiences create meaning. This can sometimes generate textual artefacts such as stories, displays or films, for example. In this way, I have worked with a group of girls to write a story about the second-world-war and ghosts, called 'Reunion'. This is written up in my book *Materializing Literacies* (2014b). The story became a means to express ideas of history, belonging and the importance of family and grandparents. The focus on narrative and text making and their relationship to the everyday through the formation of identity and feelings of belonging are central to my research. As part of the 'Making Meaning Differently' project, I decided to work with a school council in a Rotherham secondary school. The school council is part of the infrastructure of a school and has become a popular way to represent young people in the day-to-day running of school business. Most school councils use a democratic election process with individual students representing constituent groups. As the project's overarching aim was to explore how people are represented in politics with a focus on localism, I felt that a close analysis of power relations within the relatively closed system of a school could surface thinking on real and apparent influence. Using embedded research approaches, I aimed to provide space for the school council's concerns to emerge without adult intervention or manipulation. Young people would then work with a filmmaker to co-produce a film that would be used as an advocacy tool to try and generate a discussion about change.

In my work, I am concerned with representational practices as well as how to create spaces where young people can articulate their concerns outside the confines of mainstream media, drawing on the work of John Potter (2012). These spaces for alternative narratives were interesting to me in the context of representation. Talking to the school council, we quickly became interested in how aware the group was of their limitations as a school council to achieve change. Conversations about their achievements were checked by the realisation that there were many issues within school that they could not influence. For example, the school council could make suggestions about specific aspects of the school uniform. They had suggested using clip-on ties to keep boys from getting strangled, yet the decision to wear ties was pre-decided by school governors and not up for debate. Through long discussions about the role of the school council, the idea of representation crystallized in the school's approach to policing student footwear.

The 'Trainers' project involved the school council, who had been lobbying for uniform regulations to change, so that students would be allowed to wear black trainers. Current policy required students to wear smart black shoes, and there seemed to be issues and ambiguity around the definitions of a shoe and a trainer. The young people saw the 'no trainers' rule as unreasonable and were concerned primarily with fairness and justice. The 'Trainers' rule was a symbol for the limitations of student voice within the school system. The school council saw our project as a potential to legitimise their aim to make decision-making more open and transparent and to push at the edges of control and power in order to question the role and genuine influence of the group. The questioning of power structures and people's abilities to represent others and effect change within systems was central to our project. It was interesting that the school council embraced the legitimacy of University research to further its own specific agenda, in the words of one of the school council member, "*Well, they might listen to us now – cos you're here.*" The focus on power relationships and the role of democracy within the school had grown from a set of conversations. The project team had shared their own experiences of school, of growing up, of frustration with rules and what constituted legitimate ways of challenging injustice and power. We had not entered the space with the intention of making a film or foreground filmmaking within the process. Video cameras had been used by young people to capture moments of discussion, and then a short film of a tour of the school was edited together to be used as data alongside written field notes, fragments of memory or conversation.

With the help of Steve Pool and filmmaker Martin Curry, the school council decided to make a film to represent its views to the head teacher about wearing trainers. The Council members were keen to use the profile of our research project, the collective voice of film and the context of the school council to present their case. I became aware that for the film to have an impact it would be helpful to discuss the content of the film with someone in touch with power, namely the local MP. We planned a carefully constructed sharing event that would signify the end of the project. We invited the local MP (who had shown an interest in the project), the head teacher, the deputy head and the teacher who facilitates the school council; we also involved a professor of politics from Sheffield University who also originally came from the area.

In carefully constructing a discursive space to watch the film I think we made some sense of the process of its making. The young people had a clear central message that they felt strongly about, and the film as a product was contextualised within that space. The medium enabled the young people to have a voice and to advocate for what concerned them. The 'Trainers' film was made as a textual artefact and for a specific purpose. Within the context of its being shared within the school and as an advocacy tool it had integrity and was fit for purpose. Although happy for the film to be shown in school the young people did not want the film to be shown out of context; we did not use the film within our final presentation to DCLG, and although part of our research outcomes the film has not been shown in a wider context.

The day of the film showing involved a number of negotiations; with the school, who turned out to have a ban on external files coming into the school computers and required technical help to access the film; with the head teacher and deputy head teacher who had just finished a long (and gruelling) week being inspected by Ofsted and with the MP who came in looking tired, but refreshingly, was only interested in speaking with the young people. The young people gathered round, the film was shown and the resulting discussion touched on key issues of power, how change is made, links to the House of Commons and making things happen in the world. The film was strong enough to carry a further message: that young people's voices are important. At the end of the afternoon, the head teacher was better able to explain to the school council why the school followed a strict dress code. He reiterated that nothing would change and trainers would not be permitted at that moment but the uniform code was under a constant process of review by the board of governors. The school council therefore offered a kind of agency, but it was limited in terms of the structural constraints.

The school council represents a very different space from the youth club. Modelled on democratic processes and fully committed to consultation and student voice, the school council operates within an adult framework. The film demonstrated that young people lived lives within school that are defined by rules that may appear arbitrary. There was a clear limit to the school council's ability to make changes work within the school's constraints. The school council mirrored politics outside school where representation and the appearance of accountability do not equate to people's ability to influence change. The film did provide a space to ask questions, offering a space of criticality that opened up the possibility. We were careful to consider how the film would be watched; we were clear that if we maintained control over the textual artefact, many of the problems of audience and the way things were received (that we contended with on other projects) could be mitigated.

Concluding Thoughts

In the three examples, the purpose of filmmaking was to send a message; in the first film the message was intended to inform the Head of Library services, the second was originally intended for the Civil Service (DCLG) in London, and in the last example, the message was for the head and management of a large secondary school in Rotherham. In all examples, film became a space of practice where young people could develop articulations of their lived experience and their ideas. All films are drawn from emerging conversations. Practice, ideas and thoughts grew from conversations, through 'doing' over time with young people working together. They were essentially co-produced and were all to a greater or lesser extent successful.

Our key findings from these experiences include the following points:

- Context produces both the film's meaning and its logic but needs to be considered in the process of showing the film as well as when making the film.
- Young people's representational practices are not necessarily congruent with some forms of filmmaking.
- Filmmaking can appear participatory and offer 'voice' to young people, but this is not always the case; appearances can be deceptive.
- Films can surface difficult experiences, e.g. violence, anger, emotion, more easily than other modes and can be powerful, allied to suggestive forms such as music and movement.
- Film does not automatically transmit 'findings' as a form of impact; rather it is a form of inquiry, a methodology and a visual and nuanced emotional experience in itself.
- Young people who construct and make a film should ideally have ownership about where it is shown and for what purpose. Perhaps at the stage of ethical review, ethics boards should consider who has control over the film produced and where it is shown, and young people should retain copyright.

We therefore consider that a more careful understanding of the spaces for viewing, sharing and discussion is needed. This should also be combined with an understanding that within situated meaning making context is critical and under theorized. New media can be accessed and shared so easily that it is a part of the everyday, but this does not reduce our responsibility as practitioners to the integrity behind making meaning with young people. This is especially so when this meaning is emergent, conflicted and never fully understood. We are concerned about what happens to any text when it is removed from the context of its production. In 'fast forwarding to the good bits', we threaten the integrity of the piece and do not do justice to the people involved. Even when watching films in specific and relational spaces, with careful production values and a focus on creating space and time for viewing, it is important not to diminish what the young people might say. Becky Parry (in conversation 19. 1. 2016) suggested that,

> We need to analyse and deconstruct film made in research as well as let it speak for itself. We need to find a vocabulary for doing so where we can talk about the robustness and reliability of the data and our interpretations and we need to document and include process of production in doing so.

Within the cracks of the editing, the layered narratives, for example, on the 'Shadow Dance' film, contained some unpalatable truths that were also implicitly present about how the young people felt threatened. Some of the young people expressed opinions about politics or told us things about the community that we felt should not go out into the wider public.

Representation here is a process that was negotiated in the moments of doing, as children rushed round the library on roller skates or devised ways of challenging their own sense of being judged for their behaviour. Our projects happened in after-school contexts, meaning that the young people attended voluntarily. We constituted these activities as 'research' while the young people understood the activities to be 'projects'. Our commitment to participatory and co-produced research was not entirely faithful; rather, we offered 'pockets of participation' from the work of Franks (2009), where young people were able to insert lived experience and urgent messages to those in charge. This fracturing of adult inspired talk and discourses was part of the films' urgency.

Making community films in the context of academic projects can be problematic. Academics see film as useful to display the situated nature of their research. It is used in an instrumental, illustrative way rather than seeing it as a mode of inquiry and a way of explaining complex ideas. The use of film to achieve 'impact' and as a more accessible way to share research outcomes and co-produce knowledge is gaining ground within the academies. In the case of the Library film, and 'Trainers' the young people had specific objectives, and the films remained, largely, within the realm of their spaces and contexts (although the library film was once shown to an academic audience, it was never shown again). In the case of 'Shadow Dance' the not-showing was then followed up with a research project on translation of policy across borders as described by Steve Connelly and colleagues (2015). When that team explored this with the civil service, it became apparent that the film was not taken seriously. It did, however continue to echo in our minds, and we wrote about it in a book chapter (2015) as an illustration of ways in which voice can surface within research.

We suggest, here, that audience and context are essential parts of the concept of 'voice' and 'empowerment' in community filmmaking. A practice that gets young people involved in a film, listens to them, and involves them in a shaping of a textual artefact, but does not consider the ways that artefact interacts with the world is problematic. We would like to articulate that young people as filmmakers and authors of ideas need some ways of keeping these practices within their control. They should be able to know more about, and given information on, the different possible domains where their films might be screened, and be able to understand the implications of these screenings. This might prompt a re-thinking of ethical stances within academic research, as well as an increased awareness by the academic world of the dangers of constructing the field of film outside the realms of young people's agency. This might require an approach to impact that is more informed by ethics and less informed by the dissemination of academic research, at the same time recognizing the ways in which this work is itself, the research.

Acknowledgements

With thanks to Becky Parry for being our reader.

Notes

1 See AHRC funded project Language as Talisman http://languageastalisman. group.shef.ac.uk.
2 'Policy review: 'Community Governance in the Context of Decentralisation (AH/K503435/1); or 'Making Meaning Differently'.

References

Blum-Ross, Alicia. 2015a. "Voice, Empowerment and Youth-Produced Films about 'Gangs'." *Learning, Media and Technology* 2015: 1–20.
Blum-Ross, Alicia. 2015b. "Filmmakers/Educators/Facilitators? Understanding the Role of Adult Intermediaries in Youth Media Production in the UK and the USA." *Journal of Children and Media* 9 (3): 308–324.
Bourdieu, Pierre and Loic Wacquant. 1992. *An Invitation to Reflexive Sociology*. Oxford: Polity Press.
Campbell, Elizabeth and Luke Eric Lassiter. 2015. *Doing Ethnography Today: theoretical issues and pragmatic concerns*. Oxford: Wiley-Blackwell.
Christensen, Pia and Allison James. 2008. 2nd Edition. *Research with Children: perspectives and practices*. London: Routledge.
Connelly, Stephen, Gordon Dabinett, Stuart Muirhead, Kate Pahl, K and Dave Vanderhoven. 2013. *Making Meaning Differently*. Policy Briefing: Community Governance in an Age of Decentralisation. Unpublished report for the Department of Communities and Local Government (DCLG), funded by AHRC Connected Communities programme.

Connelly, Stephen, Dave Vanderhoven, Catherine Durose, Liz Richardson, Peter Mathews, and Robert Rutherfoord. 2015. Translation across Borders: exploring the use, relevance and impact of academic research in the policy process. In *After Urban Regeneration: Communities Policy and Place*, edited by Dave O'Brien and Peter Mathews, 199–204. Bristol: Policy Press.

Franks, Myfanwy. 2009. "Pockets of Participation: revisiting child-centred participation research." *Children and Society* 25(1): 15–25.

Goodman, Steven and Carolyn Cocoa. 2013. "Youth Voices for Change: building political efficacy and civic engagement through digital media literacy." *Journal of Digital and Media Literacy*, 1(1).

Hall, Melanie, Kate Pahl and Steve Pool. 2015. "Visual Digital Methodologies with Children and Young People: perspectives from the field." In *Visual Methods with Children and Young People: academics and visual industries in dialogue*, edited by Eve Stirling and Dylan Yamada-Rice, 164–185. Basingstoke: Palgrave MacMillan.

James, Allison and Alan Prout. 2004. *Constructing and Reconstructing Childhood: contemporary issues in the sociological study of childhood*. London: Taylor and Francis.

Neuman, Susan and Donna Celano. 2001. "Access to Print in Low-Income and Middle-Income Communities: an ecological study of four neighbourhoods." *Reading Research Quarterly* 36 (1): 8–26.

Neuman Susan and Donna Celano. 2006. "The Knowledge Gap: implications of levelling the playing field for low-income and middle-income children." *Reading Research Quarterly* 41(2): 176–201.

Pahl, Kate. 2014a. "The Aesthetics of Everyday Literacies: home writing practices in a British Asian household." *Anthropology and Education Quarterly* 45 (3): 293–311.

Pahl, Kate. 2014b. *Materializing Literacies in Communities: the uses of literacy revisited*. London: Bloomsbury.

Pahl, Kate and Chloe Allan. 2011a. "I Don't Know What Literacy Is: uncovering hidden literacies in a community library using ecological and participatory methodologies with children." *Journal of Early Childhood Literacy*11(2): 190–213.

Pahl, Kate and Steve Pool. 2011b. "'Living Your Life Because It's the Only Life You've Got': participatory research as a site for discovery in a creative project in a primary school in Thurnscoe, UK." *Qualitative Research Journal* 11 (2): 17–37.

Pahl, Kate and Jennifer Rowsell. 2010. *Artifactual Literacies: every object tells a story*. New York: Teachers College Press.

Parry, Becky. 2013. *Children, Film and Literacy*. Basingstoke: Palgrave Macmillan.

Parry, Becky. 2015. "Arts-Based Approaches to Research with Children: living with mess." In *Visual Methods with Children and Young People: academics and visual industries in dialogue*, edited by Eve Stirling and Dylan Yamada-Rice, 89–92. Basingstoke: Palgrave MacMillan.

Pool, Steve and Kate Pahl. 2015. "The Work of Art in the Age of Mechanical Co-Production." In *After Urban Regeneration: Communities Policy and Place*, edited by Dave O'Brien and Peter Mathews, 79–94. Bristol: Policy Press.

Potter, John. 2012. *Digital Media and Learner Identity: the new curatorship.* New York: Palgrave Macmillan.

Rogers, Matt. 2012. "Contextualizing Theories and Practices of Bricolage Research." *The Qualitative Report* 2012 Volume 17, T&L Art. 7: 1–17. http://www.nova.edu/ssss/QR/QR17/rogers.pdf.

Rowsell, Jennifer. 2013. *Working with Multimodality: rethinking literacy in a digital age.* London: Routledge.

Rowsell, Jennifer and Kate Pahl. 2007. "Sedimented Identities in Texts: instances of practice." *Reading Research Quarterly* 42, (3): 388–401.

Soep, Elisabeth. 2014. *Participatory Politics: next-generation tactics to remake public spheres.* Cambridge, MA: MIT/MacArthur Foundation.

Uprichard Emma. 2008. "Children as 'Being and Becoming': children, childhood and temporality." *Children and Society* 22: 303–313.

Wood, Elizabeth. 2015. "Ethics, Voices and Visual Methods." In *Visual Methods with Children and Young People: academics and visual industries in dialogue,* edited by Eve Stirling and Dylan Yamada-Rice, 129–139. Basingstoke: Palgrave MacMillan.

Conclusion
Embracing the Complexity of Community Filmmaking and Diversity

Sarita Malik, Caroline Chapain and Roberta Comunian

Complexity theory and complexity science have been recognised in the past few decades as promising and powerful frameworks for understanding the workings and dynamics of a range of systems from biological to computational or social (e.g. Byrne 1998, Holland 1998, Kauffman 1995). Wanting to overcome the limits of reductionist approaches, complexity theory engages with the diverse components and systems within the field of study and looks at how they interact in space and time. One of the key premises is that most phenomena or systems we study cannot really be understood simply by considering their components and elements. Instead, to understand their work and impact, we as researchers have looked at the multiple interactions and interdependencies that are taking place at all times and across different scales. While this brief comment does not provide all the background needed to understand complexity theory (see Byrne 1998 for a clear translation of its value within social sciences), it is important to note that it is not a single unified theory, but rather a framework (and set of methodological approaches) for studying complex systems that can lead to a more integrated understanding of social phenomena. Thus, a key element of our approach within this book is to recognise that, in order to understand community filmmaking and how it supports cultural diversity, we need to embrace a multidimensional and multidisciplinary approach. This is discussed in the introduction and illustrated in the various parts of the book. This conclusion brings together the findings and ideas from the chapters of the book, and offers an interconnected picture of agents, relationships, motivations and feedback mechanisms in the understanding of community filmmaking and diversity.

Taking a complexity perspective as a premise and looking at the range of chapters in this collection, we can see community filmmaking itself as a spatial and temporal practice of the work and interactions of a dynamic network of agents (the filmmaker, the communities involved, the funders and the audiences, for example.) who are moved by both individual interests (for example, generating visibility, aesthetic expression, career goals) and collective interests (for example, civic agency, local place-making, community representation). Within these networks, changes and feedback take place continuously throughout the development of projects and practices but also on various scales. In particular, we can identify three levels of development of community filmmaking projects and practices (Figure C.1) in relation to cultural diversity.

At the **micro** level, we find community filmmakers and participants taking part in community filmmaking projects. Here cultural diversity is a negotiation between the range of communities involved and the way filmmakers translate their engagement in terms of film process. The positionality of the community filmmaker her-/himself is of course important. Often, s/he is someone close or connected to the community, who brings an added level of reflexivity on the themes touched upon in the film. Sometimes, s/he is only a facilitator that needs to understand and mediate the way a variety of community voices will be represented within the film content and the production process.

At the **meso** level, the issues of representation and community engagement overlap with a range of networks and intermediaries that engage with cultural diversity and/or filmmaking. Community representatives might have different powers compared to the marginalised voices they represent and to the representatives from higher-level filmmaking and policy agendas with which they sometimes have to deal. In addition, other stakeholders (charities, local festivals for example) may also influence the shape of community film projects or, inversely, be themselves shaped by the content of the film produced and the community agendas.

Finally, at the **macro** level, all the issues and stakeholders of the previous two levels already mentioned interact with the place and policy frameworks where community filmmaking projects are taking place, be they local and/or national. While some of these interactions may be

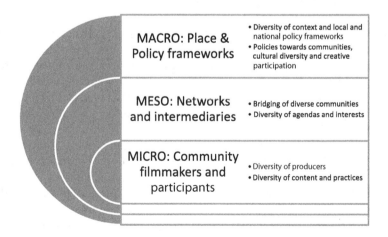

Figure C.1 Community filmmaking and diversity: a complexity perspective.

more diffuse like the inherent cultural representations and filmmaking practices embedded within particular places and their creative ecologies, other areas such as policy may impact them more directly in a top-down manner. For example, the policy attention to issues of cultural diversity from local and or national governments might affect the funding and opportunities available for intermediaries and community filmmakers to develop their work. On the contrary, policy and economic changes might restrict funding and opportunities. Of course, intermediaries and stakeholders across these levels – and their work in representing alternative voices in community film projects – might also influence new local and/or national policy agendas and initiatives.

The various contributions to be found in this book enable us to locate more precise dynamics and issues across these three levels and engage with their nuances and specificities, while overall providing a clearer picture of the complexity of a phenomenon that has so far received very little attention within academic research. The multidisciplinary nature of the research collected here also highlights the need to work across disciplines to capture the range of issues and dynamics. However, this book can only be considered a small step in drawing a bigger picture of the value that community filmmaking brings to cultural diversity and the contribution that diverse voices and communities can make to filmmaking. As mentioned in the introduction, we recognise that our collection has a greater emphasis on community filmmaking and community filmmaking contexts of the Global North than of the Global South. However, we hope that this book has the potential to provide impetus for subsequent work on the rich community filmmaking traditions of Latin America, Africa and elsewhere. The next section offers some reflections on emerging themes and directions for further research that have emerged from the rich contributions across the book, as well as our own research supported by an AHRC grant (*'Community Filmmaking and Cultural Diversity: practice, innovation and policy'* AH/K006495/1) looking at community filmmaking and cultural diversity in the UK context (Malik, Chapain and Comunian 2015).

Directions for Future Research

Our research highlights the need for more work to explore the diverse contexts of community filmmaking and its practices. In particular:

• Cultural representation plays a significant role in how community filmmakers describe their work. Broadly, community filmmakers are deeply reflexive about their practice and very conscious of ethical issues and the political contexts that surround the communities they work with. However, more research is needed to consider the positionality of community filmmakers – especially with regards to their particular position or social proximity in relation to others in 'their' communities, for example in terms of culture, ethnicity, class or gender. In general, there is little research on the community filmmakers themselves and their role in negotiating space of personal self-expression and creativity alongside community representation and facilitation work. Many chapters within this collection explore these issues, but there is scope for more research and comparative work in the future.

- Community filmmaking as a practice lives on the perceived continuum between arts and financial and commercial sustainability. It is strongly driven by the need for civic agency and mediated empowerment, in order to give a voice to a range of groups and issues from certain communities that do not reach and/or are marginalised by mainstream media. However, its financial sustainability is key to the possibility of these voices being heard (and exhibited) beyond the community filmmaking context, which itself sits on the margins of the film sector, as well as to new community filmmaking projects taking place in the future. This is an especially pressing concern given, as Isar reminds us in the Preface to this book, "the growing presence of market-driven cultural industries [which] has reduced the reach of subsidised cultural provision". Understanding better how policies and places might be able to support the development of new forms of social entrepreneurship or businesses that guarantee the viability and visibility of community filmmaking beyond the (often-unreliable) grant-aid system will become increasingly important. Exploring further the resilience of this film practice through time and place could provide further inputs in this direction. Linked to this issue, some contributions in this book argue that community filmmaking can play a key role in contributing to the cultural mapping of intangible community assets and, as such, contribute to local planning and development processes in a more formal way. This avenue of enquiry is worth exploring further.
- Community filmmaking covers a wide range of practices. It is a terrain for experimentation for filmmakers, and it can lead to various innovations in content, generating new 'authentic' stories, visually and narratively, but also in terms of funding engagement with audiences, notably through online media. However, more research is needed to explore the connection between community filmmaking projects and the mainstream film sector. While of course they are led by different agendas and objectives, some filmmakers seem to be able to navigate both community filmmaking and mainstream projects, and we believe more should be done to explore the potential connections between the two. While mainstream film would benefit from some of the innovative approaches, alternative content and approaches to diversity that are apparent in community film, community filmmaking would also benefit from platforms and opportunities to reach new audiences.

References

Byrne, David. 1998. *Complexity Theory and the Social Sciences.* London: Routledge.

Holland, John. 1998. *Emergence: from chaos to order.* Oxford: Oxford University Press.

Kauffman, Stuart. 1995. *At Home in the Universe: a search for the laws of self-organization and complexity.* New York: Oxford University Press.

Malik, Sarita, Caroline Chapain and Roberta Comunian. 2015. *Spotlight on Community Filmmaking: a report on community filmmaking and cultural diversity research.* London and Birmingham: Brunel University, the University of Birmingham and King's College London, UK.

List of Contributors

Emma Agusita is Senior Lecturer in Media, Communications & Culture at the University of the West of England. She has a background in community media as producer, editor, researcher and facilitator. Her research interests are threefold: first, exploring the role of digital technologies in creative media practices within community contexts, particularly participatory media projects and programmes involving young people – Emma's AHRC-funded collaborative PhD examined youth media production in informal educational settings; second, the investigation of creative citizenship – how people create civic value through creative networks using communication platforms; third, the research of creative entrepreneurship education.

Asier Aranzubia is Lecturer at the Carlos III University of Madrid (UC3M) and a member of the research group TECMERIN. His research interests include history and analysis of Spanish cinema. He is member of *Caimán. Cuadernos de Cine's* editorial board, and he collaborates regularly with this publication. He has collaborated also with journals such as *Revista de Occidente, Secuencias, Archivos de la Filmoteca* and *Studies in Spanish & Latin American Cinemas.* He has written, among others, *Carlos Serrano de Osma. Historia de una obsesión* (Filmoteca Española, 2007), *Alexander Mackendrick* (Cátedra, 2011) and *El mapa de la India. Conversaciones con Manolo Matji* (Cuadernos Tecmerin, 2013).

Daniel Ashton is Lecturer and MA Pathway Leader in Global Media Management in the Winchester School of Art at the University of Southampton. His research focuses on different ways of organising cultural work, including the intersections between professional and amateur media making. He has worked in partnership with UK community media organisations on digital storytelling and community radio projects. His research on digital storytelling and participatory media has been published in Media International Australia.

Alicia Blum-Ross is a Postdoctoral Research Officer in the Department of Media and Communications at the London School of Economics and Political Science (LSE). She has a PhD and MPhil in Social Anthropology from the University of Oxford. Alongside her academic research she has worked as a consultant and facilitator evaluating, managing and advising on strategic planning for media, arts and culture-based learning programmes for organisations including BAFTA, Into Film and the London Film Festival at the British Film Institute.

Casey Burkholder is a PhD Candidate at McGill University in Montreal, Canada. She became invested in the relationships among space, belonging, and civic engagement from a young age, growing up in Canada's North. In choosing a research path at the intersection of citizenship, gender, inclusion, DIY media-making and Social Studies education, Casey believes her work contributes to "research as intervention" (Mitchell, 2011) through participatory approaches to equity and social change. Her interest in cellphone video production as research method (cellphilming) has resulted in an edited collection from Sense Publishers, *What's a Cellphilm? Integrating Mobile Phone Technology into Participatory Visual Research and Activism.*

Caroline Chapain is a Lecturer at the Business School, University of Birmingham. Previously, Caroline studied and worked in France and Canada. Since 2005, she has been looking at the way creative industries emerge, operate and develop at the local and regional levels in the UK and in Europe. She has done research on topics related to creative clusters and cities, the links between creativity and innovation and creative citizenship. In the last five years she has been involved in various projects exploring the links between creative practices and online media as well as the development of creative systems for the Arts and Humanities Research Council Connected Communities Programme in the UK.

Roberta Comunian is Lecturer in Cultural and Creative Industries at the Department for Culture, Media and Creative Industries at King's College London. She is interested in relationship between public and private investments in the arts, art and cultural regeneration projects, cultural and creative industries, creativity and competitiveness. She has also undertaken research on knowledge transfer and creative industries within and has published extensively on the role of higher education in the creative economy (www.creative-campus.org.uk) and the career opportunities and patterns of creative graduates in UK (www.creative-graduates.org.uk).

Kath Dooley is a filmmaker and academic in the Department of Film, Television and Screen Arts at Curtin University, Western Australia. She recently completed a creative PhD, exploring portrayals of the body in the work of contemporary French directors Claire Denis, Catherine Breillat and Marina De Van at Flinders University, South

Australia. Kath has written a number of short and feature-length screenplays and has also directed several award-winning short films and music videos. Her current research interests include film production methodology and screenwriting in Australia and France.

Jon Dovey is Professor of Screen Media at the Faculty of Arts, Creative Industries, and Education at the University of the West of England, Bristol. In 2012 he became the Director of REACT (Research and Enterprise for Arts and Creative Technologies), one of four Hubs for the Creative Economy funded by the AHRC. Led by UWE and Watershed, REACT is an arts, technology and business collaboration aiming to produce 60 innovative media prototypes in four years (http://www.react-hub.org.uk/). His research interest is in technology and cultural form currently focused on pervasive media, documentary studies, cultural value, creative citizenship and knowledge exchange for innovation (www.dcrc.org.uk/people/jon-dovey).

Miguel Fernández Labayen is Assistant Professor at the Universidad Carlos III de Madrid, where he is a member of the research group TECMERIN and one of the two directors of the research project The Transnational Relations in Spanish-American Digital Cinema: the cases of Spain, Mexico and Argentina. His articles have appeared in *Transnational Cinemas, Journal of Spanish Cultural Studies, Studies in European Cinema*, and in several edited collections such as *A Companion to Pedro Almodóvar* (Wiley-Blackwell, 2013) and *Sampling Media* (Oxford U Press, 2014). He has curated film programs for Centro de Cultura Contemporánea de Barcelona, Seville European Film Festival and Instituto Cervantes, among others.

Yudhishthir Raj Isar is Professor of Global Communications at the American University of Paris. Isar was also the founding co-editor of the five volumes of the *Cultures and Globalization Series* (SAGE). In 2013, he was the principal investigator and lead writer for the *UN Creative Economy Report 2013. Widening Local Development Pathways*, the scientific coordinator of the European Union's inquiry Culture in EU External Relations and the principal author of its 2014 report *Engaging the World: Towards Global Cultural Citizenship*. In 2015, he edited the monitoring report on the implementation of the 2005 cultural diversity Convention entitled *Re|Shaping Cultural Policies*. Earlier, at UNESCO, he was notably the executive secretary of the World Commission on Culture and Development, director of both cultural policies and the International Fund for the Promotion of Culture.

Aitor Iturriza is a PhD student in Applied Research to Mass Media at Universidad Carlos III de Madrid. He went to the ESCAC film school and combines his studies with directing short films and documentaries.

His first short film, *Una hora, un paso,* was premiered in the San Sebastian International Film Festival and was screened in over 80 festivals around Europe, Asia, Africa and America. Since 2015 he also works as press officer for the political party Podemos in the Basque Country.

Sharon Karsten is a Canadian media arts developer and cultural policy scholar. As Director of an Artist-Run Media Centre (Quickdraw Animation in Calgary 2004–2008), and of a regional public art gallery (Comox Valley Art Gallery 2011 – present), Sharon developed a series of media access programmes for and with marginalised youth. Her interest in social justice via media and culture extends into her scholarly pursuits – as a PhD student through SFU's School of Communication, Sharon explores the potential of media as a change agent within municipal settings – looking at ways in which new and emergent cracks within the dominant planning paradigm might allow for social-democratic and creative planning manifestations to emerge.

Eileen Leahy is an independent researcher, living in Dublin, Ireland. She received her doctorate in 2014, from the department of Film Studies at Trinity College Dublin, as Government of Ireland, Irish Research Council Postgraduate Scholar. Her doctoral thesis examined community filmmaking in Ireland, with a focus on the relationship between community film and national cinema, the emergence of community filmmaking and recent community films made in contexts of urban regeneration in Dublin. Her current research interests include Irish cinema, community, youth and marginal identities onscreen. She has recently taken up a position with the Irish Youth Justice Service at the Department of Children and Youth Affairs.

Sarita Malik is Professor of Media, Culture and Communications at Brunel University London. Her research explores questions of social change, inequality, communities and cultural representation. She has published widely on representations of black and Asian communities on British television and also on diversity and broadcasting policy. Malik is currently leading a large international research project, funded by the UK government's Arts and Humanities Research Council, examining how disenfranchised communities use the arts, media and creativity to challenge marginalisation.

Roberta Mock is Professor of Performance Studies and Director of the Graduate School at Plymouth University, with specific expertise in artistic practice-research methodologies. Her research, which includes both written publications and creative outputs, focuses on the intersection of performance, bodies, gender and sexuality.

Virginia Murray lectures in the School of Communication and Creative Arts at Deakin University, Australia. She has a background in the creative industries as a filmmaker and editor. Her research interests are diverse: screenwriting, cinema production cultures, cinema history and the economic and social effects of celebrity. Her most recent publication is 'Who am I? 52 Tuesdays, Intimacy and the Search for an Authentic Life' in *Sex Education*.

Daniel H. Mutibwa is Associate Professor in Creative Industries at the Department of Culture, Film and Media at the University of Nottingham. Daniel researches and teaches in the areas of the Political Economy of Information and Communication Technologies, Media and Cultural/Creative Industries, Cultural Studies, Creative Entrepreneurship, Research Methods, Digital Culture, Community-led Research and Third Sector/Civil Society Studies.

Kate Pahl is Professor of Literacies in Education at the University of Sheffield. Her work is concerned with the cultural context of civic engagement and with everyday literacies. She has done research on artists in community contexts, on everyday writing, on language and dialect and on civic engagement and culture. Her book *Materializing Literacies in Communities* (Bloomsbury Academic 2014) is concerned with how literacies in the everyday are understood and recognised. Many of her studies are co-produced and involve university/community partnerships with a focus on culture.

Kayla Parker is Lecturer in Media Arts with Plymouth University, where she convenes the Moving Image Arts (MIA) research group. Kayla is an artist filmmaker, with over 25 years' experience in participatory filmmaking, whose research interests centre on subjectivity and place, embodiment and technological mediation from feminist perspectives.

Steve Pool is a visual artist originally trained as a sculptor; he now works in different mediums to realise ideas. He collaborates regularly with academics on projects that explore and critique how knowledge is produced and reproduced. He is interested in how cultural can be placed at the heart of building new and diverse critical public space. He is a founder member of the think tank The Poly-technic that explores the current state of things through visual art.

Steve Presence is Research Fellow at the University of the West of England (UWE) Bristol. His research interests include political film culture, documentary and British film and television. He is the founding co-director of the Bristol Radical Film Festival, convenor of the Radical Film Network (RFN) and Associate Editor of *Screenworks*, the peer-reviewed publication for screen-based practice research. Current projects include the AHRC-funded RFN project, Sustaining Alternative Film Cultures; Bristol Film and TV, a study of Bristol's film and television cluster funded by the Higher Education Innovation Fund and Success in the European Television Industries, an investigation of film and television production companies in four European countries, which is funded by the Norwegian Research Council.

Alistair Scott is Associate Professor in Film and Television at Edinburgh Napier University and Director of Screen Academy Scotland, a partnership between Edinburgh Napier and Edinburgh College of Art. He was a community video worker in the 1970s going on to post-graduate study at the National Film and Television School. He worked within the independent film and video workshop movement in the 1980s and spent over 20 years working in broadcast television directing a number of programmes about local communities. Since 2005 he has worked in higher education. His PhD thesis investigated *Raploch Stories* (2002) and *Raploch Stories Revisited* (2007), a longitudinal documentary series portraying a Scottish working-class community in Stirling, which he directed for BBC Scotland.

Shawn Sobers is Associate Professor of Lens Based Media at University of the West of England and lectures in photography and filmmaking. He has carried out a wide range of research projects spanning diverse topics, and principles relating to community media and participatory practice underpin much of his work. Most recently Shawn worked as co-investigator on two large-scale AHRC Connected Communities projects, Media, Community and the Creative Citizen and Walking Interconnections. As a filmmaker and photographer his work has been exhibited and screened nationally and internationally, and he has directed and produced documentaries for BBC1, ITV and Channel 4.

Ruth Way is Associate Professor and Associate Head of the School of Humanities & Performing Arts at Plymouth University. Her research focuses on exploring connections between somatic movement practice and the sentient body in her performance and film practice. She is a certified Somatic Movement Educator through Eastwest Somatics Institute and registered with ISMETA.

Index

school council and youth
representation 255–7
Schwab-Cartas, Josh 55
Schwarz, Andreas 35
Scifo, Salvatore 132
Scotland: community filmmaking
in 12, 60–74; factual television in
68–69; launch of Channel 4, 65–68
Scott, Alistair 12, 24
Scott, Ridley 32
Scott Free Productions 27
Scottish Association of Workshops 66
Scottish Mental Health Arts and Film
Festival 73
screendance 192
Screen Education Edinburgh 71
Screen Education Scotland 72
Second Light 72
Segovia, Ana 109
self-awareness and Canadian
community video movement
176–7
self-representation 131
'Shadow Dance' film 253–5, 259
Shea, Jack 64
Sheffield City Council 251
Sheffield University 251
Shepherd, Phil 128
Shepherds of Berneray, The (film) 64
Shohat, Ella 103
silent filmmaking 61
Sinfonía de Tetuán 106
Sobers, Shawn 13
social change 23
social entrepreneurship 266
social exclusion 45, 47, 158–9
Social Foundation of La Caixa 108
social innovation and community
media 114–28
social laboratory of community
filmmaking 132, 141
social media integrated with
community filmmaking 70–71
Social Sciences and Humanities
Research Council (Canada) 180
Somers, Margaret 79
Sony Portapak 63, 66, 175, 228
South Australian Film Corporation
(SAFC) 83, 84
South Blessed collective 14, 114,
116–28; citizen benefit of 124–8;
participatory culture of 126–7;
transforming subjects 117–21

space: being occupied by capitalism
163–4; being produced through the
body 199–201
Spain's community filmmaking 13,
98–111
SQIFF (Scottish Queer International
Film Festival) 73
stakeholders influencing community
filmmaking 264–5
Stam, Robert 103
Station House Media Unit (SHMU) 72
Stephens, Elizabeth 194
Stewart, Sue 169
storytelling 46
Stratham Productions 138–9, 143,
144–6, 149–50, 151
STV Edinburgh 72
STV Glasgow 72
subjects' transformation in *South
Blessed* collective 117–21
subsidy of community filmmaking
139–40, 143; degree of autonomy
and 149–51
Subversive Festival 212
Summerhall TV 72
Summers, Claire 194
Summerton, Bec 91
Sundance Film Festival 92

Take One Action 212
Talisman Project 250
television of Scottish community 72–73
Tesco Riots 119, 120
Tetuán 106
textual artefacts 255–7, 260
*Thematic Report on Ethnic
Minorities, The* 46
Then and Now (film) 71
11th Hour 66
third-sector organisations as a
constituency in community
filmmaking 7, 116–17
Thomas, V. 83
Torchin, Leshua 212
Tosh, Mike 65
touch and resulting empathy 195
Toulouse 107–8
'Trainers' project 255–7
transgender family experiences 89
transgender groups networking
globally in *52 Tuesdays* 89–91
transgender identity in community
filmmaking 84

natives 226–7, 238–9; distant
relationship to government 252–5;
engaging them in filmmaking
228–30; engaging them with the
community 232–3, 239; libraries
facilitating literacy in 248–50;
occupation of public places 232;
as politically apathetic 226, 233–5,
237–8; represented in politics
and localism 255–7; sense of
space and place 232–3; voice and
participation 250–5

youth filmmaking 17; audience
and community representation
in 247–8; shifting contexts in
248–50; in United Kingdom
226–40; developing skills for
the future 235–7; history of
228–31; justifications for 231–40;
self-expression 233–5, 239
youth voice 233–5, 238, 239, 246–7
YouTube 27–28, 31, 36

Zielinski, Ger 212

Printed in the United States
by Baker & Taylor Publisher Services